Lecture Notes in Computer Science 11433

Commenced Publication in 1973
Founding and Former Series Editors:
Gerhard Goos, Juris Hartmanis, and Jan van Leeuwen

Editorial Board Members

Harri Oinas-Kukkonen ·
Khin Than Win · Evangelos Karapanos ·
Pasi Karppinen · Eleni Kyza (Eds.)

Persuasive Technology

Development of Persuasive and Behavior Change Support Systems

14th International Conference, PERSUASIVE 2019
Limassol, Cyprus, April 9–11, 2019
Proceedings

 Springer

Editors
Harri Oinas-Kukkonen
University of Oulu
Oulu, Finland

Khin Than Win
University of Wollongong
Wollongong, NSW, Australia

Evangelos Karapanos (iD)
Cyprus University of Technology
Limassol, Cyprus

Pasi Karppinen
University of Oulu
Oulu, Finland

Eleni Kyza
Cyprus University of Technology
Limassol, Cyprus

ISSN 0302-9743   ISSN 1611-3349 (electronic)
Lecture Notes in Computer Science
ISBN 978-3-030-17286-2   ISBN 978-3-030-17287-9 (eBook)
https://doi.org/10.1007/978-3-030-17287-9

LNCS Sublibrary: SL3 – Information Systems and Applications, incl. Internet/Web, and HCI

This Springer imprint is published by the registered company Springer Nature Switzerland AG
The registered company address is: Gewerbestrasse 11, 6330 Cham, Switzerland

Preface

Persuasive technology is a vibrant interdisciplinary research field, focusing on the study, design, development, and evaluation of information technologies aimed at influencing people's attitudes or behaviors through open and transparent means. The International Conference on Persuasive Technology series brings together researchers, designers, practitioners, and business people from various disciplines and a wide variety of application domains. The research community seeks to facilitate healthier lifestyles, make people feel or behave more safely, reduce consumption of renewable resources, among other notable goals, by, for instance, designing software applications, monitoring through sensor technologies, analyzing obtained data, and providing various types of coaching for users.

The 14th International Conference on Persuasive Technology was hosted by the Department of Communication and Internet Studies at the Cyprus University of Technology in Limassol, Cyprus, in April 2019, and organized in collaboration with the University of Oulu, Finland, and the University of Wollongong, Australia. In previous years, similar highly successful conferences were organized in Waterloo (Canada), Amsterdam (The Netherlands), Salzburg (Austria), Chicago (USA), Padua (Italy), Sydney (Australia), Linköping (Sweden), Columbus (USA), Copenhagen (Denmark), Claremont (USA), Oulu (Finland), Palo Alto (USA), and Eindhoven (The Netherlands). The conference addressed a wide variety of topics regarding the development of persuasive and behavior change support systems. This year papers were also solicited for two specific topics, namely, personal informatics and gamification and gamified persuasive technologies.

This volume contains the scientific papers that were presented at the Limassol meeting. A total of 80 completed research papers were submitted for evaluation; one submission was withdrawn before starting the review process, resulting in 79 papers going through the double-blind peer-review process. Papers were submitted by 185 authors from 29 countries, with the UK, The Netherlands, and Canada having the most active submitters. Methodologically, the largest single group of submitted papers was quantitative empirical papers, but a good number of empirical qualitative and mixed-method papers as well as conceptual-theoretical and design science papers were submitted, too.

In the end, 29 papers were, accepted for publication in this volume (36.7% acceptance rate), which required the dedication of 67 skillful reviewers from 17 different countries (on average three reviews were written per submitted manuscript) and some tough decisions.

The accepted papers were subsequently grouped based on their content into ten sessions in the conference and in these proceedings: Motivation and Goal-Setting; Self-Monitoring and Reflection; User Types and Tailoring; Personality, Age, and Gender; Social Support; Systems Development Process; Ethical and Legal Aspects; Drones and Automotives; Special Application Domains; and Terminologies and

Methodologies. These categories, and the papers therein, show the diversity of research works and multi-paradigmatic approaches utilized in the field; furthermore, the published papers, on par with knowing how challenging it is to get a paper accepted in this conference, demonstrate that the field of persuasive technology is gaining maturity. Posters, demos, symposia, doctoral consortium papers, workshop papers, and tutorial descriptions were printed in separate adjunct proceedings.

The main program for the two full days of the conference, Wednesday and Thursday, was a single track with the aforementioned ten paper sessions, two panels, one on methods and tools and one on bridging theory and design, and keynotes. A doctoral consortium that gathered together doctoral students and seasoned professors from the field took place on Monday, and tutorials and conjunct workshops were organized on Tuesday.

We would like to thank all authors, both of accepted papers and also of papers that did not make it this time, for their contributions, and the reviewers for their very valuable feedback. Furthermore, we wish to thank all of our colleagues and students who were involved in organizing the many facets of this conference.

April 2019

Harri Oinas-Kukkonen
Khin Than Win
Evangelos Karapanos
Pasi Karppinen
Eleni Kyza

Organization

General Chair

Karapanos Evangelos   Cyprus University of Technology, Cyprus

Organizing Chair

Kyza Eleni   Cyprus University of Technology, Cyprus

Program Chairs

Oinas-Kukkonen Harri   University of Oulu, Finland
Win Khin   University of Wollongong, Australia

Special Session Chair, Personal Informatics

Meyer Jochen   OFFIS Institute for Information Technology, Germany

Special Session Chair, Gamification and Gameful Persuasive Technologies

Nacke Lennart   University of Waterloo, Canada

Program Committee Members

Ali Raian	Bournemouth University, UK
Arakawa Yutaka	Nara Institute of Science and Technology, Japan
Baghaei Nilufar	Otago Polytechnic, New Zealand
Berkovsky Shlomo	Macquarie University, Australia
Beun Robbert Jan	Utrecht University, The Netherlands
Boger Jennifer	University of Waterloo, Canada
Brinkman Willem-Paul	Delft University of Technology, The Netherlands
Burri Gram-Hansen Sandra	Aalborg University, Denmark
Chatterjee Samir	Claremont Graduate University, USA
Chittaro Luca	University of Udine, Italy
Corbett Jacqueline	Laval University, Canada
Davis Janet	Whitman College, USA
De Ruyter Boris	Philips Research, The Netherlands
De Vries Peter	University of Twente, The Netherlands
Felfernig Alexander	Graz University of Technology, Austria

Fogg BJ	Stanford University, USA
Gamberini Luciano	University of Padua, Italy
Gretzel Ulrike	University of Southern California, USA
Ham Jaap	Eindhoven University of Technology, The Netherlands
Hamari Juho	Tampere University, Finland
Hasle Per	University of Copenhagen, Denmark
Intille Stephen	Northeastern University, USA
Iyengar M. Sriram	Texas A&M University Health Science Center, USA
Kaipainen Kirsikka	Tampere University, Finland
Kaptein Maurits	Tilburg University, The Netherlands
Karapanos Evangelos	Cyprus University of Technology, Cyprus
Karppinen Pasi	University of Oulu, Finland
Kelders Saskia	University of Twente, The Netherlands
Klaassen Randy	University of Twente, The Netherlands
Langrial Sitwat	Sur University College, Oman
MacTavish Tom	IIT Institute of Design, USA
Meschtscherjakov Alexander	University of Salzburg, Austria
Midden Cees	Eindhoven University of Technology, The Netherlands
Millonig Alexandra	Vienna University of Technology, Austria
Orji Rita	Dalhousie University, Canada
Ruijten Peter	Eindhoven University of Technology, The Netherlands
Spagnolli Anna	University of Padua, Italy
Stibe Agnis	ESLSCA Business School Paris, France
Tikka Piiastiina	University of Oulu, Finland
Torning Kristian	PricewaterhouseCoopers, Denmark
Tscheligi Manfred	University of Salzburg, Austria
van Gemert-Pijnen Lisette	University of Twente, The Netherlands
Vassileva Julita	University of Saskatchewan, Canada
Wilson E. Vance	Worcester Polytechnic Institute, USA
Yetim Fahri	FOM University of Applied Sciences, Germany

Additional Reviewers

Abbas Roba	University of Wollongong, Australia
Anwar Ahm Mehbub	University of Wollongong, Australia
Ehrenbrink Patrick	TU Berlin, Germany
Kekkonen Markku	University of Oulu, Finland
Mayora Oscar	Fondazione Bruno Kessler, Italy
McCallum Claire	University of Glasgow, UK
Meedya Shahla	University of Wollongong, Australia
Mohd Hassan Naffisah	University of Teknologi Mara, Malaysia
Oduor Michael	University of Oulu, Finland

Ogie Robert	University of Wollongong, Australia
Prezenski Sabine	TU Berlin, Germany
Schmidt-Kraepelin Manuel	Karlsruhe Institute of Technology, Germany
Schueller Stephen	University of California Irvine, USA
Shevchuk Nataliya	University of Oulu, Finland
Su Yung-Yu	National Quemoy University, Taiwan
Tondello Gustavo	University of Waterloo, Canada
Vlahu-Gjorgievska Elena	University of Wollongong, Australia

Sponsoring Universities

Cyprus University of Technology, Cyprus
University of Oulu, Finland
University of Wollongong, Australia

Cyprus University of Technology

Cyprus University of Technology (CUT) is one of three state universities in the Republic of Cyprus. Founded in 2003, Cyprus University of Technology aspires to develop itself into a modern, pioneering university able to offer education and high-level research in leading branches of science and technology which have a high impact on the economic, technical, and scientific sectors. In less than 10 years of operation, CUT has occupied high positions in international rankings. Specifically, in the 2017–2018 Times Higher Education World University Rankings (THE), CUT was ranked 351–400 worldwide, and the highest ranked University in Cyprus and Greece.

University of Oulu

The University of Oulu is an international university famous for its arctic attitude toward science and research. The University of Oulu is committed to creating innovative ideas and products for the future. At the heart of University of Oulu research are well-being, sustainability, and knowledge creation through high-quality research and education. Founded in 1958, the University of Oulu is the most multidisciplinary university in Finland.

UNIVERSITY OF WOLLONGONG AUSTRALIA

University of Wollongong

The University of Wollongong (UOW), founded in 1957, is an Australian public research university ranked among the top modern universities in the world. Located in the coastal city of Wollongong, New South Wales, approximately 80 kilometres south of Sydney, the University of Wollongong (UOW) has a strong reputation for its multidisciplinary approach toward research and a personalized approach to teaching and learning. UOW's Innovation Campus gives innovative companies and organizations the opportunity to collaborate with leading research institutes within the university.

Contents

Ethical and Legal Aspects

Special Application Domains

Motivation and Goal Setting

Terminologies and Methodologies

Questioning Our Attitudes and Feelings Towards Persuasive Technology

Robby van Delden[(✉)], Roelof A. J. de Vries, and Dirk K. J. Heylen

University of Twente, Enschede, The Netherlands
{r.w.vandelden,r.a.j.devries,d.k.j.heylen}@utwente.nl

Abstract. Definitions regarding Persuasive Technology are often introduced with the accompanying remark: without using coercion and deception. For this position paper, we investigated, evaluated, and discussed the term Persuasive Technology and its connotations. We invesstigated whether Persuasive Technology is perceived with negative connotations such as coercive and deceptive, and, how in comparison, similar labels (such as Behavior Change Support System and Digital Behavior Change Intervention) were perceived. We conducted an online survey where participants (N = 488) rated their attitude towards these systems in the context of a system description, indicated to what extent they agreed with 10 descriptors (such as, manipulative, motivating, or supportive) in the context of a system description, and whether this system in general, is at risk of being perceived as coercive, manipulative, deceptive, or propagandistic. We found that when considering risks of systems in general, labeling them as PT results in them being perceived significantly more forceful than all other labels, and switching the labeling of a system to Digital Behavior Change Intervention results in them being perceived significantly more captivating compared to a neutral system label. The findings suggest that when choosing labels to use for technology or systems it is essential to consider the impact labels can have on how the system or technology is perceived, regardless of the actual function of the system. These findings are relevant for the field of Persuasive Technology and the Persuasive Technology conference specifically. This paper is meant to spark further discussion in the field and at the conference.

Keywords: Persuasive Technology · Behavior Change Support Systems · Digital Behavior Change Interventions · Terminology

1 Introduction

"An attempt to change attitudes or behaviors or both *(without using coercion or deception)*" is Fogg's definition of persuasion [6, p. 15]. He adds (between parentheses) that some people might confuse it with *coercion* (i.e., forceful instead of voluntary), or with *deception* (i.e., with the use of false information instead of transparency). This is noteworthy—not only because more than a decade later this definition is still used—but even more so because it seems the confusion

© Springer Nature Switzerland AG 2019
H. Oinas-Kukkonen et al. (Eds.): PERSUASIVE 2019, LNCS 11433, pp. 3–15, 2019.
https://doi.org/10.1007/978-3-030-17287-9_1

about the term remains and the part that used to be within parentheses is still needed to describe persuasive technologies.

In this paper, we investigate the term Persuasive Technology (PT) and its connotations. One of the questions central to this paper is whether this previously described confusion with more negative connotations indeed remains, including the link to coercion and deception, even though the field intended to place coercion and deception outside of PT. To answer this question we carried out a survey where participants had to rate their attitude towards and perceptions of PT and similar systems, such as Behavior Change Support Systems (BCSS) [12] and Digital Behavior Change Interventions (DBCI) [19]. We argue that answering this question is relevant, interesting, and timely, which we will explain in the following sections by quoting relevant literature, but also by sharing anecdotes from within the community.

1.1 Investigating Attitude Towards PT is Relevant

We argue that PT has a negative connotation for some people, and therefore investigating this connotation is *relevant*. If people have a negative attitude towards PT, labeling 'our' work as Persuasive Technologies can have negative consequences. After all, Cialdini in his book *Pre-suasion* shows how small changes in, among other things, wording might be used to—even before there is a true interaction—prompt people to focus on certain parts (e.g., negativity - are you *unhappy* versus are you *happy*, or by making it more personal - *they* might versus *you* might) in order to subsequently influence their attitude or behavior in an intended direction [4]. The PT label, or alternatives, are likely to be used throughout our daily practice as researchers and might prompt people (e.g., practitioners, participants, or users) to focus on certain aspects of our design, development, theory-forming, and evaluation practices.

1.2 Investigating Attitude Towards PT is Interesting

Spahn, explains how in a communicative act being truthful and honest is essential in building trust [14]. Spahn argues that a PT twisting the truth, presenting misinformation, or exaggerating feedback might be powerful on the short term but can have negative effects on PT in the long term as well as impact the truthfulness. To exemplify that the question of how the PT label is being perceived is of *interest* for our research community, we refer to the brief discussion of a possible name change and anticipated effects during 2018's (open) steering committee meeting of Persuasive Technology conference. Several points relating to the PT brand were discussed for possible opportunities for growth of the conference. Although the general consensus was that PT was a strong brand, several attendees stated they found it an *'awful'* and *'aggressive'* term. Alternative terms were mentioned but most seemed to be perceived as less strong or less related to the technological background, interests, and profiling of several researchers.

1.3 Investigating Attitude Towards PT is Timely

We also consider the matter to be *timely*. With a rising number of PT's we are also getting in contact with more PT that could be considered unethical. Recently, Kampik et al. even argued that due to the rise of coercive and deceptive PT the definition of PT itself should be updated to include this [9]. In their investigation leading up to that conclusion, they mention the use of deceptive headlines, coercive strategies such as purposeful disempowerment to reach the persuasive goal, Facebook's reluctance to limit the spread of miss-information, as well as social media's coercive effect related to the fear of missing out. Based on the work of Spahn we can see that the negative effects of PT can affect the technology itself, the designer of the PT, or the implementing party [14]. Additionally, we have recently seen an impact on a more personal level for the researchers of PT. For instance, the authors of this paper listened to an invited talk from a pioneer in the PT and persuasive profiling field that felt the need to distinguish himself and his work from the recent scandals around Facebook with Cambridge Analytica. Moreover, Fogg publicly defended himself this year from a piece on Medium[1], that as he described it, 'mischaracterized' his work[2]. In conclusion, the investigation of attitude towards PT is a *timely* matter.

1.4 Approach to Investigate Attitudes and Feelings Towards PT

Numerous publications have revolved around the ethics and ethical guidelines behind PT (e.g., [6,14]), questions relating to voluntariness and intentionality of PT [13], and reviewing, redefining or adding terminology to PT [2,6]. In this paper, we are interested in the attitude towards and perceptions of PT from a wider set of people. We investigate this by letting people rate their attitude towards one of two representative scenarios containing one of four labels. Moreover, we ask people to rate these systems on dimensions that could inform how forceful or captivating these technologies are perceived to be.

2 Survey: Attitudes Toward System Labels

To investigate attitudes and feelings toward system labels, we designed an online survey study. The survey was carried out through Amazon Mechanical Turk[3] (AMT) on SurveyMonkey[4].

---

[1] The tendency of the piece was roughly that hidden influencing techniques are applied in gaming and social media context to lure children away of real-life activities, see: https://medium.com/@richardnfreed/the-tech-industrys-psychological-war-on-kids-c452870464ce, last accessed 25-11-2018.

[2] For the response of Fogg see: https://medium.com/@bjfogg/the-facts-bj-fogg-persuasive-technology-37d00a738bd1, last accessed 25-11-2018.

[3] https://requester.mturk.com/.

[4] https://www.surveymonkey.com/.

2.1 Labels and Terminology

In order to investigate the attitude towards PT or alternative terms, we needed to select alternative labels that were used in the field to include in the survey. We selected two alternative terms that are used in the field: Behavior Change Support System and Digital Behavior Change Intervention.

The term Behavior Change Support System, introduced by Oinas-Kukkonen is defined as follows: *"(BCSS) is a sociotechnical information system with psychological and behavioral outcomes designed to form, alter or reinforce attitudes, behaviors or an act of complying without using coercion or deception"* [12, p. 1225].

Yardley et al. in their special issue on Digital Behavior Change Interventions (DBCI) defined them as follows: *"'DBCI' is used to refer to an intervention that employs digital technology to promote and maintain health, through primary or secondary prevention and management of health problems"* [19, p. 814].

For our purposes, where we want to explore possible alternative labels for PT that hopefully implicitly exclude several negative connotations that people might have (such as coercion and deception), it seems the term BCSS is suitable. Furthermore, DBCI seems to be a term that relates both to the technological side, as it starts with the digital component, and it does fit the various types of PT research, although the informed reader might know the focus on health care. We were mainly interested in pre-existing connotations so no explanation was given about the used labels.

2.2 Descriptors of Accompanying Connotations Towards PT

Investigating the 'without coercion and deception' component of PT that was explained in the introduction, we wanted descriptors more specific for the forcefulness of PT and other feelings relating to PT. Based on our research interests and related work we selected a set of ten terms, these terms were transformed into the following adjectives: manipulative [13,14], deceptive [1,12–14], propagandistic [14], coercive [1,12–14,17], steering [5], convincing [14], motivational [5,12,14,17,18], persuasive [1,5,12,14,17], influencing [5,9,17] and supportive [1,12]. We are well aware that these choices include some personal preferences regarding terminology (e.g. supportive and steering), that the references can be selective, or that the choices exclude other terms such as nudging, which we found less related to a connotation or a feeling.

2.3 Scenario Selection

We chose to write two 'scenarios' in which to use the labels based on systems presented at the Persuasive Technology conference. To make this selection we looked at the most cited papers over the last 5 years. The first scenario we chose is a system related to health in the form of physical activity by Herrmanny et al. [7], and the second scenario we chose is a system to promote 'customer engagement in sharing feedback' by Stibbe and Oinas-Kukkonen [16]. Based on the description found in the title, abstract and conclusion, we compiled the two scenarios of systems to be investigated, see Table 1.

2.4 Participants

The sample size consisted of 600 respondents. We set the following AMT requirements for the respondents: completed more than 100 tasks, >98% approved, and located in the US. We received (partial) data of 720 respondents (due to respondents opening a survey but never completing it). We excluded 172 respondents based on attention checks (clicking on the right scenario and labels to proceed to next page) most of which (116) were from the neutral system condition (see the Discussion section for an explanation). Moreover, we excluded 21 based on an incomplete questionnaire, 31 based on an unrealistic quick answer time (<90 s), and 8 because they used the same IP-address. The final sample included 488 respondents (216 female, 271 male, and 1 other). The minimum age was 19 and the maximum was 75, the average age was 37.73 (SD = 11.92) and the median was 35. One respondent rated his English level as average, all other participants rated this as either good or very good, 12 respondents did have a non-English native language. With respect to reported education, 8 obtained a PhD, 67 obtained a masters degree, 225 obtained a college degree, 137 respondents received some college education, 42 completed their high school, and 9 received other types of education.

2.5 Conditions and Measures

The study was set up as a four (system labels: BCSS, PT, DBCI, neutral system) by two (scenarios: one involving sharing feedback (SF) and one involving physical activity tracking (PA), see Table 1) between-subjects study.

For the measures we used the 5-item Attitude toward the Brand [15] measure (from here on Attitude toward the System), which asks participants to describe their overall feelings about the system described on a 7-point semantic differential scale with anchors: Unappealing – Appealing, Good – Bad, Unpleasant – Pleasant, Favorable – Unfavorable, and Unlikeable – Likeable. Moreover, we asked how well the previously introduced 10 descriptor-list (see Sect. 2.2) fit the system description on a 7-point Likert item response format (i.e. Strongly disagree – Strongly agree). Lastly, we asked if the system label they just read, *in general* (so without considering the previous scenario), is at risk of being perceived as Forceful, which we operationalized with the four descriptors coercive, manipulative, deceptive, and propagandistic (e.g., "Persuasive Technologies, in general, are at risk of being perceived as") on the same 7-point Likert item response format.

2.6 Procedure

At the start of the survey participants had to fill in a consent form and demographics. This was followed by a short instructions page and a follow-up page that directed them randomly to either survey SF or survey PA. The version of the system label (i.e., BCSS, PT, DBCI, neutral system) that the participant

Table 1. The two scenarios with two example system labels each.

Sharing Feedback scenario, inspired by [16]

This Behavior Change Support System, in order to collect feedback from their customers, draws upon design principles intended to change customer engagement in sharing feedback. For that purpose, an information system consisting of social influence design principles of Behavior Change Support Systems was implemented on large public screen displays.

This Persuasive Technology, in order to collect feedback from their customers, draws upon design principles intended to change customer engagement in sharing feedback. For that purpose, an information system consisting of social influence design principles of Persuasive Technologies was implemented on large public screen displays.

Activity Tracking scenario, inspired by [7]

This Digital Behavior Change Intervention implements goal setting as its core principle to support users in setting effective goals in activity tracking. It uses two Digital Behavior Change Intervention strategies to support users in setting realistic goals, namely reference routes and personal recommendation calculation, as well as manual goal input.

This system implements goal setting as its core principle to support users in setting effective goals in activity tracking. It uses two strategies to support users in setting realistic goals, namely reference routes and personal recommendation calculation, as well as manual goal input.

would get within the survey (i.e., SF or PA) was chosen randomly. We introduced the systems with, *'the following paragraph describes the system we want you to consider'*. We asked participants to complete the Attitudes toward the System measure and the 10-item descriptor-list. After, they were asked to answer whether the same label of systems (e.g., PT), in general, is at risk of being perceived as Forceful. The participants were debriefed and given a completion code to fill in on AMT to receive payment. The survey took about 3 min to complete. Participants were compensated 0.6 US dollars for their participation.

3   Data Analysis

The distribution of the included participants over the conditions after attention check (N = 488) was as follows: in total, 245 participants were in the SF condition, split between BCSS (80), PT (67), DBCI (69), and the neutral system (29), and 243 participants in the PA condition, split between BCSS (65), PT (73), DBCI (83), and the neutral system (22).

The reliability of the Attitude toward the System [15] measure was very good and similar to original findings (cf. two separate measurements .97 and .94), with a Cronbach's alpha of .93. Moreover, a principal components analysis (PCA) was carried out on the 10-item descriptor-list selected to measure the connotations of the systems described in the scenario. Following [10], the suitability of PCA was assessed prior to analysis. Inspection of the correlation matrix showed that all variables had at least one correlation coefficient greater than 0.3. The overall

Kaiser-Meyer-Olkin (KMO) measure was 0.86 with individual KMO measures all between .84 and .90, classifications of 'meritorious' according to [8]. Bartlett's test of sphericity was statistically significant ($p < .0005$), indicating that the data was likely factorizable.

PCA revealed two components that had eigenvalues greater than one and which explained 37.8% and 33.2% of the total variance, respectively. Visual inspection of the scree plot indicated that four components should be retained [3]. In addition, a two-component solution met the interpretability criterion. As such, two components were retained.

The two-component solution explained 71.1% of the total variance. A Varimax orthogonal rotation was employed to aid interpretability. Interpretation of the data suggests two dimensions of connotations of systems. One dimension with strong loadings on items could be interpreted to describe to what degree autonomy is supported by the system, i.e., Perceived Forcefulness (PF) measured with the items Manipulative, Deceptive, Propagandistic, and Coercive (these items were also selected a-priori to measure systems, *in general*, being at risk for Perceived Forcefulness (GPF)). The other dimension with strong loadings on items could be interpreted to describe to what degree the system is Perceived as Captivating (PC), measured with the items Supportive, Motivating, Influencing, Persuasive, and Convincing. Component (or dimension) loadings and communalities of the rotated solution are presented in Table 2. Of note is that the Steering descriptor loaded on both dimensions and was therefore left out of either. The Supportive descriptor also loaded on both dimensions, however, it loaded negatively on the PF dimension, and quite strongly on the PC dimension and was therefore kept in the dimension. Moreover, the subsequent reliability analysis showed that leaving out Supportive decreased the PC reliability score, while leaving out Steering increased the PF reliability score. The final reliability of our four selected terms to measure the PF of the described system was very good, with a Cronbach's alpha of .89. The final reliability of our five selected terms to measure the PC of the described system was very good, with a Cronbach's alpha of .87. Moreover, the reliability of our four selected terms (Manipulative, Deceptive, Propagandistic, and Coercive) to measure systems *in general* being at risk for PF was also very good, with a Cronbach's alpha of .93.

Table 2. Extraction Method: Principal Component Analysis. Rotation Method: Varimax with Kaiser Normalization. Rotation converged in 3 iterations.

Rotated Component Matrix

Items	C1	C2	Comm.	Items	C1	C2	Comm.
Manipulative	.894	-.107	.811	Convincing	.869		.762
Deceptive	.849	-.149	.744	Motivating	-.277	.827	.761
Propagandistic	.832		.697	Persuasive	.124	.826	.697
Coercive	.820	.113	.685	Influencing	.290	.774	.684
Steering	.569	.470	.545	Supportive	-.459	.712	.718

4 Results

We ran four two-way ANOVA's to determine the effects of our two independent variables (scenario version: SF or PA and system label: BCSS, PT, DBCI, and neutral system) on our four dependent variables (Attitude toward the System, PF, PC, and systems in general being at risk for PF). For all four ANOVA's, there were no statistically significant interactions between scenario version and system label for the separate dependent variables, see Table 3. Therefore, we can investigate the main effects of the two scenario versions and the four system labels on the four dependent variables.

Table 3. Tests of Between-Subjects Effects for four dependent variables.

Indep. var.	Dep. var.	Type III SoS	df	Mean Square	F	Sig.	Partial η_p^2
Scenario * Label	AttS	4.289	3	1.430	.758	.518	.005
	PF	4.093	3	1.364	.618	.604	.004
	PC	5.736	3	1.912	1.089	.353	.007
	GPF	14.777	3	4.926	1.938	.122	0.012
Scenario	AttS	76.628	1	76.628	40.628	<**.001**	.078
	PF	182.643	1	182.643	82.671	<**.001**	.147
	PC	21.112	1	21.112	12.022	**.001**	.024
	GPF	86.933	1	86.933	34.210	<**.001**	0.067
Label	AttS	6.959	3	2.320	1.230	.298	.008
	PF	13.948	3	4.649	2.104	.099	.013
	PC	15.129	3	5.043	2.872	**.036**	.018
	GPF	65.792	3	21.931	8.630	<**.001**	0.012

Following [11], it is generally recommended to still keep the interaction term in the model when looking at the main effects. For the main effects, we found that the scenario version had a statistically significant effect on all dependent variables (see Table 3 and Figs. 1 and 2). For the system label, there was no statistically significant main effect on Attitude toward the System. Moreover, there was no statistically significant main effect of system label on PF. However, there was a statistically significant main effect of system label on PC. For further analysis (see also Table 4), we use the estimates and pairwise comparisons tables, as we have an unbalanced design and need to use unweighted marginal means (and Type III sums of squares). As is shown in Table 4 and Fig. 2, the DBCI label is Perceived significantly more Captivating than the neutral system label.

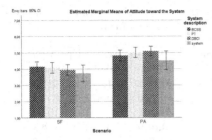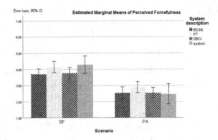

Fig. 1. The estimated marginal means for attitude towards the System (L) and Perceived Forcefulness (R) for the scenario versions and the four system labels.

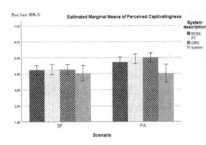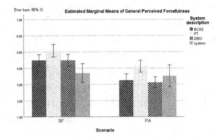

Fig. 2. The estimated marginal means for Perceived Captivatingness (L) and the General Risk for Perceived Forcefulness for the scenario versions and the four system labels.

Table 4. Six pairwise comparisons based on estimated marginal means for the Captivating measure, Bonferroni adjusted.

System 1	System 2	Mean diff.	Std. Error	Sig. ($p < 0.05$)	Lower CI	Upper CI
	BCSS	-0.450	0.218	0.234	-1.027	0.126
neutral	PT	-0.570	0.218	0.056	-1.149	0.008
	DBCI	-0.605	0.216	**0.032**	-1.178	-0.032
PT	BCSS	0.120	0.158	1.000	-0.297	0.537
	DBCI	-0.034	0.156	1.000	-0.447	0.378
DBCI	BCSS	0.155	0.155	1.000	-0.255	0.564

Regarding the risk of PF of systems in general (GPF), there was also a statistically significant main effect. As is shown in Table 5 and Fig. 2, the Persuasive Technology label is at risk of being Perceived as significantly more Forceful than all the other system labels.

Table 5. Six pairwise comparisons based on estimated marginal means for the perceived risk of systems in general on PF measure, Bonferroni adjusted.

System 1	System 2	Mean diff.	Std. Error	Sig. ($p < 0.05$)	Lower CI	Upper CI
	BCSS	-0.264	0.262	1.000	-0.958	0.429
neutral	PT	-0.990	0.263	**0.001**	-1.686	-0.294
	DBCI	-0.188	0.260	1.000	-0.877	0.501
PT	BCSS	0.725	0.189	**0.001**	0.224	1.227
	DBCI	0.802	0.187	**0.000**	0.306	1.298
DBCI	BCSS	-0.076	0.186	1.000	-0.569	0.416

5   Discussion

We found that when considering risks of systems in general, labeling them as PT will result in them being Perceived significantly more Forceful compared to the other labels. Moreover, we found that when switching the labeling of a system to DBCI in a scenario makes it score significantly higher Perceived Captivatingness compared to the neutral label. Although we could not see a similar effect of the PT label after the Bonferroni correction, we do want to point out that there might be a positive trend regarding PC compared to the neutral label. For the other comparisons we saw no significant effects on PC, PF, or Attitude toward the System.

Based on these results it seems there is a risk for PT *in general* to be perceived as PF, something that we as research community want to prevent. However, this effect of PF when labeling something PT was not present when rating this in context of the two actual scenarios from our research field. What does that mean? Although we can only speculate, perhaps this means that PT *can* be perceived to be more PF, but that this is not necessarily so when properly explained, including being transparent about some of the applied strategies/design principles, see Table 1. Or perhaps, as Kampik et al. discussed, coercion and deception might have become part of the general public's interpretation of PT.

Both explanations in turn, would mean we need to be careful to describe ourselves as PT, as there are negative connotations for the general public regarding risks of general (not well described and explained) PT. On the other hand, this might mean that we need to accurately describe the systems, taking into account but perhaps not focusing on the risks per se, so connotations might disappear due to the effect of explaining of the system. Another interpretation could be that our scenarios were not representative of PT, and therefore resulted in different ratings compared to asking for PT specifically.

The results can also be considered in a different light, as first we asked whether the descriptors (including PF and PC) were descriptive of the system in the scenario, something that might be interpreted as how *they* viewed the system, where later we asked whether in general systems were at risks of being perceived in certain ways (including only PF), something that might interpreted as how *they* thought how the *general public* would view the system. Alternatively, the additional questions might have given less focus on PF for the scenarios, which in turn could have influenced the ratings of the participants on PF. In retrospect this selective questioning also shows we started with somewhat negative expectations to the label PT, which also made us look less into other perhaps more (positive) outcomes of using the PT label. Apart from this, we think our study was reasonably representative for a point of view relevant to this conference.

An important limitation to the current setup of our study was that the attention check was harder for the neutral situation than the other labels. In retrospect, we see that participants with the neutral label might have thought they were expected to *interpret* the system by giving it a certain label. Of the original respondents (N = 720) rating the neutral system label (N = 170), 17 interpreted it as a BCSS, 17 as a PT, 7 as DBCI, and 75 as 'a description using none of the above terms'. Only 54 interpreted it correctly as a neutral system label (3 more of this set were excluded for other reasons). This might have also influenced the results as perhaps only the more well reading participants remained.

Another limitation is that only two scenarios were used. The type of scenario had a significant effect on PC and PF. It is uncertain how these results regarding scenarios would generalize over different types of scenarios. We do not yet know if actual scenario descriptions with more 'risky' use of technology would also rate higher on PF when using the label PT instead of the other labels. It is also unknown if these more risky scenarios might have had an effect on Attitude toward the System. Furthermore, even if the term PT would strengthen PF also in these risky scenarios, it is uncertain if that influences other relevant parameters such use, satisfaction, and acceptance.

All in all, for the PT community these results show ample reasons to further debate the impact of terminology in PT, as well as a need to do so.

6   Conclusion

As part of a position paper we investigated, evaluated, and discussed the term Persuasive Technology (PT) and its connotations. With this effort, we tried to answer the question of whether PT is linked to negative connotations such as coercive and deceptive, but also, how similar labels (such as BCSS and DBCI) were perceived. We conducted a survey where participants had to rate their attitude towards these systems, indicate to what extent they found 10 descriptors (such as, manipulative, motivating, or supportive) descriptive of these systems, and whether these systems in general, were at risk of being perceived coercive, manipulative, deceptive, or propagandistic.

Our main results are that (1) when considering risks of systems in general, labeling them as PT results in them being Perceived significantly more Forceful (measured by Coercive, Manipulative, Deceptive, and Propagandistic); (2) when switching the labeling of a system to DBCI in a scenario results in them being Perceived significantly more Captivating compared to the neutral system label (measured by Supportive, Motivating, Influencing, Persuasive, and Convincing).

Overall, the findings suggest that, when choosing labels to use for technology or systems it is essential to consider the importance these labels can have on how the system or technology is perceived, regardless of the actual function of the system. Only the additional wording of Persuasive Technology or Digital Behavior Change Intervention can have a significant impact on how Forceful or Captivating the system or technology is perceived.

Acknowledgements. We thank Randy Klaassen & Dennis Reidsma for their contributions, and students River & Thomas for their exploratory literature review, and the PT research community for inspiring this research.

References

1. Adaji, I., Vassileva, J.: Perceived effectiveness, credibility and continuance intention in e-commerce: a study of Amazon. In: de Vries, P.W., Oinas-Kukkonen, H., Siemons, L., Beerlage-de Jong, N., van Gemert-Pijnen, L. (eds.) PERSUASIVE 2017. LNCS, vol. 10171, pp. 293–306. Springer, Cham (2017). https://doi.org/10.1007/978-3-319-55134-0_23
2. Atkinson, B.M.C.: Captology: a critical review. In: IJsselsteijn, W.A., de Kort, Y.A.W., Midden, C., Eggen, B., van den Hoven, E. (eds.) PERSUASIVE 2006. LNCS, vol. 3962, pp. 171–182. Springer, Heidelberg (2006). https://doi.org/10.1007/11755494_25
3. Cattell, R.B.: The scree test for the number of factors. Multivar. Behav. Res. **1**(2), 245–276 (1966). https://doi.org/10.1207/s15327906mbr0102_10
4. Cialdini, R.: Pre-Suasion: A Revolutionary Way to Influence and Persuade. Simon and Schuster, New York City (2016)
5. van Delden, R., Moreno, A., Poppe, R., Reidsma, D., Heylen, D.: A thing of beauty: steering behavior in an interactive playground. In: Proceedings of the 2017 CHI Conference on Human Factors in Computing Systems, pp. 2462–2472. ACM (2017). http://doi.org/10.1145/3025453.3025816
6. Fogg, B.J.: Persuasive Technology: Using Computers to Change What We Think and Do. Morgan Kaufmann Publishers, San Francisco (2003)
7. Herrmanny, K., Ziegler, J., Dogangün, A.: Supporting users in setting effective goals in activity tracking. In: Meschtscherjakov, A., De Ruyter, B., Fuchsberger, V., Murer, M., Tscheligi, M. (eds.) PERSUASIVE 2016. LNCS, vol. 9638, pp. 15–26. Springer, Cham (2016). https://doi.org/10.1007/978-3-319-31510-2_2
8. Kaiser, H.F.: An index of factorial simplicity. Psychometrika **39**(1), 31–36 (1974). https://doi.org/10.1007/BF02291575
9. Kampik, T., Nieves, J.C., Lindgren, H.: Coercion and deception in persuasive technologies. In: 20th International Trust Workshop, pp. 38–49 (2018)
10. Laerd Statistics: Principal components analysis (PCA) using SPSS statistics (2015). https://statistics.laerd.com/
11. Laerd Statistics: Two-way ANOVA using SPSS statistics (2015). https://statistics.laerd.com/
12. Oinas-Kukkonen, H.: A foundation for the study of behavior change support systems. Pers. Ubiquit. Comput. **17**(6), 1223–1235 (2013). https://doi.org/10.1007/s00779-012-0591-5
13. Smids, J.: The voluntariness of persuasive technology. In: Bang, M., Ragnemalm, E.L. (eds.) PERSUASIVE 2012. LNCS, vol. 7284, pp. 123–132. Springer, Heidelberg (2012). https://doi.org/10.1007/978-3-642-31037-9_11
14. Spahn, A.: And lead us (not) into persuasion...? Persuasive technology and the ethics of communication. Sci. Eng. Ethics **18**(4), 633–650 (2012). https://doi.org/10.1007/s11948-011-9278-y

15. Spears, N., Singh, S.N.: Measuring attitude toward the brand and purchase intentions. J. Curr. Issues Res. Advert. **26**(2), 53–66 (2004). https://doi.org/10.1080/10641734.2004.10505164
16. Stibe, A., Oinas-Kukkonen, H.: Using social influence for motivating customers to generate and share feedback. In: Spagnolli, A., Chittaro, L., Gamberini, L. (eds.) PERSUASIVE 2014. LNCS, vol. 8462, pp. 224–235. Springer, Cham (2014). https://doi.org/10.1007/978-3-319-07127-5_19
17. Verbeek, P.P.: Ambient intelligence and persuasive technology: the blurring boundaries between human and technology. Nanoethics **3**(3), 231 (2009). https://doi.org/10.1007/s11569-009-0077-8
18. de Vries, R.A.J., Zaga, C., Bayer, F., Drossaert, C.H.C., Truong, K.P., Evers, V.: Experts get me started, peers keep me going: comparing crowd-versus expert-designed motivational text messages for exercise behavior change. In: 11th EAI International Conference on Pervasive Computing Technologies for Healthcare, pp. 155–162. ACM (2017). https://doi.org/10.1145/3154862.3154875
19. Yardley, L., Choudhury, T., Patrick, K., Michie, S.: Current issues and future directions for research into digital behavior change interventions. Am. J. Prev. Med. **51**(5), 814–815 (2016). https://doi.org/10.1016/j.amepre.2016.07.019

Effects of a Virtual Model's Pitch and Speech Rate on Affective and Cognitive Learning

Sofia Fountoukidou$^{(\boxtimes)}$, Uwe Matzat, Jaap Ham, and Cees Midden

Eindhoven University of Technology,
513, 5600 MB Eindhoven, The Netherlands
s.fountoukidou@tue.nl

Abstract. Various nonverbal behaviors – often referred to as nonverbal immediacy - of both human and virtual teachers have been shown to play a crucial role in student learning. However, past literature provides limited evidence of the effect of a virtual agent's vocalization, as a nonverbal immediacy cue, on learning outcomes. Even less is known about the effect of nonverbal immediacy on learning when used in conjunction with virtual behavioral modeling. Earlier research provides evidence that virtual behavioral modeling could be an effective instructional method to facilitate learning in multimedia learning environments. The current work investigated the effects of a virtual model that used stronger vs. weaker vocal nonverbal immediacy on affective learning and cognitive learning (both perceived and objective). The operationalization of the virtual model's vocal nonverbal immediacy has been realized by manipulating the agent's vocal parameters of pitch and speech rate. We predicted, that a virtual model with stronger vocal nonverbal immediacy (i.e., higher pitch and faster speech rate) would be more effective in influencing individuals' learning outcomes, as compared to a virtual model with weaker vocal nonverbal immediacy (i.e., lower pitch and slower speech rate). In accordance with our hypotheses, results revealed that participants who received instructions from a virtual model that used stronger vocal nonverbal immediacy showed greater affective learning, and increased perceptions of learning. Support was also found for an effect on participants' recall. Results and implications of the study's findings are discussed.

Keywords: Nonverbal immediacy · Vocalization · Virtual modeling · Learning

1 Introduction

Persuasion is a way to influence attitude change and/or corresponding behavior change. Typically, persuasion aims at influencing through communication [1]. Although often associated with verbal information, only a small percentage of communication involves words and sentences. In fact, a substantial portion of our communication is nonverbal. The term "nonverbal" is commonly used to describe all human communication events that go beyond the spoken or written word, such as facial expression, spatial behavior

© Springer Nature Switzerland AG 2019
H. Oinas-Kukkonen et al. (Eds.): PERSUASIVE 2019, LNCS 11433, pp. 16–27, 2019.
https://doi.org/10.1007/978-3-030-17287-9_2

gesture, and nonverbal vocalization. According to earlier research, more than 65% of the information exchanged during a face-to-face conversation occurs in a nonverbal band [2, 3].

Especially in the area of instructional communication, which is the domain of the study's persuasive implementation, teachers' nonverbal communication behaviors, play a crucial role in student learning. Nonverbal communication in educational settings is often referred to as nonverbal immediacy. Specifically, nonverbal immediacy has been conceptualized as the ability of teachers to create a psychological closeness with their students through nonverbal communication [4, 5]. This concept is grounded in approach-avoidance theory [4], which asserts that "people approach what they like and avoid what they do not like" (p. 22). Several nonverbal immediacy cues of teachers have been found to play a crucial role in student's learning, such as proximity, eye gaze, gestures, body position, facial expression, and vocalization. Cumulative evidence revealed that teachers' nonverbal immediate behaviors lead to better affective learning, perceived learning and cognitive learning of students [6].

Besides humans, persuasive technologies also have the capacity to employ verbal and nonverbal cues, especially when they take on the role of a social agent. In fact, the potential of replacing human teachers with virtual agents – on-screen animated characters - in multimedia learning environments has been the target of increasing research interest. Their inclusion represents an attempt to introduce more instructional support and persuasive elements in digital settings [7]. Virtual agents are expected to facilitate learning because of their ability to simulate social interaction [8].

Earlier research has provided evidence of the powerful role of a virtual agent's nonverbal communication behavior in enhancing learning (i.e., [9]). However, earlier studies examined the potential impact of agent's nonverbal cues on learning in isolation of other conditions under which an agent could facilitate learning, such as, its instructional method. Drawing on recent findings on the effectiveness of virtual agents to increase learning when used as behavioral models [10], the goal of the current research is to take one step further and examine whether nonverbal immediacy cues of a virtual behavioral model could influence learning outcomes.

Virtual behavioral modeling pertains to the employment of a virtual agent that verbally explains and physically accomplishes a task, thereby showing the learner how to successfully complete it [10]. It is argued that behavioral modeling influence learning via the four underlying processes of attention, retention, production, and motivation [11]. What is more, it has been suggested that the extent to which a learner attends to the modeled behavior is influenced by various characteristics of the model [11]. However, there is limited research on the effects of a (human or virtual) model's nonverbal characteristics on learning. To date, the most closely related research to the examination of a model's nonverbal cues for learning pertains to a model's level of expertise and similarities with the learner (i.e., sex, race, gender) [12]. As a result, there is a lack of specific guidelines on how to design nonverbal cues of virtual models.

There is a number of factors to be taken into consideration when constructing a virtual agent's verbal and nonverbal behavior, in order to facilitate learning (i.e., learners' characteristics, agent's teaching function, learning environment) [13].

In this study, taking into account the role of a virtual agent as a behavioral model, we decided to examine the effect of a virtual model's vocalization as a nonverbal immediacy cue on learning.

In the current study, the virtual model's vocalization was operationalized by manipulating the agent's vocal parameters of pitch and speech rate (i.e., to create stronger or weaker vocal nonverbal immediacy). Our selection of these vocal parameters was based on earlier findings suggesting that the combination of temporal (i.e., speech rate) and expressive features (i.e., pitch) of a speaker's voice exert the strongest effects on both emotions and cognition [14]. In more detail, pitch is defined as the degree of highness or lowness of a tone, which is determined by the vibration of the vocal folds (i.e., the faster the vibration per second (Hz), the higher the pitch). It is generally measured as the fundamental frequency of the sound wave. Speech rate is the term given to the speed at which one speaks. It is calculated by the number of words spoken in a minute [15].

Our focus on an artificial model's vocalization rests on the cognitive theory of multimedia learning [16]. According to this theory, the human information processing system includes dual channels for visual and verbal processing. Since each of these two systems has limited processing capacity, it has been suggested that instructional methods should aim at balancing the processing demands between these two channels [17]. Due to the fact that behavioral modeling requires a substantial amount of processing to take place in the visual channel (i.e., due to demonstration), we argue that the inclusion of vocal nonverbal cues (i.e., as opposed to visual nonverbal cues, like facial expressions) could further assist the development of learners' mental model of the observed behavior.

Overall, the current study aims at contributing to the topic of virtual agent's vocal nonverbal immediacy for learning, which has received limited attention (i.e. [18]), as well as extending findings, by examining the issue of nonverbal cues of a virtual model that remains unexplored.

1.1 Current Work

In the current research, we examined whether a virtual agent that models a behavior while using enhanced vocalization, operationalized as pitch and speech rate and thus strong nonverbal immediacy, could influence learning outcomes. To test our research question, we compared a virtual model that used more enhanced vocalization (i.e. stronger vocal immediacy condition), as compared to a virtual agent that used less enhanced vocalization (i.e., weaker vocal immediacy condition).

We predicted that a virtual model that used stronger vocal immediacy would be more effective in improving individuals' affective learning (H1) and cognitive learning (both perceived and objective) (H2). In addition, we explored whether the use of stronger vocal immediacy by a virtual model would influence how people perceive their interaction with this virtual agent (i.e., evaluation of agent's perceived qualities of anthropomorphism, animacy, and likeability).

2 Methodology

2.1 Participants and Design

One-hundred-forty-four individuals participated in the study. The participants were recruited using a local participant database, and most of them were students from Eindhoven University of Technology. Of these participants, 55 were females (38%) and 89 males (62%). Ninety-two participants (63%) were educated to undergraduate level or higher, 45 participants (31.2%) had completed high school and seven participants (4.86%) chose not to disclose their educational level. The vast majority of the participants (82%), reported using computers on a daily basis, with a computer use of more than 12 h per week. More than half of the participants (54.2%) reported no previous experience with using computer-based assistive technologies (i.e., software and/or hardware).

The study employed a between-participants design, with the participants being randomly assigned to one of the two experimental conditions: virtual modeling with stronger vocal immediacy and virtual modeling with weaker vocal immediacy.

The study's dependent variables were affective learning and cognitive learning. Inclusion criteria were participants' fluency in English. The duration of the experiment was approximately 30 min, for which participants received five euros as compensation for their participation.

2.2 Materials

The 3D animated virtual agent, implemented in this study, was created using the CrazyTalk 8 software.

The study's instructional script refers to an eye-tracking software, called Gaze-TheWeb (GTW). GTW is a web-browser, developed to be controlled solely with the eyes, using eye-tracking hardware (see [19]).

The actor's voice was recorded using Audacity software. Afterwards, pitch analysis of these audio recordings was performed using Praat software.

Virtual Agent. The image of the virtual agent (i.e., the design of its upper body) was designed to resemble participants' characteristics in terms of appearance, according to the guidelines derived from the earlier literature [12]. Since the majority of the participants were students at a Dutch University, the agent was designed to be young (<30 years old), attractive (as manipulated by the agent's facial features) and "cool" (as manipulated by the agent's clothing and hairstyle). Lastly, intense facial expressions of the agent were lacking.

Concerning its function, the agent as a virtual model appeared to use the GTW system to demonstrate its functionalities by moving his head and eyes, while providing verbal explanations at the same time (see Fig. 1).

Fig. 1. Virtual agent modeling the behavior: on the left side, the light blue highlights the effect of the agent's action (i.e., typing); on the right side, the agent appeared to perform this action while providing verbal explanations. (Color figure online)

Instructional Script. The first step of the study was to create an instructional script, which introduced participants to the use of a new, eye-controlled web browser (GTW). This novel technology was unfamiliar to the study's participants. Then, two instructional versions were developed. In particular, the second instructional version was an exact replica of the first version, except that it differed in terms of pitch and speech rate. A male actor, who lent his voice to the virtual model, spoke out loud both instructional versions. The voice actor was selected because of his clear English accent and pronunciation, and also because he had attended voice training in the past.

Vocal Nonverbal Immediacy. In the current study, we manipulated the agent's vocal parameters of pitch and speech rate, so as to create stronger or weaker vocal nonverbal immediacy.

The optimal pitch tone varies depending on factors such as culture or context [20]. Nonetheless, according to general guidelines, the average fundamental frequency of a male adult's speech is 120 Hz [21–23]. Thus, the pitch tone boundary we set in the study to distinguish between stronger and weaker vocal immediacy was around 120 Hz. Overall, we calculated that the average pitch tone for the stronger vocal immediacy condition was 260 Hz, while the average pitch tone for the weaker immediacy condition was at 115 Hz.

In addition to the pitch tone, we also manipulated pitch variation (i.e., intonation). This is, there was more pitch variation (i.e., voice rises and then falls before it rises again), in the stronger vocal immediacy condition than in the weaker vocal immediacy condition. Thus, the weaker vocal immediacy condition, besides its lower pitch tone, was also designed to be more "flat" in terms of pitch variation. The pitch variation in the stronger vocal immediacy condition was carefully constructed to be congruent with important concepts presented during virtual modeling. Pitch manipulation was intentionally prepared so as to emphasize, both, affective nonverbal communication (i.e., speaker's feeling and attitude conveyance) and cognitive nonverbal communication (i.e., help in the encoding of new information) [24].

Speech rate is calculated by the number of words spoken in a minute. A normal number of words per minute (wpm) can vary hugely. Studies show speech rate alters depending on the speaker's culture, geographical location, subject matter, gender, emotional state, fluency, profession or audience [15]. Nonetheless, some general guidelines are that conversational speech generally falls between 120 wpm at the slow end, to 160–200 wpm in the fast range [25]. Slow speech is usually regarded as less than 110 wpm. Overall, we calculated that the speech rate in the stronger vocal immediacy condition was 133 wpm, as opposed to 119 wpm in the weaker vocal immediacy condition. Inevitably, this manipulation resulted in a relatively small difference in the video duration between the two conditions. Therefore, the video in the stronger vocal immediacy condition lasted for 9, 30 min, while, the video in the weaker vocal immediacy condition lasted for 10 min.

Measures. To check the success of our manipulation, participants were asked to estimate two components of the virtual agent's nonverbal behavior. The first component consisted of three items and assessed participants' objective perceptions of the agent's vocal parameters of pitch and speech rate (i.e., use of high vs. low tone of voice; use of vocal variety vs. flat voice; use of fast vs. slow speech rate). The second component, consisted of six items, assessing participants' subjective perceptions of the agent's vocal immediacy (i.e., pleasant vs. unpleasant voice, enthusiastic vs. boring voice etc.). Both components were administered through a 7-point semantic differential scale. These scales were adapted from earlier questionnaires measuring not only vocal but a range of other nonverbal immediacy cues (i.e., facial expressions) [5, 26–29]. We constructed an acceptable measure of participants' objective perceptions of vocal parameters (Cronbach's $a = .68$), as also, a reliable measure of their subjective perceptions of vocal immediacy (Cronbach's $a = .87$), by averaging participants' answers to each set of questions.

The main dependent variable for the first hypothesis was affective learning. Participants were asked to evaluate: (1) their affect towards the instructional content; (2) their affect towards the (virtual) model; (3) the likelihood of following the same virtual instructor for other similar videos in the future. These components of affective learning were administered through a 7-point semantic differential scale [5, 30]. We constructed reliable measures of participants' affect towards the content (Cronbach's $a = 0.86$) and towards the (virtual) model (Cronbach's $a = 0.88$), as also the likelihood of following the virtual instructor for other videos (Cronbach's $a = 0.90$), by averaging participants answers to each set of questions.

The main dependent variable for the second hypothesis was cognitive learning. Cognitive learning was assessed both objectively (i.e., with a test) as well as subjectively (perceived learning assessment). In more detail, immediate recall of the instructional content was assessed as an index of objective cognitive learning, and it was measured with a self-constructed test. Specifically, recall was assessed with a fill-in-the-blanks test consisted of nine recall items and a multiple-choice test of 18 questions[1]. For the fill-in-the-blanks test, participants were requested to recall missing keywords (exact words or synonyms) related to what it was actually spoken by the virtual model during the video, and fill in the blanks of the written transcript. For the multiple choice test, participants were asked to answer a series of questions by selecting the correct amongst four optional answers. We constructed two measures of cognitive learning by counting participants' number of correct answers to each test separately.

---

[1] The self-constructed test measuring immediate recall can be requested from the first author.

The cognitive performance scores were calculated by two researchers independently. There was a 100% agreement on the performance scores between the two raters.

Additionally, perceived learning was assessed by asking participants' responses on two, 7-point scale, questions [27]. A "learning loss" score was then computed by subtracting the score on the first question (i.e., *How much did you learn during the video lesson?*) from the score of the second question (i.e., *How much do you think you could have learned from this video had you had this ideal instructor?*), indicating a learner's overall perceived learning score. Reliability using this measure in previous research was reported at .94 [31]. Overall, learning loss score has been widely used in communication research as an index of cognitive learning (e.g., [32]).

Finally, for exploratory reasons participants were asked to indicate their perceptions of the agent's animacy, anthropomorphism, and likability. These three questionnaires are part of the "Godspeed" questionnaire, developed to assess key concepts of Human-Computer interaction [33]. The questionnaires were administered in a 7-point semantic differential, scale. We constructed reliable measures of anthropomorphism (Cronbach's $a = .83$), animacy (Cronbach's $a = .79$), and likeability (Cronbach's $a = .93$) by averaging participants' answers to each set of questions.

2.3 Procedure

Participants were welcomed in the central hall of the lab building. Each participant was asked to read and sign an informed consent form, stating the general purpose of the research and their willingness to participate in this study. Then, participants were randomly assigned to one of the two outlined experimental conditions and they were asked to watch an instructional video on how to use the GTW browser. The video was split into the following two screens: on the right-hand side, a virtual model appeared to use the GTW system by moving the head and eyes, while providing verbal explanations of the system functionalities that was demonstrating; the left-hand side of the screen contained a display of the system, exposing participants to the progressive effects of the agent's actions in real time (i.e., Fig. 1). The instructional video in both conditions was identical in terms of wording, and demonstrations, with the only difference being the strength of the vocal parameters of pitch and rate.

After the end of the instructional videos, participants were requested to answer an online survey and to complete a cognitive test. Lastly, they were debriefed, paid and thanked for their participation.

3 Results

Manipulation check: A one-way multivariate analysis of variance (MANOVA) was conducted to check the study's manipulation of vocal nonverbal communication (measured as objective perceptions of vocal parameters and subjective perceptions of vocal immediacy). The results revealed a statistically significant treatment effect on the two dependent variables combined, Wilk's $\Lambda = .61$, $F(2, 141) = 44.385$, $p < .001$, $\eta_p^2 = .38$. Separate univariate ANOVAs on the outcome variables revealed a significant treatment effect on: (1) objective perceptions of the agent's vocal parameters,

$F(1,142) = 84.84$, $p < .001$, $\eta_p^2 = .37$, with participants' objective perceptions of vocal parameters to be more positive in the stronger vocal immediacy condition ($N = 78$, $M = 3.7$, $SD = .96$), as compared to participants in the weaker vocal immediacy condition ($N = 66$, $M = 2.3$, $SD = .84$); (2) subjective perceptions of the agent's vocal immediacy, $F(1,142) = 50.55$, $p < .001$, $\eta_p^2 = .27$, with participants' subjective perceptions of vocal immediacy to be more positive in the stronger vocal immediacy condition ($N = 78$, $M = 4.5$, $SD = 1.0$), as compared to participants in the weaker vocal immediacy condition ($N = 66$, $M = 3.3$, $SD = .87$).

Affective learning: A one way multivariate analysis of variance (MANOVA) was conducted to examine the effect of the level of strength of a virtual model's vocal nonverbal immediacy on individuals' affect towards the instructional content, towards the virtual model as also their likelihood of following the same virtual instructor for other instructional videos. The results revealed a statistically significant effect of the level of strength of the virtual model's vocal nonverbal immediacy on the three dependent variables combined, Wilk's $\Lambda = .85$, $F(3,140) = 7.88$, $p < .001$, $\eta_p^2 = .14$. In line with our hypothesis, separate univariate ANOVAs on the outcome variables revealed a significant treatment effect on: (1) affect towards the instructional content, F $(1, 142) = 7.23$, $p < .01$, $\eta_p^2 = .48$, with participants' evaluation to be more positive in the stronger vocal immediacy condition ($N = 78$, $M = 5.6$, $SD = .98$), as compared to participants in the weaker vocal immediacy condition ($N = 66$, $M = 5.1$, $SD = 1.0$); (2) affect towards the virtual model, $F(1, 142) = 21.39$, $p < .001$, $\eta_p^2 = .13$, with participants' evaluation to be more positive in the stronger vocal immediacy condition ($N = 78$, $M = 5.4$, $SD = 1.1$), as compared to participants in the weaker vocal immediacy condition ($N = 66$, $M = 4.5$, $SD = 1.1$); 3) likelihood of following the same virtual instructor for other instructional videos, $F(1,142) = 17.82$, $p < .001$, $\eta_p^2 = .11$, with participants' evaluation to be more positive in the stronger vocal immediacy condition ($N = 78$, $M = 4.4$, $SD = 1.5$), as compared to participants in the weaker vocal immediacy condition ($N = 66$, $M = 3.3$, $SD = 1.4$).

Cognitive learning: A one-way multivariate analysis of variance (MANOVA) was conducted to examine the effect of the level of strength of a virtual model's vocal nonverbal immediacy on individuals' immediate recall. Recall was measured with a fill-in-the-blanks test and a multiple-choice test. The results revealed a statistically significant effect of the level of strength of the model's vocal nonverbal immediacy on the two dependent variables combined, Wilk's $\Lambda = .94$, $F(2, 141) = 4.33$, $p = .01$, $\eta_p^2 = .6$. In line with our hypothesis, separate univariate ANOVAs on the outcome variables revealed a significant treatment effect on fill-in the-blanks test, $F(1, 142) = 5.25$, $p = .02$, $\eta_p^2 = .36$, with participants' recall performance to be better in the stronger vocal immediacy condition ($N = 78$, $M = 7.9$, $SD = 2.7$), as compared to participants in the weaker vocal immediacy condition ($N = 66$, $M = 6.9$, $SD = 2.2$). Results showed a non-significant treatment effect on the multiple-choice test, $F(1, 142) = .31$, $p > .05$, between participants in the stronger vocal immediacy condition ($N = 78$, $M = 10.4$, $SD = 2.8$) and participants in the weaker vocal immediacy condition ($N = 66$, $M = 10.6$, $SD = 2.9$).

Perceived learning (learning loss): An independent sample t-test was conducted to examine the effect of the level of strength of a virtual model's vocal nonverbal immediacy on individuals' perceptions of learning. Results revealed a statistically significant effect, $t(142) = -2.36$, $p = .02$, $r = .20$, with participants in the stronger vocal immediacy condition ($N = 78$, $M = .41$, $SE = .11$) to report less learning loss (therefore more perceived learning), as compared to participants in the weaker vocal immediacy condition ($N = 66$, $M = .83$, $SE = .13$).

Agent's qualities: A one-way multivariate analysis of variance (MANOVA) was conducted to examine the effect of the level of strength of a virtual model's vocal nonverbal immediacy on individuals' judgments about the agent's qualities of likeability, animacy, and anthropomorphism. The results revealed a statistically significant effect of the level of strength of the model's vocal nonverbal immediacy on the three dependent variables combined, Wilk's $\Lambda = .85$, $F(3, 140) = 7.55$, $p < .001$, $\eta_p^2 = .14$. As expected, separate univariate ANOVAs on the outcome variables revealed a significant treatment effect on: (1) agent likeability, $F(1, 142) = 19.75$, $p < .001$, $\eta_p^2 = .12$, with participants' judgments on the agent's likeability to be more positive in the stronger vocal immediacy condition ($N = 78$, $M = 5.4$, $SD = 1.0$), as compared to participants in the weaker vocal immediacy condition ($N = 66$, $M = 4.6$, $SD = 1.0$); (2) agent animacy, $F(1, 142) = 9.12$, $p < .001$, $\eta_p^2 = .06$, with participants' judgments on the agent's animacy to be more positive in the stronger vocal immediacy condition ($N = 78$, $M = 3.7$, $SD = 1.1$), as compared to participants in the weaker vocal immediacy condition ($N = 66$, $M = 3.2$, $SD = 0.8$); (3) agent anthropomorphism, $F(1,142) = 8.85$, $p < .001$, $\eta_p^2 = .06$, with participants' judgments on the agent's anthropomorphism to be more positive in the stronger vocal immediacy condition ($N = 78$, $M = 3.7$, $SD = 1.2$), as compared to participants in the weaker vocal immediacy condition ($N = 66$, $M = 3.1$, $SD = 0.9$).

4 Discussion

The current research investigated the persuasive effect of a virtual model that used stronger vocal nonverbal immediacy, as compared to the (same) virtual model that used weaker vocal nonverbal immediacy, on individuals' affective and cognitive learning. Vocal nonverbal immediacy was operationalized by manipulating agent's vocal parameters of pitch and speech rate.

The study's results supported our first hypothesis, showing that a virtual model that used stronger vocal immediacy enhanced individuals' affective learning, as compared to a virtual model that used weaker vocal immediacy. Specifically, participants in the stronger vocal immediacy condition showed an increased affect towards the subject matter, the virtual model, as also increased likelihood to continue learning from the same instructor. These findings are in line with past work that highlighted the crucial role of a (human) teacher's nonverbal immediacy to influence students' affective learning [6]. What is more, the study's results add to earlier literature (i.e., [9]) by providing further evidence that, similar to a human teacher, a virtual agent that uses nonverbal immediacy cues (i.e., vocalization) can influence people's affective learning. Nonetheless, the current study not only supports, but, also extends these findings, by revealing that a virtual agent acting as a behavioral model can amplify students' affective learning by providing oral explanations augmented with strong vocal immediacy cues (i.e., pitch and speech rate).

Furthermore, we found mixed results for our second hypothesis. In more detail, participants in the stronger vocal immediacy condition showed better recall when they were assessed with the fill-in-the-blanks test, compared to participants in the weaker vocal immediacy condition. To the contrary, no evidence for a difference between the two conditions was found when recall was assessed with a multiple-choice questions test.

We suggest several potential explanations for these mixed results. One possible reason pertains to the educational assessment used for evaluation (i.e., fill-in-the-blanks vs. multiple-choice questions), as it seems to influence students' performance. According to recent literature, one of the basic disadvantages of a multiple-choice assessment is the possibility of guessing the answer. To the contrary, evidence suggests that the fill-in-the-blanks test is more objective and can overcome the possibility of guessing [34]. Moreover, another reason for these mixed results could be related to the virtual behavioral modeling. This is, virtual modeling could have provided participants with visual information (in addition to verbal explanations), helping them to recognize, instead of recalling, the correct answer in the multiple-choice question test. On the other hand, the fill-in-the-blanks assessment required participants to rely solely on their recall of the model's oral instructions in order to supply the correct answer. In sum, we suggest that a fill-in-the-blanks test, assessed specific knowledge acquired only through verbal explanations, while the multiple-choice questions test assessed more general knowledge acquired also through visual task demonstration. Overall, the study extends earlier literature, by providing evidence that a virtual model that uses strong vocal immediacy cues when demonstrating a task, can further enhance recall of specific knowledge.

Next, we found evidence that a virtual model with stronger vocal immediacy cues also affects perceived learning. In more detail, the study's findings showed that participants in the stronger vocal immediacy condition, as compared to those in the weaker vocal immediacy condition, indicated increased perceptions of having learned from the instructional video.

Lastly, since the research pertained to a virtual agent as a model (using stronger vs. weaker vocal nonverbal immediacy), we explored the effect of the study's treatment on individuals' perceptions of the agent's key qualities. As expected, participants in the stronger vocal immediacy condition indicated higher perceptions of the agent's anthropometrism, animacy, and likeability, compared to participants in the weaker vocal immediacy condition. Overall, these findings provided evidence that, in addition to improving the learner-teacher relationship, nonverbal immediacy cues (i.e., vocalization) positively affected human-technology interaction.

Despite the study's clear evidence on the effect of vocal immediacy cues of a virtual model on learning, caution is needed in generalizing these findings beyond the study's population characteristics. This is because nonverbal immediacy cues are highly inferential and they vary culturally and contextually [15]. What is more, although we adopted a single-cue approach, the study's vocal immediacy was comprised of both pitch and speech rate. Future research could examine the single effect of each vocal parameter on learning outcomes. Finally, little is known about the underlying mechanisms of the effects of nonverbal immediacy on affective and cognitive learning. Future research could investigate whether motivation and attention, proposed by earlier research (i.e., [35, 36]), mediate the effect of nonverbal immediacy on learning outcomes.

Overall, the current findings revealed that a virtual model's vocal non-verbal immediacy can enhance learners' affective and cognitive learning, and also affect their perceptions of the agent's qualities. The study contributes to the field of persuasive technologies, showing that taking into consideration non-verbal cues (i.e., vocalization) can increase the power of virtual agents as technological persuaders. Furthermore, the study's findings also have practical implications for the design and use of virtual models in digital settings. Similarly, these results contribute to the development of effective artificial voice assistants that will be found more and more in our societies like Alexa, Siri, and Google assistant.

References

1. André, E., et al.: Non-verbal persuasion and communication in an affective agent. In: Cowie, R., Pelachaud, C., Petta, P. (eds.) Emotion-Oriented Systems. Cognitive Technologies. Springer, Berlin (2011). https://doi.org/10.1007/978-3-642-15184-2_30
2. Morris, D.: Gestures, Their Origins and Distribution. Stein & Day Pub, New York (1979)
3. Knapp, M.L., Hall, J.A., Horgan, T.G.: Nonverbal Communication in Human Interaction. Cengage Learning, Boston (2013)
4. Mehrabian, A.: Silent Messages. Wadsworth, Belmont (1971)
5. Andersen, J.F.: Teacher immediacy as a predictor of teaching effectiveness. Ann. Int. Commun. Assoc. 3(1), 543–559 (1979)
6. Witt, P.L., Wheeless, L.R., Allen, M.: A meta-analytical review of the relationship between teacher immediacy and student learning. Commun. Monogr. 71(2), 184–207 (2004)
7. Clark, R.E., Choi, S.: Five design principles for experiments on the effects of animated pedagogical agents. J. Educ. Comput. Res. 32(3), 209–225 (2005)
8. Reeves, B., Nass, C.: The Media Equation: How People Treat Computers, Television, and New Media. Cambridge University Press, Cambridge (1997)
9. Johnson, W.L., Rickel, J.W., Lester, J.C.: Animated pedagogical agents: face-to-face interaction in interactive learning environments. Int. J. Artif. Intell. Educ. 11(1), 47–78 (2000)
10. Fountoukidou, S., Ham, J., Matzat, U., Midden, C.: Using an artificial agent as a behavior model to promote assistive technology acceptance. In: Ham, J., Karapanos, E., Morita, P.P., Burns, C.M. (eds.) PERSUASIVE 2018. LNCS, vol. 10809, pp. 285–296. Springer, Cham (2018). https://doi.org/10.1007/978-3-319-78978-1_24
11. Bandura, A.: Self-efficacy: toward a unifying theory of behavioral change. Psychol. Rev. 84 (2), 191 (1977)
12. Rosenberg-Kima, R.B., Baylor, A.L., Plant, E.A., Doerr, C.E.: Interface agents as social models for female students: the effects of agent visual presence and appearance on female students' attitudes and beliefs. Comput. Hum. Behav. 24(6), 2741–2756 (2008)
13. Heidig, S., Clarebout, G.: Do pedagogical agents make a difference to student motivation and learning? Educ. Res. Rev. 6(1), 27–54 (2011)
14. Breitenstein, C., Lancker, D.V., Daum, I.: The contribution of speech rate and pitch variation to the perception of vocal emotions in a German and an American sample. Cogn. Emot. 15 (1), 57–79 (2001)

15. Ngiam, J., Lee, C.C.Y., Charumilind, J., Chen, Z.: U.S. Patent No. 9,741,392. U.S. Patent and Trademark Office, Washington, DC (2017)
16. Mayer, R.E.: Multimedia Learning. Academic Press, New York (2001)
17. Mayer, R.E., Moreno, R.: Nine ways to reduce cognitive load in multimedia learning. Educ. Psychol. **38**(1), 43–52 (2003)
18. Veletsianos, G.: The impact and implications of virtual character expressiveness on learning and agent–learner interactions. J. Comput. Assist. Learn. **25**(4), 345–357 (2009)
19. Menges, R., Kumar, C., Müller, D., Sengupta, K.: GazeTheWeb: a gaze-controlled web browser. In: Proceedings of the 14th Web for All Conference on the Future of Accessible Work, p. 25. ACM (2017)
20. Gudykunst, W.B., Ting-Toomey, S., Chua, E.: Culture and Interpersonal Communication. Sage Publications Inc., Thousand Oaks (1988)
21. Hollien, H., Shipp, T.: Speaking fundamental frequency and chronologic age in males. J. Speech Lang. Hear. Res. **15**(1), 155–159 (1972)
22. Hsiao, T.Y., Solomon, N.P., Luschei, E.S., Titze, I.R.: Modulation of fundamental frequency by laryngeal muscles during vibrato. J. Voice **8**(3), 224–229 (1994)
23. Mizuno, O., Nakajima, S.Y.: A new synthetic speech/sound control language. In: Fifth International Conference on Spoken Language Processing, pp. 2007–2010 (1998)
24. Frechette, C., Moreno, R.: The roles of animated pedagogical agents' presence and nonverbal communication in multimedia learning environments. J. Media Psychol. **22**(2), 61–72 (2010)
25. What's Your Speech Rate?. https://mscra.com/whats-your-speech-rate/. Accessed 29 Nov 2018
26. Mehrabian, A.: Silent Messages, 2nd edn. Wadsworth, Belmont (1981)
27. Richmond, V.P., Gorham, J.S., McCroskey, J.C.: The relationship between selected immediacy behaviors and cognitive learning. Ann. Int. Communication Assoc. **10**(1), 574–590 (1987)
28. Richmond, V.P., McCroskey, J.C., Johnson, A.D.: Development of the nonverbal immediacy scale (NIS): measures of self-and other-perceived nonverbal immediacy. Commun. Q. **51**(4), 504–517 (2003)
29. Servilha, E.A.M., Costa, A.T.F.D.: Knowledge about voice and the importance of voice as an educational resource in the perspective of university professors. Revista CEFAC **17**(1), 13–26 (2015)
30. Scott, M.D., Wheeless, L.R.: Communication apprehension, student attitudes, and levels of satisfaction. W. J. Speech Commun. **41**, 188–198 (1975)
31. Gorham, J.: The relationship between verbal teacher immediacy behaviors and student learning. Commun. Educ. **37**(1), 40–53 (1988)
32. Chesebro, J.L., McCroskey, J.C.: The relationship between students' reports of learning and their actual recall of lecture material: A validity test. Commun. Educ. **49**, 297–301 (2000)
33. Bartneck, C., Croft, E., Kulic, D.: Measuring the anthropomorphism, animacy, likeability, perceived intelligence and perceived safety of robots. In: Metrics for HRI Workshop, Technical report, vol. 471, pp. 37–44 (2008)
34. Medawela, R.S.H.B., Ratnayake, D.R.D.L., Abeyasinghe, W.A.M.U.L., Jayasinghe, R.D., Marambe, K.N.: Effectiveness of "fill in the blanks" over multiple choice questions in assessing final year dental undergraduates. Educación Médica **19**(2), 72–76 (2018)
35. Kelley, D.H., Gorham, J.: Effects of immediacy on recall of information. Commun. Educ. **37**(3), 198–207 (1988)
36. Christophel, D.M.: The relationships among teacher immediacy behaviors, student motivation, and learning. Commun. Educ. **39**(4), 323–340 (1990)

Self-monitoring and Reflection

Are Trackers Social Actors? The Role of Self-tracking on Self-evaluation

Elçin Hancı[1]([✉]), Peter A. M. Ruijten[1], Joyca Lacroix[2],
Elisabeth T. Kersten-van Dijk[1], and Wijnand A. IJsselsteijn[1]

[1] Eindhoven University of Technology,
P.O. Box 513, 5600 MB Eindhoven, The Netherlands
{e.hanci,p.a.m.ruijten,e.t.v.dijk,
w.a.ijsselsteijn}@tue.nl
[2] Philips Research, High Tech Campus 34,
5656 AE Eindhoven, The Netherlands
joyca.lacroix@philips.com

Abstract. Despite the increased usage and potential benefits of self-tracking technologies for pursuing healthy lifestyles, the relationship that users have with these personal devices has remained under-studied. The current paper presents a field study to explore the perceived role of self-tracking devices as social actors. Participants received a pedometer which they carried on their person for one day. Users' access to numerical feedback and the feeling of being tracked were manipulated, and users were interviewed afterwards regarding their experiences and their perceived social relationship to the tracker. Results of a thematic analysis indicated that in general, the feeling of being tracked led to higher self-awareness regarding participants' walking activity. In particular, having access to agent feedback gave rise to more frequent self-evaluative reports towards one's performance as well as a closer relationship between the device and its user. The results extend the CASA (Computers As Social Actors) paradigm by demonstrating that the capturing (and feeding back) of data can make a device be perceived as a social actor and be described in relational terms, even in the absence of clear social cues.

Keywords: Self-tracking · Social actor · Self-evaluation

1 Introduction

The acceleration of technological advancements have allowed technologies to be smaller and more ubiquitous, allowing just-in-time adaptive interventions (JITAIs) and context relevant persuasion [13]. Self-tracking technologies are one of the promising products of these advancements [1]; their ubiquitous nature combined with their capability of tracking a wide range of behaviours and bodily states has allowed self-tracking devices to play an active role in influencing one's lifestyle. Despite of the potential benefits, the effects of continuous tracking and constantly having access to feedback on the user's self-evaluation are under-researched. The current study is designed to explore these effects.

H. Oinas-Kukkonen et al. (Eds.): PERSUASIVE 2019, LNCS 11433, pp. 31–42, 2019.
https://doi.org/10.1007/978-3-030-17287-9_3

2 Background

2.1 Self-tracking Technology

By means of monitoring one's behaviour and delivering timely feedback, self-tracking devices aim to increase a user's self-knowledge and ultimately help to support a healthy lifestyle by facilitating long term behaviour change [9]. This is a long-term endeavour that starts with elevation of self-awareness with respect to the targeted behaviours. To give an example, measuring number of steps directs individuals' attention towards the quantified output, and hence facilitates self-reflection about one's walking activity. In other words, self-tracking, through the help of quantification, allows a relatively mundane activity to become the center of a user's attention [18]. Once an increase in self-awareness is experienced, users become more likely to gain relevant insights through quantified feedback. Literature shows that continuous engagement with self-tracking helps users in their attempts to make healthier choices; for example, monitoring calorie intake enables people to be more aware of their eating behavior, and counting steps stimulates people to put extra effort into reaching their daily goal of ten thousands steps [3, 4]. Moreover, findings that are more recent show that self-tracking can support the fulfilment of psychological needs thereby illustrating that the role of trackers can go beyond that of merely stimulating behavior change [8].

Despite their popularity and potential benefits, self-tracking is not without its drawbacks. Recent work by van Dijk and colleagues pointed out that self-tracking technologies may have unintended negative side effects such as stimulation of excessive self-focus [22]. Indeed, literature reports mixed findings regarding the effectiveness of self-tracking technologies [4]. In a recent longitudinal study of 6 months where the effectiveness of different types of weight loss interventions was compared, results indicated that participants who were exposed to the technology-enhanced intervention had less weight loss compared to those who were exposed to the standard weight loss intervention [7]. One possible explanation for these unexpected findings was that the constant feedback could have been perceived as a reminder of how much participants were behind in comparison to their stated goals, and eventually got demotivated.

In another study, Etkin manipulated the accessibility of quantified feedback for participants walking with a pedometer [5]. Those who had access to the pedometer's numerical feedback demonstrated an increase in performance, yet at the same time reported a decrease in their enjoyment related to the activity. The underlying explanation was that the numerical feedback made participants perceive the activity of walking more like work rather than as an enjoyable activity they voluntarily choose to engage in. This study thus illustrates that using such devices can have seemingly paradoxical effects on people's behavior on the one hand and the experience of that behavior on the other hand. Considering that subjective experiences associated with a behavior play a key role in maintaining that behavior over a longer period of time, it is crucial to gain a better understanding of the experiential effects related to self-tracking devices that monitor behavior and provide feedback to the user. This paper focuses on exploring such experiential effects for walking behavior and in particular its effect on self-evaluation processes.

The wide acceptance and use of self-tracking technologies in our daily lives brings along fundamental changes in terms of the kinds of feedback we receive, the behavioral and physiological scope of the feedback, as well as the frequency and format of such feedback. Today, the use of self-tracking devices provides a constant reminder as to how well we are doing at reaching our goals. In contrast to a decade ago where bathroom scales were the most accessible way of tracking one's weight in a not so-precise way, today one can track a host of bodily and behavioral variables with great precision and with a constant flow of feedback.

Another change that comes along with self-monitoring technology is the evolving level of intimacy that is being formed between user and device. Physical closeness of the device (i.e., sensors worn on the body) together with the intimate nature of the behavioral and bodily signals it captures set it apart from other measurement devices such as weighting scales. This level of physical intimacy resembles the closeness and the function of human embodied biological senses, making human senses and digi-talized sensors harder to separate psychologically [18]. Given the novelty of this new fashion of intimacy and the personal importance of the feedback users are exposed to, the key question that arises is how users evaluate themselves as a consequence of this feedback, and what kind of psychological relationship they build with such physically intimate technology. In this paper, we present a first exploration to elucidate this relationship.

2.2 Technology as a Social Actor

Social relationships in human-computer interactions have been studied for a few decades already. One influential paradigm, Computer as Social Actor (CASA), was established in the mid-1990s [15, 16]. Its' central claim is that the social heuristics of interpersonal relationships are also witnessed in human-computer interaction [20]. Several studies have demonstrated that individuals attribute similar social behaviors and attitudes to technology as they would to humans. This includes reciprocating help to computers when they were helpful to the users before or by attributing gender roles to the computers when they have 'female' vs. 'male' voices [14].

Similar observations have been made with other advanced technologies such as embodied conversational agents and robots. Attributing some level of social agency to the aforementioned technologies is relatively straightforward as the cues they express are reminiscent of humans; computers respond to users by using personable language, embodied agents have facial expressions and robots have humanoid bodies, with faces and limbs that can mimic human movements. As we are fundamentally social beings, our brains are especially attuned to processing social cues, even when such cues are simulated or degraded versions of interpersonal interactions. In this paper, we explore the question whether, and to what extent, a self-tracking device, which is devoid of such overt social cues, will be processed in a way that is fundamentally social, or whether it will be perceived as an information display without social properties or impact.

2.3 Self-tracking Technology as a Socially Present Agent

Self-tracking devices typically communicate with their users by displaying numerical feedback on a tiny screen without giving any verbal or non-verbal social cues. However, we hypothesize here that the physical closeness, the personal relevance of the feedback it provides together with its' ubiquitous nature create enough room to develop a more personal relationship between the user and the self-tracking technology. This would be expressed, for example, by users attributing personality traits to the device and perceiving it, implicitly or explicitly, as a social actor. In line with this reasoning, in one recent study, an application about calorie intake monitoring was evaluated as oppressive and "punishy", thus clearly attributing intentionality and agency to the system [17].

Perceiving a self-tracking device as a social agent is of importance since such perception changes the nature and intensity of the confrontation with one's personal data. If the device is perceived as a social agent, this simultaneously adds the concept of social presence as a new dimension in evaluating user experience as well as giving the device a new additional role as an observer.

The concept of social presence was introduced by Short, Williams and Christie [21] and described as a 'degree of salience of the other person in the interaction and the consequent salience of the interpersonal relationships...' (p. 65). While the concept of social presence has been widely studied in the context of video-mediated communication and online environments, we argue that it is relevant to evaluate social presence in relation to self-tracking as well. The bodily data gathered is not only passively monitored by the device; the mere possibility to rather easily connect a judgement to the measurement (due to agreed standards in social communities, e.g. it is a good thing to take 10000 steps per day) may already be sufficient for the device itself to indirectly interpret the data [12]. This room for interpretation allows to form a more organic relationship with the device where the perceived interaction is bilateral.

Perceiving the device as a socially present actor brings along its role as an observer of the user monitoring his/her own performance. Literature shows that the mere presence of an observer can bring both advantages and drawbacks to oneself. The notion of social facilitation, developed by Zajonc, explains that the mere presence of an audience can facilitate task performance on simple, well-learned tasks [24]. Studies also showed that the presence of an audience may stimulate evaluation apprehension by triggering impression management processes [11]. If self-tracking devices are perceived as socially present agents, this can lead towards improved performance when it is relatively easy to reach one's goals. At the same time, wearing a tracker may also trigger users to evaluate their own performance in a more judgmental way due to the anticipated social-evaluative threat the tracker encompasses.

2.4 Current Study

In order to explore the perceived social presence of a self-tracking technology, we designed a study in which people carried a pedometer for one day. By means of manipulating the accessibility of numerical feedback and the feeling of being tracked, and interviewing participants afterwards, we aimed to get an understanding of how people experienced being tracked and how they evaluated the pedometer. We expected that self-tracking, regardless of the exposure to the numerical feedback, would increase self-awareness. If the device is perceived as socially present agent, then people will be likely to hold more of a self-evaluative attitude towards their performance.

3   Method

3.1   Participants and Design

One hundred and sixteen participants from Eindhoven University of Technology (TU/e) were recruited using JFS database, a participant database open to all registered students and employees of the university. 6 participants were excluded before the analysis as they did not show up for the second part of the experiment. In total, there were 110 participants (45 female), ranging in age from 19 to 35 years (mean age = 24). Inspired by the design of the third study from Etkin's paper, we used a between subjects design with three conditions [5]. The three conditions were (1) being tracked and receiving feedback, (2) being tracked but not receiving feedback, and (3) just wearing the device but not being tracked or receiving feedback. In the feedback condition, participants received a pedometer and were told that they were free to check the numbers if they wanted, but it was not part of the protocol. In the no feedback condition, participants wore the pedometer but had no access to the monitored data (i.e., the pedometer was sealed). Participants in this condition were told that the study focused on the usability of the device and numbers were irrelevant to the study. Please take note that in the no feedback condition, although participants were not able to see the numbers, they were still aware that the device was functioning and they were being tracked. In order to explore any differences which may occur from merely being tracked vs. not, we added an additional 'no battery' condition. In this condition, participants received a pedometer with the lid shut like in the no feedback condition, but they were told that the experimenter had removed the battery and hence the device was not functioning.

3.2   Materials and Procedure

To objectively measure walking behavior, all participants wore a Yamax Digi-WalkerTM SW200 (YDWP) pedometer to record the number of steps taken. The SW 200 pedometer is reliable and has been validated in previous studies [2, 23]. In order to explore our hypotheses, we used a creative writing task with 2 open-ended questions. Choosing a creative writing task rather than a more traditional method such as interviews has allowed participants to preserve their anonymity while answering the questions. This has diminished the degree to which the experimenter is involved in the procedure and therefore has made participants' responses less susceptible to social desirability bias. Additionally, it has also allowed participants to take their time as answers to both questions required reflective thinking.

Aim of the first question was to ask, albeit indirectly, to what extent 'walking' played a role in the participant's day whilst wearing the pedometer: *Could you write a short bed time story about your adventures of the day?* The second question targeted the user's relationship with the tracker more directly and aimed to understand whether seeing the numbers vs. not would make any difference on how people evaluated the pedometer itself: *If this pedometer you have worn today was a friend of yours, how would you describe your friendship with her/him?* In addition, a set of usability questions targeting the device were added in order to make our cover story more credible and divert participant's attention from the concept of 'walking'. Answers to the usability questions were not of interest to the current study and will not be analyzed further. In addition, we also assessed participants' motivation towards walking using the SIMS scale [6], which will be reported elsewhere.

The study consisted of 2 brief on-site (lab) sessions, with at least 6 h of wearing the device between the two sessions. The first session took place in the morning (9 am–12 pm). Upon arrival to the lab, participants were told a cover story that the study was about the usability testing of the pedometer which they were going to wear for the next six hours. Participants were randomly assigned to one of the three conditions. They were given the same instructions as used by Etkin [5]: For the feedback condition, participants were told, "If you are interested in how many steps you have taken, feel free to look at the counter, but it is not a required part of the study". Participants in the no feedback condition were told, "We are only interested in whether the pedometer is comfortable to wear and so the lid has been taped shut". In the additional no battery condition, they were told that the experimenter removed the battery from the device. In order to make participants believe that the battery of the device was really removed, the experimenter had scattered the pieces of the pedometer and a few extra batteries on the desk. Participants in all conditions were asked to wear the pedometer on their belt and not to take it off until they arrived to the lab for the second session. Lastly, those who were wearing any smartwatches or trackers prior to the study were kindly asked to take them off until the end of the experiment. All participants then left the lab and continued their day. Participants returned to the lab for the second session after 6 h (3 pm–6 pm). Upon arrival, participants handed over their pedometer to the experimenter, who discretely took note of the number displayed on the screen. They completed the creative writing task and answered a set of usability questions.

3.3 Analysis

Answers from the creative writing task were analyzed by conducting a thematic analysis. First, answers from all participants were read carefully and repeatedly. In order to avoid any possible bias, the coder was not aware of the conditions of the participants until the coding was completed. The data were analyzed using Nvivo (12th edition), which helps code larger amounts of data in an organized and structured way. Initially 16 codes were generated for question 1 and 11 codes for question 2 based on the recurring patterns in the data. Lastly, themes and subthemes were formed. Intercoder reliability of the qualitative data set was tested by an independent coder: there was 86% agreement for the first question and 81% for the second question.

4   Results and Discussion

Findings of the thematic analysis for both questions demonstrated that the presence or absence of feedback and the feeling of being tracked led to differences in how participants perceived their day as well as how they evaluated their relationship with the device. In the following section, the themes that emerged from the answers to both questions and their interpretations are discussed in detail.

4.1   Thematic Analysis 1: Tell Me About Your Day

By asking the question 'Could you write a short bed-time story about your adventures of the day?' we wanted to know the role of pedometer in participants' day. If seeing the feedback or the feeling of being tracked would have any effect on their perception of the day, we would expect it to be reflected in terms of the way participants described their day. Although the experiment was conducted at different times of the days, many participants, regardless of the conditions, only talked about their day while having the device. What happened during the participant's day before receiving the pedometer or what was likely to happen after handing in the pedometer was mostly skipped.

Value Judgement Based on Walking

Although it is clearly explained during the instructions that the purpose of the study was not related to any physical activity performance, many participants still reported their walking activities. However, the level of detail of their evaluations and the justifications provided of their lack of walking performance varied across the conditions.

Figure 1 demonstrates a difference between the conditions (feedback, no feedback and no battery) in terms of participants' value-based judgements of their walking performance. Participants who were aware of being tracked mention their 'walking performance' more frequently than those who were unaware, regardless of their accessibility of the numerical feedback: *"...The thing was, I did not take many steps that day...This was a pretty regular day for me, so the step counter may not have counted many steps"* (P103). While the feeling of being tracked seems to make people more self-aware of their walking, those who could see the numbers became more self-evaluative and reported a variety of reasons as justifications of their performance; *"I did a little less walking than usual due to an intense work schedule for the day"* (P61), *"I just thought I won't be walking that much. Unfortunately, I kept my key inside my home and came out and locked the main door. I was walking the whole day and steps count came approximately to 5800 steps in last six hours:)))"* (P70). In contrast to these two conditions, those who were unaware of being tracked were much less frequently mentioning their walking performance. When they mentioned walking, however, the focus was more on the experience than on the performance itself; *"Whenever I get frustrated or bored, I go for a walk along the Dommel River. ... the walk was very pleasant and my day continued with pleasant times."* (P64). It is of importance here to mention that while many of the participants in the feedback condition were talking about their 'expectations' and how they felt they fell short of those expectations in terms of their walking performance, the actual experiment, as far as they were told, had nothing to do with their walking performance and the numbers were irrelevant. Despite of having this information, when the numerical feedback turned out lower than their expectations, they were not satisfied and sometimes even felt guilty about themselves. In a way, they were trying to reach a goal which was not explicitly set.

Another difference observed across the conditions is the context in which walking activity was mentioned (see Fig. 1). 'Walking as a task' is a subtheme that stands for reporting solely one's walking when it is being isolated from one's environment as positioning it, so to speak, as a main task of the day; "...I walked to the Spar super-market... I went out for a 10-min walk and then walked back to the library..." (P35). 'Walking as an experience' on the other hand, stands for mentioning walking without centralizing it as a main task of the day: "Walking down the streets with lots of trees on the side, a pleasant walk to remember" (P52). Those who reported walking more as a task were also more likely to pair it with time of the day: "...Around 12.00 I walked to the building...and walked back around 13.00. Around 13.45 I packed my bag and cycled to work" (P102).

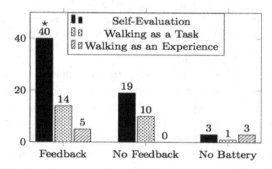

Fig. 1. The frequency of coding references for each subtheme across the conditions for the theme Value Judgement Based on Walking. The values with a Pearson adjusted residual greater than ±1.96 are indicated with a (*).

Results of this analysis showed that tracking one's steps increased self-evaluation towards walking. In turn, the increased self-focus has oriented users towards justifying their behavior in objective terms rather than being immersed in the experience itself, making them more self-critical. People become self-aware of their walking even when there was no access to the numbers. Receiving the numerical feedback in particular, however, made participants more performance oriented, with a heightened focus on numbers in general (e.g., time of day, duration of a walk, number of steps). On the other hand, the absence of self-tracking appeared to give participants more freedom to enjoy the activity for its own sake, in line with Etkin's interpretations of her results [5]. Sharing time of the day and other numerical information, accompanied with lack of shared subjective experiences indicate that users appear to be *accounting for their performance*, or lack thereof, rather than sharing their day. One interpretation of this seemingly defensive attitude is that users felt they were being held accountable, implying an observing social agent to whom one is held accountable. These findings suggest that access to the numerical feedback can make the device be perceived as a social agent, at least to the extent that people feel a need to explain themselves and become more self-critical about their own performance, even during a relatively open and natural "Tell me about your day" creative writing task.

4.2   Thematic Analysis 2: Describe Your Relationship with the Pedometer

The purpose of asking the question 'If this pedometer you have worn today was a friend of yours, how would you describe your friendship with her/him?' was to obtain insight about the participant's perceived relationship with the pedometer, and specifically the extent to which this relationship was perceived as friendly or intimate.

Evaluation and Attributions of Friendship

Many participants, across the conditions, described their friendship based on their perceived level of closeness with the pedometer. Figure 2a shows that the majority of participants who described this relationship as close were those who had access to the numbers; "*I would say he/she is a close friend*" (P27). Whereas people in the no feedback condition generally seemed to consider the device as more distant from them: "*...need more time to develop our friendship*" (P45). It is worth mentioning that participants who did not have access the numerical feedback, yet were still aware of the fact that the device was tracking them, evaluated the friendship in similar terms to those who believed that the device was not functioning at all. It seems that receiving numerical feedback aids in forming a more intimate bond between the device and the participant. Perhaps this is similar to human interpersonal relationships, where having shared a secret with a friend brings the two people closer together. The "secret" in this case would be the intimate nature of the bodily data collected by the device, which seems to add a new, intimate dimension to the evaluation of the user-device relationship by changing the dynamics of the friendship.

After indicating their level of closeness, people stated reasons for perceiving the device as a close or distant friend. The majority of participants who perceived the pedometer as a helpful friend belonged to the people in the feedback condition (see Fig. 2b). The pedometer was perceived as helpful mainly because of two reasons; it is informative and it is motivating: "*...the friend stimulates me to walk even more than I already do*" (P14), "*...I would say he's a helpful friend. Someone who knows me and gives advice*" (P109). None of the people who did not have access to the numbers have evaluated the potential friendship as close. These same participants also evaluated the 'friend' as silent, even more than those who thought the device was not functioning, making its passive role much more salient. Even though people in both the No Feedback and No Battery conditions could not see the numbers, it appears that for participants in the No Feedback condition, being aware of the fact that tracking data is available in principle yet inaccessible to them, may have increased their interaction expectations and therefore heightened their feelings of disappointment compared to others.

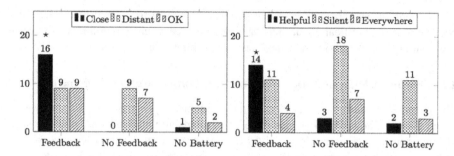

Fig. 2. The frequency of coding references for each subtheme across the conditions for the themes *Evaluation of Friendship* (left) and *Attributions of the Friend* (right). The values with a Pearson adjusted residual greater than ±1.96 are indicated with a (*).

5 Conclusion

The current paper aimed to explore whether the presence of a self-tracking device would be perceived as a social entity and if so, how it affects the user-device relationship, in terms of self-evaluation and perceived social relationship to the tracker. This is a relevant question, both from a research perspective of understanding the psychology of self-tracking and other personal technological artefacts, as well as from an applied design-perspective, where we want to support positive behavior change based on an adequate understanding of the user's experience.

In our research, we used a creative writing task to elicit reflections of the role of self-tracking data in relation to self-evaluation. The results of the thematic analysis indicated, in line with the literature [10], that self-tracking increases self-awareness. The elevated self-awareness seems to trigger a process of self-evaluation particularly when people have access to numerical feedback. This may be due to social components attributed to the devices' capability to perceive the walking behavior. Higher numbers of self-evaluative comments made in the Feedback condition, compared to the No Feedback condition, suggests that it is the feedback of the captured data that is of primary social significance. More importantly perhaps, participant's descriptions of the tracking technology, especially when numerical feedback was available, was strongly framed in social terms, with the tracking technology described as a close and helpful friend.

Whilst this study presents a first exploration which is not without its limitations, it is one of the first empirical works that explores the perception of self-tracking devices as social entities. Results of the current study may thus be seen to extend the CASA paradigm [20] and suggest that despite the lack of overt social cues, self-tracking technologies may elicit significant social perceptions, which has consequences four our self-evaluative processes, as well as the relationship we build with our tracking devices.

Acknowledgements. We would like to thank Heleen Rutjes for her help as independent coder in order to assess inter-coder reliability. This work is part of the project "Mobile Support Systems for Behavior Change", supported by Netherlands Organization for Scientific Research (NOW). For more information see http://behaviour-change.eu/.

References

1. Asimakopoulos, S., Asimakopoulos, G., Spillers, F.: Motivation and user engagement in fitness tracking: heuristics for mobile healthcare wearables. Informatics **4**(1), 5 (2017)
2. Barfield, J.P., Rowe, D.A., Michael, T.J.: Interinstrument consistency of the Yamax Digi-Walker pedometer in elementary school-aged children. Meas. Phys. Educ. Exerc. Sci. **8**(2), 109–116 (2004)
3. Bravata, D.M., et al.: Using pedometers to increase physical activity and improve health: a systematic review. J. Am. Med. Assoc. **298**(19), 2296–2304 (2007)
4. Burke, L.E., Swigart, V., Warziski Turk, M., Derro, N., Ewing, L.J.: Experiences of self-monitoring: successes and struggles during treatment for weight loss. Qual. Health Res. **19** (6), 815–828 (2009)
5. Etkin, J.: The hidden cost of personal quantification. J. Consum. Res. **42**(6), 967–984 (2016)
6. Guay, F., Vallerand, R.J., Blanchard, C.: On the assessment of situational intrinsic and extrinsic motivation: the situational motivation scale (SIMS). Motiv. Emot. **24**(3), 175–213 (2000)
7. Jakicic, J.M., et al.: Effect of wearable technology combined with a lifestyle intervention on long-term weight loss: the IDEA randomized clinical trial. JAMA **316**(11), 1161–1171 (2016)
8. Karapanos, E., Gouveia, R., Hassenzahl, M., Forlizzi, J.: Wellbeing in the making: peoples' experiences with wearable activity trackers. Psychol. Well-Being **6**, 4 (2016)
9. Kersten-van Dijk, E.T., Westerink, J.H.D.M., Beute, F., IJsselsteijn, W.A.: Personal informatics, self-insight, and behavior change: a critical review of current literature. Hum.-Comput. Interact. **32**(5–6), 268–296 (2017)
10. Kersten-van Dijk, E., IJsselsteijn, W.A.: Design beyond the numbers: sharing, comparing, storytelling and the need for a quantified us. Interact. Des. Archit. J. **29**, 121–135 (2016)
11. Kowalski, R.M., Leary, M.R.: Strategic self-presentation and the avoidance of aversive events: antecedents and consequences of self-enhancement and self-depreciation. J. Exp. Soc. Psychol. **26**(4), 322–336 (1990)
12. Kristensen, D.B., Ruckenstein, M.: Co-evolving with self-tracking technologies. New Media Soc., 1–17 (2018)
13. Nahum-Shani, I., et al.: Just-in-time adaptive interventions (JITAIs) in mobile health: key components and design principles for ongoing health behavior support. Ann. Behav. Med. **52**(6), 446–462 (2016)
14. Nass, C., Moon, Y.: Machines and mindlessness: social responses to computers. J. Soc. Issues **56**(1), 81–103 (2000)
15. Nass, C., Moon, Y., Fogg, B.J., Reeves, B., Dryer, D.C.: Can computer personalities be human personalities? Int. J. Hum.-Comput. Stud. **2**(43), 223–239 (1995)
16. Nass, C., Steuer, J., Tauber, E.R.: Computers are social actors. In: Proceedings of the SIGCHI Conference on Human Factors in Computing Systems, pp. 72–78 (1994)
17. Orji, R., Lomotey, R., Oyibo, K., Orji, F., Blustein, J., Shahid, S.: Tracking feels oppressive and "punishy": exploring the costs and benefits of self-monitoring for health and wellness. Digital Health **4** (2018)
18. Pink, S., Fors, V.: Being in a mediated world: self-tracking and the mind–body–environment. Cult. Geogr. **24**(3), 375–388 (2017)
19. Pink, S., Sumartojo, S., Lupton, D., Heyes La Bond, C.: Mundane data: the routines, contingencies and accomplishments of digital living. Big Data Soc. **4**(1) (2017)

20. Reeves, B., Nass, C.: The Media Equation: How People Treat Computers, Television, and New Media Like Real People and Places. Cambridge University Press, Cambridge (1996)
21. Short, J., Williams, E., Christie, B.: The Social Psychology of Telecommunications. Wiley, London (1976)
22. Kersten-van Dijk, E.T., Beute, F., Westerink, J.H.D.M., IJsselsteijn, W.A.: Unintended effects of self-tracking. In: Proceedings of the 33rd Annual ACM Conference on Human Factors in Computing Systems (2015)
23. Wilde, B.E., Sidman, C.L., Corbin, C.B.: A 10,000-step count as a physical activity target for sedentary women. Res. Q. Exerc. Sport **72**(4), 411–414 (2001)
24. Zajonc, R.B.: Social facilitation. Science **149**(3681), 269–274 (1965)

Supporting and Understanding Reflection on Persuasive Technology Through a Reflection Schema

Fahri Yetim[1,2(✉)]

[1] Department of Information Systems,
FOM University of Applied Sciences, Cologne, Germany
fahri.yetim@fom.de
[2] Department of Information Processing Science,
University of Oulu, Oulu, Finland

Abstract. Literature on persuasive technology acknowledges the importance of promoting reflection within design research and practice. This paper takes up a reflection framework suggested in previous research as assisting the reasoning of researchers, designers or other stakeholders concerning values, goals, actions, and their consequences in a project. It contributes to this research by demonstrating additional evidence for the applicability of the reflection framework by applying it to a published case. This work can guide researchers and practitioners by means of issues to be considered while reflecting on as well as communicating value-related aspects in a project, so that significant value choices and the rationale for actions taken to promote them are clear.

Keywords: Reflection · Discourse ethics · Value sensitive design · Research communication · Persuasive technology

1 Introduction and Background

It is a widely shared view that being sensitive in setting design goals, choosing means as well as considering the values and rights of all relevant stakeholders ensure that ethically and morally relevant considerations inform the shaping of a system [2, 3, 5, 13, 16]. Reflection is necessary to challenge assumptions and values as well as for clarifying our understanding of what is good or bad, right or wrong [5, 13]. Research in the context of persuasive technology investigates and suggests a set of principles, models and methods for the analysis, design and evaluation of such systems that aim at influencing people to change their attitudes and/or behaviors [10]. Previous research has argued that setting persuasion goals and chosen means to achieve them imply value assumptions and have consequences for those affected. They have emphasized the importance of reflection and user participation in the analysis, design and evaluation of persuasive systems [7, 9, 11, 12, 15, 17].

This paper takes up a reflection framework suggested in previous research as assisting the reasoning of researchers, designers or other stakeholders about values, goals, actions, and their consequences in a project [15]. This framework is informed by

© Springer Nature Switzerland AG 2019
H. Oinas-Kukkonen et al. (Eds.): PERSUASIVE 2019, LNCS 11433, pp. 43–51, 2019.
https://doi.org/10.1007/978-3-030-17287-9_4

the reflective concepts of discourse ethics [4, 5], - including different types of discourses such as pragmatic, ethical, and moral discourses, - and by other value-based argumentation approaches [1]. Previous publications related to this framework have argued that it can be used within the process of persuasive system development for several purposes, e.g., for supporting ideation, analysis, design, evaluation as well as publication of a system. However, the usage of the framework has so far only been partially demonstrated. For example, the framework provided guidance for the design of reflection support systems [14, 16] as well as of an argumentation-based design rationale application, a *Rationale Browser*, that implements several of the questions of the framework to enable reflections as well as to document the result of the reflections [6]. In addition, parts of the framework (i.e., aspects of the pragmatic discourse) were considered for the analysis of the communication of value sensitive design research, and demonstrated that some of the guidelines have been inherently followed by some researchers [18].

This paper extends the analysis perspective beyond pragmatic discourses and in addition considers ethical and moral discourses in order to offer an incremental contribution to the research. By applying the framework to a published case that communicates reflections on persuasive technology, this paper provides additional evidence for the applicability of the reflection framework within the practice of persuasive design research. Such an analysis of reflections can help persuasive system researchers and designers to clarify the value specific issues and significant choices, to understand the reflections and reasoning of research participants, as communicated by the researchers, as well as to identify issues that have been given no or little consideration.

In the following, we first introduce the relevant parts of the reflection framework, then present a proof-of-concept demonstration of its applicability by applying it to a published research article, and finally, provide some discussion and conclusions.

2 The Reflection Framework

Practical reasoning is the general human capacity for resolving, through reflection, the question of what one intends to do. In his discourse ethics, Habermas [4] distinguishes between the pragmatic, ethical and moral employment of practical reason and three types of practical discourses, i.e., pragmatic, ethical and moral discourses. The idea is that in practical situations the question of what one is to do can take on pragmatic, ethical, and moral meaning, requiring different kinds of answers for justifying choices among alternative available courses of action. Reflections on *pragmatic discourse* seek reasons for a rational choice of means in the light of fixed goals, or of rational assessments of goals in the light of existing value preferences. *Ethical discourse* involves reflection on what is good for oneself or for a cultural community. Finally, *moral discourses* seek what is "equally good for all" and thus just.

To provide further refined guidance for reflections in relation to these three types of discourses, previous research [15] has distinguished two usage options for discourses: for identifying ideas (identifying mode) and for evaluating decisions/regulations (checking mode). In addition, a set of critical questions for each discourse are provided to support the reasoning/reflection of researchers, designers or other stakeholders.

Habermas [5] considers practical decisions to be legitimate if they result from a deliberative process that involves a fair consideration of the interests, values and valid norms. We consider persuasive system design research as a practice that has to deal with the practical, the good and the just. Consequently, its results can be considered legitimate if they are justified from the standpoint of pragmatic, ethical, and moral reasons, - a process requiring iterations between discourses in both identifying and checking modes for creating and examining ideas [16]. In this paper we limit our attention to the usage of discourses in the checking mode, as shown in Table 1, and leave the usage of discourses in the identifying mode to another paper.

Table 1. Discourses and related questions in the checking mode [15]

Pragmatic Discourse
Goal-Value: Reflect on the goal and its value
1.   Is the value V proposed indeed a legitimate value?
2.   Is goal G possible?
3.   Will goal G realize (or at least be consistent with) the value intended?
4.   Are there other goals considered that might conflict with goal G?
5.   Are there alternative goals to promote the same value?
Action-Goal: Reflect on the preferred action (means) to achieve the goal
6.   Is it possible to do action A?
7.   Will action A bring about the desired goal G?
8.   Are there alternative ways of realizing the same goal?
Action-Value: Reflect on the value consequences of the action
9.   Will doing action A promote the value intended?
10. Will doing action A promote some other value?
11. Will doing action A have a side effect which demotes the value intended?
12. Will doing action A have a side effect which demotes some other value?
13. Will doing action A preclude some other action which would promote some other value?
14. Are there alternative ways of realizing the same value?

Ethical Discourse
Values: Reflect on the compatibility of final decisions with ethical values
15. Do the goals considered promote or violate values preferred?
16. Do the actions considered promote or violate values preferred?

Moral Discourse
Norms: Reflect on the compatibility of decisions with accepted moral norms
17. Are the values promoted in accord with norms?
18. Are the goals to be achieved in accord with norms?
19. Are the actions to be taken in accord with norms?

Reflections in *pragmatic discourse* assess the choice of means in the light of fixed goals, or of goals in the light of existing value preferences. The questions for pragmatic discourses were mainly based on the concept of value-based practical reasoning [1]. In the context of persuasive systems, this kind of reasoning in checking mode can support the examination of existing practices or systems.

The goal of an *ethical discourse* is first and foremost to critically evaluate the goodness of ends ([5], p. 161). In the checking mode we considered those questions that help to assess whether the choices of goals and actions (i.e., results of pragmatic discourse) are in line with the values preferred. Two questions are included so as to critically evaluate the goodness of the results of pragmatic discourse, i.e., checking the goals and the actions taken with respect to their compatibility with the values preferred. They accommodate Habermas's [5] requirement that practical decisions should be compatible with ethical values to be considered legitimate.

Moral discourses deal with the moral rightness of norms of actions or regulations. Norms and values differ in their reference to obligatory rule-following and in their absolute versus relative bindings, as Habermas [5] states: "In the light of norms, I can decide what action is commanded; within the horizon of values, which behavior is recommended." (p. 256). Moral discourses can be entered into to find a norm or regulation that is just (identifying mode) or to assess the morally rightness of the results of other discourses (checking mode). For the checking mode we considered those questions that critically assess the results of other discourses. They can prompt researchers to examine whether the values promoted, goals set or actions taken are in accord with accepted norms and if they are in line with the requirement that the results of pragmatic and ethical discourses should be compatible with the moral norms in order to be considered legitimate [5].

To conclude, the schema recommends researchers reflect on and communicate the issues. Next, we apply these questions to analyze a research case in order to understand whether they have been inherently followed in a somewhat coherent way.

3 An Example of Reflective Research Communication

3.1 Purpose and Method

To demonstrate the applicability of the framework, we examined a published research article echoing the work other researchers [8] have done who used secondary data in the form of published cases to demonstrate the applicability of their guidelines. A published article can be viewed as an artifactual outcome of a reasoning process. We consider the article by Purpura et al. [12], which discusses some ethical and socio-cultural considerations involved in the design. It thus represents a good example of reasoning on the practical issue of "what one is to do" and provides evidence for pragmatic, ethical and moral reasoning. Our main goal is to determine if the descriptions, explanations, and justifications provided by the authors are classifiable according to the concepts of the framework.

Our analysis followed interpretive research method principles [8]. We marked sentences that express concepts of the schema, i.e., goals, actions, explicit value terms (e.g., privacy, surveillance, helpful, useful), and value consequences, and interpreted them through the lens of the questions. In the presentation of the analysis, we use Q# to refer to the related questions of the schema, where applicable. Indeed, multiple readings and interpretations of a text can be generated. The analysis draws on the text in its own right. We do not challenge its authors, nor undertake a critical evaluation of the quality of the articles. Yet, by analyzing the articles in the light of the framework we also demonstrate how authors, reviewers, and editors can apply it.

3.2   The Fit4Life Case

This case deals with a fictional, critical design, whose goal is not to provide a clear solution to a problem but to provoke reflection about ethical and conceptual limits of persuasive computing. For this purpose, Purpura et al. [12] first took the persuasive technology and obesity research literature at their word and implemented their logic and recommendations in a system called Fit4Life. Then they used the system as an example for reflecting on persuasive computing. The Fit4Life system "encourages individuals to address the larger goal of reducing obesity in society by promoting individual healthy behaviors." Its goal is to make users aware of situations that might negatively impact on their maintaining their ideal weight and to cause a change in their eating and exercise behaviors. The persuader is, on one level, the system designers. On another level, the Fit4Life system allows other individuals on social networks to become persuaders and influence each user (e.g. by generating wall posts to notify others to provide encouragement).

We employed the framework to analyze researchers' critical reflections on the design of Fit4Life and persuasive computing. Table 2 illustrates example statements as evidence used for the reflections relating to some of the questions. Concerning the pragmatic discourse, the researchers reflected on the societal goal of reducing obesity and the value of its achievement (Q3), i.e., improving the health of people and also making them attractive and socially acceptable. They criticized the design goals of the previous research and suggested alternative design goals to promote the same value (Q5). The researchers also argued for a design to foster mindfulness, challenged the appropriateness of existing actions for this purpose (Q7), and suggested alternative ways of achieving the desired goals effectively (Q8). Finally, they reflected on value consequences or side-effects of actions, for example, stating that the use of a specific model narrows our understanding of healthiness (Q11), that the use of a quantitative measuring method discards the value of personal experience (Q12), and that the system suggesting what to do precludes users from deciding on appropriate actions and improving their self-reflection ability (Q13).

Ethical discourse involves reflections on values and value conflicts as well as the assessment of whether actions and goals are in line with the preferred values. The example sentences illustrate researchers' evaluation/checking of Fit4Life against some accepted values. While reflecting on a broader, pervasive rationalization of our lives, they criticized Fit4Life for representing a rationalistic, objective worldview and denying our humanity (Q15), and that the mechanism used (i.e., the beacon) is coercive, forcing users to act involuntarily (Q16).

Moral discourse involves reflections on the rightness of actions or decisions. For example, the researchers raised moral issues with respect to enforcing the social good over the individual good through unpleasant pressure (Q17), setting goals for changing

Table 2. Reflections on the design of the Fit4Life system

Pragmatic Discourse

Goal-Value: Reflect on the goal and its value

Q3: "Optimizing the system to achieve the user-in-societal goal of reducing obesity will not only improve the health of working Americans, making them more productive, but, also has the effect of helping each participant become more attractive, and, therefore, more socially acceptable." (p. 424)

Q5: "While we used the terminology and design practices of the persuasive computing movement, the complete Fit4Life product [...] highlights a need for reflection through non-judgmental means rather than persuasion to achieve an ideal. In this way, it suggests that an ideal system might be a subjective one that would allow users to define their own meanings and values." (p. 428)

Action-Goal: Reflect on the preferred action (means) to achieve the goal

Q7: "If Fit4Life were designed to foster mindfulness, it might not discuss calories, schedules, and exercise in minutes at all." (p. 431)

Q8: "[...] exercise and diet planning regimes could be more effective [...] By exposing rather than covering seams [...] in the abilities of calorie or exercise tracking, [...] users would be encouraged to reflect on how they feel." (p. 431)

Action-Value: Reflect on the value consequences of the action

Q11: "One issue with the formal models derived from sensed data used in Fit4Life is that positive behavior is identified solely with reducing BMI. In choosing such a fixed model, the system reinforces a narrow conception of what it means to be healthy or fit." (p. 429)

Q12: "By focusing on quantitative measures the system also discards the value of personal experiences and emotions for a utilitarian position on the value of food and exercise." (p. 429)

Q13: "[The System] provides explicit verbal suggestions when specific foods should be eaten or avoided [...] The user no longer has to calculate calories consumed [...]to determine for themselves whether they are within their daily calorie allowance [...] we took away the user's ability to reflect on their situation and decide on appropriate action." (p. 430)

Ethical Discourse

Values: Reflect on the compatibility of final decisions with ethical values

Q15: "Fit4Life represents an incursion of a rationalistic, objective view of the world that is often hidden in the agendas of persuasive designers. [...] By seeking to reduce basic human flaws (or characteristics [...]), the persuasive agenda embodied in this design is dehumanizing." (p. 429)

Q16: "But when viewed critically, the beacon appears as both a signal for help and an element of shame. While soliciting support for the user it also highlights his or her nonconformity to personal and social norms and an inability to stick to plan. We believe that this shame [...] is coercive [...]." (p. 428)

Moral Discourse

Norms: Reflect on the compatibility of decisions with accepted moral norms

Q17: "Fit4Life's design decisions frequently sacrificed individual good for the social good— by providing avenues for unpleasant peer pressure, for example." (p. 428)

Q18: "More broadly, persuasive computing raises questions on the ethics of changing another's attitude, belief or behavior. In considering an ethical boundary situated around a user's intent we must ask if a choice can even honestly be made to take away one's choices." (p. 428)

Q19: "[...] persuasive technologies [...] often aim to enforce sublimated social goals. Is it ethical to exploit fears and anxieties in service of such goals? Are users allowed witness to the origin and full extent of these changes?" (p. 428)

another's attitude, belief, or behavior (Q18) and using fears and anxieties as a means for achieving social goals (Q19).

We should note that multiple interpretations of a statement are possible. For example, a statement that emphasizes rationalization through a persuasive system can be interpreted from a pragmatic perspective (i.e., the effectiveness of rationalization through the system), from an ethical perspective (i.e., the goodness of rationalization through the system), or from a moral perspective (i.e., the rightness of rationalization through the system). Similarly, statements that criticize preferences for social goods (or goals) over individual goods (or goals) and vice versa may be viewed from the perspective of goodness (ethical) or rightness (moral).

In summary, the analysis illustrates how the researchers used arguments to present and justify their work that matches some of the questions in the framework, and that the main ideas of the framework are inherently considered within their research communication practice.

4   Discussion and Conclusion

Acknowledging that persuasive systems imply value assumptions and have consequences for those affected, previous research has already emphasized the importance of reflection and user participation in the analysis, design and evaluation of such systems. In this paper we have taken a reflective perspective and considered a reflection framework which was informed by discourse ethics, in particular by three types of practical discourses, as well as by other value-focused approaches. The framework includes a set of refined discourse-type specific guiding questions for supporting the reasoning of researchers, designers or other stakeholders in practical discourses. The questions aim to create an awareness of important aspects and to prompt discourse participants to think about them.

The demonstration of the framework by applying it to a prior case have provided evidence of its applicability as well as showing its practical relevance for communicating research results. The analysis of the article on persuasive technology shows that researchers' reflections on the main concerns – including the desirability of changing a behavior to a specific direction, the effectiveness of methods chosen, and the value implications – instantiate concepts of the framework such as values, goals and actions at different levels of abstraction.

This work offers several benefits to research and practice. First, it provides refined structures for documenting the reasoning of researchers throughout different stages of a project. Second, it complements general guidelines for communicating reflective research results by making dimensions such as goal-value or action-value with associated critical questions explicit, so that researchers can use the framework as a guide to reason about the content they want to communicate in different sections of an article, including the goals, actions (methods) and associated values at different levels of granularity. Third, the framework can be used for ex post analysis and evaluation of published works. By asking questions researchers can critically evaluate ideas and identify further research issues which have gained less attention or been ignored. Nevertheless, we do not argue for a too strict consideration of the questions, as this may not always be practical for different reasons, including limits to an article's length, its thematic focus, as well as the background of researchers. Fourth, this work may also be of value in a review process. Reviewers can consider the concepts and questions of the framework so as to assess the validity of a value sensitive design research study as well as the reporting of its results. In this way, the reviewers participate in and continue practical discourses leading to an agreement or a revision of the research and/or the organization of the paper's content.

The suggested questions are by no means complete. Researchers can investigate additional questions for promoting reflection and guiding research communication. Moreover, further proof-of-use analyses can follow once we see how these ideas are applied in future research publications.

References

1. Atkinson, K., Bench-Capon, T., McBurney, P.: Computational representation of practical argument. Synthese **152**(2), 157–206 (2006)
2. Davis, J., Nathan, L.P.: Value sensitive design: applications, adaptations, and critiques. In: van de Poel, I., Vermaas, P., van den Hoven, J. (eds.) Handbook of Ethics, Values and Technological Design, pp. 11–40. Springer, Dordrecht (2015). https://doi.org/10.1007/978-94-007-6970-0_3
3. Friedman, B., Kahn Jr., P.H., Borning, A.: Value sensitive design and information systems. In: Zhang, P., Galletta, D. (eds.), Human-Computer Interaction in Management Information Systems: Foundations, pp. 348–372. New York (2006)
4. Habermas, J.: Justification and Application. Polity Press, Cambridge (1993)
5. Habermas, J.: Between Facts and Norms. Polity Press, Cambridge (1996)
6. Haghighatkhah, A., Oinas-Kukkonen, H., Yetim, F.: An argumentation-based design rationale application for reflective practice. In: Proceedings of the 22nd European Conference on Information Systems (ECIS), 9–11 June 2014, Tel Aviv, Israel (2014)
7. Halttu, K., Oinas-Kukkonen, H.: Persuading to reflect: role of reflection and insight in persuasive systems design for physical activity. Hum.-Comput. Interact. **32**(5–6), 381–412 (2017)
8. Klein, H.K., Myers, M.D.: A set of principles for conducting and evaluating interpretive field studies in information systems. MIS Q. **23**, 67–94 (1999)
9. Kuonanoja, L., Meedya, S., Win, K., Oinas-Kukkonen, H.: Ethical evaluation of a value sensitive persuasive system: case milky way. In: Proceedings of the Twenty-Second Pacific Asia Conference on Information Systems, pp. 1983–2825 (2018)
10. Oinas-Kukkonen, H., Harjumaa, M.: Persuasive systems design: key issues, process model, and system features. Commun. Assoc. Inf. Syst. **24**, 485–500 (2009)
11. Ploderer, B., Reitberger, W., Oinas-Kukkonen, H., van Gemert-Pijnen, J.: Social interaction and reflection for behaviour change. Pers. Ubiquit. Comput. **18**(2), 1667–1676 (2014)
12. Purpura, S., Schwanda, V., Williams, K., Stubler, W., Sengers, P.: Fit4Life: the design of a persuasive technology promoting healthy behavior and ideal weight. In: Proceedings of the 27th International Conference on Human Factors in Computing Systems, New York, NY, USA, pp. 423–432. ACM (2011)
13. Yetim, F.: Acting with genres: discursive-ethical concepts for reflecting on and legitimating genres. Eur. J. Inf. Syst. **15**(1), 54–69 (2006)

14. Yetim, F.: Critical examination of information: a discursive approach and its implementations. Informing Sci. **11**, 125–146 (2008). http://inform.nu/Articles/Vol11/ISJv11p125-146Yetim212.pdf

15. Yetim, F.: A set of critical heuristics for value sensitive designers and users of persuasive systems. In: Proceedings of the 19th European Conference on Information Systems (ECIS 2011), 9–11 June 2011, Helsinki, Finland (2011)

16. Yetim, F.: Bringing discourse ethics to value sensitive design: pathways to toward a deliberative future. AIS Trans. Hum.-Comput. Interact. **3**(2), 133–155 (2011)

17. Yetim, F.: Critical perspective on persuasive technology reconsidered. In: Proceedings of the ACM SIGCHI Conference on Human Factors in Computing Systems (CHI-2013), 27 April–02 May 2013, Paris, pp. 3327–3330. ACM, New York (2013)

18. Yetim, F.: Applicability of a reflection model for communicating value sensitive design research. In: Proceedings of the 24th European Conference on Information Systems (ECIS), 12–15 June 2016, Istanbul, Turkey (2016)

Designing Representations of Behavioral Data with Blended Causality: An Approach to Interventions for Lifestyle Habits

Kenny K. N. Chow[✉]

School of Design, The Hong Kong Polytechnic University,
Hung Hom, Hong Kong
sdknchow@polyu.edu.hk

Abstract. Many personal informatics systems present users' behavioral data in numbers or graphs for their reflection, which may not be effective on a daily basis because people do not always act like data scientists. Representation of behavioral data in virtual environments can provide information at a glance. Grounded in conceptual blending theory, insights from social psychology, and existing persuasive design principles, this article is conceptual-theoretical. It argues that representations should be designed like virtual consequences of behavior and related to users' existing knowledge of comparable cause-effect relationships in order to prompt one's imaginative beliefs about the behavioral-virtual causality. It proposes a framework that guides designing representations of behavioral data, including (1) identifying scenarios with comparable causality, (2) examining and grounding the mappings in embodied experiences, (3) performing blends between the behavior and the identified scenario, with different virtual consequences corresponding to different user behaviors, and (4) rendering virtual consequences as feedback that dynamically anchors the scenario for similar blends in users. Design cases are presented and analyzed to demonstrate how embodied mappings can be constructed for interventions for lifestyle habits.

Keywords: Behavior change · Personal informatics · Blending theory

1 Introduction

People today can use technology to track personal data related to various facets of daily life, from vitals (heart rate, blood pressure, body temperature), physical activity (step counts, travel distance, exercise minutes, active energy burnt), to lifestyles (sit-stand hours, sleep-wake patterns, alcohol or tobacco consumption, meditation exercise minutes), and others. Computational analyses of these data inform individuals of respective health or wellness. The systems that help people collect and reflect on this "personally relevant information" are called "personal informatics" [1]. Many of these systems present the analytics in numbers or graphs. Yet, the reflection on a daily basis may not be effective, because people do not always act like rational data scientists [2] and many of them are not data-savvy [3]. Representation of "raw" data is recommended [4], and "stylized representations" that map tracked data to images particularly

H. Oinas-Kukkonen et al. (Eds.): PERSUASIVE 2019, LNCS 11433, pp. 52–64, 2019.
https://doi.org/10.1007/978-3-030-17287-9_5

make information more "attractive", distinctive, and perceivable at a glance [5]. Non-numerical, non-literal, and figurative representations have been explored in earlier studies, such as Fish'n'Steps [6], UbiFit [7], UbiGreen [8], Playful Bottle [9], and Eco-island [10]. These representations typically map values of tracked data to states of on-screen virtual items like fish, flowers, trees, a garden, or an island. Yet, some representations seem like an abstract sign, rather than a natural outcome, of a behavior, because the causality between the behavior and the virtual outcomes is not related to users' existing knowledge. For example, why do the fish (in Fish'n'Steps) or the flowers (in UbiFit) grow when the user walks more? Why does the tree (in Playful Bottle) grow when the user drinks less water? There are probably some cause-effect links (e.g., maybe walking to collect food from surroundings for the fish?), yet they are untold, indirect, or conceptually distant to users. The virtual outcomes should be designed like natural, yet distinct (as in virtual environments) outcomes of the performed behavior. To enable users to make sense of the causality, designers should tap into users' existing knowledge of comparable scenarios, as informed by the embodied cognition thesis [11, 12]. The thesis holds that our understanding of a concept (e.g., a cause-effect relationship) is structured by our existing knowledge built on experiences in the world via the body. Major theories include conceptual blending, which refers to the understanding or generation of new knowledge by combining two or more structurally comparable concepts. To apply blending to causality, designers should imagine and identify a cause-effect scenario from another domain that is known to users, and then blend it with the behavior. The effects of the action in the scenario will suggest the design of possible outcomes in virtual environments, which will be experienced and imagined by users to be the consequences of the performed behavior.

This article is conceptual-theoretical. It argues that representation of behavioral data should be designed and rendered like outcomes of a behavior by blending with another scenario from a different domain, which prompt users' imaginative beliefs about the "blended causality". It first relates to existing persuasive design principles and insights from social psychology on behavioral consequences and motivation, and then provides the theoretical framework of imaginative understanding grounded in embodied cognition. It proposes to ground the mappings between the behavior and the scenario in embodied experiences. An extended set of guidelines is provided, including construction and evaluation of the mappings, blending of the behavior with the scenario, and rendering the blended causality as feedback that dynamically anchors the scenario for similar blends in users. To demonstrate how to use the guidelines, three design cases related to lifestyle habits are presented. The first one is to assist smoking cessation by blending with scenarios of virus or other life-threatening chemical leaks. The second one is to prevent smartphone overuse by blending with scenarios of keeping your companion awake with lights. The third one is to motivate users to stand up while sitting too long. It is blended with scenarios of incubating eggs.

2   Theoretical Framework

Representations of behavioral data should be designed like behavioral consequences. Insights from social psychology theories and persuasive design principles indicate that beliefs about the consequences are major motivators for performing or changing a behavior. Furthermore, for virtual outcomes to be seen and imagined to be behavioral consequences, the virtual outcomes should be related to users' knowledge of comparable causality, based on the embodied cognition thesis.

2.1   Beliefs About Behavioral Consequences

Fogg's Behavior Model (FBM) [13] considers both immediate outcomes (e.g., pleasure vs. pain) and foreseeable consequences (e.g., hope vs. fear), in addition to social influence, as major motivators for performing a behavior. Oinas-Kukkonen and Harjumaa [14] extend the model and develop a framework comprising specific principles for designing persuasive software systems. The list includes supporting self-monitoring, simulating the cause-effect link of a behavior, providing virtual rewards, being visually attractive, and many others. Midden et al. [15] discuss the roles of technology in behavioral intervention and particularly point out that virtual environments can create sensory and affective experiences of distant or indirect cause-effect relationships regarding a behavior. These major thoughts in persuasive design largely support the approach of representing tracked behavioral data as behavioral outcomes in virtual environments.

Research results in social psychology indicate that human behavior depends on both conscious intention and non-conscious automaticity. Theory of Planned Behavior (TPB) [16] sees one's beliefs about the consequences of a behavior as one major reason for performing that behavior. Yet, many of our everyday behaviors are interfered by the automatic environment-perception-behavior link [17] (e.g., we may thoughtlessly dry our hands with tissue paper after toilet). Habits are products of the two intertwined threads of thinking [18], which are learned, functional acts initially goal-directed (e.g., drying hands after toilet for hygiene and convenience) but later turned automatic in response to specific cues (e.g., a paper towel within reach), even though that may not be intentional on occasions (e.g., having a handkerchief in the pocket). People sometimes intend to change, but they need supportive interventions. In case of strong habits, people can be less attentive to new information or options [18]. Stimulating triggers are required to provoke one into conscious thinking. Metaphorical design promises to shift users' focus of attention and stimulate conscious awareness [19]. Metaphorical mappings of the behavior with a scenario from a different domain become promising.

2.2   Imaginative Beliefs About Virtual Consequences

For virtual outcomes to be seen as behavioral consequences, they should be related to users' knowledge of comparable causality, as informed by embodied cognition. Embodied cognition believes that human understanding of a concept, such as causality [20], are built on and structured by physical experiences in the world via the body and the brain. One fundamental and pervasive way of understanding is via "metaphor" [21].

Initially informed by linguistic studies, followed by empirical evidence from experimental psychology and neuroscience research results [22], metaphor theory sees metaphor (e.g., Good Is Up, as in the common phrase "high quality") cognitively as structural mappings between two conceptual domains (e.g., the abstract domain Quality and the concrete domain Verticality). Primary metaphors (e.g., Affection Is Warmth) are those entrenched by regularly co-occurring experiences (e.g., we touch or hug others with affection and simultaneously feel warm). Combining metaphors or other existing knowledge generates new understanding or ideas, technically called "blends". Blending emergently combines two (or more) mental simulations of particular scenarios as enacted, perceived, remembered, or imagined, into new one [23]. When we throw a crumpled sheet in a parabola into a wastebasket, we cognitively combine waste disposal (as enacted) with basketball playing (as remembered) into an imagined scenario of trashcan basketball [24]. In short, metaphor and blends are grounded in embodied experiences, which scaffold many concepts and support everyday understanding, such as imaginative beliefs (e.g., one momentarily believes that the wastebasket is the basket for basketball).

Consider if a habitual action (e.g., sitting too long) can be mapped with the action in a comparable scenario (e.g., over-incubating), technology-enabled co-occurrence (via embedded sensors and displays) of the behavior and the virtual outcomes (e.g., death of newly hatched virtual chicks) can enable imaginative blends that prompt momentary beliefs about the behavioral-virtual causality (e.g., sitting too long suffocates virtual chicks). The imaginative beliefs about the virtual consequences reinforce motivation to change (e.g., stand up).

3 The Guidelines

Designing representations of behavioral data with blended causality have four steps: (1) identifying comparable scenarios from different domains; (2) examining the mappings of scenarios with the behavior; (3) performing blends between the behavior and the scenario; elaborating different virtual consequences corresponding to different user behaviors; and (4) rendering the blended behavioral consequences as feedback that dynamically anchors the scenario for similar blends in users.

3.1 Identify Scenarios

Designers need to look for scenarios from different domains that have causes and effects comparable to the behavior and its consequences. This process can benefit from previous guidelines for metaphorical design. Madsen [19] offers guidelines for generating metaphors for interactive systems, including (1) attend to how users say about a system; (2) build on existing metaphors; (3) make use of old artifacts; and (4) look for real events with similar aspects. All four guidelines are applicable to designing representations of behavioral data. To identify cause-effect scenarios from different domains, designers can consider the following extensions.

(1) The vernacular: Designers can involve target users in focus-group interviews, showing them with relevant concepts via photo-mockups, videos, or other digital prototypes, which stimulate their thoughts and invite verbal responses from them. Verbal expressions often reveal mental associations, providing examples of comparable scenarios. Sometimes, vernacular naming in everyday communication can be insightful too, for instance, the smartphone on/off button is called "sleep/wake button", which makes users associate with the scenario of waking someone up.

(2) Existing metaphors: Designers can revisit existing metaphors pertaining to the behavior (e.g., a common expression in Cantonese describing the act of sitting too long as incubating). Some existing metaphors may be culturally specific; yet visualizing the scenarios (e.g., hatching an egg) via technology may work for people from other cultures. This is because metaphors that survive in a culture are often grounded in embodied experiences (e.g., sit on something and produce heat) that can be felt with the universal body. Technology can create similar experiences.

(3) Physical artifacts: Designers should always look at current or even old physical artifacts that people may use when performing the behavior (e.g., peak flow meter for checking lung capacity). Artifacts used in other domains can be related too (e.g., egg candler for checking the development status of an egg). These artifacts often remind users of familiar actions (e.g., blow at a peak flow meter or scan at an egg) and outcomes. Designers can tap into users' knowledge and enable them to recall similar scenarios (related or unrelated to the behavior) via the representation.

(4) Anecdotes: Designers can refer to anecdotes of theirs or others and look for perceived or remembered events that are seemingly unrelated to the behavior, but they have comparable causes and effects. For example, smoking is hazardous to health. The hazard can evoke memories of events like virus or bacteria infection. Also consider overuse of smartphones. The excessive screen light hurts the eyes, which echoes incidents of distracting roommates with the lights on. Designers need to check if the events are part of users' knowledge. Measures are discussed in Sect. 3.4.

3.2 Examine Mappings

Designers need to examine the mappings between the behavior and the comparable cause-effect scenario. The mappings should be grounded in embodied experiences. Embodied experiences are bodily experiences, whose primitive patterns, called schemas [22] (e.g., spatial relations like Up-Down, Near-Far, Contact-Noncontact, etc.), structure many basic concepts (e.g., metaphors like Good Is Up, Intimacy Is Close, Engagement Is Physical Contact, etc.). Some developed concepts have more culturally elaborate structures, called frames [25] (e.g., a light sign on means something is ongoing). Embodied schemas and cultural frames structure mental simulations of perceived or imagined scenarios, called mental spaces [23], which are mapped and combined in blending. Each mental space consists of elements of the scenario, such as actors, objects, their spatial relations, motions, or changes. A structural mapping links actors to actors, objects to objects, motion paths to motion paths, orientation to orientation, duration to duration, and the like. For example, sitting and incubating are comparable in duration (both cannot be too long), orientation (one on the other), and contact (both generating warmth). One may start with "trivial" mappings (e.g., daily floors climbing mapped with hiking). It is then the various imaginative consequences (e.g., a stunning view for climbing 9 floors, or discovering a new species of butterfly after accumulating 100 stair flights) making the metaphor novel and engaging.

3.3   Perform Blends and Elaborate Virtual Consequences

After examining and choosing a scenario with embodied mappings, the processes continue with performing blends between the habitual behavior and the comparable scenario, yielding imaginative behavior-consequence relationships.

(1) Blend actions: Map the habitual action (and the object to be effected) with the action in the comparable scenario (and the object to be effected), and compress them into new action in the resulting blended concept. Grounded in embodied experiences, the blended action is "felt" as one by users at the sensorimotor and cognitive levels. For example, sitting on a task chair is mapped with incubating, forming an imaginative act of incubating during work. Turning on the phone screen is mapped with switching on the room lights, forming an imaginative act of switching on the phone-room lights.

(2) Elaborate consequences: Map behavioral data with effects of the action in the comparable scenario. Different data analytics, which imply different degrees or frequencies of the behavior, should correspond to different stages or variations of the imaginative consequences. The mappings require considerations of the user experiences over the course of the behavioral journey. For example, locking up the lighter for longer time (in hours and then days) results in a stronger avatar; yet taking the lighter out immediately makes the avatar sick. Increasing continuous sit time (in hours) develops the chick inside a virtual egg, until it hatches; additional sit time then leads to suffocation and death of the chick; regularly standing up gives birth to a variety of birds. The initial blend with embodied mappings yields intuitive representations and allows elaboration of nontrivial and even unexpected outcomes to keep users' attention.

(3) Render consequences: Project effects of the action in the comparable scenario onto the blend, which are rendered in virtual environments via technology and become virtual consequences of the blended action. The virtual consequences can be imagined by users to be natural outcomes of the blended action, as long as the rendering preserves the natural coupling, that is, co-occurrence of physical acts and virtual outcomes in time and location, and congruence in direction, dynamics, and modalities. For example, a blow at the phone results in an immediate lung capacity test performance represented in the avatar's health status. Pressing the physical button on the phone switches on the room lights "inside" the phone. Pointing the phone at the seat shows the scan of the virtual egg in it.

3.4   Anchor Blends for Users

The blend so far takes place at the designer's side. The output is a blended mental space combining the performed behavior with the comparable scenario. It contains a blended action and its virtual consequences. A user performs the habitual action, sees the virtual outcomes, and feels the sensorimotor experience of the causality. To ensure consistent blends at the user's side, co-occurrence and congruence of the virtual outcomes with the habitual action are necessary conditions. The user experiences the blended causality, which evokes a scenario from a domain similar to the designer's intended one. The virtual outcomes and the physical artifacts dynamically anchor the user's imaginative understanding to the designer's blends. Chow [26] proposes the liveliness framework, which includes a protocol of cognitive processes, guiding prediction and examination of user experiences for coherent imaginative blends propagated from designers. With the earlier work focusing on the processes of converging designers' proposals and users' responses, this article offers design guidelines that centers on the processes of generating the proposals for the user evaluation.

4   Design Cases

To demonstrate how the guidelines assist designers in making design choices, three design cases are presented. The ideas of the first and the third cases originated from design students' projects led and guided by the author; the second case is one of the author's latest projects. All the design concepts have been developed by the author with reflection based on the proposed guidelines. The user experience studies and results of the first case (in the laboratory) and the second case (in the field) published elsewhere [27, 28] provide empirical evidence for the proposed approach. The third case has also been evaluated via video prototyping. This article focuses on the application of the proposed guidelines.

4.1   Lock up

Lock Up is a design concept originated from a design student (Lui Yan Yan) under the author's supervision. It aims to assist users in smoking cessation. The design includes a mobile app that turns the phone into an imaginative peak flow meter, together with a smart case that holds the user's lighter. When the user blows at the phone (the meter), the level on the screen moves up, followed by a virtual character starting with a skeleton indicating the poor health status. If the user locks up the lighter for some time and then blows at the phone again, the character's appearance improves for every time interval. If the user takes the lighter out, the character quickly relapses.

1. Identify scenarios: The designers first related the smoking behavior to health checks such as lung capacity tests, which typically involved a peak flow meter. This physical artifact evoked a scenario of someone breathing out air into the meter. Health-threatening events from news, hearsay, or movies, included infectious viruses or radioactive chemicals leaks that spread and kill people. These dangerous items were initially locked in a danger box; yet someone released them.

2. Examine mappings: The actions taken around the smoking behavior included opening the case and taking out the lighter, followed by putting back to the case and sometimes performing lung tests. The actions in comparable scenarios included opening and closing the danger box and performing health checks. The matching of embodied experiences across the mapping included spatial relation (in/out the container), physical contact (touch the item), proximity (far from the item), and force (blowing hard at the meter/phone).

3. Perform blends: (1) The above actions were mapped and compressed into an imaginative act of taking out and touching the life-threatening lighter or e-cigarette, putting it back to the case, and breathing out air to the peak flow meter/phone. (2) The smart case detected and tracked the continuous amount of time with the lighter or e-cigarette in the case, and not in the case. This data was mapped with results of the lung capacity checks, which were represented as different appearances of the character showing its health status. The favorable condition was the lighter or e-cigarette in the case, while the unfavorable condition was having it taken out. The continuous time of the favorable condition elevated the character's health status. The period of time corresponding to each level of the health status could be configured according to individual users' needs. For example, the health status could go up one level every four hours. To the contrary, the unfavorable condition dragged down the health status, and the time could be very short. For example, it could drop one level every five minutes. The configuration aimed to let users experience that building up took time while destruction was like a flash. (3) Results of the lung capacity checks, which are visualized in terms of the character's health status, were projected onto the blend, becoming virtual consequences of the habitual act of smoking. Other inherent feedback of the habitual act that could be projected included the lock up of the lighter or e-cigarette, which set a physical barrier from it and functioned like a protective shield in the blended scenario. The virtual consequences preserve the natural coupling in time and dynamics (e.g., the force of blowing to the phone moved the meter level in real time).

4.2 Lights Out (aka Time Off)

Lights Out is a design emerged from the author's project. It aims to prevent users from excessive use of smartphones. It is a mobile application that turns the phone into a room for the user's imaginative "little" companion. It presents a virtual character on the screen, together with a physical jacket for the phone. When the user turns on the screen and uses the phone for too long, the character becomes tired, asks (via notification messages) to turn off the light or wants to hide in the jacket. If the user continues to use the phone (and keeps the screen on), the character gets sick and finally leaves the phone (the room). If one turns off the screen for a while, the character starts to recover. Yet, turning on the screen again prevents the character from full recovery. In other words, both continuous and cumulative screen time data are considered.

1. Identify scenarios: The designers first looked closely at the basic actions of using smartphones, including holding the phone and pressing the physical "sleep/wake button" to "wake" it up. Based on the metaphor "Wake It Up Is Turn It On", the

designers extended to "Keep It Awake Is Keep Using It". The sleep/wake button on the phone was comparable to a light switch. Turning on the phone screen was like switching on the light in a room. The screen light was annoying to the character "inside" the phone just like the room light to someone in the room. One could not rest and might become sick. When the situation became unbearable, one would leave the room. This sounded like a familiar incident to many people.

2. Examine mappings: The action of smartphone use was turning on the screen. The comparable action was switching on the room light. The matching of embodied experiences across the mapping includes immediate feedback (the screen light and the room light), spatial relation (the character "inside" the phone and someone in the room), and physical contact (touch the sleep/wake button and the light switch).

3. Perform blends: (1) The habitual action of turning on the screen was mapped with the action of switching on the room light. They were compressed into an imaginative act of switching on the phone-room light. (2) The tracked data was the amount of time with the screen turned on, which implied the phone was in use. The analytics included the time of every continuous session. Increase in the continuous time of the current session incrementally made the character sick. The length of continuous time bringing the character to the next state could be configured based on individual users' conditions. For example, the character might start to feel unwell after 30 min of continuous use, followed by changing to next state every other five minutes. The analytics also included the cumulative net time that was cumulative screen-on time minus cumulative screen-off time. This net time informed whether the character (and the user too) got enough time to rest and recover (the longer the time of use, the longer the time needed for recovery). Exceedingly long continuous time of one session or having the cumulative net time over a threshold (not enough time to recover) would make the character leave the phone. The configuration was intended to give users a sense that the little companion tried to endure or to recover, as long as time was given. (3) Effects of the action of switching on the room light on somebody were projected onto the blend and visualized in the character's state, becoming virtual consequences of excessive smartphone use. The inherent heat up of the phone after exceedingly long sessions of use could be projected onto the blend as a sign of the character's fever. Overall, the imaginative act of switching on the phone-room light for too long would result in virtually the character's illness and inherently the fever heat. The virtual consequences preserve the natural coupling in time and spatial relation (e.g., the phone-room was like a miniature "inside" the phone).

4.3 Sit-Hatch

Sit-Hatch is a design concept emerged from a mini project by two design students (Kulasumpankosol Wagi and Dai Liyi) under the author's guidance. It attempts to motivate users to stand up while sitting too long during work. This sedentary style is common but unhealthy. The design comes with a mobile app that turns the phone into an imaginative egg candler (a device that cast light on eggs for examining the embryo development). A smart cushion is provided for the user to put on the work chair. If the user sits on it and works for too long (e.g., more than 60 min continuously), it starts to vibrate briefly and sends notifications to the phone. The user can aim the phone's camera at one's lap and see an egg in the app, which shows that the chick inside is well developed and about to hatch. If the user continues to sit and work, the hatched chick finally suffocates (Fig. 1).

Fig. 1. The user sits for one hour; the cushion vibrates and the app shows a translucent image of an egg. If the user stands up, the chick hatches out; otherwise, the chick is suffocated.

1. Identify scenarios: The designers drew on the vernacular Cantonese saying "Sit Too Long Is Incubate Eggs". A physical object related to natural incubating was the nest. For a counterpart in the workplace, the designers considered a cushion on the seat. Another related physical artifact, the egg candler, also came to the mind. This device allowed the user to illuminate the inner of an egg. The translucent effect revealed the development status of the embryo. While the egg was typically kept in the incubator, the designers imagined that the user incubated the egg by his or her body heat while sitting. The user regularly monitored the embryo development by an egg candler until the chick hatched out. This was not a common, everyday event to many people, but should be imaginable with the experience created by the design.
2. Examine mappings: The habitual actions consisted of mainly the act of continuously sitting and occasionally checking the phone. The comparable scenario included actions like sitting on eggs, producing heat by body temperature, scanning the eggs under the thighs by an egg candler. The matching of embodied experiences across the mapping includes continuous time period (time of sitting and incubating), spatial relation (cushion and eggs underneath the thighs), haptic (the heat produced in sitting and incubating).
3. Perform blends: (1) The habitual action of continuously sitting during work was mapped with the action of sitting on the nest to incubate the eggs. The habitual action of checking the phone was mapped with the action of scanning the eggs by the egg candler. They were compressed into an imaginative act of incubating eggs and monitoring the egg development during work. (2) The tracked data was mainly the current continuous sitting time (in minutes). The first 60 min of sitting could be favorable, and that was mapped with the gradual development of the embryo inside the virtual egg before hatching. The user could use the egg candler-phone to check the translucent image of the egg intermittently. Other feedback of incubating included vibrations from the egg, which should be increasingly frequent when the hatching time was approaching. After 60 min, the chick hatched out and vibrations

under the hip became very vigorous. The continuous sitting then became unfavorable, which was mapped with suffocation of the newborn chick in a short period of time (e.g., 5 min). If one continued to sit, more other chicks were suffocated. Once the user stood up, the count reset and the user could sit to hatch again after a while. This configuration applied to general people in order to put them into the recommended period of sitting. (3) Results of the action of incubating were projected onto the blend and visualized in the translucent image of egg development and vibrations under the thighs. The inherent heat under the thighs was brought to the blend too, as it matched perfectly with the scenario of incubating. Overall, the imaginative act of incubating during work brought virtual eggs to hatching and then probably suffocating. The virtual consequences preserve the natural coupling in time, spatial relation, and modalities.

5 Conclusion

The proposed approach will instill imaginative beliefs about virtual consequences of behavior. Previous user studies in the laboratory and in the field provide evidence that imaginative blends did emerge in participants. This article focuses on the idea generation and examination at the designer side. The author invites other researchers to use the framework and conduct more empirical studies. Suggested work includes evaluation of users' intuitive associations with scenarios based on unfamiliar knowledge (e.g., metaphor in another culture), their extended interpretations of nontrivial consequences contingent on different behaviors, and the correlation with any behavior change.

Acknowledgements. This research benefits from projects supported by The Hong Kong Polytechnic University and Tung Wah Group of Hospitals.

References

1. Li, I., Dey, A., Forlizzi, J.: A stage-based model of personal informatics systems. In: CHI 2010, Proceedings of the SIGCHI Conference on Human Factors in Computing Systems. ACM Press (2010)
2. Rooksby, J., Rost, M., Morrison, A., Chalmers, M.: Personal tracking as lived informatics. In: CHI 2014, Proceedings of the SIGCHI Conference on Human Factors in Computing Systems, pp. 1163–1172. ACM (2014)
3. Wilson, G.T., Bhamra, T., Lilley, D.: The considerations and limitations of feedback as a strategy for behaviour change. Int. J. Sustain. Eng. **8**, 186–195 (2015)
4. Rooksby, J., Asadzadeh, P., Rost, M., Morrison, A., Chalmers, M.: Personal tracking of screen time on digital devices. In: CHI 2016, Proceedings of the SIGCHI Conference on Human Factors in Computing Systems, pp. 284–296. ACM Press (2016)
5. Consolvo, S., Klasnja, P., McDonald, D.W., Landay, J.A.: Designing for healthy lifestyles: design considerations for mobile technologies to encourage consumer health and wellness. Found. Trends Hum.-Comput. Interact. **6**, 167–315 (2014)

6. Lin, J.J., Mamykina, L., Lindtner, S., Delajoux, G., Strub, H.B.: Fish'n'Steps: encouraging physical activity with an interactive computer game. In: Dourish, P., Friday, A. (eds.) UbiComp 2006. LNCS, vol. 4206, pp. 261–278. Springer, Heidelberg (2006). https://doi.org/10.1007/11853565_16

7. Consolvo, S., et al.: Activity sensing in the wild: a field trial of UbiFit garden. In: CHI 2008, Proceedings of the SIGCHI Conference on Human Factors in Computing Systems, pp. 1797–1806. ACM Press (2008)

8. Froehlich, J., et al.: UbiGreen: investigating a mobile tool for tracking and supporting green transportation habits. In: CHI 2009, Proceedings of the SIGCHI Conference on Human Factors in Computing Systems. ACM Press (2009)

9. Chiu, M.-C., et al.: Playful bottle: a mobile social persuasion system to motivate healthy water intake. In: Ubicomp 2009. ACM Press (2009)

10. Shiraishi, M., Washio, Y., Takayama, C., Lehodonvirta, V., Kimura, H., Nakajima, T.: Using individual, social and economic persuasion techniques to reduce CO2 emissions in a family setting. In: Persuasive 2009. ACM (2009)

11. Varela, F.J., Thompson, E., Rosch, E.: The Embodied Mind: Cognitive Science and Human Experience. MIT Press, Cambridge (1991)

12. Lakoff, G., Johnson, M.: Philosophy in the Flesh: The Embodied Mind and Its Challenge to Western Thought. Basic Books, New York (1999)

13. Fogg, B.J.: A behavior model for persuasive design. In: Persuasive 2009 (2009)

14. Oinas-Kukkonen, H., Harjumaa, M.: A systematic framework for designing and evaluating persuasive systems. In: Oinas-Kukkonen, H., Hasle, P., Harjumaa, M., Segerståhl, K., Øhrstrøm, P. (eds.) PERSUASIVE 2008. LNCS, vol. 5033, pp. 164–176. Springer, Heidelberg (2008). https://doi.org/10.1007/978-3-540-68504-3_15

15. Midden, C.J.H., Kaiser, F.G., McCalley, L.T.: Technology's four roles in understanding individuals' conservation of natural resources. J. Soc. Issues 63, 155–174 (2007)

16. Ajzen, I.: From intentions to actions: a theory of planned behavior. In: Kuhl, J., Beckman, J. (eds.) Action-Control: From Cognition to Behavior, pp. 11–39. Springer, Heidelberg (1985). https://doi.org/10.1007/978-3-642-69746-3_2

17. Bargh, J.A., Chartrand, T.L.: The unbearable automaticity of being. Am. Psychol. 54, 462–479 (1999)

18. Verplanken, B., Aarts, H.: Habit, attitude, and planned behaviour: is habit an empty construct or an interesting case of goal-directed automaticity? Eur. Rev. Soc. Psychol. 10, 101–134 (1999)

19. Madsen, K.H.: A Guide to metaphorical design. Commun. ACM 37, 57–62 (1994)

20. Mandler, J.M.: How to build a baby: II. Conceptual primitives. Psychol. Rev. 99, 587–604 (1992)

21. Lakoff, G., Johnson, M.: Metaphors We Live by. University of Chicago Press, Chicago (2003)

22. Lakoff, G.: Explaining embodied cognition results. Top. Cogn. Sci. 4, 773–785 (2012)

23. Fauconnier, G., Turner, M.: The Way We Think: Conceptual Blending and the Mind's Hidden Complexities. Basic Books, New York (2002)

24. Coulson, S., Fauconnier, G.: Fake guns and stone lions: conceptual blending and privative adjectives. In: Fox, B., Jurafsky, D., Michaelis, L. (eds.) Cognition and Function in Language. CSLI, Palo Alto (1999)

25. Fillmore, C.J.: Frames and the semantics of understanding. Quaderni di Semantica 6, 222–254 (1985)

26. Chow, K.K.N.: Sketching imaginative experiences: from operation to reflection via lively interactive artifacts. Int. J. Des. 12, 33–49 (2018)

27. Chow, K.K.N.: Lock up the lighter: experience prototyping of a lively reflective design for smoking habit control. In: Meschtscherjakov, A., De Ruyter, B., Fuchsberger, V., Murer, M., Tscheligi, M. (eds.) PERSUASIVE 2016. LNCS, vol. 9638, pp. 352–364. Springer, Cham (2016). https://doi.org/10.1007/978-3-319-31510-2_30

28. Chow, K.K.N.: Time off: designing lively representations as imaginative triggers for healthy smartphone use. In: Ham, J., Karapanos, E., Morita, P.P., Burns, C.M. (eds.) PERSUASIVE 2018. LNCS, vol. 10809, pp. 135–146. Springer, Cham (2018). https://doi.org/10.1007/978-3-319-78978-1_11

Systems Development Process

Scrutable and Persuasive Push-Notifications

Kieran Fraser$^{(\boxtimes)}$, Bilal Yousuf, and Owen Conlan

ADAPT Centre, School of Computer Science and Statistics,
Trinity College Dublin, Dublin 2, Ireland
{kfraser,yousufbi,owen.conlan}@scss.tcd.ie

Abstract. Push-notifications have the potential to reinforce positive behaviours when applied in an intelligent manner. This paper explores a method of improving the delivery process of push-notifications by extracting scrutable persuasive features and refining prediction of notification outcomes. Additionally, a method is proposed for generating recommended notifications, based on the extracted persuasive features, to maximise potential engagement for scenarios such as behavioural interventions. The results illustrate that the persuasive features extracted contributed toward improved push-notification action prediction and that the personalised persuasive notifications recommended vastly increased the *Click Through Rate* (CTR) of notifications.

Keywords: Push-notifications · Synthetic data · Scrutable persuasion

1 Introduction and Related Work

In today's attention economy, an abundance of information is pushed from every direction and device, seeking to constantly engage regardless of the emotional state or health of those targeted. Push-notifications are an example of a powerful design tool used to persuade engagement [8]. The intent of a push-notification is to add timely value, however due to their inherent design and unintelligent management, notifications contribute toward adverse smartphone use and behaviours resulting in poor digital health (e.g. NoMoPhobia, FOMO). This paper investigates a means of improving the design and subsequent engagement behaviours associated with push-notifications by: (1) Extracting scrutable persuasive features from notifications; (2) Using the extracted persuasive features to improve prediction of open/dismissal of notifications; (3) Generating personalised persuasive notifications which can be used for positive behavioural change interventions.

This research is supported by the ADAPT Centre for Digital Content Technology under the SFI Research Centre's Program (Grant 13/RC/2106) and is co-funded under the European Regional Development Fund.

© Springer Nature Switzerland AG 2019
H. Oinas-Kukkonen et al. (Eds.): PERSUASIVE 2019, LNCS 11433, pp. 67–73, 2019.
https://doi.org/10.1007/978-3-030-17287-9_6

Push-notification were a topic of recent study by Morrison et al. [7] whereby the impact of timing and frequency of notifications on user responses and subsequent use of a health-intervention app was explored. Similarly, Smith et al. [9] studied the impact of personality on choosing a persuasion type for personalised reminders in melanoma patients. Cialidini's 6 principle's of behaviour [1] were used for identifying the suitability of a reminder in a given situation. Comparably, Thomas et al. [5], also use Cialdini's principles to craft personalised messages for encouraging healthy eating. This paper uses Cialdini's principle's in an identical manner, in the sense of generating personalised persuasive notifications, but also leverages the scrutable facets they offer for enabling transparency and explainability.

2   Method

2.1   Data Collection

A smartphone application was created to capture push-notifications in-the-wild for the purposes of identifying negative notification-engagement behavioural patterns and developing intelligent systems which could improve behaviour toward notifications. 15 participants (2 female, 13 male; all Android users) engaged with the WeAreUs app over a period of 4 months allowing for the collection of over 30,000 push-notifications as well as 291 questionnaires. The questionnaire was used to identify and verify features such as the sender of the notification (using the participants contact list) and the subject of the notification. For this study, the WeAreUs data set is limited to 11 users (male; aged 21–64) as 4 of the participants had under 100 notifications logged (due to notification settings of their device). During the study, the participants were not restricted to any particular smartphone activity (e.g. business or leisure).

2.2   Feature Engineering

The original notification features captured through the WeAreUs app are as follows: {*app, category, priority, subject, time, day, updates, contactSignificantTo-Context, action (open/dismiss)*}. *Dismiss* is defined as a user removing (swiping away) a notification without opening (clicking) it. On inspection, these features do not easily reveal whether a push-notification will be persuasive. An objective of this study is to enable end-users to identify persuasive facets of notifications they receive in order to promote improved self-awareness of notification-engagement behaviour and prevent addictive habits forming. Therefore, 6 features of persuasiveness (P1–P6) are derived with respect to push-notifications using Cialidini's 6 principle's as a guide and the original features as seed. Cialidini's principles are as follows: **Scarcity**: people will place higher value on something that is rare; **Authority**: people follow and respect requests made by an authority; **Reciprocity**: people feel obliged to return a favour; **Commitment and Consistency**: people tend to follow through on their word and uphold behaviours associated with their own self-image; **Liking**: people will follow what they like; **Social Proof**: people will do what they see their peers doing. These principle's are applied to push-notifications as follows (P1–P6 scores are weighted evenly, and sum to a max value of 6):

1. P1 (Authority) - a combined measure of (a) priority; (b) number of updates; and (c) a contact's significance to a given context; indicates persuasiveness. Assumptions: *the app is considered an authority on knowing how important a notification is; an associated contact is an authority if found relevant to the context.*
2. P2 (Scarcity) - a measure of how rare a notification is, indicates persuasiveness. Assumption: *notifications which are rarely seen are more tempting to open.*
3. P3 (Liking) - a measure of previously liked feature content, taking the action 'opened' as an indicator of likeness, indicates persuasiveness. Assumption: *users are persuaded by notifications which contain content they like.*
4. P4 (Social Proof) - a measure of similar notifications opened by other users indicates persuasiveness. Assumption: *users tend to act similarly to their peers.*
5. P5 (Commitment and Consistency) - a measure of similar notifications opened by the user (essentially their habits), indicates persuasiveness. Assumption: *users tend to behave consistently with their notifications.*
6. P6 (Reciprocity) - a measure of how recently content was consumed in an app before the app sent a notification, indicates persuasiveness. Assumption: *if content was recently consumed in an app, the user acknowledges they received value and are more likely to be persuaded to open a notification from it.*

2.3   Prediction and Generation

Once extracted, the 6 persuasive principle's (P1–P6) derived with respect to push-notifications were evaluated using a selection of machine learning algorithms to ascertain the effectiveness of the facets toward predicting whether an incoming push-notification is opened or dismissed. Additionally the persuasive features were also evaluated using *Mean Decrease Impurity* (MDI) [6] for identifying the level of importance of each feature when predicting open or dismiss. The hypothesis being that the derived persuasive features should improve the performance of predicting a notification's *Click Through Rate* (CTR), as highly persuasive notifications should indicate a higher likelihood of opening a notification. Subsequently, the persuasive features should also be identified as of higher importance when attempting to predict opens/dismissals for this same reason, highlighting their value toward prediction performance.

Assuming the persuasive features are a good indication of CTR, synthetic notifications generated with a high combined sum of P1–P6 should be opened more frequently by the receiver. A conditional *Wasserstein Generative Adversarial Network with Gradient-Penalty* (WGAN-GP) [4] was used to synthetically generate push-notifications with combined P1–P6 values of between 5 and 6. The synthetic notification data was first evaluated using the *Train on Real, Test on Synthetic* (TRTS) [2] method to ensure convincing samples were being generated. Subsequently, the synthetic notifications were then classified as opened or dismissed by the selection of machine learning algorithms trained on the original notification data (simulating a real world scenario) and the results were compared against a random benchmark and the original notification data.

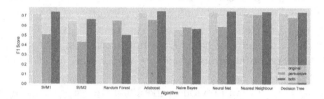

Fig. 1. F1 scores of selected algorithms when predicting notification action

3   Results and Discussion

Figure 1 illustrates the results obtained when a selection of algorithms were used to predict the open or dismissal of a notification. Three scenarios are shown for comparison. In the *original* scenario, each algorithm was trained and tested using only the original features of the notification. In the *persuasive* scenario, only the extracted persuasive features (P1–P6) were used for training and testing. The last scenario, *both*, is the union of all features used in the first two scenarios. The F1 score was taken as the metric for measuring performance due to the necessity for balancing *Precision* and *Recall*. Stratified 10-fold cross validation was used for each scenario. As can been seen from the results, the scenario in which both the original and persuasive features were used together yields best performance across all algorithms but for Naive Bayes and Random Forrest, in which the persuasive scenario performs best. While only a marginal increase in most cases over use of original features alone, this demonstrates that the persuasive features add value in performing predictions of open/dismissal of notifications.

Additionally, the persuasive features add a scrutable element as they were derived based on well defined principle's of persuasion. Therefore, a system implementing features P1–P6 could illustrate their values to end-user's when explaining automated decisions or facilitating self-reflection and steering behavioural change. For example, Fig. 2 illustrates categories of notifications with associated P1, *Authority*, values. The chart highlights that notifications with categories *msg* and *reminder* generally have a high *Authority* persuasion factor. Armed with this information, user's could adjust their behaviour by ensuring they don't open notifications of this type simply because they feel they are authoritive.

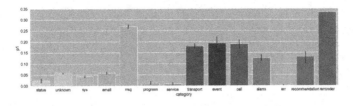

Fig. 2. P1 values (in the range 0–1) of notifications split by category

Although the combination of original and persuasive features performed best, by ascertaining feature importance via MDI implemented through the Scikit-Learn *ExtraTreesClassifier*, select persuasive features were identified as most important. P3 and P6, *Liking* and *Reciprocity* respectively, were ranked highest for 8 of the users while original features such as the app and the day of the week were ranked most important in only 2.

The WGAN-GP was chosen for synthetic generation as it shows enhanced training stability and enables categorical, as well as continuous, feature generation. The generated data was evaluated using TRTS, such that all algorithms were first trained on the real notification data and then tested using the generated data. By comparing the resultant F1 scores with those from Fig. 1, the similarity between the synthetic and real data could be evaluated. The Root Mean Squared Error (RMSE) calculated across F1 scores of all algorithms identified the scores differing in the range of 0.02–0.07, illustrating that convincing samples were generated. Discrepancies in prediction performance using synthetic data could be attributed to a loss of nuance generated within the data, whereby the real distribution of all features was not mapped fully to the generator's latent space. For each user, 1000 notifications with a combined P1–P6 sum of between 5 and 6 were generated using the conditional WGAN-GP generator as an example of an intelligent system which can recommend highly personalised and persuasive notifications on demand. The recommended notifications were then tested using the selected algorithms which were trained on real notification data for each user. A data set of 1000 randomly generated notifications was used as a benchmark and the original notifications were also used for comparison. Figure 3 depicts the CTR of each scenario for all user's and illustrates that the synthetically generated persuasive recommendations typically have a much higher CTR than those randomly generated, or those originally sent to the user. The result of this means that persuasive notifications can be generated, based on Cialidini's principle's, such that users will open them. Notifications such as these could be used to motivate positive behavioural change at opportune moments while ensuring, through the scrutable persuasive features, that the user is aware of the type of persuasion they are subjected to.

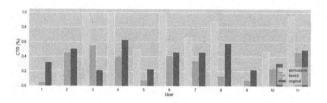

Fig. 3. Comparison of CTR of users using differing notification data sets.

4 Limitations, Future Work and Conclusion

Due to the intimate nature of notifications, encouraging participation in a study such as this is challenging [3], hence the dataset of 11 male users is a limiting factor of this study. Similarly, technological restrictions regarding notification monitoring set in place on iOS devices prevented those users being included in the study. However, this was used as motivation for generating synthetic notifications, a method of which is proposed in this paper. Future work will aim to improve synthetic notification generation with respect to persuasive notifications as well as extraction of additional features which indicate persuasive strategies. In addition, measuring extracted persuasiveness against that perceived by the user and identifying actions which follow is also proposed for future work.

In conclusion, the goal of this paper was to evaluate a method of extracting scrutable persuasive features from push-notifications for the purpose of improving predicted action outcomes and enabling users to reflect on the persuasive characteristics. The results illustrated that persuasive features could be extracted and visualised and that performance in predicting notification action outcomes could be improved using the persuasive features. Recommended persuasive notification could also be generated on demand and were also shown to increase the Click Through Rate (CTR) of users when simulated.

References

1. Cialdini, R.B.: Influence, vol. 3. A. Michel, Port Harcourt (1987)
2. Esteban, C., Hyland, S.L., Rätsch, G.: Real-valued (medical) time series generation with recurrent conditional GANs. arXiv preprint arXiv:1706.02633 (2017)
3. Fraser, K., Yousuf, B., Conlan, O.: Synthesis and evaluation of a mobile notification dataset. In: Adjunct Publication of the 25th Conference on User Modeling, Adaptation and Personalization (2017)
4. Gulrajani, I., Ahmed, F., Arjovsky, M., Dumoulin, V., Courville, A.C.: Improved training of Wasserstein GANs. In: Advances in Neural Information Processing Systems, pp. 5767–5777 (2017)
5. Thomas, J.R., Masthoff, J., Oren, N.: Personalising healthy eating messages to age, gender and personality: using Cialdini's principles and framing. In: Proceedings of the 22nd International Conference on Intelligent User Interfaces Companion (2017)
6. Louppe, G., Wehenkel, L., Sutera, A., Geurts, P.: Understanding variable importances in forests of randomized trees. In: Advances in Neural Information Processing Systems, pp. 431–439 (2013)

7. Morrison, L.G., Hargood, C., Pejovic, V., et al.: The effect of timing and frequency of push notifications on usage of a smartphone-based stress management intervention: an exploratory trial. PloS ONE **12**(1), e0169162 (2017)
8. Oulasvirta, A., Rattenbury, T., Ma, L., Raita, E.: Habits make smartphone use more pervasive. Pers. Ubiquit. Comput. **16**(1), 105–114 (2012)
9. Smith, K.A., Dennis, M., Masthoff, J.: Personalizing reminders to personality for melanoma self-checking. In: Proceedings of the 2016 Conference on User Modeling Adaptation and Personalization, pp. 85–93. ACM (2016)

Applications for Persuasive Technologies in Participatory Design Processes

Max Jalowski$^{(\boxtimes)}$ (iD), Albrecht Fritzsche (iD), and Kathrin M. Möslein (iD)

Chair of Information Systems, Innovation and Value Creation,
Friedrich-Alexander-Universität Erlangen-Nürnberg (FAU),
Nuremberg, Germany
max.jalowski@fau.de

Abstract. This paper studies the possibilities to support participatory design processes with persuasive technologies. Drawing on extant work by Elizabeth Sanders, it introduces a comprehensive framework for participatory design which highlights challenges for collaborative attitudes and behavior. To see how persuasive technologies can answer these challenges, the paper reviews the proceedings of the PERSUASIVE conferences since 2010. It identifies 186 application cases, which can be related to twelve different technology platforms. Following a design science research approach, the paper introduces an online navigator to explore different scenarios to support participatory design processes resulting from the findings of the literature review. The navigator can be applied together with Fogg's eight-step design process for creating persuasive technology. To evaluate the navigator, two artificial evaluation iterations are conducted: ex ante a criteria-based analysis to show its theoretical efficacy and ex post problem-centered interviews with experts to gain further insights. The results contribute to a better understanding of the role that persuasive technologies can play in participatory design activities.

Keywords: Participatory design · Co-design ·
Applications of persuasive technology · Design science research ·
Technology channels

1 Introduction

Co-creation and co-design workshops are popular means to integrate external knowledge into the innovation processes of an organization. Popular examples include workshops or hackathons. While technology is often the subject of such workshops, innovation processes at the workshop are usually driven solely by direct human interaction. Technology support, which is otherwise very common in collaborative (open) innovation processes [1] is often missing. At the same time, workshop activities with non-professional designers are often accompanied by problems regarding the motivation or distraction of the participants. Existing research determines challenges concerning the efficiency of collaboration [2] and identifies the need for concepts to motivate and support participants [3, 4]. Researchers from other domains designed methods for integrating and motivating participants in open innovation processes [1, 5].

© Springer Nature Switzerland AG 2019
H. Oinas-Kukkonen et al. (Eds.): PERSUASIVE 2019, LNCS 11433, pp. 74–86, 2019.
https://doi.org/10.1007/978-3-030-17287-9_7

Furthermore, persuasive strategies and design principles have already been developed to minimize negative side effects of digital motivation on teamwork [6].

Persuasive technology as a research area focuses on technologies, concepts, design principles, theories, evaluation, strategies, etc. that change attitudes or behaviors of users by using persuasive technologies [7, 8]. According to Fogg [9] a behavior change consists of three factors: motivation, ability and triggers. While research on persuasive technology has already produced numerous results, particularly in the area of health-care applications and influence on social behavior, the application of persuasive technologies to stimulate and propel the collaboration between different actors has so far received little attention in this community. Torning and Oinas-Kukkonen [10] already identified knowledge work and collaboration as a challenging field in 2009. Yet there are still only a few studies in this field, for example [11, 12]. Our research will therefore focus on creating an application navigator showing different applicable persuasive technologies for participatory design processes to engage collaboration between people. To our best knowledge and a systematic search in the proceedings of the PERSUASIVE conferences since 2006 for keywords such as *co-creation, co-design, collaboration, cooperation* and *participatory design* no comparable work has so far been undertaken. To propose an approach for persuasive technologies in participatory design, this study addresses the following research question: *How can persuasive technologies be applied to change attitudes and behavior in participatory design processes?*

2 Conceptual Background: Co-design and Participatory Design

The following section describes the conceptual foundations for this study. First, an overview about co-design and participatory design is presented, followed by success factors for the engagement in such processes.

Co-design in the narrower sense is describing the collaboration of designers. In a broader sense, the term is not limited to design professionals and it can be seen as collective creativity during a design process [13]. Customer co-creation and lead user integration in co-creative activities address questions of co-design, but are mainly researched as processes between producers and customers [1, 14]. Participatory design today means the inclusion of non-professional designers in a co-design process [15]. Muller, Wildman and White provide a taxonomy of participatory design practices [16]. A similar approach is pursued by Sanders, Brandt and Binder [15], who created a framework for practicing participatory design. In this framework a cycle of activities in participatory design processes is presented: making, enacting and telling [15, 17]. These can be seen as sequencing or connected activities in co-designing. Making refers to creating tangible things, this describes the use of hands to transform ideas into physical artifacts [17]. Enacting consists of acting, enacting and playing, this "refers to the use of the body (...) to express ideas about future experience" [17]. Telling refers to talking, telling and explaining, e.g. verbal descriptions of ideas or future artifacts [17].

Participatory design processes require motivated and focused users. One known way to motivate users is to make them feel co-owners of the result, this can be achieved by techniques that help users to express themselves and keep these expressions in the results [18]. Others state that cooperation in a community, learning of new things, entertainment and good support by the supervisors improve motivation in collaborative processes [3]. Interventions by supervisors need the right timing and must be clearly formulated in order to have a positive effect on cooperation [4]. Hagen and Robertson [19] found out that social technologies, such as Facebook, Twitter, personal blogs and discussion platforms are promoting participation in design. Jarvela and Jarvenoja [2] developed 14 challenge scenarios to identify motivation regulation in collaborative learning. These challenges address five challenge categories: personal priorities, work & communication, teamwork, collaboration and external constraints. Their research shows that participants applied the following motivation regulation strategies: task structuring, social reinforcing, efficacy management, interest enhancement, socially shared goal-oriented talk and handicapping of group function [2].

3   Research Design

In order to answer the research question, we use a design science research approach, which generates insight into a problem by working on its solution [20, 21]. We create a navigator as an IT artifact to support the application of persuasive technologies in participatory design. The navigator is focused on the integrability into Fogg's eight-step design process, especially the steps 4–6: choice of familiar technology channel, identification of relevant examples and imitation of successful examples [8]. We chose a quick and simple evaluation strategy, since our design is with low social and technical risk [22]. IT artifacts can be evaluated regarding e.g. functionality, completeness, consistency, accuracy, and usability [21]. We conducted two artificial evaluation iterations: ex ante a criteria-based analysis to show the theoretical efficacy and ex post problem-centered interviews [23] to validate the artifact with researchers and professionals working on participatory design or persuasive technology [22, 24].

For building the knowledge base of the artifact, we started with a literature-based search. Two researchers reviewed and analyzed the proceedings of the PERSUASIVE conferences from 2010 to 2018. For these 222 papers an abstract and title screening was carried out. In the following step, papers that describe, use, or create a persuasive technology were reviewed in detail, which covers a set of 139 papers describing 186 different applications of persuasive technologies. By categorizing and grouping of the persuasive technologies, twelve different technology platforms could be identified. In a second step we conducted a database search in Scopus and Google Scholar with the terms "Persuasive Technology" and the respective identified technology platform to find relevant papers and validate the technology platforms outside the persuasive technology community. Then, we categorized all identified papers regarding technology or technology concept, keywords and domain, topic or field of the appliance.

To answer the research question, we developed an artifact with application scenarios for each of the twelve technology platforms. These scenarios were divided into four different dimensions (cf. Fig. 1), three of them are activities originating from Elizabeth Sanders' framework for practicing participatory design: *making, telling, enacting* [15, 17]. These activities contain existing tools, techniques and methods for

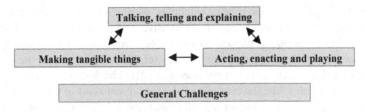

Fig. 1. Overview of the underlying structure of the artifact (cf. [2, 15, 17])

participatory design processes. We added a fourth dimension, *general challenges*, e.g. motivation, work and communication, external constraints, to our artifact since these processes require motivated and focused users (cf. Sect. 2). Figure 1 shows an overview of the underlying structure of the artifact with its four dimensions.

4 Artifact Description and Evaluation

4.1 Persuasive Technology Platforms

The analysis of the selected literature shows 186 technology applications that can be categorized in twelve different persuasive technology platforms. Table 1 gives an overview about the platforms, a description or an example and the number of mentions.

Table 1. Overview of identified technology platforms

Technology platform	Description/example	Σ
AR & VR	Augment physical settings or show 3-D mock-ups	12
Displays, Lights & Sound	Show information or influence participant behavior	14
Games	Serious games to reflect opinions or enable learning	21
Online Collaboration Tools	e.g. video conferences, collaborative blogs, wikis	2
(Persuasive) Messages	(Text) messages to remind or influence people	21
Physical Tags	e.g. QR codes or RFID tags to enhance activity	2
Prototyping Toolkits	e.g. (electronic) toolkits with persuasive strategies	1
Robotics	(Humanoid) robot assistant	5
Sensors, Analytics & IoT	e.g. wearables, sensors, IoT devices or analytic-tools	29
Smartphone App	Applications on smartphones, tablets or similar devices	29
Virtual Agent & AI	Artificial intelligence to monitor and recommend actions	18
Web & Social Network	Show additional data or provide social components	32

4.2 Applications for Persuasive Technologies in Participatory Design

The identified technology platforms and examples from the selected papers were mapped to four dimensions (cf. Fig. 1). The results contain application examples for the different persuasive technology platforms. Based on the existing examples in other application domains, we derived application scenarios for persuasive technologies in participatory design processes. These examples were extended by suitable system features of persuasive technologies and persuasive principles as described by [25]. Each application scenario is mapped to or adapted from one of the existing tools, techniques and methods for participatory design (cf. [15, 17]) or one of the challenge categories for collaborative design processes (cf. [2]). The following paragraphs and Tables 2, 3, 4 and 5 describe the contents of the four dimensions of the navigator. The online implementation of the artifact including additional data, for example persuasive principles for each scenario, is available at: http://pt-navigator.innovationresearch.eu.

Table 2 lists the application scenarios for the making activity. Augmented reality and virtual reality applications can be used to add virtual and interactive mock-ups to physical or digital participatory design settings to improve prototyping possibilities. Classical prototyping methods can be extended by using technology-focused prototyping toolkits.

Table 2. Overview of persuasive technology platforms for making tangible things

Technology platform	Application scenario	Existing example(s)
AR & VR	Virtual 3-D mock-ups	Virtual bike tutorial [26]; Virtual kitchen [27]
Prototyping Toolkits	Technology-focused prototyping	Littlebits [28]; Prototyping tools that encourage co-creation [29]

Table 3 gives an overview about application scenarios for enacting. AR, VR, displays, lights and sound can be implemented to provide further information to facilitate the phase for the participants. Games are already mentioned by Sanders, Brandt and Binder, in their framework [15], existing games can be extended by persuasive strategies as it is already in use e.g. in learning scenarios. Robotics, virtual agents and artificial intelligence are capable of monitoring participants' behavior to further influence passive or distracted participants to facilitate acting, enacting and playing. Web and social networks can connect online and offline settings to improve collaboration inbetween.

Table 4 shows identified application scenarios for telling activities. AR and VR can play a supporting role by putting participants directly in future scenarios. Online collaboration tools, smartphone apps, web and social networks can be used to digitize elements of the design process. This can reduce barriers and persuade people to share their opinions. Robots, smartphone apps, sensors, analytics and IoT can further support some of the existing tools, techniques and methods, e.g. documentaries, self-observations or timelines (cf. [17]). Persuasive messages can act as reminders to perform certain actions or guide through conversations to improve the quality of the content. Tags, like QR codes may be used in particular to facilitate participation at specific locations.

Table 3. Overview of persuasive technology platforms for acting, enacting and playing

Technology platform	Application scenario	Existing example(s)
AR & VR	Enhancing acting and enacting by displaying additional information	Digitally augment a plate of food by showing information [30]
Displays, Lights & Sound	Ambient lighting or displays for influencing participant behavior	Ambient lighting for energy-efficient behavior [31]; LED displays for influencing crowds [32]
Games	Influence users to participate, reflect opinions, or to enable learning	Reflection for healthy eating through gaming [33]; Persuasive learning [34]
Robotics	(Humanoid) robot persuading people to enact	Social robot monitoring certain actions [35]; Education game [36]
Virtual Agent & AI	Virtual Agent or AI monitors participation and persuades passive people	Argumentation-based recommendation techniques [37]; Empower individuals, facilitate decision making [38]
Web & Social Network	Augment offline playing or interactions with an online component	Online Tool for learning and increasing energy awareness [39]

Table 4. Overview of persuasive technology platforms for talking, telling and explaining

Technology platform	Application scenario	Existing example(s)
AR & VR	Facilitate telling by putting participants in virtual or augmented scenarios	Simulated experiences in VR concerning awareness of personal fire safety issues [40]
Online Collaboration Tools	Virtualize talking, telling and explaining methods, by using e.g. video conferences, collaborative blogs, wikis, etc.	Using ICT to approach cross-cultural communication [41]
(Persuasive) Messages	Structure and guide through conversations with persuasive messages	Text messages to reduce electricity consumption [42]; Auditory messages for influencing crowds [32]
Physical Tags	Trigger location-based participation	QR codes on products to simplify purchase and to give additional information [43]
Robotics	(Humanoid) robot guiding through processes or assisting e.g. observations	Social robot monitoring certain actions [35]; Robot assistant [44]
Sensors, Analytics & IoT	Simplify e.g. timelines and self-observations	Monitor activities and health condition [45]; Track behavior via self-reporting [46]
Smartphone App	Digitizing various talking, telling and explaining activities by using smartphone apps	e-coaching system to support organizational processes and lifestyle changes [47]
Web & Social Network	Motivate participants by virtualizing parts of the design process using a persuasive social network	Motivate users to generate and share feedback [48]; Persuasive Q&A social networks [49]

The fourth dimension (cf. Table 5) mainly deals with general challenges, e.g. motivation, work and communication, external constraints [2], especially with detecting and involving passive people. Displays, lights and sound are able to avoid confusion and to guide concretely through the process and display explanations and reminders. Robots and smartphone apps may play a similar role to support this part of the process. Online collaboration tools can link an offline to an online setting and include remote participants. Physical Tags, like QR codes or RFID tags can increase activity and provide additional information and help e.g. in combination with web and social networks. Persuasive messages can involve passive people and encourage them to participate. Sensors, analytics, IoT and virtual agents can also use wearables such as smartwatches to monitor participants and encourage them to become more active, or to monitor and control the process in a targeted manner.

Table 5. Overview of persuasive technology platforms to address general challenges, e.g. motivation, work and communication, external constraints, etc.

Technology platform	Application scenario	Existing example(s)
Displays, Lights & Sound	Guide trough processes and show adaptive reminders	Adaptive reminders for safe work [50]
Online Collaboration Tools	Bridge online offline gap and include remote participants	Use video conferences, collaborative blogs, wikis, forums and Google Docs [41]
(Persuasive) Messages	Involve passive people	Persuasive videos to encourage physical activity [51]; Collect logs and send reminders [52]
Physical Tags	Enhance activity by including QR codes or RFID tags in the design process and e.g. displaying additional information	QR codes on products to simplify purchase and to give additional information [43]
Robotics	Robot guides through design process	Robot assistant [44]; Robot guides through education game [36]
Sensors, Analytics & IoT	Track activity data of participants and encourage activity	Feedback on participation levels during meetings [53]; Smartwatch-based system for supporting group cohesion in physical activity [54]
Smartphone App	Improve collaboration by supporting decision making and explaining or recommending actions	Phone-based recommendation system [55]; Facilitate decision making [38]
Virtual Agent & AI	Monitor progress and suggest following actions	Monitor health condition, connect users and recommend activities [45]
Web & Social Network	Show additional data or background information about selected items	Online tool for learning and increasing energy awareness [39]

4.3   Evaluation

In this study, an application navigator was developed (cf. Tables 2, 3, 4 and 5) to facilitate the application of persuasive technologies in participatory design processes. Beyond that an online implementation (http://pt-navigator.innovationresearch.eu) was created. In an artificial ex ante evaluation, we assigned the identified technology platforms together with suitable examples from the literature set to the four dimensions of the navigator. In order to evaluate the theoretical efficacy in the individual dimensions, a criteria-based analysis was conducted [24]. The goal was, for each persuasive technology platform, to show the application in at least one of the four dimensions. Based on the selected examples, application scenarios in the respective dimensions were developed. These were evaluated with respect to their relation to the tools, techniques and methods in the activities of the underlying framework [15] or the challenge categories and motivation regulation strategies in [2]. Tables 2, 3, 4 and 5 show the results of the criteria-based analysis. The described application scenarios show theoretical efficacy in participatory design processes. Afterwards, an ex post evaluation was performed. The evaluation was carried out regarding the functionality, completeness, consistency, accuracy, and usability of the artifact [21]. We conducted four problem-centered interviews [23] with researchers and professionals from different institutions working on participatory design or persuasive technology. The interview guideline followed steps 4–6 of Fogg's eight-step design process [8]. The questions in each step were designed in order to evaluate the plausibility and applicability of the navigator, including the four dimensions, the technology platforms and the examples. The interviewees were provided with the online implementation of the navigator and the tables from this paper. In sum, the interviews lasted approximately five hours and were documented in audio recording or writing and afterwards systematically reviewed, structured and categorized.

The overall feedback of the interviewees underlines the applicability of the navigator. In order to facilitate the selection of possible technology platforms, the clear presentation and usability were pointed out. One interviewee remarked that a subdivision into further dimensions could be helpful, such as, if the technology is addressing a single person or a group of participants or whether it can be used more in a goal- or process-oriented way. Regarding the identification of technology platforms to address the activities or challenges, the interviewees noted that they are familiar with the dimensions from their own experience and that the separation therefore seems reasonable. Beyond that, it was stated that there are overlaps and correlations between the dimensions, which could be clarified in the future. One interviewee remarked that especially the use of smartphones could have a counter-productive effect on participants, as they might be distracted by e.g. push messages. For the third step, the identification and imitation of successful examples, the presentation and selection of the examples were regarded as comprehensible and helpful. For the future, respondents noted that concrete implementation scenarios with more detailed and tested examples would further improve applicability. In addition, the focus on persuasive design principles could be increased. The online implementation of the navigator was initially perceived as overloaded in some places, then the explanatory texts, the overall presentation and the relation to the eight-step design process were improved.

5 Discussion and Conclusion

By reviewing extant literature, we were able to differentiate twelve categories for persuasive technology platforms which can be used as channels for the intervention [8]. Previous research identified similar platforms, for instance, Orji and Moffatt [56] categorized persuasive technologies in seven different (six plus one category for others) platforms: mobile and handheld devices; game; web and social network; desktop; sensors and wearable devices; ambient and public display; and other specialized devices. Most of the frequently used technology platforms in this study are similar to the ones by Orji and Moffatt. We want to point out that it makes sense to list persuasive messages as a separate category, although of course they need a medium to be transmitted, e.g. a display, but a display itself can also act as a persuasive technology without using persuasive messages. Virtual agents and artificial intelligence are as well frequently used and can definitely add value in participatory design settings. Augmented reality and virtual reality are often used in the persuasive technology community, especially to simulate (future) situations, which can also be useful in design workshops. According to Fogg it is a challenge to choose the right technology that is suitable for the target behavior [8]. For this purpose our navigator contains descriptions, examples and persuasive principles for the respective technology platforms.

The second part of our findings is embodied in the navigator artifact, which puts the findings from literature into a common context of practical application. Such a compilation has not yet been implemented in the community. Participatory design is not much underpinned by technology so far, especially in workshop settings, so we can offer an added value in this context. As the interviews have confirmed, the navigator supports the steps "find relevant examples of persuasive technology" and "imitate successful examples" of Fogg's eight-step design process [8]. This simplifies the implementation of persuasive technologies in participatory design. For three of the four dimensions we used an accepted framework for practicing participatory design [17]. Most of the identified examples are fitted directly to one of the existing elements of this framework. Users can continue to select elements for their workshops or other processes as usual and replace or enhance them by one of the identified persuasive technologies. As in the original framework, less examples could be found for the category "making tangible things". This might be caused by its focus on creating physical objects. The fourth dimension also offers clear added value as it addresses common problems from collaborative design processes (cf. [2]). Persuasive technologies can be used to detect disruptions or guide through processes and to provide support for the participants. Thus the quality of the things to be designed can be increased. All success factors for engagement mentioned in Sect. 2 can be addressed by our navigator, especially the motivation regulation strategies as described by [2]: task structuring (e.g. Robotics, Virtual Agent & AI), social reinforcing (e.g. Virtual Agent & AI, Physical Tags, Smartphone App), efficacy management (e.g. Sensors, Analytics & IoT, Persuasive Messages), interest enhancement (e.g. AR & VR, Web & Social Network), socially shared goal-oriented talk (cf. Table 4) and handicapping of group function (cf. Tables 4 and 5).

This paper is currently still quite theoretical-conceptual and will have to be underpinned by concrete implementation concepts in the future. Another limitation of the contribution results from the exclusive focus on Sanders' original framework, which is a seminal contribution to research, but could be updated and extended regarding newly emerging formats and environments of interaction. Furthermore, the period and scope of the literature search offers potential for expansion, particularly regarding the extant discussion in the field of participatory design. Nevertheless, we believe that our work adds an important new facet to research on persuasive technology, opening up interesting new directions for future studies.

References

1. Von Hippel, E.: Democratizing Innovation. The MIT Press, Cambridge (2005)
2. Jarvela, S., Jarvenoja, H.: Socially constructed self-regulated learning and motivation regulation in collaborative learning groups. Teach. Coll. Rec. **113**, 350–374 (2011)
3. Antikainen, M., Mäkipää, M., Ahonen, M.: Motivating and supporting collaboration in open innovation. Eur. J. Innov. Manag. **13**, 100–119 (2010)
4. Goos, M., Galbraith, P., Renshaw, P.: Socially mediated metacognition: creating collaborative zones of proximal development in small group problem solving. Educ. Stud. Math. **49**, 193–223 (2002)
5. de Vreede, T., Nguyen, C., de Vreede, G.-J., Boughzala, I., Oh, O., Reiter-Palmon, R.: A theoretical model of user engagement in crowdsourcing. In: Antunes, P., Gerosa, M.A., Sylvester, A., Vassileva, J., de Vreede, G.-J. (eds.) CRIWG 2013. LNCS, vol. 8224, pp. 94–109. Springer, Heidelberg (2013). https://doi.org/10.1007/978-3-642-41347-6_8
6. Algashami, A., Shahri, A., McAlaney, J., Taylor, J., Phalp, K., Ali, R.: Strategies and design principles to minimize negative side-effects of digital motivation on teamwork. In: de Vries, P.W., Oinas-Kukkonen, H., Siemons, L., Beerlage-de Jong, N., van Gemert-Pijnen, L. (eds.) PERSUASIVE 2017. LNCS, vol. 10171, pp. 267–278. Springer, Cham (2017). https://doi.org/10.1007/978-3-319-55134-0_21
7. Fogg, B.: Persuasive computers. In: Proceedings of SIGCHI Conference on Human Factors Computer and Systems - CHI 1998, pp. 225–232 (1998)
8. Fogg, B.: Creating persuasive technologies: an eight-step design process. In: Proceedings of 4th International Conference on Persuasive Technology - Persuasive 2009 (2009)
9. Fogg, B.: A behavior model for persuasive design. In: Proceedings of 4th International Conference on Persuasive Technology - Persuasive 2009 (2009)
10. Torning, K., Oinas-Kukkonen, H.: Persuasive system design: state of the art and future directions. In: Proceedings of 4th International Conference on Persuasive Technology - Persuasive 2009 (2009)
11. Stibe, A., Oinas-Kukkonen, H.: Designing persuasive systems for user engagement in collaborative interaction. In: Twenty Second European Conferences of Information Systems, pp. 1–17 (2014)
12. Stibe, A., Oinas-Kukkonen, H., Lehto, T.: Exploring social influence on customer engagement: a pilot study on the effects of social learning, social comparison, and normative influence. In: 2013 46th Hawaii International Conference on System Science, pp. 2735–2744 (2013)
13. Sanders, E.B.-N., Stappers, P.J.: Co-creation and the new landscapes of design. CoDesign **4**, 5–18 (2008)

14. Piller, F., Ihl, C., Vossen, A.: A Typology of customer co-creation in the innovation process. SSRN Electron. J. (2010). https://doi.org/10.2139/ssrn.1732127

15. Sanders, E.B.-N., Brandt, E., Binder, T.: A framework for organizing the tools and techniques of participatory design. In: Proceedings of 11th Biennial Participatory Design Conference - PDC 2010, p. 195 (2010)

16. Muller, M.J., Wildman, D.M., White, E.A.: Taxonomy of PD practices: a brief practitioner's guide. Commun. ACM **36**, 24–28 (1993)

17. Sanders, E.B.-N.: Perspectives on participation in design. In: Mareis, C., Held, M., Joost, G. (eds.) Wer Gestaltet die Gestaltung? Praxis, Theorie und Geschichte des Partizipatorischen Designs, pp. 65–78. Transcript Verlag, Bielefeld (2013)

18. van Rijn, H., Stappers, P.J.: Expressions of ownership: motivating users in a co-design process. In: Tenth Anniversary Conference on Participatory Design 2008, pp. 178–181 (2008)

19. Hagen, P., Robertson, T.: Dissolving boundaries: social technologies and participation in design. In: Proceedings of 21st Annual Conference of the Australian Computer-Human Interaction Special Interest Group: Design: Open 24/7 - OZCHI 2009, pp. 129–136 (2009)

20. Peffers, K., Tuunanen, T., Rothenberger, M.A., Chatterjee, S.: A design science research methodology for information systems research. J. Manag. Inf. Syst. **24**, 45–78 (2007)

21. Hevner, A.R., March, S.T., Park, J., Ram, S.: Research essay design science in information systems research. MIS Q. **28**, 75–105 (2004)

22. Venable, J., Pries-Heje, J., Baskerville, R.: FEDS: a framework for evaluation in design science research. Eur. J. Inf. Syst. **25**, 77–89 (2016)

23. Witzel, A., Reiter, H.: The Problem-Centred Interview. Sage, London (2012)

24. Sonnenberg, C., vom Brocke, J.: Evaluation patterns for design science research artefacts. In: Helfert, M., Donnellan, B. (eds.) EDSS 2011. CCIS, vol. 286, pp. 71–83. Springer, Heidelberg (2012). https://doi.org/10.1007/978-3-642-33681-2_7

25. Oinas-Kukkonen, H., Harjumaa, M.: A systematic framework for designing and evaluating persuasive systems. In: Oinas-Kukkonen, H., Hasle, P., Harjumaa, M., Segerståhl, K., Øhrstrøm, P. (eds.) PERSUASIVE 2008. LNCS, vol. 5033, pp. 164–176. Springer, Heidelberg (2008). https://doi.org/10.1007/978-3-540-68504-3_15

26. Wunsch, M., et al.: What makes you bike? Exploring persuasive strategies to encourage low-energy mobility. In: MacTavish, T., Basapur, S. (eds.) PERSUASIVE 2015. LNCS, vol. 9072, pp. 53–64. Springer, Cham (2015). https://doi.org/10.1007/978-3-319-20306-5_5

27. Barral, O., et al.: Covert persuasive technologies: bringing subliminal cues to human-computer interaction. In: Spagnolli, A., Chittaro, L., Gamberini, L. (eds.) PERSUASIVE 2014. LNCS, vol. 8462, pp. 1–12. Springer, Cham (2014). https://doi.org/10.1007/978-3-319-07127-5_1

28. Bdeir, A.: Electronics as material. In: Proceedings of the 3rd International Conference on Tangible and Embedded Interaction - TEI 2009, p. 397 (2009)

29. Boukhris, A., Fritzsche, A., Möslein, K.M.: Towards the design of a persuasive technology for encouraging collaborative prototyping. In: CEUR Workshop Proceedings, vol. 1582, pp. 126–131 (2016)

30. Ganesh, S., Marshall, P., Rogers, Y., O'Hara, K.: FoodWorks: tackling fussy eating by digitally augmenting children's meals. In: Proceedings of the 8th Nordic Conference on Human-Computer Interaction: Fun, Fast, Foundational - Nordic 2014, pp. 147–156 (2014)

31. Lu, S., Ham, J., Midden, C.J.H.: Using ambient lighting in persuasive communication: the role of pre-existing color associations. In: Spagnolli, A., Chittaro, L., Gamberini, L. (eds.) PERSUASIVE 2014. LNCS, vol. 8462, pp. 167–178. Springer, Cham (2014). https://doi.org/10.1007/978-3-319-07127-5_15

32. de Vries, P., Galetzka, M., Gutteling, J.: Persuasion in the wild: communication, technology, and event safety. In: Spagnolli, A., Chittaro, L., Gamberini, L. (eds.) PERSUASIVE 2014. LNCS, vol. 8462, pp. 80–91. Springer, Cham (2014). https://doi.org/10.1007/978-3-319-07127-5_8

33. Tikka, P., Laitinen, M., Manninen, I., Oinas-Kukkonen, H.: Reflection through gaming: reinforcing health message response through gamified rehearsal. In: Ham, J., Karapanos, E., Morita, P.P., Burns, C.M. (eds.) PERSUASIVE 2018. LNCS, vol. 10809, pp. 200–212. Springer, Cham (2018). https://doi.org/10.1007/978-3-319-78978-1_17

34. Gram-Hansen, S.B., Ryberg, T.: Acttention – influencing communities of practice with persuasive learning designs. In: MacTavish, T., Basapur, S. (eds.) PERSUASIVE 2015. LNCS, vol. 9072, pp. 184–195. Springer, Cham (2015). https://doi.org/10.1007/978-3-319-20306-5_17

35. Rapoport, M.: Persuasive robotic technologies and the freedom of choice and action. In: Nørskov, M. (ed.) Social Robots: Boundaries, Potential, Challenges, pp. 219–238. Taylor and Francis, Abingdon (2017)

36. Henkemans, O.A.B., et al.: Design and evaluation of a personal robot playing a self-management education game with children with diabetes type 1. Int. J. Hum. Comput. Stud. **106**, 63–76 (2017)

37. Heras, S., Rodríguez, P., Palanca, J., Duque, N., Julián, V.: Using argumentation to persuade students in an educational recommender system. In: de Vries, PW., Oinas-Kukkonen, H., Siemons, L., Beerlage-de Jong, N., van Gemert-Pijnen, L. (eds.) PERSUASIVE 2017. LNCS, vol. 10171, pp. 227–239. Springer, Cham (2017). https://doi.org/10.1007/978-3-319-55134-0_18

38. Chow, K.K.N., Harrell, D.F., Yan, W.K.: Designing and analyzing swing compass: a lively interactive system provoking imagination and affect for persuasion. In: MacTavish, T., Basapur, S. (eds.) PERSUASIVE 2015. LNCS, vol. 9072, pp. 107–120. Springer, Cham (2015). https://doi.org/10.1007/978-3-319-20306-5_10

39. Hedin, B., Zapico, J.: Kilowh.at – increasing energy awareness using an interactive energy comparison tool. In: de Vries, P.W., Oinas-Kukkonen, H., Siemons, L., Beerlage-de Jong, N., van Gemert-Pijnen, L. (eds.) PERSUASIVE 2017. LNCS, vol. 10171, pp. 175–185. Springer, Cham (2017). https://doi.org/10.1007/978-3-319-55134-0_14

40. Chittaro, L., Zangrando, N.: The persuasive power of virtual reality: effects of simulated human distress on attitudes towards fire safety. In: Ploug, T., Hasle, P., Oinas-Kukkonen, H. (eds.) PERSUASIVE 2010. LNCS, vol. 6137, pp. 58–69. Springer, Heidelberg (2010). https://doi.org/10.1007/978-3-642-13226-1_8

41. O'Brien, A.J., Alfano, C., Magnusson, E.: Improving cross-cultural communication through collaborative technologies. In: de Kort, Y., IJsselsteijn, W., Midden, C., Eggen, B., Fogg, B. J. (eds.) PERSUASIVE 2007. LNCS, vol. 4744, pp. 125–131. Springer, Heidelberg (2007). https://doi.org/10.1007/978-3-540-77006-0_17

42. Alharbi, O., Chatterjee, S.: BrightDark: a smartphone app utilizing e-fotonovela and text messages to increase energy conservation awareness. In: MacTavish, T., Basapur, S. (eds.) PERSUASIVE 2015. LNCS, vol. 9072, pp. 95–106. Springer, Cham (2015). https://doi.org/10.1007/978-3-319-20306-5_9

43. Basten, F., Ham, J., Midden, C., Gamberini, L., Spagnolli, A.: Does trigger location matter? The influence of localization and motivation on the persuasiveness of mobile purchase recommendations. In: MacTavish, T., Basapur, S. (eds.) PERSUASIVE 2015. LNCS, vol. 9072, pp. 121–132. Springer, Cham (2015). https://doi.org/10.1007/978-3-319-20306-5_11

44. Hammer, S., Lugrin, B., Bogomolov, S., Janowski, K., André, E.: Investigating politeness strategies and their persuasiveness for a robotic elderly assistant. In: Meschtscherjakov, A., De Ruyter, B., Fuchsberger, V., Murer, M., Tscheligi, M. (eds.) PERSUASIVE 2016. LNCS, vol. 9638, pp. 315–326. Springer, Cham (2016). https://doi.org/10.1007/978-3-319-31510-2_27

45. Costa, A., Heras, S., Palanca, J., Jordán, J., Novais, P., Julián, V.: Argumentation schemes for events suggestion in an e-Health platform. In: de Vries, P.W., Oinas-Kukkonen, H., Siemons, L., Beerlage-de Jong, N., van Gemert-Pijnen, L. (eds.) PERSUASIVE 2017. LNCS, vol. 10171, pp. 17–30. Springer, Cham (2017). https://doi.org/10.1007/978-3-319-55134-0_2

46. Chow, K.K.N.: Lock up the lighter: experience prototyping of a lively reflective design for smoking habit control. In: Meschtscherjakov, A., De Ruyter, B., Fuchsberger, V., Murer, M., Tscheligi, M. (eds.) PERSUASIVE 2016. LNCS, vol. 9638, pp. 352–364. Springer, Cham (2016). https://doi.org/10.1007/978-3-319-31510-2_30

47. Nooitgedagt, A., Beun, R.J., Dignum, F.: e-Coaching for intensive cardiac rehabilitation. In: de Vries, P.W., Oinas-Kukkonen, H., Siemons, L., Beerlage-de Jong, N., van Gemert-Pijnen, L. (eds.) PERSUASIVE 2017. LNCS, vol. 10171, pp. 31–42. Springer, Cham (2017). https://doi.org/10.1007/978-3-319-55134-0_3

48. Stibe, A., Oinas-Kukkonen, H.: Using social influence for motivating customers to generate and share feedback. In: Spagnolli, A., Chittaro, L., Gamberini, L. (eds.) PERSUASIVE 2014. LNCS, vol. 8462, pp. 224–235. Springer, Cham (2014). https://doi.org/10.1007/978-3-319-07127-5_19

49. Adaji, I., Vassileva, J.: Persuasive patterns in Q&A social networks. In: Meschtscherjakov, A., De Ruyter, B., Fuchsberger, V., Murer, M., Tscheligi, M. (eds.) PERSUASIVE 2016. LNCS, vol. 9638, pp. 189–196. Springer, Cham (2016). https://doi.org/10.1007/978-3-319-31510-2_16

50. Hartwig, M., Scholl, P., Budde, V., Windel, A.: Adaptive reminders for safe work. In: MacTavish, T., Basapur, S. (eds.) PERSUASIVE 2015. LNCS, vol. 9072, pp. 135–140. Springer, Cham (2015). https://doi.org/10.1007/978-3-319-20306-5_12

51. Clinkenbeard, D., et al.: What's your 2%? A pilot study for encouraging physical activity using persuasive video and social media. In: Spagnolli, A., Chittaro, L., Gamberini, L. (eds.) PERSUASIVE 2014. LNCS, vol. 8462, pp. 43–55. Springer, Cham (2014). https://doi.org/10.1007/978-3-319-07127-5_5

52. Daskalova, N., Ford, N., Hu, A., Moorehead, K., Wagnon, B., Davis, J.: Informing design of suggestion and self-monitoring tools through participatory experience prototypes. In: Spagnolli, A., Chittaro, L., Gamberini, L. (eds.) PERSUASIVE 2014. LNCS, vol. 8462, pp. 68–79. Springer, Cham (2014). https://doi.org/10.1007/978-3-319-07127-5_7

53. DiMicco, J.M., Bender, W.: Group reactions to visual feedback tools. In: de Kort, Y., IJsselsteijn, W., Midden, C., Eggen, B., Fogg, B.J. (eds.) PERSUASIVE 2007. LNCS, vol. 4744, pp. 132–143. Springer, Heidelberg (2007). https://doi.org/10.1007/978-3-540-77006-0_18

54. Esakia, A., McCrickard, D.S., Harden, S.M., Horning, M.: FitAware: channeling group dynamics strategies with smartwatches in a physical activity intervention. In: Proceedings of 2017 CHI Conference on Extended Abstracts on Human Factors in Computing Systems - CHI EA 2017, pp. 2551–2559 (2017)

55. Reddy, V., et al.: Influencing participant behavior through a notification-based recommendation system. In: Ham, J., Karapanos, E., Morita, P.P., Burns, C.M. (eds.) PERSUASIVE 2018. LNCS, vol. 10809, pp. 113–119. Springer, Cham (2018). https://doi.org/10.1007/978-3-319-78978-1_9

56. Orji, R., Moffatt, K.: Persuasive technology for health and wellness: state-of-the-art and emerging trends. Health Inform. J. **24**, 66–91 (2018)

Is ArguMessage Effective? A Critical Evaluation of the Persuasive Message Generation System

Rosemary J. Thomas[1]([✉])(iD), Judith Masthoff[1,2]([✉]), and Nir Oren[1]([✉])

[1] University of Aberdeen, Aberdeen, UK
rosemaryjthomas@acm.org, n.oren@abdn.ac.uk
[2] Utrecht University, Utrecht, The Netherlands
j.f.m.masthoff@uu.nl

Abstract. This paper describes an investigation into the effectiveness of ArguMessage, a system that uses argumentation schemes and limited user input to semi-automatically generate persuasive messages encouraging behaviour change that follow specific argumentation patterns. We conducted user studies in the domains of healthy eating and email security to investigate its effectiveness. Our results show that ArguMessage in general supported users in generating messages based on the argumentation schemes. However, there were some issues in particular with copying the example messages, and some system improvements need to be made. Participants were generally satisfied with the messages produced, with the exception of those produced by two schemes ('Argument from memory with goal' and 'Argument from values with goal') which were removed after the first study.

Keywords: Persuasion · Argumentation schemes · Message generation

1 Introduction and Related Work

The process of creating and confirming the validity of persuasive messages is a cumbersome and time consuming task, particularly given the lack of domain independent tools for the purpose of message generation. For example, Thomas et al. [15] manually created and validated healthy-eating messages for each of Cialdini's principles of persuasion[1] using a time-consuming process. They suggested that argumentation schemes could be used to partially automate the process of message creation after message types have been validated, as these schemes have a clear structure that can accommodate modifiable and replaceable variables. This would allow domain experts to easily create messages which

---

[1] A study was conducted to group messages into the six principles with over 150 participants and the measure used for effective validation of their messages was the Free-Marginal Kappa [13].

© Springer Nature Switzerland AG 2019
H. Oinas-Kukkonen et al. (Eds.): PERSUASIVE 2019, LNCS 11433, pp. 87–99, 2019.
https://doi.org/10.1007/978-3-030-17287-9_8

follow a particular argumentation pattern, removing the need for message validation. A corpus of such messages can then be incorporated by, for example, intelligent agent software or used in user studies. There is some existing research that uses persuasive strategies and argumentation together to motivate people to make changes in their behaviour. For example, 'Daphne' [8] and 'Portia' [11] use a conversational agent based on argumentation for behaviour change.

Much existing research illustrates guidelines for persuasive message design and communication, mainly in the domain of health promotion [3,6,9,20] and— to a lesser extent—within the cyber-security domain [2]. Table 1 shows a sample of studies within the health domain with examples of the messages used. Note that the messages produced in these studies were all manually created by the researchers and were not validated before they were used in the evaluation studies. Message creation and validation is a time intensive task depending on the number of messages that are required.

Thomas et al. [15] claimed that automating the process of creating valid persuasive messages could be accomplished by integrating Cialdini's principles of persuasion [4] and argumentation schemes[2] [12,19]. They created a system called ArguMessage [17], built on the basis of the mapped Cialidini's principles and argumentation schemes (see Table 2) intended to make the process of generating persuasive messages easier, and proposed using the system to generate healthy eating messages. Additionally, Thomas et al. proposed to implement the system in the cyber-security domain, focusing on email security and phishing to generate messages to help users protect themselves against malicious emails [14].

In this paper, we evaluate the effectiveness of ArguMessage across these two domains to ensure the results are generalisable. We present two user studies one for each domain, to answer the following research questions:

RQ1. How easy is it to produce messages using ArguMessage?
RQ2. How satisfied are participants with the messages generated?

The goal of this work is to investigate whether ArguMessage is easy enough to use for people who are not experts in argumentation to produce messages, and whether the messages generated by the system are natural enough for users to be satisfied with them.

The remainder of the paper is structured as follows: Sect. 2 describes the studies' design; Sects. 3 and 4 describes the results studies into the generation of healthy eating and email security messages respectively; and Sect. 5 draws conclusions and proposes future work.

---

[2] Argument schemes are commonly used defeasible patterns of reasoning, for example arguing that something is the case because an expert stated so.

Table 1. Studies that created messages for evaluation with example messages

Reference	Domain	Example messages	Creation	Validated
[1]	Health education messages	People who eat too much fat have more chance of getting cardiovascular diseases If your intake of folic acid is below 8 mg per day, your risk of having a child with a neural tube disorder is 50% higher	Hand crafted	No
[18]	Educational dietary messages	People who do eat enough F & V often have an adequate intake of dietary fibres and therefore more chance of healthy bowels People who eat too much fat have more chance of staying unfit or feeling less energetic	Hand crafted	No
[5]	Health messages	Suntanning helps to maintain vitamin D levels, but causes skin cancer Suntanning gives you an attractive tanned skin, but causes wrinkles	Hand crafted	No
[7]	Dietary habits	If you eat at least 5 portions of FV a day. You will be provided with vitamins and mineral salts which perform the fundamental role of protecting the body. If you do not eat at least 5 portions of FV a day. It may trigger diseases such as cancer	Hand crafted	No
[10]	Public health messages	When you're in a hurry, have a quick and healthy breakfast. FV provide nutrients, fiber, and substances like antioxidants that help guard against the threat of disease	Hand crafted	No

Table 2. Cialdini's principles mapping to argumentation schemes [14]

Cialdini's principles	Argumentation schemes
Commitments and consistency	Argument from commitment with goal
	Practical reasoning with goal
	Argument from waste with goal
	Argument from sunk cost with action
	Argument from values with goal
Social proof	Argument from popular opinion with goal
	Argument from popular practice with action
Liking	Practical reasoning with liking
	Practical reasoning with goal and liking
	Argument from position to know with goal and liking
Authority	Argument from expert opinion with goal
	Argument from rules with goal
	Argument from position to know with goal
	Argument from memory with goal

2   Studies' Design

We used ArguMessage to conduct two studies to generate corpora of healthy eating and email security messages. Both studies had the same design.

Step 1: Argument from waste with goal

Please read the recipe and the sample message given below. Do not worry if you do not fully understand the recipe, as these can be quite hard to read.

> **Recipe:** Argument from waste with goal
> **Major Premise:** If Actor A stops trying to realise **Goal G** now, all of **Actor A's** previous efforts to realise **Goal G** will be wasted.
> **Minor Premise:** If **Actor A's** previous attempts to realise **Goal G** are wasted, that would be a bad thing.
> **Conclusion:** Therefore, **Actor A** ought to continue trying to realise **Goal G**.
>
> **Sample Message for User**
> If you stop trying to check for poor spelling and grammar in received emails now, all your previous efforts will be wasted. Therefore, you ought to continue trying to do that.

The sample user message above is to give you an example of the message finally generated. **Please don't copy it.** Now let us create your own email security message using this recipe.

What is the goal of the user?

The goal of the user is to [check for genuine links in incoming emails] .

[Create Message]

Fig. 1. Explanation of argumentation scheme and questions

Participants were first given instructions explaining what they were required to do, namely generate three persuasive messages using three "recipes" (argumentation schemes); they were then asked to answer some questions to help ArguMessage generate the messages. Next, the description of a "recipe" was shown (including an example of the message it generates) along with a set of questions which the participant needed to answer to generate a message. Once the participant was happy with their answers, ArguMessage used template-based natural language generation to create a message and present it to the participant. Finally, participants indicated their satisfaction level with the message generated on a 5-point Likert scale and provided feedback. This was repeated 3 times, for 3 randomly chosen recipes, leading to the generation of 3 messages per participant. The recipes were based on the 14 argumentation schemes shown in Table 2 (with 9 schemes used in the second study as explained below).

Table 3. Healthy eating domain: mean user satisfaction rating of generated messages within argumentation schemes and p-values for Z-test comparing the mean to 3, and for those not-significantly above 3, to 2

Argumentation scheme	Rating (1–5)	>3	>2
Argument from expert opinion with goal	4.15	***	
Argument from position to know with goal and liking	4.07	***	
Argument from popular opinion with goal	4.06	***	
Argument from position to know with goal	4.00	***	
Argument from sunk cost with action	4.00		***
Practical reasoning with goal and liking	3.93	*	
Practical reasoning with liking	3.89	*	
Practical reasoning with goal	3.84	**	
Argument from popular practice with action	3.63	*	
Argument from commitment with goal	3.42		***
Argument from waste with goal	3.20		***
Argument from rules with goal	3.16		***
Argument from memory with goal	2.57		
Argument from values with goal	2.23		

*** $p < 0.001$; ** $p < 0.01$; * $p < 0.05$

After the first study, the system was improved (see below). An illustration of the completed participant input is shown in Fig. 1. In this instance, the message generated would be "If you stop trying to check for genuine links in incoming emails now, all your previous efforts will be wasted. Therefore, you ought to continue trying to do that".

3   Generation of Messages: Healthy Eating Domain

Participants. We conducted a user study using ArguMessage with lay people recruited via Amazon Mechanical Turk who had an acceptance rating of at least 90% and were located in the United States. This yielded 72 participants, of which 31 were males (5 aged 18–25, 19 aged 26–40, 6 aged 41–65 and 1 aged over 65); and 41 were females (2 aged 18–25, 24 aged 26–40, 13 aged 41–65 and 2 aged over 65). Table 4 shows the participants' attitude, behaviour and knowledge in the healthy eating domain. Participants generated a total of 216 messages.

Table 4. Healthy eating domain: participants' attitude, behaviour and knowledge

Attitude	%	Behaviour	%	Knowledge	%
Extremely important	18.1	Everyday	9.7	Extremely knowledgeable	6.9
Considerably important	38.9	Frequently	41.7	Considerably knowledgeable	38.9
Somewhat important	34.7	Sometimes	43.1	Somewhat knowledgeable	44.4
Slightly important	6.9	Rarely	5.6	Slightly knowledgeable	9.7
Not important at all	1.4	Never	0.0	Not knowledgeable at all	0.0

Table 5. Healthy eating domain: rejected messages

Unexpected user interactions	Total
Copied	50
Copied and not followed instructions	13
Not followed instructions	22
Partly out of domain (but correct message)	1
Different domain (but correct message)	19
Different domain and grammar issues	3
Different domain and punctuation issues	4
Different domain and spelling issues	1

Copied messages include messages which were exactly copied or matched closely with the sample messages

Participants' Satisfaction Rating. We calculated the mean of all messages rated under the specific argumentation scheme to determine satisfaction. The highest rated scheme was 'Argument from expert opinion with goal' with a mean of 4.15 and the lowest rated was 'Argument from values with goal' with a mean of 2.23 (see Table 3). For this analysis, all 216 messages were used. For almost all argumentation schemes, satisfaction with the generated messages was rated significantly above the midpoint of the scale for 8 argumentation schemes (see Table 3), and at the midpoint of the scale for 4 schemes. However, satisfaction was below the midpoint of the scale for 'Argument from memory with goal' and 'Argument from values with goal'. This answers Research Question RQ2, demonstrating that on the whole, users were satisfied with the messages.

Unexpected User Interactions. Out of 216 messages obtained, we rejected 113 (see Table 5) and approved 61. In addition, there were 42 messages that had minor grammatical (10 messages), spelling (3), typing (1), punctuation (16) and multiple (12) mistakes which could be considered for approval[3].

As shown in Table 5, there were three main reasons for rejection. First, some participants produced messages that were clearly not about healthy eating, but for example about physical exercise (noted in the table as 'Different domain'). Second, there were messages where participants had not provided information in the format requested (for example, in Fig. 1, the participant is asked to complete the phrase 'the goal of the user is to', and a participant may have written a full message instead of completing the phrase (this is noted in the table as 'Not followed instructions'). Third, there were messages that were identical to the sample messages provided with the scheme (noted in the table as 'Copied' if they followed instructions, and 'Copied and not followed instructions' if for example they copied parts of the sample message as answers for the wrong question).

Table 6 shows the distribution of the number of messages produced with the 14 argumentation schemes used in the system. The 'total approved' is calculated by combining the 'approved' and 'considered to be approved' messages. The table does not include all rejected messages, as most were copied or different domain (so, unrelated to a difficulty with using a particular argumentation scheme, but rather to the instructions for the system as a whole), however the number of cases where instructions were not followed may point towards a difficulty with a particular scheme. Overall, the proportion of messages for which people managed to follow the instructions of the argumentation schemes was 84% (86% if excluding copied messages). The proportion was worst for 'Argument from memory with goal', where it was 76%. This answers Research Question RQ1: the system was quite easy to use, but the experimental setup was not clear enough with some participants copying the example message or producing messages which were not about healthy eating.

---

[3] These were approved after post-processing, and the system changed (as explained below) to do this automatically in future.

Table 6. Healthy eating domain: distribution of messages within the schemes

Argumentation schemes	Total	Instructions not followed	Approved	Considered to be approved	Total approved
Arg. from sunk cost with action	6	0	2	1	3
Practical reasoning with liking	9	2	2	2	4
Arg. from expert opinion with goal	13	1	3	4	7
Arg. from values with goal	13	2	2	0	2
Arg. from position to know with goal and liking	14	0	4	7	11
Practical reasoning with goal and liking	14	1	5	0	5
Arg. from waste with goal	15	1	4	0	4
Arg. from position to know with goal	17	1	5	1	6
Arg. from popular opinion with goal	18	1	2	9	11
Arg. from commitment with goal	19	2	7	4	11
Arg. from popular practice with action	19	1	3	6	9
Arg. from rules with goal	19	3	7	5	12
Practical reasoning with goal	19	2	11	1	12
Arg. from memory with goal	21	5	4	2	6
Total	216	22	61	42	103

Mitigation to Unexpected User Interactions. The system was modified to pre-process most of the unexpected user interactions. The system was revised by adding functions to remove or avoid most language mistakes[4]. Additionally, a training module was incorporated for participants to practice to get an idea of the working of the system before they proceeded to the actual study; they could try it multiple times. The instruction not to copy the example message was emphasized.

Before running the email security study, we also removed the two lowest rated argumentation schemes, i.e., 'Argument from memory with goal' and 'Argument from values with goal', and the three argumentation schemes that involved liking (i.e., 'Argument from position to know with goal and liking', 'Practical reasoning with goal and liking' and 'Practical reasoning with liking'). The latter was done partially because 'liking' is harder to conceptualize in the email security domain and partially because previous studies suggested that messages based on liking were rated lowest on perceived persuasiveness [15, 16].

---

[4] For example, converting capital letters to lower case, removing additional full-stops, and converting 2nd and 3rd person usage to 1st person usage.

Table 7. Email security domain: mean user satisfaction rating of generated messages within argumentation schemes and p-values for Z-test comparing the mean to 3, and for those not-significantly above 3, to 2

Argumentation scheme	Rating (1–5)	>3	> 2
Argument from position to know with goal	3.80	***	
Argument from rules with goal	3.80	*	
Argument from commitment with goal	3.60	*	
Argument from popular opinion with goal	3.36		**
Argument from popular practice with action	3.33		**
Argument from waste with goal	3.33		**
Practical reasoning with goal	3.33		***
Argument from expert opinion with goal	3.00		*
Argument from sunk cost with action	2.79		*

*** $p < 0.001$; ** $p < 0.01$; * $p < 0.05$

4   Generation of Messages: Email Security Domain

Participants. The study was conducted with participants who have some knowledge or experience with anti-phishing. The link to the study was shared on mailing lists and known contacts. The invitation to take part (without the link) was shared on social media which helped to find domain knowledgeable participants. The study had 40 participants, of which 23 were males (2 aged 18–25, 14 aged 26–40, 5 aged 41–65 and 2 aged over 65), 15 females (1 aged 18–25, 10 aged 26–40 and 4 aged 41–65), and 2 undisclosed. Table 8 shows the participants' attitude, behaviour and knowledge in the email security domain. 106 messages were generated.

Participants' Satisfaction Rating. We calculated the mean of all messages rated under the specific argumentation scheme to determine the satisfaction. The highest rated schemes were 'Argument from position to know with goal' and 'Argument from rules with goal' with a mean of 3.80, and the lowest rated 'Argument from sunk cost with action' with a mean of 2.79 (see Table 7). For this analysis, all 106 messages were used. Satisfaction ratings for the messages produced by the different schemes are not similar between the two studies, and seem a bit lower in this study. This is likely an impact of the domain. However, for all argumentation schemes, satisfaction with the generated messages was still rated significantly above the midpoint of the scale for 3 argumentation schemes (see Table 7), and at the midpoint of the scale for 6 schemes. This answers Research Question RQ2.

Table 8. Email security domain: participants' attitude, behaviour and knowledge

Attitude	%	Behaviour	%	Knowledge	%
Extremely important	57.5	Everyday	15.0	Extremely knowledgeable	25.0
Considerably important	35.0	Frequently	32.5	Considerably knowledgeable	47.5
Somewhat important	5.0	Sometimes	32.5	Somewhat knowledgeable	20.0
Slightly important	0.0	Rarely	15.0	Slightly knowledgeable	7.5
Not important at all	2.5	Never	5.0	Not knowledgeable at all	0.0

Table 9. Email security domain: rejected messages

Unexpected user interactions	Total
Copied	24
Copied and not followed instructions	3
Partly out of domain (but correct message)	4
Different domain (but correct message)	8
Not followed instructions	8

Copied messages include messages which were exactly copied or matched closely with the sample messages

Table 10. Email security domain: distribution of messages within the schemes

Argumentation schemes	Total	Instructions not followed	Approved	Considered to be approved	Total approved
Arg. from sunk cost with action	14	1	4	0	4
Arg. from expert opinion with goal	10	1	3	3	6
Arg. from waste with goal	12	1	2	3	5
Arg. from position to know with goal	10	1	4	1	5
Arg. from popular opinion with goal	11	0	7	0	7
Arg. from commitment with goal	15	0	9	3	12
Arg. from popular practice with action	9	0	7	0	7
Arg. from rules with goal	10	2	3	1	4
Practical reasoning with goal	15	2	7	1	8
Total	106	8	46	12	58

Unexpected User Interactions. Out of 106 messages obtained, we rejected 47 (see Table 9) and approved 46. In addition, there were 12 messages with minor grammar (9 messages) and spelling (3) mistakes which could be considered for approval. These mistakes may be fixed by including further post-processing into the system. Table 10 shows the distribution of the number of messages produced with the 9 argumentation schemes used in the system. As before, the 'total approved' is calculated by combining the 'approved' and 'considered to be approved' messages.

Overall, the proportion of messages for which people managed to follow the instructions of the system was 90%. This answers Research Question RQ1: the system was quite easy to use. The changes we had made after the first study had a positive effect on ease of use. Nevertheless, there were still some participants copying the example message or producing messages which were not about email security.

5 Conclusions

This paper investigated the effectiveness of ArguMessage, a system that can semi-automatically generate persuasive messages based on argumentation schemes. We investigated the effectiveness of ArguMessage in two domains: healthy eating and email security. Whilst the studies used lay people, the intention ultimately is for the system to be used by domain experts, to guarantee that the messages produced have domain validity.

We ran the studies with lay people to check that the system is easy enough to use, and does produce messages which are natural enough to satisfy the users. Lay people were used, as domain experts are hard to get, and also would spend considerable time worrying about the correctness of the content of the messages (for example, a dietitian may need substantial time to ensure dietary advice is accurate). This would make studies with experts very time consuming. The studies in this paper ensure that the usability of the system will be good enough for experts to use; if even lay people can produce messages that adhere to an argumentation scheme then so will domain experts.

There were some clear issues when our participants used the system. First, a substantial amount of copying from the sample messages took place. This shows that some participants were not clear enough about what was expected from them. After we added some training and made it more explicit not to copy (by bolding the words) in Study 2, the rate of copying reduced from 29% to 25%, which is still substantial. This indicates that a longer, more detailed training session will be needed (before deploying the system, we could for example add a video tutor). Second, some participants produced messages that were outside of the domain. This is an issue which would not occur with domain experts. Based on the results, we modified the system slightly between the studies, to add some post-processing, and based on the second study we plan to add some more post-processing. Overall, the effectiveness of generating messages was good when considering those participants who produced original messages applicable to the domain; there were only a limited number of cases were instructions of the scheme were not followed, and there was no scheme that was particularly bad for this. Participants were also generally satisfied with the messages produced, with the exception of two schemes ('Argument from memory with goal' and 'Argument from values with goal') which were removed after Study 1. ArguMessage uses the argumentation schemes that were all adapted from Walton et al. [19]. Given that Walton et al.'s schemes are mainly created for broad purposes, it is plausible for ArguMessage to use domain specific argumentation schemes. So, schemes particularly for healthy eating and cyber-security could be created and integrated [17]. In addition, we are running a study to investigate the extent to which argumentation experts agree that the messages produced match the argumentation schemes. The system is not yet designed to handle all spelling, typing, and other grammatical issues, though we incorporated some post-processing already. Future work would include exploring the possibilities to incorporate full Natural Language Processing to mitigate these issues. ArguMessage is currently only used to generate individual persuasive messages. One could also extend the system to produce messages suitable for a dialogue system.

We only evaluated ArguMessage and were not able to compare it against another system as no other systems currently exist that can semi-automatically generate persuasive messages. A future study could compare the efficiency and effectiveness of using ArguMessage to a manual process of message generation. We also intend to perform a qualitative study with domain experts to get their opinions on the usefulness of ArguMessage and further improvements required, as well as a study where domain experts use ArguMessage to produce messages that will be used in practice.

Acknowledgements. The work on cyber-security in this paper was supported by EPSRC award EP/P011829/1.

References

1. Brug, J., Ruiter, R., Van Assema, P.: The (IR)relevance of framing nutrition education messages. Nutr. Health **17**(1), 9–20 (2003)
2. Chipperfield, C., Furnell, S.: From security policy to practice: sending the right messages. Comput. Fraud. Secur. **2010**(3), 13–19 (2010). https://doi.org/10.1016/S1361-3723(10)70025-7
3. Churchill, S., Pavey, L.: Promoting fruit and vegetable consumption: the role of message framing and autonomy. Br. J. Health Psychol. **18**(3), 610–622 (2013). https://doi.org/10.1111/bjhp.12007
4. Cialdini, R.B.: Harnessing the science of persuasion. Harv. Bus. Rev. **79**(9), 72–79 (2001)
5. Cornelis, E., Cauberghe, V., De Pelsmacker, P.: Being healthy or looking good? The effectiveness of health versus appearance-focused arguments in two-sided messages. J. Health Psychol. **19**(9), 1132–1142 (2014). https://doi.org/10.1177/1359105313485310
6. Dijkstra, A.: The psychology of tailoring-ingredients in computer-tailored persuasion. Soc. Pers. Psychol. Compass **2**(2), 765–784 (2008). https://doi.org/10.1111/j.1751-9004.2008.00081.x

7. Godinho, C.A., Alvarez, M.J., Lima, M.L.: Emphasizing the losses or the gains: comparing situational and individual moderators of framed messages to promote fruit and vegetable intake. Appetite **96**, 416–425 (2016). https://doi.org/10.1016/j.appet.2015.10.001

8. Grasso, F., Cawsey, A., Jones, R.: Dialectical argumentation to solve conflicts in advice giving: a case study in the promotion of healthy nutrition. Int. J. Hum.-Comput. Stud. **53**(6), 1077–1115 (2000). https://doi.org/10.1006/ijhc.2000.0429

9. Kreuter, M., Farrell, D., Olevitch, L., Brennan, L.: Tailoring Health Messages: Customizing Communication With Computer Technology. Routledge, Abingdon (2012)

10. Latimer, A.E., et al.: Promoting fruit and vegetable intake through messages tailored to individual differences in regulatory focus. Ann. Behav. Med. **35**(3), 363–369 (2008). https://doi.org/10.1007/s12160-008-9039-6

11. Mazzotta, I., de Rosis, F., Carofiglio, V.: Portia: a user-adapted persuasion system in the healthy-eating domain. IEEE Intell. Syst. **22**(6), 42–51 (2007). https://doi.org/10.1109/MIS.2007.115

12. Mazzotta, I., de Rosis, F.: Artifices for persuading to improve eating habits. In: AAAI Spring Symposium: Argumentation for Consumers of Healthcare (2006)

13. Randolph, J.J.: Free-marginal multirater kappa (multirater k[free]): an alternative to fleiss fixed - marginal multirater kappa. In: Joensuu Learning and Instruction Symposium 2005 (2005)

14. Thomas, R.J., Collinson, M., Masthoff, J.: Caught by phishing emails? How can argumentation schemes be used to protect users? In: Proceedings of AISB Annual Convention 2018 Symposium on Digital Behaviour Intervention for Cyber Security (2018)

15. Josekutty Thomas, R., Masthoff, J., Oren, N.: Adapting healthy eating messages to personality. In: de Vries, P.W., Oinas-Kukkonen, H., Siemons, L., Beerlage-de Jong, N., van Gemert-Pijnen, L. (eds.) PERSUASIVE 2017. LNCS, vol. 10171, pp. 119–132. Springer, Cham (2017). https://doi.org/10.1007/978-3-319-55134-0_10

16. Thomas, R.J., Masthoff, J., Oren, N.: Personalising healthy eating messages to age, gender and personality: using Cialdini's principles and framing. In: IUI 2017 Companion. ACM (2017). https://doi.org/10.1145/3030024.3040986

17. Thomas, R.J., Oren, N., Masthoff, J.: ArguMessage: a system for automation of message generation using argumentation schemes. In: Proceedings of AISB Annual Convention 2018 18th Workshop on Computational Models of Natural Argument, pp. 27–31 (2018)

18. Van Assema, P., Martens, M., Ruiter, R.A.C., Brug, J.: Framing of nutrition education messages in persuading consumers of the advantages of a healthy diet. J. Hum. Nutr. Diet. **14**(6), 435–442 (2001). https://doi.org/10.1046/j.1365-277X.2001.00315.x

19. Walton, D., Reed, C., Macagno, F.: Argumentation Schemes. Cambridge University Press, Cambridge (2008). https://doi.org/10.1017/CBO9780511802034

20. Wilson, B.J.: Designing media messages about health and nutrition: what strategies are most effective? J. Nutr. Educ. Behav. **39**(2, Suppl), S13–S19 (2007). http://www.sciencedirect.com/science/article/pii/S1499404606006518

Drones and Automotives

"I Am the Eye in the Sky – Can You Read My Mind?" How to Address Public Concerns Towards Drone Use

Anne Oltvoort[1], Peter de Vries[1(✉)], Thomas van Rompay[2], and Dale Rosen[3]

[1] Psychology of Conflict, Risk and Safety,
University of Twente, Enschede, The Netherlands
{a.b.a.oltvoort,p.w.devries}@utwente.nl
[2] Communication Science, University of Twente, Enschede, The Netherlands
t.j.l.vanrompay@utwente.nl
[3] BMS Lab, University of Twente, Enschede, The Netherlands
dalerosen15@gmail.com

Abstract. Inspired by recent debates on drone technology and privacy protection, this research examines how negative consequences of drone usage can be mitigated by tailoring information about drone employment to the environmental context in which they are used. Additionally, this study seeks to clarify the role of information needs people have when confronted with drones in different settings. Using virtual reality environments and a dedicated virtual app providing opportunities for the public to learn more about drone usage, participants were confronted with drone surveillance at either a business area, at a park, or during an event, and received transparent information on drone usage or a neutral message proving no information on drone usage. Additionally, participants could obtain more information on drone usage by clicking on one or more information buttons in the app. Results show that, compared to an event, participants were less acceptant of drones in a business area and even less so at the park. Further analyses indicated that heightened transparency perceptions resulted in higher levels of trust, perceived control, and drone acceptance. Finally, participants particularly sought information on how drones are used in the business area and park environment, whereas a need for privacy information stood out in the park context. These findings testify to the importance of careful consideration of the environmental context and related communication needs people have when informing the public about drone usage.

Keywords: Drones · Acceptance · Transparency

1 Introduction

Drones are steadily finding their way into everyday life. Apart from consumers using drones for entertainment purposes, drones are also increasingly deployed by a wide variety of (governmental) organizations and event organizers to improve detection and prevention of crime, and to enable enhanced data collection for incident management

H. Oinas-Kukkonen et al. (Eds.): PERSUASIVE 2019, LNCS 11433, pp. 103–114, 2019.
https://doi.org/10.1007/978-3-030-17287-9_9

purposes [1]. Consider for instance drones used by firefighters which are equipped with cameras and sensors that are able to collect information about possible toxic substances in the air. Live video footage and information about air composition could allow firefighters to better anticipate and prepare for upcoming emergencies. Despite such evident advantages however, organisations such as local governments, police forces, and event organisers are often hesitant to deploy drones [2]. Not only may members of the public infer that something is amiss – something especially event organisers want to avoid at all cost - people might also feel that their privacy is at stake. Several recent cases indeed suggest that civilians are becoming increasingly suspicious and hostile when confronted with drones humming overhead [3], in some cases even triggering explicit acts of violence and aggression (e.g., shooting a drone from the sky [4]).

Inspired by the division between proponents of drone use, who are mainly attuned to the opportunities which drones provide for enhancing public safety and security and opponents and critics, who have pointed out aforementioned privacy concerns and weariness regarding drone usage, the current research seeks to find middle ground by proposing that concerns and fears regarding drone usage can be remedied by context-specific information disclosure strategies. More specifically, we will argue that feelings and fears regarding drone use vary with context, and that therefore different information-disclosing strategies are needed across different types of settings. Furthermore, we seek to gain insight into information needs triggered by drone perception across environmental settings. For instance, are needs for (additional) privacy information less prevalent in settings where drones are typically common and expected (e.g., a large event where safety management is obviously an issue of concern) compared to settings where surveillance feels out of place (e.g., at a public park where people come to unwind and reboot)?

In other words, negative effects and consequences of drone usage may be remedied when tailoring information disclosure strategies to the specific information needs civilians have across different environmental settings. Hence our research question:

How does acceptance of drones vary with environmental context and what information disclosure strategy contributes to the acceptance of government's use of drones?

2   Background

Several negative effects of drone use have been noted across studies in recent years. Rahman, for instance, mentions 'Orwellian' fears of 'being followed' and mass surveillance, concerns over abuse or misuse of footage, and growing perceptions of ever more impersonal and distant relationships with police and law enforcers [5]. Furthermore, Custers [6] lists a number of negative effects with respect to privacy, including the 'Chilling effect', 'Function creep', and 'Privacy of location and space'. The chilling effect is a term used to describe people being more self-conscious and less free-wheeling when they know they are being watched by authorities. Function creep refers to governments initially using drones for acceptable purposes, such as a missing-person search, but gradually shifting towards more controversial purposes, such as mass surveillance. Privacy of location and space refers to the right a person has not be identified or monitored when moving in public, semi-public or private places.

Literature suggests that the effects of drone use on safety perceptions vary with the extent to which a context is experienced as private. Indeed, Taylor [7] found people to feel less safe when filmed in private environments rather than in public places. Thus, being (almost) alone in a peaceful park may feel like a relatively private experience, and observing an 'out of place' drone overhead may negatively affect safety perceptions by signaling that something is amiss.

Other research points to the importance of people's inferences with respect to drone use. Van Rompay et al. [8], for example, showed that CCTV camera presence in a city center positively impacted participants' affective evaluation of the environment as it is interpreted as a sign of good intent. Specifically, in such an 'appropriate' setting, camera presence elicited positive inferences about law enforcers and policy makers and their intentions (e.g., "They know what is going on, they know what they are doing, and they do it with citizen safety in mind"). Similarly, Taylor [7] showed that individuals who had no difficulties in accounting for the presence of CCTV cameras ("The CCTV is there to prevent crime", p. 309) were also less likely to experience problems with their presence. On the other hand, when camera presence is not perceived as appropriate or natural (e.g., in everyday public settings where risk perceptions are low or non-existent), people have been found to behave more negatively as CCTV is interpreted as a sign of distrust [7].

Thus, when it is difficult for people to come up with logical reasons or inferences as to why drones are employed in a specific context (e.g., drones employed at a peaceful park), drones may readily inspire confusion and weariness, and may for that reason inspire distrust and an overall negative attitude. On the other hand, when drones are readily perceived as contributing to safety and security (e.g., at a large event), attitude formation takes an altogether different route and safety perceptions and feelings of wellbeing are arguably enhanced. In sum, the context in which a drone is employed might well be a crucial factor to consider when seeking to enhance public acceptance of drones. Whereas the need for information might be lower or non-existent in settings where drone usage is expected, it might be particularly important for organisations such as local governments and police units to invest in information-disclosure strategies in settings where drones are perceived as less commonplace. In these cases, transparency, i.e., informing members of the public about the true reasons behind drone use, might be essential to avert incorrect inferences and belief formation which may be detrimental for the public's acceptance of drones.

Transparency is believed to be an underlying factor in this process of acceptance, because it could (re)establish trust in organisations [9–13] and it could evoke a sense of perceived control [14]. Transparency is considered to consist of three underlying concepts: disclosure, clarity and accuracy. *Disclosure* is defined as the perception that relevant information is received in a timely manner [e.g., 15, 16]. This implies that information should be shared openly (without holding back) and timely. *Clarity* is defined as the perceived level of lucidity and comprehensibility of information received from a sender [17]. Information should be presented clearly and in a concrete (rather than overly abstract) manner by organizations for it to be transparent. *Accuracy* is defined as the perception that information is correct to the extent possible given the relationship between sender and receiver [17]; information cannot be seen as transparent when it is purposefully biased or unfoundedly contrived [13]. In short, information about drones that is timely, comprehensible, and accurate may (re)establish trust in the organisation (i.e., the sender of the communication).

Trust, in turn, plays a major role in overcoming risk perceptions and in the acceptance of new technologies [e.g., 18, 19]. Trustworthiness of an organisation is based on attributed *goodwill (or: benevolence), integrity,* and *competence* [20]. Goodwill refers to *"the extent to which a trustee is believed to want to do good to the trustor, aside from an egocentric profit motive"* [20, p. 718]. Integrity refers to *"the trustor's perception that the trustee adheres to a set of principles that the trustor finds acceptable"* [20, p. 719]. Competence refers to *"the group of skills, competencies, and characteristics that enable a party to have influence within some specific domain"* [20, p. 717]. Thus, effectively communicating an organisation's goodwill, integrity and competence may positively affect trust in that organisation, and, probably, acceptance of drones it deploys.

Transparent information from an organisation (e.g., about the course of implementation and by addressing possible concerns about the impact of a new technological innovation) may boost user involvement [14]; user involvement, in turn, has been shown to increase a sense of control and acceptance. Mills and Krantz [21], for instance, showed that moderate levels of choice and information provided to blood donors proved effective for coping with stress, arguably because they experienced higher levels of control over the situation.

2.1   The Current Study

Participants were exposed to a Virtual Reality (VR) environment – a park, business area, or a festival – and, as part of the VR scenario, watched a drone fly overhead. In VR, participants had a (virtual) smart phone with an app; transparency was manipulated by providing the option to look for information about the drone. Several menu options were provided, each representing different types of information (e.g., information on the 'why' and 'how' of drone usage and privacy information). The effects of context and transparency on trust, control and acceptance was measured. By logging the use of these menu options, we aimed to determine which kinds of information people preferred in the different environmental settings. The conceptual model is shown in Fig. 1.

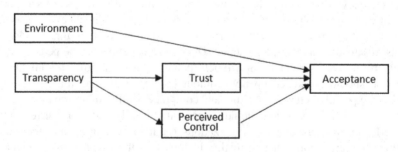

Fig. 1. Conceptual model

3 Method

3.1 Participants and Design

120 participants (69 F, 51 M, M_{age} = 24.30, SD = 6.58, range = 19–61 y) participated in this study. They were randomly assigned to distributed across the cells of a 2 (Transparency: yes versus no) * 3 (Context: event versus business area versus park) between-participants design with acceptance as dependent variable.

Fig. 2. Environment conditions: event (top), park (middle), and business area (bottom).

3.2 Procedure

First of all, participants received an introductory text about the experiment, and were assigned to one of the virtual environments.

Environment. Participants were given a VR head set and placed in a virtual environment. The VR scenario that unfolded was either situated at an event, in a park, or at a business area. Participants were positioned in a fixed spot, where they could look around freely. After a short time they could hear and see a drone overhead; they had been informed beforehand that the drone belonged to the Enschede Municipality. Figure 2 shows screenshots of each condition.

Transparency. After 30 s participants received a push notification of the 'Municipality of Enschede Drone App'. In the transparent condition, this app conveyed information related to drone use. Participants could obtain this information by clicking on six menu options: 1. Who (explicating the Enschede municipality to be the organisation responsible for the drone deployment), 2. Why (making clear that drones are used to make [the specific environment] a pleasant and safe place for everyone), 3. How (briefly explaining that security personnel will be alerted if risky situations or behaviours are detected), 4. Privacy (underscoring that visitors' privacy is taken very seriously and that the drone is incapable of detecting actual individuals), 5. Images/map (showing what kind of footage is collected with the drone, and where), and 6. Feedback (offering the possibility to ask questions or give feedback).

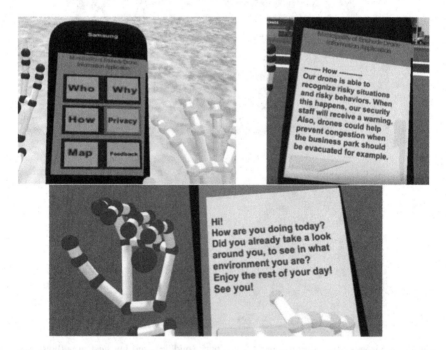

Fig. 3. Transparency conditions: transparency (top row) and no transparency (bottom)

Participants could click on as many options as they wanted. Their choices and the time they spent reading the specific information were logged. In the control condition (no transparency) participants did not receive a push notification of the 'Municipality of

Enschede Drone App', but instead received a neutral message (e.g., *'Hi! How are you doing today? Did you already take a look around you, to see in what environment you are?'*). After approximately 2 min the smart phone disappeared; subsequently, the drone appeared in the sky and flew over the terrain for about 2 min. Figure 3 shows the Transparency conditions.

After answering the questions pertaining to the dependent variables, participants were debriefed and thanked.

Materials. The materials for this experiment were created with the help of the University of Twente's BMS Lab. The three environments were created in 3D; characters were built with Reallusion Iclone7 and Character Creator 2. Oculus CV1 was used to immerse participants in the VR environments.

Measures

Perceived Transparency. The level of Perceived Transparency (regarding the Municipality of Enschede), was measured using a 7-point Likert scale (ranging from 1 = *strongly disagree* to 7 = *strongly agree*), using items from Rawlings [22]. Participants rated their level of agreement on four items such as *"The municipality of Enschede wants to understand how its decisions affect people like me"* (Cronbach's $\alpha = .69$; Guttman's $\lambda_2 = .70$).

Trust. To determine the participant's level of Trust in the organisation thirteen items from Rawlings [22] were used, using a 7-point Likert scale (ranging from 1 = *strongly disagree* to 7 = *strongly agree*). A distinction was made between the three dimensions of trust (goodwill, integrity and competence) and overall trust. Goodwill was measured with three items (e.g., *"I believe the municipality of Enschede takes the opinions of people like me into account when making decisions"*), Integrity with four items (e.g., *"The municipality of Enschede treats people like me fairly and justly"*), and Competence with three items (e.g., *"I feel very confident about the skills of the municipality of Enschede"*). Overall trust was measured with three items (e.g., *"I trust the municipality of Enschede to take care of people like me"*; $\alpha = .87$ and $\lambda_2 = .88$).

Perceived Control. Perceived control was measured with five items, based on items from Ouwehand, De Ridder and Bensing [23], on a 10-point Likert scale (1 = *Not at all* to 10 = *A great deal*). A sample item is *"To what extent did you feel you could predict the situation?"* ($\alpha = .74$ and $\lambda_2 = .75$).

Acceptance. The Acceptance Scale [24] was slightly adjusted to reflect the extent to which participants accepted government's use of drones, using nine Likert items (e.g., *"My judgements of the drone of the municipality of Enschede is are...: Pleasant - Unpleasant"* ($\alpha = .86$ and $\lambda_2 = .88$).

In addition, participants were asked to indicate to what extent they considered drone usage appropriate and understandable at an event, at a park, and in a business area. Five questions of demographic data were asked (age; gender; level of education; residence; frequency of visiting Enschede).

4 Results

4.1 Effects of Context and Transparency on Acceptance

A Multivariate Anova was conducted, with Context and Transparency as independent variables and Perceived transparency, Trust, Perceived control and Acceptance as dependent variables. The results showed non-significant main effects of Context (F (8, 222) = 0.68, ns., Wilks' Lambda = .95 and Transparency (F (4, 111) = 0.90, ns., Wilks' Lambda = .97). Also, no significant interaction was found (F (8, 222) = 0.98, ns., Wilks' Lambda = .93). The lack of effect of the Transparency manipulation on Perceived transparency clearly shows that the manipulation did not produce the desired result. We therefore decided to proceed our analyses in a more exploratory manner, using Perceived transparency as the independent variable.

4.2 Mediation Analysis

A mediation analyses was conducted to exploratively test whether the relationship between Perceived transparency and Acceptance can be explained by Trust and/or Perceived control. Figure 4 shows the result of this mediation analysis. As can be seen here, the initial significant direct effect of Perceived transparency on Acceptance (showing that perceived transparency increased acceptance; $B = 0.32$, $p < .005$) was reduced to insignificance ($B = -0.02$, n.s.) when the proposed mediators Trust and Perceived Control were added to the model. Subsequent Sobel tests show that both indirect paths (i.e., via Trust and Perceived control) are significant (Trust: Sobel $z = 3.64$, $p < .001$; Perceived control: Sobel $z = 2.59$, $p = .010$). These results suggest that the effect of Perceived transparency on Acceptance are mediated by both Trust and Perceived control.

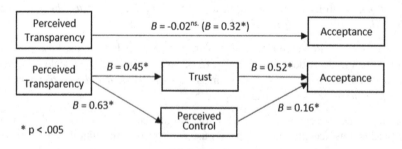

Fig. 4. Mediation analysis

4.3 Effects of Environment on Acceptance

Participants were asked to indicate the extent to which they considered drone usage appropriate and reasonable in different contexts (event, business area and park). A repeated measures Anova was conducted to compare the acceptance rates among the three contexts. The analysis showed the contexts differed significantly from each other,

F (2, 118) = 121.08, $p < .001$, Wilks' Lambda = .33. Pairwise comparisons indicated drones were significantly more accepted during events compared to business areas ($M_{difference}$: 1.58, $SE = 0.13$, $p < .001$) and compared to parks ($M_{difference} = 2.01$, $SE = 0.13$, $p < .001$). Drones were also significantly more accepted at business areas compared to parks ($M_{difference} = 0.43$, $SE = 0.12$, $p = .001$).

4.4 Effects of Environment on Information Use

The need for information participants experienced (as a function of the context in which the drone appeared), was analyzed with a multivariate repeated-measures Anova with the time spent reading the information provided by each of the six app buttons as dependent variables and Environment as independent variable. This resulted in a significant main effect of Environment, F (12, 106) = 2.44, $p = .008$, Wilks' Lambda = .609. Univariate analyses revealed effects of Environment on How (F (2, 57) = 5.66, $p = .006$) and Privacy (F (2, 57) = 6.13, $p = .004$).

Follow-up analyses with the time spent reading 'How' information revealed a significant difference between the Event and Park condition: in the former participants spent more time reading the information than in the latter ($M = 11.82$, $SD = 8.72$ versus $M = 3.26$, $SD = 5.26$, $p = .002$). Additionally, in the Business area condition reading times were higher than in the Park condition ($M = 8.91$, $SD = 9.85$ versus $M = 3.26$, $SD = 5.26$, $p = .033$). No differences were found between the Event and Business area conditions ($p = .264$). Apparently, both in the Event and the Business area condition participants were interested in finding out how the drone operated. Reversely, analyses relating to the time spent reading Privacy information showed that the need for this information was lower in the Event than in the Park condition ($M = 10.67$, SD = 10.35 versus $M = 20.53$, $SD = 15.74$, $p = .013$). This need was also lower in the Business area condition compared to the Park condition ($M = 7.58$, $SD = 9.61$ versus $M = 20.53$, $SD = 15.74$, $p = .001$). Hence, in the park condition, the need for privacy information stood out. No difference was found between the Event and Business area conditions ($p = .427$).

5   Conclusions and Discussions

The current study examined whether the acceptance of drones differs among contexts and whether transparent information disclosure increases acceptance of drones. Although direct manipulations of context and transparency failed, more explorative analyses did provide useful insights. First, the degree to which people thought drone deployment was appropriate or reasonable was shown to vary between contexts: drones were more acceptable during events compared to business areas and to parks, and more acceptable at business areas compared to parks.

Second, perceived (rather than manipulated) transparency proved to have positive effects on trust in the organization utilizing the drones (i.e., the municipality), on the degree of control they perceived to have, and on the willingness to accept drones. Additional analyses showed that, in conformance with expectations, the relationship between transparency and acceptance can be explained by trust and perceived control.

It should be noted however that these findings are purely correlational, necessitating cautious interpretation of the causality of these relationships.

Interestingly, the need for information participants experienced also depended on the context in which the drone appeared, especially information pertaining to 'privacy' and to 'how' the drone and the system behind it functioned. For both types of information, presented after pushing the respective app buttons, the event and business area contexts stood out against the park context. In the former two contexts, the time spent reading how-information was higher and time spent reading privacy information was lower than in the latter. The findings relating to privacy tie in with literature about effects of CCTV. Taylor [7], for instance, found people to feel less safe when filmed in private environments than in public places and have a higher need for information remedying such negative feelings. By extension, being at a park may feel like a relatively private experience, and observing a drone overhead may inspire feelings of being watched and related privacy concerns, resulting in an enhanced need for privacy information. The event and business area contexts were likely judged as less private (and drone presence as more appropriate), which may have reduced participants' need for privacy information. As to why reading times for the 'how' of drone usage were higher in the event and business area conditions (as opposed to the park condition), our results do not provide a straightforward answer. Perhaps, when drone presence comes across as appropriate, reasonable and for the safety of all, people are intrinsically motivated to learn more about drones, and hence may more readily click the 'How' button. In the park context where fears and privacy concerns take centre stage, a corresponding inclination to click on the 'Privacy' button may transpire.

Because of various practical problems connected to real-life drone use for research purposes, we decided to administer the scenarios in Virtual Reality. One may argue that this would confront participants with inherently artificial environments, and that this likely leads to artificial findings. In answer to this we would like to point out that there are quite some studies providing convincing support for ecological validity of scenario studies in general [25, 26], and studies employing Virtual Reality specifically [27]. After explicitly comparing the experiential qualities of real and VR environments, Kuliga et al. [27] concluded VR to have strong potential to be used as an empirical tool in psychological research.

Having said so, it is of course true that VR environments (including ours) usually lack fully immersive atmospherics, social dynamics, and multi-sensory stimulation which are typical of real-life settings and of events in particular (where people gather partly because of social dynamics and sensations of many kinds). Although as such, these are shortcomings of our VR manipulation, in all likelihood enriching future VR encounters along these lines could be expected to lead to even stronger effects. Hence, future research could involve more realistic virtual environments, for instance with more detailed graphic rendering, additional environmental sounds, more people moving about, and incorporate an actual rather than a virtual smartphone app. This way, future research could also incorporate more realistic and subtle ways of informing people by, for instance, automatically sending a message to people's phones who are near a drone [cf. 28].

In conclusion, our findings underscore the importance of being responsive to the needs and values of specific target audiences while communicating about drone usage [cf. 29]. Findings of the current research may provide a first step to compose effective communication and provide indications as to what specific information needs should take precedence in which settings.

References

1. Winkler, S., Zeadally, S., Evans, K.: Privacy and civilian drone use: the need for further regulation. IEEE Secur. Priv. **16**, 72–80 (2018)
2. de Vries, P., Galetzka, M., Gutteling, J.: Persuasion in the wild: communication, technology, and event safety. In: Spagnolli, A., Chittaro, L., Gamberini, L. (eds.) PERSUASIVE 2014. LNCS, vol. 8462, pp. 80–91. Springer, Cham (2014). https://doi.org/10.1007/978-3-319-07127-5_8
3. Jolly, J.: 'Never, ever try to shoot at a drone.' Neighborhoods buzz with complaints over pesky drones. USA Today (2018). https://eu.usatoday.com/story/tech/columnist/2018/09/03/drone-gripes-mount-homeowners-complain-breached-privacy-annoyance/1117085002/
4. Witteman, J.: Wanneer schendt een drone uw privacy? De Volkskrant (2017). https://www.volkskrant.nl/cultuur-media/wanneer-schendt-een-drone-uw-privacy-~b91d9c53/
5. Rahman, M.F.A.: Security Drones: is the Singapore Public Ready? (2016)
6. Custers, B. (ed.): The Future of Drone Use: Opportunities and Threats from Ethical and Legal Perspectives. ITLS, vol. 27. T.M.C. Asser Press, The Hague (2016). https://doi.org/10.1007/978-94-6265-132-6
7. Taylor, E.: I spy with my little eye: the use of CCTV in schools and the impact on privacy. Sociol. Rev. **58**, 381–405 (2010)
8. Van Rompay, T.J.L., De Vries, P.W., Damink, M.T.: "For your safety": effects of camera surveillance on safety impressions, situation construal and attributed intent. In: MacTavish, T., Basapur, S. (eds.) PERSUASIVE 2015. LNCS, vol. 9072, pp. 141–146. Springer, Cham (2015). https://doi.org/10.1007/978-3-319-20306-5_13
9. Bennis, W., Goleman, D., O'Toole, J.: Transparency: How Leaders Create a Culture of Candor. Wiley, Hoboken (2008)
10. Fombrun, C.J., Rindova, V.P.: The road to transparency: reputation management at Royal Dutch/Shell. Expressive Organ. **7**, 7–96 (2000)
11. Jahansoozi, J.: Organization-stakeholder relationships: exploring trust and transparency. J. Manag. Dev. **25**, 942–955 (2006)
12. Tapscott, D., Ticoll, D.: The Naked Corporation: How the Age of Transparency Will Revolutionize Business. Simon and Schuster, New York City (2003)
13. Walumbwa, F.O., Avolio, B.J., Gardner, W.L., Wernsing, T.S., Peterson, S.J.: Authentic leadership: development and validation of a theory-based measure. J. Manag. **34**, 89–126 (2008)
14. Baronas, A.-M.K., Louis, M.R.: Restoring a sense of control during implementation: how user involvement leads to system acceptance. MIS Q. **12**, 111–124 (1988)
15. Bloomfield, R., O'Hara, M.: Market transparency: who wins and who loses? Rev. Financ. Stud. **12**, 5–35 (1999)
16. Clark Williams, C.: Toward a taxonomy of corporate reporting strategies. J. Bus. Commun. **1973**(45), 232–264 (2008)
17. Schnackenberg, A.K., Tomlinson, E.C.: Organizational transparency: a new perspective on managing trust in organization-stakeholder relationships. J. Manag. **42**, 1784–1810 (2016)

18. Gefen, D., Karahanna, E., Straub, D.W.: Trust and TAM in online shopping: an integrated model. MIS Q. **27**, 51–90 (2003)
19. Pavlou, P.A., Gefen, D.: Building effective online marketplaces with institution-based trust. Inf. Syst. Res. **15**, 37–59 (2004)
20. Mayer, R.C., Davis, J.H., Schoorman, F.D.: An integrative model of organizational trust. Acad. Manag. Rev. **20**, 709–734 (1995)
21. Mills, R.T., Krantz, D.S.: Information, choice, and reactions to stress: a field experiment in a blood bank with laboratory analogue. J. Pers. Soc. Psychol. **37**, 608 (1979)
22. Rawlins, B.R.: Measuring the relationship between organizational transparency and employee trust. Public Relat. J. **2**, 1–21 (2008)
23. Ouwehand, C., De Ridder, D.T.D., Bensing, J.M.: Situational aspects are more important in shaping proactive coping behaviour than individual characteristics: a vignette study among adults preparing for ageing. Psychol. Health **21**, 809–825 (2006)
24. Van Der Laan, J.D., Heino, A., De Waard, D.: A simple procedure for the assessment of acceptance of advanced transport telematics. Transp. Res. Part C: Emerg. Technol. **5**, 1–10 (1997)
25. Bateson, J.E., Hui, M.K.: The ecological validity of photographic slides and videotapes in simulating the service setting. J. Consum. Res. **19**, 271–281 (1992)
26. Stamps III, A.E.: Use of photographs to simulate environments: a meta-analysis. Percept. Mot. Skills **71**, 907–913 (1990)
27. Kuliga, S.F., Thrash, T., Dalton, R.C., Hölscher, C.: Virtual reality as an empirical research tool—exploring user experience in a real building and a corresponding virtual model. Comput. Environ. Urban Syst. **54**, 363–375 (2015)
28. Thomasen, K.: Beyond Airspace Safety: A Feminist Perspective on Drone Privacy Regulation (2017)
29. PytlikZillig, L.M., Duncan, B., Elbaum, S., Detweiler, C.: A drone by any other name: purposes, end-user trustworthiness, and framing, but not terminology, affect public support for drones. IEEE Technol. Soc. Mag. **37**, 80–91 (2018)

Exploring the Validity of Methods to Track Emotions Behind the Wheel

Monique Dittrich$^{(\boxtimes)}$ and Sebastian Zepf

Daimer AG Research and Development, Böblingen, Germany
{monique.dittrich, sebastian.zepf}@daimler.com

Abstract. Emotions accompany us anytime, even while driving. Thereby especially negative emotional experiences influence our driving behavior and the safety on our roads. A psychological intervention to regulate feelings is to track them, e.g. by labeling them along categories. Thus, the aim of this work is to establish an empirical base to guide the development of a system that encourages the driver to label his or her emotions. This involves asking what the relevant emotions are and how they can be validly labeled in the driving context. For this purpose, a driving study was conducted to collect data on emotional experiences in-situ. For the labeling task, three methodological approaches were used: free responses, dimensional emotion rating (DER), and categorical emotion rating (CER). As a result, while DER and CER lack validity due to ambiguity or priming effects, respectively, the free response method has practical limitations. Following, it is recommended to develop an in-car emotion tracker based on CER and use the free response data to determine the appropriate number and naming of categories that cover a significant range of emotions. An initial analysis of the free responses revealed 40 distinct categories of emotional experiences.

Keywords: Emotion labeling · Validity · Driving context

1 Introduction

People track their sleep, their steps, and the kilometers they traveled. They monitor what they eat, which exercises they do, or how they feel. The latter is also known from the treatment of depression, where emotion tracking is used to monitor emotional outbursts, for example, with smartphone applications, such as *Mood Meter* or *How is the world feeling* (Fig. 1). These applications provide an interface to label emotional experiences by speaking about them, writing them down, or rating them along provided categories. The engagement with the own feelings helps depressed as well as mentally healthy individuals to regulate their emotions, in particular negatives ones [1].

Negative as well as positive emotions accompany us anytime, even while driving. In doing so, they influence our driving behavior and the safety on our roads. For example, angry drivers show up a more aggressive driving style, tend to drive faster, and are more often involved in traffic accidents [2]. Against this background, there is the demand for a system that supports the driver in regulating his or her emotions by providing an interface to label them under the conditions of the driving task [3]. In

© Springer Nature Switzerland AG 2019
H. Oinas-Kukkonen et al. (Eds.): PERSUASIVE 2019, LNCS 11433, pp. 115–127, 2019.
https://doi.org/10.1007/978-3-030-17287-9_10

doing so, the car takes on the role of an interaction partner, who directs the driver to engage with his or her feelings [4]. Thus, the aim of this work is to establish an empirical base to guide the development of such a system. Regarding its content, this includes the question of what kind of emotions people experience while driving. With respect to the system design, it has to be considered how emotional experiences should be labeled from a methodological perspective. To answer these questions, the present work proposes an in-situ approach to collect data on emotional experiences in the wild. This contributes to research since most work dealing with the subjective measurement of emotions in the driving context is either retrospective in nature or limited in the range of considered emotions. Furthermore, there is no knowledge of which method is the most valid one to label emotions under the conditions the driving task entails.

The present paper starts with related work on the subjective measurement of emotions while driving, followed by an overview of concrete methods. Subsequent, the driving study and its results are described. Finally, the results are discussed, including recommendations for the development of an in-car emotion tracker.

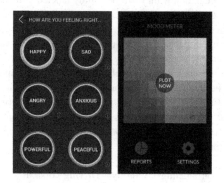

Fig. 1. Smartphone applications *How is the world feeling* (left) and *MoodMeter* (right).

2 Theoretical Background

2.1 Emotions While Driving

Most studies that deal with the nature and frequency of emotions that people experience while sitting in a car are based on retrospective methods, asking them to label their emotions *after* the ride. For instance, this can be done by writing a diary [5] or being interviewed [6]. At the expense of representativeness, however, the respondents mainly remember extreme emotions and do not report minor ones. When asking participants in-situ, their reports are as close to the emotional event as possible, why less is forgotten. An in-situ study was conducted by [7]. Within the study, the participants completed a 50 min test drive accompanied by an experimenter, who asked them to rate their emotional experiences along the categories "anger", "anxiety", "happiness", and "no emotion". As a result, anxiety (Ø2.6 times) was the most mentioned emotion during the ride, followed by anger (Ø1.5 times) and happiness (Ø1.0 times). Still, this work has limitations. First, the participants did not drive alone, which could have influenced their emotional experiences and expression [8]. Thus, the results are rather representative for trips accompanied by others, although driving alone is the most common mode of travel [9]. Second, the participants were forced to label their emotions along three emotion categories. This does not cover the whole range of emotional states possible while driving. As a reference, in [6] the authors obtained 56 affective keywords that describe emotional experiences from drivers' brainstorming.

In summary, the current state of research on emotions while driving is lacking on studies that subjectively measure emotions in-situ and give the participants the opportunity to label their full range of emotional experiences. This calls for a domain-specific emotion taxonomy for the driving context and leads to the following research question (RQ1): *What kind of emotions do people experience while driving?*

2.2   Subjective Emotion Measurement

Subsequent to the question of what kind of emotions are experienced while driving, the question arises how they can be subjectively measured. The only access to these kind of information are self-reports, either in form of *free* or *forced-choice* responses [10]. Free responses, i.e. respondents verbally describe their emotions with freely chosen terms and expressions, can be seen as the most valid method and ground truth of emotional experiences [11]. Though, these reports may be constrained, since some individuals have problems communicating their emotions and people differ in their emotional vocabulary. Regarding the forced-choice option, there are two major approaches in the field [10]: (1) the *dimensional* emotion rating (DER) and (2) the *categorical* emotion rating (CER). The CER provides the respondents with different emotion categories and asks them to choose the one that best characterizes their experience (see *How is the world feeling*). A drawback of this method is that the categories may *prime* the rating in that they "suggest responses that [the participants] might not have chosen otherwise" [10, p. 717]. Moreover, if an individual wants to answer with a category that is not provided, he or she is forced to choose the closest alternative. Consequently, CER can be seen as a valid instrument, if the following requirements are fulfilled [12]: (1) the given categories cover a significant range of relevant emotions and (2) there is a common understanding about the given categories that is not caused by priming effects. With the DER, emotional experiences are rated along bipolar and orthogonal dimensions, such as valence (positive–negative), arousal (calm–excited), and tension (tense–relaxed). Thus, emotions are described as points in a two- or three-dimensional space formed by these dimensions (see *Mood Meter*). However, the results may suffer from ambiguity, since respondents interpret and use the space individually. For example, both very fearful and a very angry individuals would indicate their experience in a similar region, namely high negative valence and high arousal [13]. Consequently, validity of DER is given under the following criteria [12]: (1) spatially close points follow a common understanding (*internal homogeneity*) and (2) points that are spatially far away from each other clearly differ in their meanings (*external heterogeneity*).

The question of which methodological approach is the right depending on the interest of research is not new. However, there is no work addressing this issue for the driving context. This leads to the second research question (RQ2): *What is a valid method to label emotional experiences while driving?*

2.3 The Regulating Effect Emotion Labeling

The aforementioned methods of subjective emotion measurement can be used to label emotions while driving. In doing so, emotion labeling not only serves the purpose of data collection, but also has an emotion regulating effect [1]. Whenever people put their feelings into words, e.g. by rating them along categories or talking about them to another person, brain regions like the parahippocampal gyrus and aspects of ventral temporal cortex are activated. This indicates that the individual is engaged in increased episodic memory retrieval and sensory processing to make meaning of the present situation. These cognitive processes disrupt and therefore downregulate the emotional experience. Furthermore, the priming effect that occurs when people label their emotions along provided categories can regulate emotional experiences. This shows up in cases of ambiguous emotional experiences. Here, predefined emotion categories can transform an ambiguous experience (e.g. excitement) into a more specific one (e.g. nervousness or joyful anticipation; [14]). These findings propose the effectiveness of an in-car system that encourages drivers to label and therefore regulate their emotions.

3 Driving Study

In order to answer the RQ a driving study was conducted, where data on emotional experiences were collected in-situ, i.e. while the participants were driving. Since human subjects were involved, the study procedure was reviewed and approved according to the Daimler Ethical Compliance Process that is accompanied by an internal IRB.

3.1 Procedure

The study was carried out from 23/07/2018 to 03/08/2018 between 8 a.m. and 7 p.m. Each trial took about 2.5 h, including two rides with a Mercedes Benz e-class (each about 25 min) and questionnaire sessions. The trials started at a lab of the Daimler AG in Böblingen, Germany. After arrival, the participants were welcomed, briefed on the procedure, and completed a questionnaire on their mood before the experiment. Then they completed the first test drive. They traveled alone guided by the navigation system. The route started and ended at the lab, including sections on the highway, the country road, and in the city. During the ride, the participants rated their emotions on a tablet application, randomized provided with one of two versions (see Sect. 3.2). The tablet (*Samsung Galaxy Tab 6*) was installed in the center console, thus it could easily be reached from the driver's seat. Before departure, the participants familiarized themselves with each version. The ride was video recorded using two *GoPro Hero 4* (one directed to the driver's face, one to the windshield), physiological data were tracked using an *Empatica Wristband E4*, and the acceleration was recorded using the tablet application *Torque Lite*. The participants were instructed to drive as they would outside of the study, e.g. they were allowed to use the radio or open the window. After they returned to the lab, they were handed out a questionnaire for the usability of the first version of the tablet application. Subsequently, similarly, the participants completed the second test drive with the other application version. Finally, the participants answered questionnaires on different personality factors influencing the experience and expression of emotions as well as on their mood after the experiment in the lab.

3.2 Emotion Labeling Data

In the further course of this paper, the focus is on the emotion labeling data. Other measures, such as the physiological and questionnaire data, are addressed in other work.

In order to collect these data, the participants were provided with a tablet application to label their emotional experiences anytime while driving (Fig. 2). They were instructed to give a rating whenever an event, whether linked to the current traffic situation (e.g. interaction with another road user) or not (e.g. personal memories), elicits a change in their emotional state. Thereby, it was emphasized that safety has the highest priority and that the tablet should only be operated if the driving situation allows it.

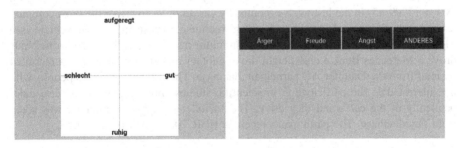

Fig. 2. Graphical interface of the tablet application showing the dimensional version (left; *Engl.* exited-calm, good-bad) and the categorical version (right; *Engl.* anger, joy, fear, other).

In order to avoid driver distraction, the application meets the following requirements: (1) only one touch is needed to submit a rating, (2) more complex answers are inputted verbally, (3) no distracting colors or images are used, (4) a maximum of 160 characters per frame is used so that the entire content can be perceived at a glance less than 2 s. (5), interaction areas are large enough to hit them from the driver's position, and (6) characters are large enough to read them from the driver's position [3]. This is in line with the German road traffic act §23, according to which a driver is allowed to use a mobile device as long as (I) the device is neither picked up nor held in hand and (II) it is operated exclusively by speech or requires just a brief gaze for interaction.

Two versions of the application were developed in German. The first version, the *Dimensional Emotion Rating* (DER), asked the participants to rate their emotional experiences by touching a point within a two-dimensional space formed by the x-axis with the poles "bad-good" (*Ger.* schlecht-gut) and the y-axis with the poles "calm-exited" (*Ger.* ruhig-aufgeregt). The naming of the poles is based on literature and common use of language [13]. The second version, the *Categorical Emotion Rating* (CER), consisted of four buttons, from which the participants could choose. Following [7], the buttons were named as "joy" (*Ger.* Freude), "anger" (*Ger.* Ärger), "fear" (*Ger.* Angst), and "other" (*Ger.* Anderes). Directly after each DER or CER, the participants were instructed to describe their emotional experience in their own words (*free response*). To trigger them to speak, a voice command was given ("Voice record started.") and a 15-s progress bar appeared. The verbal report was automatically audio recorded.

The DER data were provided in form of two points in a range of [−50; +50], one for the x-value (low values indicate "bad", high values indicate "good") and one for the y-value (low values indicate "calm", high values indicate "exited"). The CER data are outputted as a numerical value. The audio recordings were saved as mp3 files.

3.3 Participants

In total, 34 participants (20 male, 14 female) took part in the study. Their mean age was 44.6 years (*SD* = 13.8; range 21–67) and they drove an average of 25558.82 km (*SD* = 13799.85) in the last twelve months by car. In order to create the most common driving experience, only participants were recruited, whose most used vehicle is a Mercedes Benz e-class or a comparable premium mid-size car. Thus, 26 participants drove a Mercedes Benz e-class, eight drove another model. The sample was recruited by mail from the Daimler AG participant database. The database includes people, who are interested in the participation in scientific studies about automotive issues, independently of the car brand they drive. The sociodemographic information was taken from this database. The participants received EUR 70 for their participation.

4   Results

The results focus on the descriptive statistics and the validity of the emotion labeling methods. Overall, the participants gave 615 emotion ratings, 307 DER and 308 CER. 166 DER and 201 CER are linked to an audio recording, i.e. there was no additional verbal description of the emotional experience for the remaining cases. Emotional terms contained in the recordings were transcribed, including nouns (e.g. "anger"), verbs (e.g. "dislike"), adjectives/adverbs (e.g. "calm"), and claims (e.g. "super"). In total, 410 terms were extracted. The data were analyzed using *IBM SPSS Statistics 21*.

4.1   Free Response Categories (FRC)

The 410 emotional terms were classified. Hereby, terms that are based on the same root word (e.g. "anger" and "angry") or are semantically similar (e.g. "relaxed" and "serenity") were grouped to a free response category (FRC). As a result, the terms can be clustered in 40 FRC, each describing a distinct emotional experience (Fig. 3). Since the free response data can be seen as the ground truth, the FRC were used to further analyze the DER and CER. Considering the most frequently stated FRC per method, the first thing to notice is that they clearly differ. For example, for CER these are "anger" and "joy", whereas for DER these are "good/okay/alright" and "relaxation/serenity".

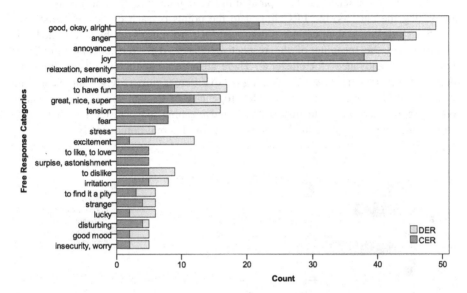

Fig. 3. Free response categories (FRC) linked to the dimensional emotion ratings (DER) and categorical emotion ratings (CER); FRC with less than five counts are not depicted.

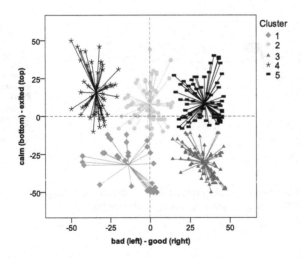

Fig. 4. Clusters of the dimensional emotion ratings (DER).

4.2   Dimensional Emotion Rating (DER)

In order to analyze the DER data, a hierarchical cluster analysis was performed based on the x-value and the y-value of each of the 307 ratings. First, the number of spatial clusters ($k = 5$) was determined using the Ward method and the squared Euclidean distances. Following, the k-mean procedure was applied to form equitable clusters. As a result, the two-dimensional space that was actually used by the participants to label their emotional experience can be separated in five regions (Fig. 4). For the purpose of interpreting the clusters, the FRC linked to the points of each cluster are examined (Fig. 5). According to their counts, a dominant FRC per cluster can be determined that may represent the meaning of the respective cluster, e.g. "relaxation/serenity" for cluster 3 or "annoyance" for cluster 2. There are also contradictory observations. In some cases one and the same FRC is assigned to different clusters (e.g. "annoyance" to cluster 2 and 4), indicating low external heterogeneity. Moreover, some clusters contain conflicting FRC according to their valence and meaning (e.g. cluster 1 or 5 include "stress" and "relaxation/serenity") that assumes low internal homogeneity.

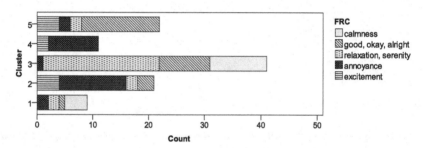

Fig. 5. Top 5 free response categories (FRC) linked to the clusters of the dimensional emotion ratings (CER) with the most counts over all clusters.

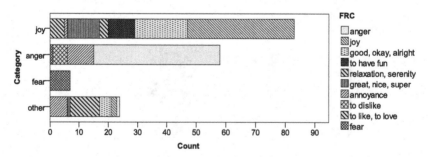

Fig. 6. Top 10 free response categories (FRC) linked to the categories of the categorical emotion ratings (DER) with the most counts over all categories.

4.3   Categorical Emotion Rating (CER)

The most frequent used category of CER is "joy" (112), followed by "anger" (101), "other" (78), and "fear" (17). Thus, in a quarter of cases the participants experienced an emotion not covered with the provided categories. In contrast, the category "fear" was used comparatively seldom. Both findings question the validity of CER regarding the requirement to cover of a significant range of relevant emotions.

In order to examine the priming effect of CER, it is hypothesized that there should be no significant difference in the nature and frequency of FRC linked to CER or DER, respectively. For this purpose, the two FRC with the largest figure linked to CER and DER are determined. As shown in Fig. 3, for DER these are "anger" (CER: 44; DER: 2) and "joy" (CER: 38; DER: 4). The dominant FRC linked to DER are "good/okay/alright" (DER: 27; CER: 22) and "relaxation/serenity" (DER: 27; CER: 13). At first glance, there is a clear difference regarding the nature of the four categories. Complementary, Fig. 6 shows that the most frequently used FRC per CER category, i.e. "joy", "anger", and "fear", corresponds to the naming of these categories in a conspicuous way. Not only with respect to the nature, but also according to the frequency distribution of these four FRC, there is a significant difference depending on whether the participants rated their emotional experience via CER or DER before their free response ($\chi^2(3) = 59.1$, $p = .000$, $n = 177$), whereby the effect is even strong (*Cramer's* $V = .578$, $p = .000$ [15]). Thus, a priming effect of CER can be assumed.

5   Discussion

In the following, the focus is on the advantages and disadvantages of the used methods, resulting in recommendations for the development of an in-car emotion tracker as well as an initial emotion taxonomy for the driving context.

5.1   Validly Labeling Emotions While Driving

According to the literature, the most valid subjective emotion measures result from free responses [10]. However, with respect to the development of an in-car emotion tracker, this method has at least two practical disadvantages. First, some people have problems freely communicating their emotions and therefore need some guidance, e.g. in form of emotion categories or dimensions. Second, the range of emotional terms resulting from free responses can be quite wide, what makes emotion tracking complex. This limitations are overcome by forced-choice measures, i.e. DER and CER. However, according to the present results, these methods lack validity. Regarding DER, the dimensions (bad-good, calm-aroused) are used very individually by the participants, leading to ambiguity. For example, some of the participants, who freely reported "annoyance", positioned their rating high on negative valence and high on arousal (cluster 4), while others set their rating high on negative valence but low on arousal (cluster 1). In other words, they used different regions of the space to indicate the same emotion. While the literature claims that it is valid to transfer a point within the space into a concrete emotion value, such a conclusion is not reasonable according to the present results [13]. In the case of CER, the provided categories (joy, anger, fear) did not cover the relevant range of emotions that people actually experience while driving. On the one hand, emotion categories are missing which is proven by the frequent use of the category "other". On the other hand, categories are redundant or incorrectly named, in particular "fear". This is supported by participants' statement saying that *"fear is a strong term in this context"* and should be replaced by "uncertainty" or similar. Moreover, the categories primed emotional experiences. This is shown by the fact, that participants' free responses were similar or even identical to the naming of the corresponding categories. For instance, most participants, who selected the category "joy", freely stated terms such as "joy" or "happy". This priming affects the interpretation of the data in two ways. First, the ratings may not reflect emotions actually experienced. Second, the counts of free response categories (FRC) that are semantically similar to the CER categories are above average.

In order to develop an in-car emotion tracker that overcomes the aforementioned limitations, it is recommended to use the CER as a basis and to enhance its validity. First, CER excels DER because two-dimensionality leads to ambiguity. Since the rating of emotions within a two-dimensional space is the fundamental idea of DER, this limitation can hardly be eliminated. Second, compared to the free response method, DER is the more practical solution. In order to enhance the validity of CER, (1) more than four categories need be offered to cover a significant range of emotions. This number should not exceed a critical threshold in terms of driver distraction. Moreover, (2) the categories have to be renamed according to the free response wordings. Thus, the categories represent actually experienced emotions and priming effects are diminished. As a consequence, further analysis of the free response data to optimize CER are needed.

5.2 Driving-Specific Emotion Taxonomy

In total, the emotion categories derived from the free responses are a base to establish a domain-specific emotion taxonomy for the driving context. These include basic emotions (e.g. "joy", "anger" [16]), affective states linked to arousal (e.g. "relaxation/serenity", "tension"; [10]), claims that express emotional experiences (e.g. "good/okay/alright", "great/nice/super"), as well as emotionally charged verbs (e.g. "to like/to love", "to find it a pity"). Overall, the categories "good/okay/alright", "anger", "annoyance", "joy", and "relaxation/serenity" are most frequently used. Interpreting the composition of these five categories, one can assume that "good/okay/alright" is an indicator of normality, i.e. the occurring event or thought did not elicit a considerable good or bad experience. Compared with this, the categories "joy" and "relaxation/serenity" have a positive valence, whereas "anger" and "annoyance" are negative in nature. To be more precise, "joy" can be seen as the comparative form of "relaxation/serenity" and, analogous, "anger" as the comparative form of "annoyance". This discussion gives a first indication of which categories an in-car emotion tracker should cover.

In any case, the results confirm the relevance of an emotion taxonomy specific to the driving context. This is justified by the fact that the set of emotional experiences identified within this study differentiates from those considered with common instruments for the subjective measurement of emotions, such as the *Geneva Emotion Wheel*

[10]. On the one hand the *Geneva Emotion Wheel* includes emotional states that were not stated by the participants in this driving study, such as "sadness", "disgust", or "hope". On the other hand, the participants reported experiences that the *Geneva Emotion Wheel* is not taking into account, e.g. "irritation", "uncertainty/worry", or "having fun".

However, the question remains if this initial emotion rating approach and taxonomy for the driving context is generalizable for individuals with different cultural backgrounds and personalities. This question is fueled by the discussion of the universality of emotions [16]. Thereby, not only emotional experiences differ across cultures, but also the local traffic conditions and thus the emotional triggers. With respect to the issue of personality, the handling of one's own emotions as well as those of others is influenced by personal traits and sociocultural development. For instance, the skill to recognize others' emotions develops in childhood and is related to these experiences [17].

6 Conclusion

This study investigated what kind of emotions people experience while driving (RQ1) and how they can be validly labeled (RQ2). In order to answer these questions, a driving study was carried out with the participants labeling their emotions in-situ. For the labeling task, they were provided with two different versions of a tablet application that included three different methodological approaches of subjective emotion measurement: the categorical emotion rating (CER), the dimensional emotion rating (DER), and free responses. The CER version included four buttons, named as "joy", "anger", "fear" and "other" from which the participants could choose. The DER was presented in form of a dimensional space that was formed by two axes with the poles "calm-exited" and "bad-good", asking the participants to rate their emotions by positioning a point within this space. After each CER and DER, the participants verbally describe their emotional experience (free response). The report was audio recorded. In total, they made 615 ratings (307 DER, 308 CER), in 324 cases a free response was given. An analysis of the free response data resulted in 40 distinct categories of emotional experiences. The most frequently mentioned categories are "good/okay/alright", "anger", "annoyance", "joy", and "relaxation/serenity". Other results point out that the DER suffer from ambiguity and the CER, on the one hand, are primed by the provided categories and, on the other hand, do not give the respondent the opportunity to fully rate his or her emotions. Compared to this, the free response method counts for the most valid solution according to literature, but is the least practicable one. Consequently, it is recommended to use the CER as the basis for the development of an in-car emotion tracker. In order to enhance the validity of this method further analysis of the free response data are required to determine the appropriate number and naming of categories.

Due to the in-situ approach, the study reveals a representative picture of the entire domain. The representativeness is even enhanced since the participants drove alone so that their emotional experiences and ratings were not influenced by the presence of an experimenter. Finally, it should be mentioned that this work is the first that empirically explores the validity of different survey methods for the labeling of emotional experiences while sitting in the car. However, the major limitation of the present investigation is that the free responses of emotional experiences are in part biased due to the priming effect. That is because the free response followed directly after the CER, whose categories caused the priming. This has to be taken into account if the free response data are used for further analysis. In order to address this limitation, an effort should be made to replicate this study with some adaptions. First, studies should use the free response method exclusively, until a valid set of emotional categories is determined. Second, the situational (e.g. number of passengers), environmental (e.g. season), and cultural (e.g. Western and Eastern countries) settings of the study should be varied to widen the picture of emotional experiences that are elicited while driving and to generalize the results. This includes the need for long-term surveys in the participants' own car. More extensive insight could also be revealed from free reports as long as the participants verbalize their emotions more consistently and in more detail. Based on future findings, the prototypical implementation of an in-car emotion tracker should be addressed.

References

1. Torre, J.B., Liebermann, M.D.: Putting feelings in to words: affect labeling as implicit emotion regulation. Emot. Rev. **10**(2), 116–124 (2018)
2. Nesbit, S.M., Conger, J.C., Conger, A.J.: A quantitative review of the relationship between anger and aggressive driving. Aggress. Violent Behav. **12**, 156–176 (2007)
3. National Highway Traffic Safety Administration: Visual-manual NHTSA driver distraction guidelines for in-vehicle electronic devices. National Highway Traffic Safety Administration, Department of Transportation, Washington, DC (2012)
4. Oinas-Kukkonen, H., Harjumaa, M.: Persuasive systems design: key issues, process model, and system features. Commun. Assoc. Inf. Syst. **24**(1), 485–500 (2009)
5. Underwood, G., Chapman, P., Wright, S., Crundall, D.: Anger while driving. Transp. Res. Part F **2**(1), 55–68 (1999)
6. Jeon, M., Walker, B.N.: What to detect? Analyzing factor structures of affect in driving contexts for an emotion detection and regulation system. In: Proceedings of the Human Factors and Ergonomics Society 55th Annual Meeting, pp. 1889–1893. Sage Publications, Los Angeles (2011)
7. Mesken, J., Hagenzieker, M.P., Rothengatter, T., de Waard, D.: Frequency, determinants, and consequences of different drivers' emotions: an on-the-road study using self-reports, (observed) behaviour, and physiology. Transp. Res. Part F **10**, 458–475 (2007)
8. Niven, K., Totterdell, P., Holman, D.: A classification of controlled interpersonal affect regulation strategies. Emotion **9**(4), 498–509 (2009)
9. DeLoach, S.L., Tiemann, T.K.: Not driving alone? American commuting in the twenty-first century. Transportation **39**(3), 521–537 (2012)
10. Scherer, K.R.: What are emotions? And how can they be measured? Soc. Sci. Inf. **44**(4), 695–729 (2005)
11. Healey, J.: Recording affect in the field: towards methods and metrics for improving ground truth labels. In: D'Mello, S., Graesser, A., Schuller, B., Martin, J.-C. (eds.) ACII 2011. LNCS, vol. 6974, pp. 107–116. Springer, Heidelberg (2011). https://doi.org/10.1007/978-3-642-24600-5_14

12. Cicchetti, D.V.: Guidelines, criteria, and rules of thumb for evaluating normed and standardized assessment instruments in psychology. Psychol. Assess. **6**(4), 284–290 (1994)
13. Crispim, C., Cruz, R.M., Baasch, D., Amorim, L., Trevisan, R.L., Da Silva, M.A.: Measurement of affect: from theoretical and instrumental perspectives. Psychol. Res. **5**(2), 96–107 (2015)
14. Brooks, J.A., Shablack, H., Gendron, M., Satpute, A.B., Parrish, M.H., Lindquist, K.A.: The role of language in the experience and perception of emotion: a neuroimaging meta-analysis. Soc. Cogn. Affect. Neurosci. **12**(2), 169–183 (2017)
15. Cohen, J.: Statistical Power Analysis for the Behavioural Sciences, 2nd edn. Lawrence Erlbaum Associates, Hillsdale (1988)
16. Ekman, P.: An argument for basic emotions. Cogn. Emot. **6**(3–4), 169–200 (1992)
17. Watling, D., Damaskinou, N.: Children's facial emotion recognition skills: longitudinal associations with lateralization for emotion processing. Child Dev. 1–16 (2018)

Persuading the Driver: A Framework for Persuasive Interface Design in the Automotive Domain

Irina Paraschivoiu[✉], Alexander Meschtscherjakov[✉],
Magdalena Gärtner, and Jakub Sypniewski

Center for Human-Computer Interaction, University of Salzburg,
Salzburg, Austria
{irina.paraschivoiu,
alexander.meschtscherjakov}@sbg.ac.at

Abstract. Designing for persuasive interfaces in cars is a challenging task, particularly considering that new systems should not distract drivers. In order to support designers in their decisions, we present a novel framework for persuasive interface design with a focus on automotive UI. It is based on existing behaviour change models and extends them with categories to support interface design decisions. It serves three purposes: (1) it provides a tool to support designers in decision making when designing persuasive interfaces; (2) it can be used to create alternatives to existing systems; (3) it allows to structure literature reviews in order to identify blind spots and serve as an inspiration to ideate new approaches. we provide an analysis of three examples based on it to illustrate its applicability.

Keywords: Automotive · Persuasion · Framework · Interface design

1 Introduction

The pervasion of technologies in cars holds great promises to help achieve desired driving behaviours. The past decade has seen a rise in the design of persuasive systems targeting safety, attention, and energy efficiency. Simultaneously, progress made in HMI and interface design allows for technologies to be tested in driving scenarios [1].

Designers need to make several important decisions when creating novel persuasive in-car interfaces. This includes choosing the goal, the strategy and concrete interface design decisions such as providing information visually or auditory. The very diversity of persuasive strategies makes it imperative to provide frameworks to support designers in prototyping persuasive systems in the car and to assess the state-of-the-art in this application area. Our contribution with this paper is to provide a novel framework which can be used by designers and researchers. While it is based on existing models, it includes a new element: it defines categories for system design with respect to the automotive domain. Our framework is theoretically informed and aims to support designers when developing new persuasive interfaces. It can also be used to create alternatives to already developed systems, for example when other persuasive strategies

H. Oinas-Kukkonen et al. (Eds.): PERSUASIVE 2019, LNCS 11433, pp. 128–140, 2019.
https://doi.org/10.1007/978-3-030-17287-9_11

need to be explored. Finally, the framework allows researchers to structure literature reviews in order to identify blind spots and ideate new approaches.

2   Related Work

In order to support the motivation to provide a novel framework, we report on the main theoretical approaches that informed its creation and reflect on ongoing research in persuasive design in the automotive domain.

2.1   Existing Persuasion Models

Fogg's work focuses on technology as a persuasive tool in behaviour change [2]. He identifies seven principles for persuasion (reduction, tunnelling, tailoring, suggestion, self-monitoring, surveillance, and conditioning) and five types of cues computers may use (physical, psychological, language, social dynamics, and social roles).

Oinas-Kukkonen and Harjumaa [3] propose the PSD model. The persuasion context contains the intent, the event, and the strategy. A central feature of the intent is the type of change aimed for: attitude or behaviour change. The event considers the use, the user, and the technology. Strategically, a message can take a direct or indirect route. Systems provide primary, dialogue, system credibility, or social support.

Both theoretical approaches do not look into the specifics of interface design. For example, they do not suggest which modality should be used or how often triggers should be employed. Especially in automotive, the design of such feedback systems is crucial because the car provides a very limited design space. The driver always has a primary task (i.e. drive safely) and interaction possibilities are very limited.

2.2   Persuasion in the Automotive Domain

Driver persuasion has a long tradition in persuasive interface design, mostly targeting safe (e.g., [4, 5]) or eco-friendly driving (e.g., [6, 7]). Meschtscherjakov et al. [8] have investigated the acceptance of different interfaces persuading the driver to reduce fuel consumption. Wilfinger et al. [9] used design-driven methods such as cultural probing to involve the user in the design process. Regarding interaction design, Roider et al. [10] have shown that visual cues can leverage the use of speech input for a driver. Diewald et al. [11] provide a review of gamified applications in cars, and a framework for developing user interfaces in vehicles.

Zhang et al. [12] review persuasive mobile applications in cars. They find that over 90% of car apps use the principles of self-monitoring, reduction, suggestion, trustworthiness, real-world feel, and expertise, while 73% implement reminders. They note that concepts in persuasive design lack standardisation and cannot easily be used for empirical studies. Vaezipour et al. [13] notice there is no comprehensible integration of safe and eco-efficient driving applications and that technology acceptance models are not explicitly stated. Steinberger et al. [14] show there is a shortage of literature reporting both design recommendations and user studies.

3   Persuasive Interface Design Framework in the Automotive Domain (PIDAF)

When proposing a persuasive system, designers are confronted with both conceptual and design choices. As Hekler et al. [15] point out, "*the use of meta-models in design requires a great deal of conceptual and formative work to translate into pragmatic design guidelines and system features*". Additionally, behavioural theories range from meta-models, to conceptual frameworks, and constructs [15].

In our empirical work, we have found three needs: (1) to understand what systems have already been developed; (2) to support designers when creating such systems with the choices they need to make; (3) to support designers when alternative options need to be explored. The framework we are proposing aims to answer these emerging issues in the field of automotive persuasion. It is based on the work of [2] and [3] and enriched it with specific categories which are helpful to understanding persuasion in cars. We focus on four levels of decision-making:

(a)	*the intent*	*(c)*	*the persuasive principles*
(b)	*the cues*	*(d)*	*the design*

This four-level model reflects four important decision areas designers usually address in their work. They define (1) the change type they target, (2) the way of influencing the user, (3) the principles employed, and (4) specifications of their designs.

The *intent* is defined by Oinas-Kukkonen and Harjumaa as a part of context analysis, involving consideration of the persuader and of the change type envisioned. The *cues* derive from Fogg's proposed taxonomy of the way computers can be used to leverage social influence. The *principles* are also based on Fogg's work and are widely acknowledged as ways of achieving desired behaviours. Finally, we contribute a detailed categorisation of the *design* options, which can support a detailed mapping of existing systems. This categorisation is based on our own empirical research in this area as well as common aspects in user interface design. We further detail each of these levels of decision making below. A visualization of the framework is represented in Fig. 1. We will further reference the framework with the acronym **PIDAF** standing for Persuasive Interface Design in Automotive Framework.

3.1   Intent

In our understanding, "*intent*" refers to the expressed change desired in the behaviour of the user. In automotive, this can be either an attitude or behaviour change (or both), and refers to the explicit domain the system is designed for (safety, eco-driving, etc.). Our definition overlaps with Oinas-Kukkonen and Harjumaa [3] who place the intent within the persuasion context. We define two sub-categories:

The **Aim** can be *Attitude* and/or *Behaviour* change. Understanding the change type is central to persuasion. Theories such as the theory of reasoned action imply that intention is the strongest predictor of behaviour [3]. However, in many cases habits override intentions and thus designers need to target what is most efficient in the respective case. For example, tackling habits, rather than perception of risk, can be more effective in improving safe driving. That is because drivers have a positive attitude towards safety but are not aware of their own risky behaviours [16].

Domain. We define three categories: *Safety*, *Eco-driving* and *Other*. In automotive, it is relevant which domain the system is focused on. In our research, we have found many systems tackle the safety or eco-efficiency areas e.g., [13] but some are exploring other themes, such as the learning of functions e.g., [11]. We propose that the latter are grouped in the sub-category *Other*.

3.2 Cues

In social signalling theory, cues are defined as features which guide future action and have the property of altering the receiver's beliefs or behaviours. Thus, "cues" are hints which influence the user towards achieving the desired outcome. Based on the work of Fogg [2] and our work in automotive persuasion, we define four categories:

Psychological cues can be either *Subliminal* or *Conscious*. Fogg proposes this category as a broad umbrella for understanding human psychology and appealing to it through different strategies. The taxonomy derives from dual process theory, whereby individuals make decisions either through a conscious or an unconscious (automatic) process.

Social dynamics refers to whether a system targets a *Single User*, *Multi-user*, uses *Competition* and/or *Cooperation*. Social dynamics looks at the patterns of people interacting with each other and is a common strategy in persuasive applications. The social component of applications enhances the user experience, either through friendly competition or cooperation [17]. In automotive, it is common for systems to be designed for single-users, but multi-user applications have been gaining ground [18].

Gamification. Applications can be *gamified (Yes)* or *not (No)*. Previous reviews have pointed at many applications in automotive use gamification tools, because of its potential to arouse sustainable motivation and strong commitment [11].

Verbal cues mean a system can use *language (Yes)* or not *(No)*. Verbal cues are broadly understood as ways of using written or spoken language to convey social presence and persuade. In automotive, applications can use language or strictly rely on visual (non-verbal), auditive, or haptic communication tools.

3.3 Persuasive Principles

Broadly, *principle* refers to "universal rules governing human behaviour" [2]. Moreover, these rules can be translated into potential system specifications and provide clearer directions for designers. Fogg's [2] taxonomy of principles is a conceptual framework which can offer more specific guidance to the design of behaviour change technology. Therefore, we include in our framework this typology as designed by Fogg:

Reduction narrows down complex activities to a few simple steps. This principle is based on making the behaviour easier for the user, which can be done through design, but also through setting default actions.

Tunnelling leads the users through a predetermined sequence of actions. Because tunnelling involves taking the users step by step through a series of actions, it is particularly relevant for high cognitive load contexts, such as driving.

Tailoring means providing relevant and personalized information. Tailoring is based on formulating a message or strategy for a particular person, and these messages are based on individual factors related to the behaviour of interest [19].

Suggestion is providing advice about which behaviour should be performed. Suggestion has been widely researched as a way to improve cognition and behaviour, and can have a long-lasting impact on the choices people make [20].

Through **self-monitoring** individuals acquire information about self-progress. Self-monitoring is based on self-efficacy theory, referring to an individual's belief in his or her ability to achieve goals [15].

Surveillance means a party's behaviour is monitored by another party. Surveillance is derived from social norms research, whereby individuals tend to abide cultural or societal expectations.

Conditioning is based on using positive reinforcements to shape behaviour. Gamified applications, in particular, are based on rewards and reinforcements, but other types of systems can also be designed bearing this principle in mind.

3.4   Design

Based on commonly known aspects and previous works in user interface design, we define a set of categories in which designers have to make choices. Our principles are a hybrid selection of this broad domain and do not claim to be exhaustive. They include 9 categories which we consider to be specifically relevant for automotive. *Ambience* is included because drivers are usually focused on the main task (driving) and thus information presented in the periphery of attention may be preferable. *Representation* is important for persuasive design, where metaphors are often used. *Feedback* immediacy is also especially relevant for driver attention and reaction time. *Integration* is relevant because cars are a limited design space. *Modality* is often considered when deciding what drivers react best to, without distracting them from driving. *Visualization* impacts the user experience and reaction. *Placement* and *mobility* reflect on the limitations of cars, how user experience and behaviour can be changed within the car or outside of it. *Frequency* is important when deciding which option can be more impactful.

The **Ambience** could be *Peripheral* or *Focal*. In peripheral ambience, the user receives input from peripheral vision or hearing, and rapidly acquires low-frequency information. A focal ambient system would require the user to direct attention towards the interface or message. For example, Shi et al. [21] use audio feedback to transmit information to the driver in a peripheral manner.

Representation can be *Concrete,* or *Metaphorical*. Metaphors are representations of events and objects from the non-computer domain [22]. A metaphorical interface uses representations to alert the driver, for example by using green leaves to signal fuel efficiency. Concrete interfaces transmit information directly to the driver, for example information about time to destination.

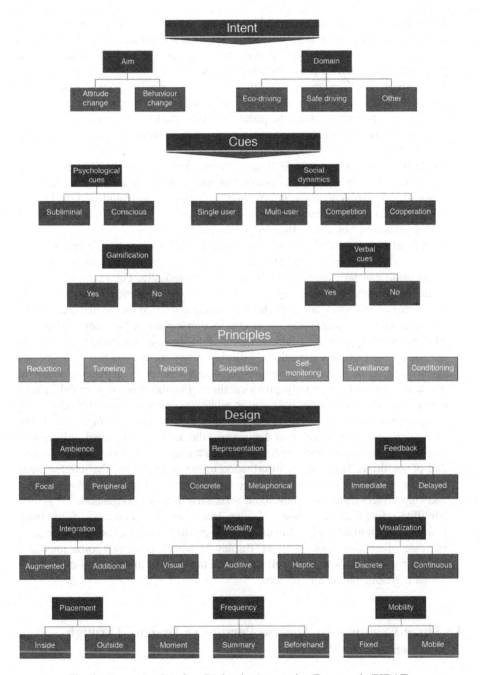

Fig. 1. Persuasive Interface Design in Automotive Framework (PIDAF)

Feedback can be *Immediate* or *Delayed*. A system can transmit information either immediately after a task is performed, or later on. An immediate feedback allows the driver to make corrections during the drive but a delayed feedback can be preferred if the intent is not to disturb the driver.

Integration: interfaces can be *Additional* or *Augment* existing interfaces. In cars, augmented interfaces could include the steering wheel (e.g. vibrating), the rear-view mirror (e.g., infrared overlay), the pedal (e.g., push back). Additional interfaces are not specific to vehicles, for example a display. A system could also be a combination of both.

Modality means output can be *Visual, Haptic,* and/or *Auditory.* Common visual interfaces in cars are displays, but mobile phone applications are also visual, if they make use of display to show information. A haptic output could be vibration, or pressure exerted by the pedal, when the driver presses it. Auditory output could be verbal messages, but also designated sound patterns.

Visualization can be *Discrete* or *Continuous*. When information is represented in a discrete way, it takes a limited number of values. In continuous representation, the information can take infinite values, at least theoretically. For example, a driver could receive either a "thumbs up" or a "thumbs down" as a performance rating (only two possible values). A driver could also see current speed on the display, and the speed can take any value, meaning the information is presented in a continuous way.

Placement of the interface could be *Inside* of the car, *Outside* the car, or both. An interface placed within car would be a display or any car element that is augmented (wheel, mirror, pedal, seat). We would consider interfaces to be placed outside the car if the information is only provided there. For example, if a mobile phone application is meant to offer information while the driver is not in the vehicle.

Frequency can be in the *Moment* of the action, as a *Summary* or *Beforehand.* The driver can receive information in the moment the action is performed. Information can also be centralized, allowing the user to see a summary of performance, after the end of the drive. Transmitting information to the driver before the journey starts could be sent to prime drivers to behave more safely, to map out alternative routes and help drivers make decisions about avoidance of traffic congestion.

Mobility refers to the possibility of using *Mobile* or *Fixed* interfaces. Some interfaces are meant to be used within the car only by the nature, cannot be mobile, as is the case of an augmented car seat, display or wheel. However, some interfaces could be used both within as well as outside the car, the most typical example of which is mobile phone applications.

4 Three Examples to Analyse Persuasive Designs Through the Lens of the PIDAF

To illustrate potential applications of the framework for existing and future persuasive interfaces in cars, we structurally analyse three existing systems based on the categorisations described above. This allows us to test the viability of the framework and the insights gained from applying it.

4.1 Auditory and Haptic System for In-car Speed Management

Intent. Adell et al. [23] detail a system to change driver behaviour to comply with speed limits. The system is composed of an active accelerator pedal, which exerts counterforce when the driver is exceeding speed limit, an auditory system, consisting of an auditory warning (BEEP), as well as a display, which shows (1) current speed limit and (2) a small red-light flashing. A mapping of the system on our framework involves starting with the intent. The paper is targeting *behaviour* and *safety*.

Cues. The system is non-gamified *(no)*, and there are no subliminal cues employed, all the information and feedback given to the driver is targeting *conscious* decisions. There are also no verbal cues *(no)* – there is only audio, haptic or visual feedback. The system is addressed to the driver only *(single-user)* – passengers are not involved in any way, and neither is the driver's social group.

Principles. The system is based on persuasive principles: *self-monitoring* is enacted through the display showing the current speed limit. The haptic and audio signals are *suggestions* for the driver to slow down when speeding.

Design. From the ambience point of view, the system is both *focal* and *peripheral*. The auditory signal and the haptic pedal are peripheral, because the driver does not need to focus on them, but the display requires driver attention for short periods of time. The system is both *concrete* and *metaphorical*. The red light, "BEEP" signal and pedal feedback are metaphors for "slow down". The information on the display (speed limit) is, however, concrete: this is the current speed limit in the area. The feedback is *immediate*, with a *momentary* frequency. The output modalities are *visual* (display), *haptic* (pedal) and *auditory* ("BEEP"). The interfaces are both *additional* (display, sound system) and *augmented* (pedal). The visualization is *discrete* – the speed limits are based on the area and pre-defined (30, 50, 70 km/h). The system is placed *inside* the car and it is *fixed*.

4.2 Subliminal System for Driver Awareness

Intent. Riener and Thaller [24] propose a subliminal system for non-conscious *behaviour* change. They expose drivers in a Lane Change Task to briefly flashed stimuli to change their steering behaviour, reduce distraction and improve *safety*.

Cues. The system consists of an overhead display in a simulator where visible stimuli (lane change requests) are doubled by *subliminal cues*, visible for only 16.67 ms (negative or positive primes). The prototype, therefore, uses subliminal cues, it targets *single users* (the drivers) and *no language* cues are employed. The system is also *not gamified*.

Principles. The technique of micro-showing future lane changes to drivers to prime them for the subsequent visual stimuli is based on the *tunnelling* principle, as it directs users towards the desired action.

Design. Driver attention is focused on the display, meaning the ambience is *focal*, but there are no metaphors used so it is *concrete*. The feedback is *immediate*, the *frequency* is *momentary*, the modality is only *visual* (the display). The prototype is based on an *additional* interface (display). The information can take only a limited number of values, namely the lanes between which the driver can change, therefore it is a *discrete* form of visualization. The system is placed *inside* the car and it is *fixed.*

4.3   Driving Miss Daisy

Intent. A gamified smartphone application for encouraging *safety* in driving, Driving Miss Daisy is a prototype designed by Shi et al. [21], where users need to drive a virtual passenger to the destination safely and smoothly. The application targets safety *behaviour*, but through different means than previous ones.

Cues. The designers opted for a *gamified* approach, a *conscious* system, which also *uses language cues*: the drivers get audio feedback in real time from "Miss Daisy" to slow down when it is the case. The application also uses *competition* as social dynamics cue, with drivers being able to compete between each other for better scores.

Principles. There are several persuasive principles at play here: *conditioning* (drivers get rewards such as virtual money), *self-monitoring* (performance data are available in the application), *tailoring* (the game level adjusts to the driver performance).

Design. The design uses both *focal* and *peripheral* cues – the driver needs to focus on the smartphone to access real-time data but feedback is peripheral when driving. The system is *metaphorical,* using the representation of a virtual passenger to convey information to the driver. Feedback is *immediate*, as Miss Daisy reacts in real-time to driver behaviour. The frequency is both *momentary* and *summary,* as drivers can visualize summaries of the game at the end of the drive. Two types of modalities are used: *visual* (smartphone screen) and *audio* (Miss Daisy). There is no augmentation of existing interfaces, but use of an *additional* one (mobile phone screen). The visualization is both *discrete* (game scores) and *continuous* (audio feedback when driving). As the interface is a smartphone, the system is *mobile*, but placed *inside* the car when collecting driving information.

5   Discussion on How to Use PIDAF in Persuasive Design

As the examples above illustrate, designers have many options – both conceptually and in terms of design – when prototyping persuasive systems in cars. The framework presented above can support them in making decisions in at least three ways.

5.1   Designing New Systems

Firstly, designers can use the framework as a starting point and process guideline for new systems, going through the different levels of decision making. The framework can serve as a checklist for of the factors that are important during the design process. It differs from other frameworks such as Oinas-Kukkonnen's [3] or Fogg's [2] in that it addresses interface design questions with a focus on automotive applications. We envision designers to go through the PIDAF step-by-step:

Typically, the *intent* is the starting point, where the aim and domain need to be considered. Very often in automotive, systems target behaviour rather than attitude. For the domain we currently use eco-driving and safety since these are the two most prominent examples. Other application areas are subsumed in the "other" category. Designers might suggest adding other categories, depending on their interests and growing importance of other domains, however it is important that both these decisions (aim and domain) are made from the very beginning.

Designers could then reflect on the different cues they want to employ and in which combination. In automotive, a large majority of applications use conscious psychological cues and many systems focus on a single user, the driver. It is important for the designer to consider, at this stage, whether the system will target the driver only, multiple driver, involve one's social circle, or create a form of competition or cooperation with other drivers. The popular application Waze, for example, does not include competition elements, but drivers do cooperate in sharing information about road conditions. Next, one or more principles can be considered, depending on what evidence supports them for that respective domain. Suggestion and self-monitoring are popular in automotive, while other principles are less used.

Finally, the several design related choices have to been made and the PIDAF may help the designers in identifying choices that have to be made. It ranges from general decision of the placement of the interface, its integration-level in existing elements and whether to use a mobile device or a fixed one, over feedback time and frequency, to important interface design decisions that have to be made such as the chosen modality, its visualization and level of ambience, or representational character.

5.2 Ideate New Designs from Existing Ones

Another way to use the framework is as a source to identify interaction alternatives to an already existing system. If user trials evaluations show no significant impact of a prototype on user behaviour, changing certain design features or testing other persuasive principles can be an option. For example, a gamified application can be targeting a single user, and use suggestion as a principle. A designer could try, as an alternative, a multi-user version or one based on competition, to see if performance improves. Features and decisions can be changed at any level and in any of the categories, and the system re-tested.

From a methodological point of view, we envision the system to be used as a categorization tool for an existing system. Similar as described in Sect. 4, the system shall be investigated through the PIDAF lens. Then a designer might deliberately change certain aspects of the design and think how the system could look like if one of these aspects is changed. That transfers the designer into a new perspective and may spark new ideas.

5.3   Identifying Blind Spots

Finally, the framework can be used as a tool for literature reviews and for mapping blind-spots in the existing research landscape, particularly which domains, cues, principles or designs are under-explored, either alone or in combination with each other. The three examples above show that some categories are hardly used in the automotive domain, whereas others are very prominent. Additionally, they also point that the categories are not mutually exclusive. A system can use multiple principles, cues, modalities at once. Researchers and designers could also use the PIDAF as an evaluation tool to compare effects of certain intents, cues, principles and designs.

In order to utilize the framework in such a way, an extensive literature analysis has to be done. Thereby, various factors can be used as given. For example, one could only investigate persuasive systems that target at eco-friendly behaviour or only real-time feedback systems. Similar to the examples in Sect. 4, each system shall be investigated with respect to every aspect of the PIDAF. Then blind-spots are easy to identify and new approaches can be envisioned.

6   Conclusions and Future Work

This paper has proposed a novel framework for assessing and making design decisions about persuasion in vehicles. Our goal was to provide designers and researchers with guidance when designing systems or evaluating them. We propose that this process consists of defining the intent, the relevant cues and principles, and making design decisions. While this process may be similar for a variety of behaviour change support systems, we have enriched our framework with categories which are particularly relevant for automotive. Therefore, we have illustrated this framework with three examples from the literature in automotive persuasion. We suggest that it can be further used to design new systems, to map out alternatives to existing ones, or to identify underdeveloped areas in automotive persuasion. Issues that require further exploration include conducting a thorough literature review in automotive using PIDAF and applying PIDAF together with designers to test and expand it where necessary.

References

1. Lo, V.E.-W., Green, P.A.: Development and evaluation of automotive speech interfaces: useful information from the human factors and the related literature. Int. J. Veh. Technol. **2013**, 1–13 (2013). https://doi.org/10.1155/2013/924170
2. Fogg, B.J.: Persuasive Technology: Using Computers to Change What We Think and Do. Morgan Kaufmann Publishers, Amsterdam, Boston (2003)
3. Oinas-Kukkonen, H., Harjumaa, M.: A systematic framework for designing and evaluating persuasive systems. In: Oinas-Kukkonen, H., Hasle, P., Harjumaa, M., Segerståhl, K., Øhrstrøm, P. (eds.) PERSUASIVE 2008. LNCS, vol. 5033, pp. 164–176. Springer, Heidelberg (2008). https://doi.org/10.1007/978-3-540-68504-3_15

4. Miranda, B., Jere, C., Alharbi, O., Lakshmi, S., Khouja, Y., Chatterjee, S.: Examining the efficacy of a persuasive technology package in reducing texting and driving behavior. In: Berkovsky, S., Freyne, J. (eds.) PERSUASIVE 2013. LNCS, vol. 7822, pp. 137–148. Springer, Heidelberg (2013). https://doi.org/10.1007/978-3-642-37157-8_17

5. Maurer, B., Gärtner, M., Wuchse, M., Meschtscherjakov, A., Tscheligi, M.: Utilizing a digital game as a mediatory artifact for social persuasion to prevent speeding. In: Meschtscherjakov, A., De Ruyter, B., Fuchsberger, V., Murer, M., Tscheligi, M. (eds.) PERSUASIVE 2016. LNCS, vol. 9638, pp. 199–210. Springer, Cham (2016). https://doi.org/10.1007/978-3-319-31510-2_17

6. Ecker, R., Holzer, P., Broy, V., Butz, A.: EcoChallenge: a race for efficiency. In: Proceedings of the 13th International Conference on Human Computer Interaction with Mobile Devices and Services – MobileHCI 2011, p. 91. ACM Press, Stockholm (2011)

7. Atzl, C., Meschtscherjakov, A., Vikoler, S., Tscheligi, M.: Bet4EcoDrive: In: MacTavish, T., Basapur, S. (eds.) PERSUASIVE 2015. LNCS, vol. 9072, pp. 71–82. Springer, Cham (2015). https://doi.org/10.1007/978-3-319-20306-5_7

8. Meschtscherjakov, A., Wilfinger, D., Scherndl, T., Tscheligi, M.: Acceptance of future persuasive in-car interfaces towards a more economic driving behaviour. In: Proceedings of the 1st International Conference on Automotive User Interfaces and Interactive Vehicular Applications – AutomotiveUI 2009, p. 81. ACM Press, Essen (2009)

9. Wilfinger, D., Gärtner, M., Meschtscherjakov, A., Tscheligi, M.: Persuasion in the car: probing potentials. In: Spagnolli, A., Chittaro, L., Gamberini, L. (eds.) PERSUASIVE 2014. LNCS, vol. 8462, pp. 273–278. Springer, Cham (2014). https://doi.org/10.1007/978-3-319-07127-5_24

10. Roider, F., Rümelin, S., Gross, T.: Using visual cues to leverage the use of speech input in the vehicle. In: Ham, J., Karapanos, E., Morita, P.P., Burns, C.M. (eds.) PERSUASIVE 2018. LNCS, vol. 10809, pp. 120–131. Springer, Cham (2018). https://doi.org/10.1007/978-3-319-78978-1_10

11. Diewald, S., et al.: Gamification-supported exploration and practicing for automotive user interfaces and vehicle functions. In: Reiners, T., Wood, L.C. (eds.) Gamification in Education and Business, pp. 637–661. Springer, Cham (2015). https://doi.org/10.1007/978-3-319-10208-5_32

12. Zhang, C., Wan, L., Min, D.: Persuasive design principles of car apps. In: Abramowicz, W., Alt, R., Franczyk, B. (eds.) BIS 2016. LNBIP, vol. 255, pp. 397–410. Springer, Cham (2016). https://doi.org/10.1007/978-3-319-39426-8_31

13. Vaezipour, A., Rakotonirainy, A., Haworth, N.: Reviewing in-vehicle systems to improve fuel efficiency and road safety. Procedia Manuf. 3, 3192–3199 (2015). https://doi.org/10.1016/j.promfg.2015.07.869

14. Steinberger, F., Schroeter, R., Foth, M., Johnson, D.: Designing gamified applications that make safe driving more engaging, pp. 2826–2839. ACM Press (2017)

15. Hekler, E.B., Klasnja, P., Froehlich, J.E., Buman, M.P.: Mind the theoretical gap: interpreting, using, and developing behavioral theory in HCI research. In: Proceedings of the SIGCHI Conference on Human Factors in Computing Systems – CHI 2013, p. 3307. ACM Press, Paris (2013)

16. Chin, H., Zabihi, H., Park, S., et al.: WatchOut: facilitating safe driving behaviors with social support, pp. 2459–2465. ACM Press (2017)

17. Khalil, A., Abdallah, S.: Harnessing social dynamics through persuasive technology to promote healthier lifestyle. Comput. Hum. Behav. 29, 2674–2681 (2013). https://doi.org/10.1016/j.chb.2013.07.008

18. Wang, C., Terken, J., Hu, J., Rauterberg, M.: "Likes" and "dislikes" on the road: a social feedback system for improving driving behavior, pp. 43–50. ACM Press (2016)

19. Hirsh, J.B., Kang, S.K., Bodenhausen, G.V.: Personalized persuasion: tailoring persuasive appeals to recipients' personality traits. Psychol. Sci. **23**, 578–581 (2012). https://doi.org/10.1177/0956797611436349
20. Michael, R.B., Garry, M., Kirsch, I.: Suggestion, cognition, and behavior. Curr. Dir. Psychol. Sci. **21**, 151–156 (2012). https://doi.org/10.1177/0963721412446369
21. Shi, C., Lee, H.J., Kurczak, J., Lee, A.: Routine driving infotainment app: gamification of performance driving. In: Adjunct Proceedings of the 4th International Conference on Automotive User Interfaces and Interactive Vehicular Applications (Automotive UI) (2012)
22. Marx, A.: Using metaphor effectively in user interface design. In: Conference Companion on Human Factors in Computing Systems - CHI 1994, pp. 379–380. ACM Press, Boston (1994)
23. Adell, E., Várhelyi, A., Hjälmdahl, M.: Auditory and haptic systems for in-car speed management – a comparative reallife study. Transp. Res. Part F: Traffic Psychol. Behav. **11**, 445–458 (2008). https://doi.org/10.1016/j.trf.2008.04.003
24. Riener, A., Thaller, H.: Subliminal visual information to enhance driver awareness and induce behavior change, pp. 1–9. ACM Press (2014)

Ethical and Legal Aspects

Do Ethics Matter in Persuasive Technology?

Raymond Kight and Sandra Burri Gram-Hansen[(✉)]

Department of Communication and Psychology, Aalborg University,
Aalborg, Denmark
rkight17@student.aau.dk, burri@hum.aau.dk

Abstract. This paper aims to discuss how ethics has been addressed within the persuasive technology field and to explore whether ethics is generally applied in persuasive technology (PT) or simply recognized by academics as an important perspective. The paper is based on a literature review of the past 13 years of Persuasive Technology conference papers. The themes identified from the literature review are presented along with summaries of defining works within the field which have contributed to the discussion of ethics. This is followed by a discussion and reflection on the findings of the literature review. Finally, we conclude that ethics does matter but we argue that ethics has not been adequately addressed in the field of PT and that ethical considerations regarding the rights of the designers need to be researched.

Keywords: Persuasion · Rights · Ethics · Freedom of speech · Rhetoric

1 Introduction

Based on a thorough review of all papers published within the Persuasive Technology conference series, this paper aims to contribute to the further development of the field by clarifying some of the issues related to the role of ethics in persuasive systems. Persuasion is generally understood as a more ethical approach to behavior change, yet the ethical implications of persuasive technologies remain a scarcely explored subject. The particular interest in exploring the role of ethics in persuasive design is motivated by the emergence of several other approaches to digital behavior design. In continuation it inspires reflections regarding the justification of referring to ethics as a defining feature of the persuasive approach. The aim of the presented study is to explore how ethics has been addressed in relation to persuasive design and persuasive technologies, particularly with regards to whether ethics or the discussion of ethics has moved from the world of academia and into the persuasive design workplace.

Early findings within the study indicate that save for a few researchers [1–3], etc., ethics appears to be an element of persuasive design that academics and designers pay a lot of lip service to without really attacking the problem. Many papers include statements such as "ethical concerns are one of the key challenges"... [4] or "no ethical issues were found" with our..." [5], yet there are no other mentions of ethics or further discussions about how such conclusions about ethics were reached. This comprises a challenge as ethics is most often referred to as a defining feature of persuasion, when related to other similar approaches to behavior design. Furthermore, the literature from

© Springer Nature Switzerland AG 2019
H. Oinas-Kukkonen et al. (Eds.): PERSUASIVE 2019, LNCS 11433, pp. 143–155, 2019.
https://doi.org/10.1007/978-3-030-17287-9_12

the persuasive design conferences is littered with suggestions and commentary on what principles or methods designers of persuasive design technologies should take into consideration with regards to ethics when creating their designs. Suggestions ranging from urging designers to follow Berdichevsky and Neuenschwander's "golden rule" [6] principle that "creators of a persuasive technology should never seek to persuade anyone of something they themselves would not consent to be persuaded of" from way back in 2006 [7] to challenging designers to step up to a "critical, ethical, and active engagement with the world" [8] or urging users to consider using approaches from Value Sensitive Design (VSD) and Participatory Design (PD) to solve ethical issues in 2009 [3]. However nowhere within the persuasive technology conference literature does there appear to be a paper where a methodological or philosophical discussion on ethics take place outside of academia. The lack of publications discussing how and when ethics has been considered and applied by practitioners, gives reason to worry if ethics in persuasive technologies have become simply an academic phrase, rather than an actual concept of the field – and furthermore if the academic issues and discussions raised within the field of persuasive technologies do in fact reach the design practitioners aiming to intentionally influence the users.

A state of the art was conducted by Kristian Torning and Harri Oinas-Kukkonen and published in 2009. They investigated the research published as full papers in the conference proceedings from the first three Persuasive Technology conferences (2006–2008), in order to generate directions for future research within the field. Amongst the findings of this study it was noted that in spite of potential noble outcomes, it was stressed that ethical considerations need far more attention, both with regards to development of systems and implementation into different contexts [9]. It is with this in mind, that this paper aims to contribute to the discussion of ethics within the persuasive technology design field.

2   Methodology: Literature Review on Ethics in Persuasive Technology Design

The research presented in this paper is borne out of a semi-structured literature review on ethics in persuasive technology design and based on themes that emerged from the review. The review included the entire body of work from the persuasive design conferences from 2006–2018 (376 papers). The Persuasive Technology conference series is recognized as a well-established scientific forum dedicated to research and practice within the area of designs for behavior change. Although the notion of persuasion, and different perspectives on persuasive design are also presented at other conferences and in academic journals, the Persuasive Technology conference proceedings constitute the most coherent collection of research on the topic [10].

A systematic overview of the papers, their themes, and the theoretical and methodological perspectives, was established by applying NVivo[1] as a tool for

---

[1] NVivo is software that supports qualitative and mixed methods research. It is designed to assist in organizing, analyzing and finding insights in unstructured, or qualitative data.

categorization, search, and analysis. Furthermore, all papers were organized chronologically by date in an excel codebook. In total 66 papers were coded which discussed ethics with more than 1 sentence. Papers which contained a sentence or less on ethics were not included in the final review, however they are considered as they are an indicator of the issues addressed here regarding the lack of applied ethics discussed in the persuasive technology literature. The papers included in the review are listed in Appendix A.

3 Immediate Findings

The immediate findings are comprised of the themes or patterns that emerged during the open coding of the literature review. Throughout the review, 3 main themes were identified establishing that the discussion on ethics was limited to one or more of the following (Table 1):

Table 1. Themes identified during ethics in persuasive technology design literature review

Theme	Sums	Explanation
Academic input	23	Ethics mentioned and/or discussed in an manner which contributes to the understanding of ethics in persuasive technology
In passing	43	Ethics mentioned in passing with no discussion

The theme descriptions may appear rather subjective in nature and clearly some papers could inhabit more than one theme, however for the purpose of this paper, they are very important as they strongly indicate that most papers only mention ethics in passing and the only people having any kind of philosophical or methodological discussion about ethics within the persuasive design field are the academics. Although it has been argued that the examination of ethics is a "key component" in persuasive technology [1], these early observations gives reason to consider if this is merely the case in academics and if ethics is even considered by practitioners.

It was also noted that there does not appear to be one single example of a researcher arguing ethical concerns for the designers of persuasive technology. It appears that our ethical concerns for designers focuses only on their responsibility of outcomes. In consideration that design comprises a particular type of computer mediated communication [2], the lack of consideration for the rights of the designers indicates a challenges which has yet to be addressed.

4 Ethics – or Lack of Ethics in Persuasive Technology

On a more detailed level, it was found that there has not been a paper within the persuasive technology design conferences that has addressed ethics on a philosophical or methodological level since 2012, however in 2013 Karppinen and Oinas-Kukkonen [11] did provide a short description of where the ethical discourse stands within the field of persuasive technology design. In the following, a brief overview is provided of the works that contributed to the discussion of ethics on a philosophical and/or a methodological level from the persuasive design conferences. The included papers distinguish themselves by being the only contributions focusing on philosophical or methodological ethics.

The vast majority of papers cite Berdichevsky and Neuenschwander [6] and/or Fogg [1] as their foundations for arguing ethical theory and application. The conducted review identified Fogg as mentioned 822 times in the 12 years of conference proceedings, however all mentions were not related to ethics. Berdichevsky and Neuenschwander are mentioned another 65 times, all of which are identified as related to ethics. As such while their contributions to the field were not published as part of the persuasive design conferences it would be remiss to ignore them considering they appear to be the foundation for ethics in persuasive technology design.

Atkinson's contribution [2] in her critical review of Fogg's work [1] suggests a higher philosophical debate on ethics while Davis' work [3] proposes methodologies for the analysis of ethics from other fields of technology design. Finally, Smids [12] doesn't discuss the philosophy behind voluntariness, his reflection is included because it offers a theory of ethics that hasn't been discussed within the persuasive technology design field before. Likewise, the reflections of Karppinen and Oinas-kukkonen [11] are included because they instantiate where ethics stands within the field right now.

4.1   Berdichevsky and Neuenschwander 1999

Berdichevsky and Neuenschwander's framework for ethics in persuasive technologies is a principle-based system with its foundation in Utilitarian ethics philosophy. It is a set of 8 principles that encompass their framework of motivation, methods, unintended outcomes, privacy, disclosure, and accuracy as areas that should be ethically considered in persuasive design. Ethics is scrutinized via the motivations and methods of the designers as the technologies are simply the "executors" of the methods developed by the designer and technology itself is devoid of intent. They stress that "why do we want to persuade" and "why this intended outcome" should be the first questions asked by designers when considering ethics and suggest that the more principles that are ignored the less ethical the design will be [6].

4.2   Fogg 2003

When initially introducing Persuasive Technologies, Fogg emphasized that ethics should potentially be considered a defining feature of persuasion and consequently also of persuasive technologies, Fogg states that a key component of captology is examining ethical issues and states that ethical issues in persuasive technology can be found in the intentions, methods, and intended outcomes. He cites coercion and deception as always unethical, Operant conditioning and surveillance as areas that could be either ethical or unethical (Red Flags) as well as the targeting of vulnerable groups such as children or the mentally challenged. Furthermore, Fogg cites his former students (Berdichevsky and Neuenschwander) in stating that ethics can be "assessed" by investigating intended and unintended outcomes of persuasive technology systems.

Fogg finishes his foray into the ethics of persuasive technology by offering a 7-step stakeholder analysis framework as a methodology for the analysis of ethics in persuasive technology systems [1].

4.3   Atkinson 2006

Atkinson's contribution to ethics in persuasive technology design revolves around her critical review of Fogg's book from 2003 [1] where she posits that a fundamental ethic of persuasion design or captology is that the designer's intent be exposed at the beginning of user engagement with a program and that Fogg's ethical reminders are "not soundly, philosophically and theoretically, incorporated into his discourse". She goes on to state that what is missing is "a rigidly defined context of what constitutes an ethical application of persuasion principles".

Speaking on the differences between macrosuasion and microsuasion the author nominates a new term, 'compusuasion' as the ethical term that would describe the unintended, unforeseen, or induced behavioral change phenomena that go along with persuasive technology, thus accepting the responsibility.

On the topic of altering social behavior she states that there are ethical issues and in describing methods for reduction of the unintended and unforeseen consequences of social planning the author also notes that it is possible to gauge the impact "by current established philosophical, ethical, moral and human rights principles". The author defines ethical principles as "right and responsible action" and suggests that a study of moral and ethical principles as well as human rights can take us beyond subjective individualism. She asks is computer mediated persuasion ethical and feels that anything that obstructs an individual's right to freedom (choice) can be considered unethical. However, she goes on to say that it could be argued that persuasion that operates without the user being aware of the programmers' intent could be ethical "if the change in attitude, behavior or belief is motivated from the perspective of wisdom, benevolence and genuine care for others" but then asks if it wouldn't be better if the benevolence was used through advocacy or education where intent is known from the outset. She concludes that devising "appropriate guiding principles" is the true purpose of ethical and philosophical enquiry and that ethical safeguards are required for captology which could be fulfilled if the intent of the persuasion is exposed from the outset of engagement with a program. Finally, Atkinson makes clear the distinction between education and persuasion relating to Fogg's work where she states that "Persuasion is associated with rhetoric [2].

4.4   Davis 2009

Davis starts by giving a short overview of the work done by Berdichevsky and Neuenschwander [6], and Fogg [1] and then argues that these principles or guidelines are not enough and that persuasive designers should look to the human computer interaction community for methods that "help designers uncover and address ethical issues" as she concludes that ethical issues faced by persuasive systems are not unique to the field. Furthermore, Davis states that there are "lessons to be learned from how philosophers and designers have analyzed and accounted for such ethical issues in information systems beyond persuasive technology".

Davis suggests that methods are needed to structure the efforts of designers to enact ethical principles since designers cannot possibly predict all outcomes, cannot guarantee privacy or how privacy is even defined nor, can they guarantee the persuaders' intent. She argues that methods will help designers know what to do when principles are "inadequate" and to "structure their efforts to enact ethical principles". She cites Atkinson [2] in support of methods for ethical design via "public consultation", "social learning", and "multi-stakeholder negotiation" as a way of reducing "unintended and unforeseen" consequences as well as persona's and scenarios. She argues that work in persuasive technology has recently taken a user centered approach but from a persuasive effectiveness approach rather than an ethical one and since the persuasive technology ethical issues are not unique one can draw from the information technology field which does in fact engage with ethics. According to Davis, Value Sensitive Design (VSD) comes from the perspective of "human values" such as "privacy", "autonomy", and "moral beliefs of the technology" rather than the usability and that Participatory Design allows the users to be part of the design process and "is very much concerned with social learning and multi-stakeholder negotiation". She goes on... "VSD emphasizes values of moral import—values such as fairness, autonomy, privacy, and human welfare—and thus speaks to ethical concerns in technology design" and thinks that VSD could contribute to the design of ethical persuasive computing in many meaningful ways. She goes on to basically say that that the VSD method is better than the stakeholder's analysis at being able to uncover the ethical implications of a system in that it is more concerned with the "welfare of the indirect stakeholders, provides additional guidance in identifying values at stake, and reveals situations in which designers must make tradeoffs between conflicting value concerns."

Davis concludes that she believes that VSD and PD offer frameworks that "support the designer in engaging stakeholders and uncovering and addressing ethical issues" and that she urges other designers and researchers to consider VSD and PD approaches to solving ethical problems [3].

4.5   Smids 2012

Smids states that voluntariness is the most important ethical question regarding persuasive technology and then he goes on to cite Oinas-Kukkonen 2010, that in persuasive technology research "ethical considerations have been largely unaddressed". He then cites Berdichevsky and Neuenschwander [6] and Fogg [1] in stating that "the intentions of the persuaders, behavioral and attitudinal aims of the persuasive technologies and methods of persuasion" should be considered. Speaking of persuasive profiling the author feels that there is a need for more "ethical reflection" than can be done in his paper. Later, on the topic of subliminal feedback the author makes the claim that "ethical design cannot change subliminal feedback into persuasion" and while there might be situations where subliminal feedback is ethical it should not be called persuasion. Smids goes on to reassert his claim "that the most important ethical question regarding persuasive technologies is the voluntariness of changes they bring about" and recommends that an assessment of voluntariness is performed by all persuasive technology designers on the persuasive technologies they create.

4.6   Karppinen and Oinas-Kukkonen 2013

Karppinen and Oinas-Kukkonen state that when developing persuasive systems there are oftentimes ethical questions that arise and that there is no easy way to address ethical issues in all cases. They state that it is the purpose of their paper to analyze and define possible ways of addressing ethical questions in persuasive design and suggest that there are in fact 3 possible approaches to doing this which are by "guidelines, stakeholders' analysis, and involving users". The authors cite Davis [3], stating that it is something of an ethical minefield trying to change users' behaviors and attitudes through these types of systems. They cite Berdichevsky/Neuenschwander and Fogg [1, 6] as those responsible for the first academic work on ethics in persuasive technology design and then go on to give honorable mentions to a host of other academics for their "growing" interest in persuasive ethics but while claiming that these academics have contributed "convincing pieces of work" they state that they all differ in their suggestions for resolving ethical issues.

- Berdichevsky/Neuenschwander: Eight moral principles for designers to follow [6]
- Davis and Yetim: Designers and stakeholders should find consensus on ethical issues [3, 13]
- Smids: Voluntariness [12]
- Spahn: validity claims of speech acts [14]
- Fogg: Stakeholder analysis for examining ethics in complicated situations [1]
- Gram-Hansen: ethics as an intuitive result of human nature, rather than reason-based rule [15]

The authors suggest that designers can learn from these studies but argue that how to best systematically approach ethics is left open. Later the authors argue that it is possible for indirect persuasion to be ethical by stating that being unaware does not necessarily make persuasive technology manipulative. The authors continue showing contradictions and paradoxes between the differing arguments of what is ethical in persuasive design for a while before finally claiming "that all persuasive acts during the change process do not need to be voluntary or fully transparent". The authors then argue that a system isn't automatically on "solid ethical ground" just because of its transparency or voluntariness based on their belief that behavior change requires commitment and compliance from the user. The paper continues with the outline for their ethical framework which include the guidelines and analysis concepts from various academics before finally stating that guideline-based approaches are subjective. A designer and user may have two differing views on what is ethical. They go on say that the stakeholder analysis approach is used in business ethics and that values vary from one situation to the other and there are no easy answers with this approach. Furthermore, they make clear that a stakeholder analysis does not mean "that suggested ethical guidelines have no meaning". They then argue that there are too FEW published studies on ethical issues and that they believe as new ethical approaches are published that they will be able to be mapped to the authors presented framework. In Chap. 5 the authors continue by stating they presented a framework from which a designer can choose a suitable ethical approach to their designs and then go on to state that that stakeholder's analysis only works when the design is targeted at a specific and predefined group and argue that user consensus does not automatically make a system ethical. They then argue while "moral values should be emphasized" it should not be at the neglect of other values. They go on to state that ethical considerations should be made along the way with any design as they all have a target group in mind. They argue that guidelines can be thought of as checklists and that there are no experimental approaches that have the "ability to solve all questions of morality and ethics". They go on with stating that the framework of 3 categories (guideline-based, stakeholder analysis, and user involvement) is "unique to persuasive design" and rather than coming from the philosophical traditions it is built from the design perspective and that persuasive design still requires ethical design study [11].

5 Reflection – Discussion

Although acknowledging the quality of the work already published, there are several issues with the way ethics has been addressed over the last 12 years. Firstly, there have been no studies investigating how designers in the workplace address ethics. The identified contributions constitute academic theories and methodologies and a hope that they transition to the workplace. We have yet to explore if the stakeholder analysis proposed by Fogg [1] works in practice or not, and if Berdichevsky and Neuenschwander principles are followed. We don't know if the designers have any input where ethics are concerned, or if the role and standards of ethics is merely determined by management. Secondly, ethics has not been a distinct topic of discussion within the persuasive technology conference series since 2013. Based on the conducted review, it is as if the field has gotten complacent with regards to ethics in persuasive technology design. As to why this is, one can only speculate, but it could be that the field hasn't tried hard enough to move out of the utilitarian approach to ethics. As Atkinson stated in 2006, devising "appropriate guiding principles" is the true purpose of ethical and philosophical enquiry [2]. Maybe it is time to look at other theories of ethics in order to move towards a practical application of the research conducted so far. Davis [3] proposed user involvement methodologies based in value theory from the fields of Value Sensitive Design and Participatory Design and Gram-Hansen [15] suggested that ethical reflections might be considered as intuitive and personal. Consequently we should create technologies that we as designers find ethically acceptable e.g. based in Aristotle's virtue principles, particularly in the areas of practical wisdom (phronesis) and intuitive understanding or intellect (nous) [16]. In continuation, we have voluntariness as proposed by Smids [12] which has its foundations in Contractarianism, yet it would appear no one has decided to address these theories. As far as the literature review goes there does not appear to be an agreed upon approach to ethics within the field. It may be that the field is happy with the way ethics has been addressed as it is. However, it could also be that no one really cares about ethics?

6 Conclusion

Do ethics matter in persuasive technology? We would argue that it does.

Even though social media might not be designed as persuasive in intent they are in fact used for persuasive purposes as are all technologies [17]. It is with this in mind that we use Facebook as an example of how society at large does care about ethics even if we as designers have not given it sufficient attention. As has been seen in recent news accounts Facebook was brought before the US Senate as well as international councils to answer questions about their handling of user data [18]. Since then Facebook has been in the news and under scrutiny from the American judiciary for a range of ethical violations (e.g. violations of child privacy laws [19], violations of election laws [20], and censorship [21]). These ethical breeches affect everyone, designers and users alike and illustrate what happens when ethics are not considered. They also illustrate what happens when consequences are not considered. Furthermore, they exemplify the change in how technologies are applied over the past decade and the user mentality. Technologies are now far from simple tools that facilitate users during their daily tasks, they have become a pervasive and personal force in the lives of many. Moreover, users have a greater understanding of technologies and are increasingly becoming able to consider technologies both critically and constructively. Therefore, it is most important to find out what ethical conversations practitioners are having in the workplace and outside of academics. Particularly as it would appear that ethical considerations is becoming a specification considered by users when they decide which technologies to apply and which to disregard.

Recognizing the new tendencies in both the role of technologies and of the users, gives reason to also consider a second concern. Future research within the persuasive technology field should potentially strive to ensure that ethics is applicable not only for academic researchers, but also the design practitioners. With the rapid development in persuasive technologies, research should look further into the rights of designers rather than focusing simply the user. All ethical discussions thus far focus on securing the rights of the users and placing responsibility on the designers. If as Atkinson claims that freedom is a fundamental inalienable right [2] why is it only afforded to the users and not the designers? If design as suggested is a particular type of communication, shouldn't there be an ethical discussion on a designers right to free speech which would include the right to persuade?

Appendix A

See Tables 2 and 3.

Table 2. Reviewed papers providing academic contribution to ethics in persuasive technology

Authors (Date)	Contribution
IJsselsteijn et al. (2006)	Ethical guidelines in the field will encourage "morally responsible" design of persuasive technology
Khaled et al. (2006)	Ethics is a challenge of designing persuasive technologies for well being
Lucero et al. (2006)	Improving the motivation for children to read and write is ethical using captology
Atkinson (2006)	Designers intent is exposed at the beginning of user engagement with persuasive technologies
Jespersen et al. (2007)	From a historical and cultural context, a discussion on the ethical perspectives of surveillance and persuasive technology
Daniel Fallman (2007)	Ethics is one of the many challenges facing the HCI field
K. Torning and H. Oinas-Kukkonen (2009)	Illustrates the shortcomings of ethics within the persuasive design field
Davis (2009)	Discussion of the value of using methodologies from Value Sensitive Design and Participatory Design to address ethics in Persuasive Design
A. M. Ranfelt et al. (2009)	Discussion on ethics as it applies to persuasive design within the development of Autism Spectrum Disorder Technology
J. Davis (2010)	Autonomy and consent are just as important as ethical implications of the designs themselves
M. Kaptein and D. Eckles (2010)	Discussion of the ethical considerations with regards to adaptive persuasive technologies
J. Z. Daae and C. Boks (2011)	Discussion of the ethical implications of coercion from the product design perspective
S. B. Gram-Hansen et al. (2012)	The required action in the notion of Kairos is ethical
Jiles Smids (2012)	Voluntariness as the biggest ethical question facing persuasive technology design
P. Karppinen and H. Oinas-Kukkonen (2013)	A presentation of a design framework for ethics based on guidelines, stakeholder analysis, and user involvement
O. Barral et al. (2014)	Discussion of voluntariness as the ethical standard in covert persuasion systems
F. Basten et al. (2015)	Discussion of the ethicality of subliminal triggers
J. Timmer et al. (2015)	Discussion on ethics with integration of persuasive technologies in "smart environments"

(*continued*)

Table 2. (*continued*)

Authors (Date)	Contribution
S. B. Gram-Hansen (2016)	Discussion of constructive ethics as a focus during each step of the presented Explore, Design, Implement, Evaluate (EDIE) method
A. Krischkowsky et al. (2016)	Discussion on ethics in the framework of persuasive design as it relates to appropriation of the technology
A. Stibe and B. Cugelman (2016)	Discussions on dark patterns, unethical applications, backfiring, etc.
E. Twersky and J. Davis (2017)	The benefits of using methods from Value Sensitive Design to resolve ethical issues most specifically a look at human values with regards to language
S. B. Gram-Hansen et al. (2018)	Discusses persuasive technology design from the perspective of classical rhetoric and less ethical approaches to influencing the receiver (peithenanke)

Table 3. Reviewed papers mentioning ethics in passing

1. Gasser et al. (2006)	23. Lockton et al. (2009)
2. B. J. Fogg (2006)	24. Jaap Ham and Cees Midden (2010)
3. Redström (2006)	25. Harri Oinas-Kukkonen (2010)
4. G. Cornelissen et al. (2006)	26. Yamabe et al. (2010)
5. Redström et al. (2006)	27. Martha G. Russell (2011)
6. A. Meijnders et al. (2006)	28. Ruijten et al. (2011)
7. Goessens et al. (2006)	29. Appel et al. (2011)
8. van Bronswijk (2006)	30. Morten Aagaard and Peter Øhrstrøm (2012)
9. P. Barr et al. (2006)	31. Burleson et al. (2012)
10. Zhu (2007)	32. Muller et al. (2012)
11. R. Khaled et al. (2007)	33. Tim Marsh and Brigid Costello (2013)
12. Teddy McCalley and Alain Mertens (2007)	34. J. Masthoff et al. (2013)
13. Gable (2007)	35. A. Schmeil and L. Suzanne Suggs (2014)
14. O'Brian et al. (2007)	36. S. Langrial et al. (2014)
15. Duane Varan and Steve Bellman (2007)	37. K. Torning (2014)
16. Cugelman et al. (2008)	38. S. Burri Gram-Hansen and T. Ryberg (2015)
17. Harri Oinas-Kukkonen and Marja Harjumaa (2008)	39. M. M. Mustaquim and T. Nyström (2015)
18. Brenda Laurel (2009)	40. A. Algashami et al. (2017)
19. Nikki Serapio and B. J. Fogg (2009)	41. A. Caraban et al. (2017)
20. Ham et al. (2009)	42. Sandra Burri Gram-Hansen (2018)
21. Lasse Burri Gram-Hansen (2009)	43. K. Rogers and M. Weber (2018)
22. B. J. Fogg (2009)	

References

1. Fogg, B.J.: Persuasive Technology: Using Computers to Change What We Think and Do. Morgan Kaufmann Publishers, San Francisco (2003)
2. Atkinson, B.M.C.: Captology: a critical review. In: IJsselsteijn, W.A., de Kort, Y.A.W., Midden, C., Eggen, B., van den Hoven, E. (eds.) PERSUASIVE 2006. LNCS, vol. 3962, pp. 171–182. Springer, Heidelberg (2006). https://doi.org/10.1007/11755494_25
3. Davis, J.: Design methods for ethical persuasive computing. In: Persuasive 2009, 4th International Conference on Persuasive Technology, Paper 6, New York, NY, USA. ACM (2009)
4. IJsselsteijn, W., de Kort, Y., Midden, C., Eggen, B., van den Hoven, E.: Persuasive technology for human well-being: setting the scene. In: IJsselsteijn, W.A., de Kort, Y.A.W., Midden, C., Eggen, B., van den Hoven, E. (eds.) PERSUASIVE 2006. LNCS, vol. 3962, pp. 1–5. Springer, Heidelberg (2006). https://doi.org/10.1007/11755494_1
5. Gasser, R., Brodbeck, D., Degen, M., Luthiger, J., Wyss, R., Reichlin, S.: Persuasiveness of a mobile lifestyle coaching application using social facilitation. In: IJsselsteijn, W.A., de Kort, Y.A.W., Midden, C., Eggen, B., van den Hoven, E. (eds.) PERSUASIVE 2006. LNCS, vol. 3962, pp. 27–38. Springer, Heidelberg (2006). https://doi.org/10.1007/11755494_5
6. Berdichevsky, D., Neuenschwander, E.: Toward an ethics of persuasive technology. Commun. ACM 42, 51–58 (1999)
7. Khaled, R., Barr, P., Noble, J., Fischer, R., Biddle, R.: Our place or mine? Exploration into collectivism-focused persuasive technology design. In: IJsselsteijn, W.A., de Kort, Y.A.W., Midden, C., Eggen, B., van den Hoven, E. (eds.) PERSUASIVE 2006. LNCS, vol. 3962, pp. 72–83. Springer, Heidelberg (2006). https://doi.org/10.1007/11755494_11
8. Laurel, B.: Meeting people where they are. In: Persuasive 2009, 4th International Conference on Persuasive Technology, New York, NY, USA, pp. 1–2. ACM (2009)
9. Torning, K., Oinas-kukkonen, H.: Persuasive system design : state of the art and future directions. In: Persuasive 2009, 4th International Conference on Persuasive Technology, Cordura Hall, New York, NY, USA. ACM (2009)
10. Gram-hansen, S.B.: Persuasive designs for learning - learning in persuasive design: exploring the potential of persuasive designs in complex environments, p. 181. Aalborg Universitetsforlag (2016)
11. Karppinen, P., Oinas-Kukkonen, H.: Three approaches to ethical considerations in the design of behavior change support systems. In: Berkovsky, S., Freyne, J. (eds.) PERSUASIVE 2013. LNCS, vol. 7822, pp. 87–98. Springer, Heidelberg (2013). https://doi.org/10.1007/978-3-642-37157-8_12
12. Smids, J.: The voluntariness of persuasive technology. In: Bang, M., Ragnemalm, E.L. (eds.) PERSUASIVE 2012. LNCS, vol. 7284, pp. 123–132. Springer, Heidelberg (2012). https://doi.org/10.1007/978-3-642-31037-9_11
13. Yetim, F.: A set of critical heuristics for value sensitive designers and users of persuasive systems. In: ECIS 2011 Proceedings, Helsinki (2011)
14. Spahn, A.: And lead us (not) into persuasion…? Persuasive technology and the ethics of communication. Sci. Eng. Ethics 18, 1–18 (2011)
15. Gram-Hansen, S.B.: Towards an approach to ethics and HCI development based on Løgstrup's ideas. In: Gross, T., et al. (eds.) INTERACT 2009. LNCS, vol. 5726, pp. 200–203. Springer, Heidelberg (2009). https://doi.org/10.1007/978-3-642-03655-2_24
16. Kraut, R.: Aristotle's Ethics. The Stanford Encyclopedia of Philosophy (2018)

17. Redström, J.: Persuasive design: fringes and foundations. In: IJsselsteijn, W.A., de Kort, Y.A.W., Midden, C., Eggen, B., van den Hoven, E. (eds.) PERSUASIVE 2006. LNCS, vol. 3962, pp. 112–122. Springer, Heidelberg (2006). https://doi.org/10.1007/11755494_17
18. Yurieff, K.: Your Facebook data scandal questions answered. CNN Business (2018)
19. n/a. Facebook's Messenger Kids app accused of violating children's privacy law. Business Standard (2018)
20. Associated Press: Facebook is accused of violating election law in Seattle. The Telegraph (2018)
21. Tynan, D.: Facebook accused of censorship after hundreds of US political pages purged. The Guardian (2018)

The Ethics of Persuasive Technologies in Pervasive Industry Platforms: The Need for a Robust Management and Governance Framework

Gustav Borgefalk$^{(\boxtimes)}$ and Nick de Leon

Royal College of Art, Kensington Gore, London SW7 2EU, UK
gustav.borgefalk@network.rca.ac.uk,
nick.leon@rca.ac.uk

Abstract. A growing challenge for owners, board members, executive managers, and regulators is how to regulate and manage pervasive industry platforms which use persuasive technologies. The persuasive technology community has intentionally steered clear of researching technologies used for coercion or deception. Yet, we now see different shades of persuasive technology used for coercion and deception in the market, causing problems and possibly harm to people. In this article, we will argue that the persuasive technology research community is uniquely positioned to deal with the ethical and moral challenges with pervasive industry platforms and that it has a responsibility to proactively address these challenges. We propose an interdisciplinary research approach, combining knowledge from persuasive technologies, governance, and management studies, to arrive at a framework that can provide direction for future research as well as indicate potential solutions. We introduce the reader to some of the managerial challenges with persuasive technologies used in pervasive industry platforms using an illustrative case study of Facebook and propose three future research directions.

Keywords: Persuasive technology · Governance · Management ·
Service design · Persuasive platforms · Facebook

1 Introduction

In the past two decades, we have seen the rise and proliferation of pervasive, digital industry platforms that use strategies and tactics from the fields of persuasive technology and persuasive design to attract and engage users and clients. Out of the top ten most valuable companies on the Fortune 500, five[1] base their business models on digital platforms and related ecosystems of products and services [15]. In information system literature, these would be described as *dominant industry platforms* or *platform leaders*, which set the standards for other actors in their respective ecosystems [16]. Together with thousands of less influential platforms these platforms make up the lion

---

[1] Apple, Amazon, Alphabet, Microsoft, Facebook, as of March 29, 2018.

© Springer Nature Switzerland AG 2019
H. Oinas-Kukkonen et al. (Eds.): PERSUASIVE 2019, LNCS 11433, pp. 156–167, 2019.
https://doi.org/10.1007/978-3-030-17287-9_13

share of our digital experience, a *system of systems* mediating the human experience: intentionally and unintentionally, directly and indirectly influencing the lives of billions of people.

Since the inception of the field, the methods, impact and design of persuasive technologies and systems (here denoted persuasive technologies) has been in focus in the persuasive technology literature. However, a growing challenge is how to *regulate and manage* emerging, pervasive industry platforms which base their competitive advantage on persuasive technologies. For businesses and organizations, persuasive technologies offer a compelling value proposition, because they guide people's actions and choices and can influence attitudes and values [7]. By implementing persuasive features in digital products and platforms, companies can gain competitive advantage and differentiate from their competitors [26]. In the past decades, we have experienced unprecedented growth in the number and scale of businesses using persuasive technologies in digital platforms. A key driver of platform growth has been the deliberate use of strategies and tactics from the field of persuasive technologies to attract and engage users and clients. The focus of this article, however, is neither on designers, nor on product managers, but on *senior decision makers* in companies, organizations and governments who oversee strategic planning and daily operations of platforms using persuasive technologies. These include owners, board members, managing executives, politicians, investors or other stakeholders who *shape leadership, strategies and organizational structures and cultures* that directly or indirectly influence the emergence and management of pervasive industry platforms.

Despite a vibrant ethical discussion in the persuasive technology community, there are still valid concerns about the growing influence of persuasive platforms, where, the *ethical* and *moral* aspects of persuasion, the intentional act of trying to influence people's behaviors and attitudes, has recently become the subject of stinging criticism, from academia, governments and non-governmental organizations. The persuasive technology community has intentionally steered clear of research on technologies used for coercion or deception. Yet, we now see different shades of persuasive technologies used for coercion and deception in the market, causing problems and possibly harm to people. In this article, we will argue that the persuasive technology research community is uniquely positioned to deal with the ethical and moral challenges with pervasive industry platforms and that it has a *responsibility* to address and act on these challenges. We propose an interdisciplinary research approach, combining knowledge from persuasive technologies, governance and management studies, to arrive at a framework that can provide directions for future research as well as indicate potential solutions.

2 Responsible Implementation of Persuasive Technologies

2.1 Who Is Responsible When the Research Leaves the Lab?

Why do we need an updated, more holistic view on how to govern persuasive systems in more ethical ways and what is missing from existing literature? Since the inception of the field of persuasive technologies nearly two decades ago, technological systems and ecosystems have become vastly more complex and the computing substrate that persuasive software runs on has changed character. A computer is no longer a grey box tucked in under our desks, but cloud-based, global, invisible, multi-modal systems embedded in our environments. An updated definition of computer hardware and software also require updated research into new forms of persuasion. Timmer et al. describe this process as *proliferation* of persuasion (the range of contexts in which they can be applied expands) and *integration* of persuasive technologies in the physical environment [29]. New directions of research such as personalized persuasion and persuasion profiling [20], ambient persuasion [34] and subliminal persuasion [9, 25] has been proposed in recent years and have contributed to a better understanding of persuasion in the emerging computing landscape. In parallel with the ethical discussions in the persuasive technology community, large and small platform companies, as well as governments, are struggling with understanding and controlling their influence. Following on a series of events involving deceptive applications of persuasive technologies, there is now a flourishing debate in media, about the growing influence of persuasive technologies and platforms. Following on the Facebook/Cambridge Analytica scandal, the governments in the US and UK have initiated public hearings with digital platform providers such as Facebook and Twitter, to better understand how to understand and regulate digital platform companies on a national level [30, 31]. In 2018, the General Data Protection Regulation (GDPR) was introduced in the EU, to strengthen regulation and protection of citizens' privacy.

Still, significant regulatory and managerial challenges remain with pervasive industry platforms. These are a few examples of areas where research has indicated that persuasive technologies may be causing people harm:

Exploiting People's Attention. A common critique against pervasive industry platforms using persuasive technologies is that they are exploiting people's biological and psychological vulnerabilities. In his book 'Stand out of our light', Williams makes the case for how these platforms are fundamentally designed to prey on human attention and calls for more ethical practices and better governance [37]. Another critic of persuasive technologies is Tristan Harris, a former design ethicist at Google, who launched the Time Well Spent movement in 2013. In 2018, Harris founded the Center for Humane Technology, to work with issues related to persuasive technology and design.

Deception and Breach of Privacy. Psychographic targeting and behavioral advertisement are the subjects of growing criticism. Matz et al. demonstrated that psychological targeting can possibly be used for mass persuasion. In an experiment with 3.5 million participants, they tailored marketing messages using their psychological profiles and saw a significant increase in actions taken where the methods were used [22]. In 2015, Epstein et al. presented a study with the results from five experiments suggesting the existence of a Search Engine Manipulation Effect (SEME) that could shift voter preferences of undecided voters [11]. The hidden influence of ambient persuasive technologies and the mediating effects described by Verbeek, is making it increasingly difficult for people to notice if they are being persuaded, which may lead to deception [33].

Negative Influence on Wellbeing or Health. Social media are a class of platforms which use persuasive technologies to engage platform users. Although evidence has shown both positive and negative impact on well-being, there are strong indications that the use of social media, at least for certain groups, is making people depressed. In 2018, Hunt et al. claimed a casual correlation between depression and social media use, after studying how reduced social media use influenced a group of students [19]. Another study by Primack et al. connected increased social media use with increased depressive symptoms [24].

In this article, we do not intend to give a complete account of all challenges related to the use of persuasive technologies. However, these examples demonstrate a few emerging and unresolved problems which can potentially be linked to the use of persuasive technologies in pervasive industry platforms, which needs to be addressed.

2.2 Governance and Management

To clarify and motivate our choice of approach, we will briefly explain the concepts of governance and management. In 1999, Wolfensohn, former President of the World Bank stated that "*the proper governance of companies will become as crucial to the world economy as the proper governing of countries*" [38]. The term governance was minted in political science, but the concept has been translated into many different contexts. Governance is defined in the Cambridge dictionary as "the way that organizations or countries are managed at the highest level, and the systems for doing this" [8]. Governance and management are two overlapping concepts describe two perspectives on how an organization is led and managed. While *governance* is considered a higher-level system for goal-setting and control, *management* concern operational decision regarding organizational resource use.

2.3 Governance and Management Concepts in Persuasive Technology Literature

Obviously, there is no lack of literature about organizational management, management of information systems or platform ecosystems. However, in our view, these theories lack the in-depth knowledge about persuasive technologies to provide sufficient guidance for decision makers. Recently, there have been a few calls for further interdisciplinary research in the intersection between persuasive technology, ethics, and business management. Shao et al. called for a closer integration of persuasive technologies and business management studies [26]. The authors outline how persuasive technologies could contribute to the competitive advantage of companies. They focused on turning product-based advantage to cost-based competitive advantage of persuasive technologies, and to contribute with a better understanding of the costs involved in integrating persuasive features into digital services and platforms. In addition, they outlined four research directions based on cost-based competitive advantage and its relation to persuasive technologies: (1) understanding the costs associated with persuasive technology development, (2) strategic cost analysis for persuasive technology development, (3) empirically validating the cost strategy and (4) theory development.

Aagaard et al. explored how persuasive technologies can be used to facilitate sustainable innovation and business model innovation and speculate on how 5G as an enabling infrastructure could transform business models. They highlighted the need for good governance for persuasive business models and that further research is needed to ensure that these platforms are secure [1]. In 2018, Lindgren introduced the concept of *persuasive businesses* and *persuasive business models (PBMs)*, defined as *"an inter-active, dynamic business model and business model innovation strategy vision, mission and goal(s) where the PBM seeks to achieve impact on business models including users, customers, and technologies – all dimensions of other business models."* [21].

Apart from these pioneers, the territory is largely unexplored, and it is evident that there is a need for further inquiry into the way platforms are governed and managed.

2.4   Ethics in Persuasive Technology Literature

Ethics has always been an important aspect of persuasive technology research, but it has arguably risen in importance as the influence of digital industry platforms and ecosystems grow. Ethical questions related to machines and computers in relation to human beings have been around for long. In 1950, at the dawn of the computer era, the Cybernetic researcher Norbert Wiener published The Human Use of Human Beings, where he predicted that: *"...society can only be understood through a study of the messages and the communication facilities which belong to it; and that in the future development of these messages and communication facilities, messages between man and machines, between machines and man, and between machine and machine, are destined to play an ever-increasing part."* [35].

The earliest ethical theories specifically devised for *persuasive technologies* were developed by Fogg. Fogg's ethical work was influenced by the Human-Computer interaction-researchers Friedman and Kahn and their extensive research on Human Values, Ethics and Design [14]. In Fogg's seminal textbook on Persuasive Technologies, he identifies six ethical challenges that are unique for computers as persuasive technologies [7]. In one of the most cited ethics articles in persuasive technology research, Berdichevsky and Neuenschwander introduced seven 'commandments' and a 'golden rule', stating that "creators of a persuasive technology should never seek to persuade anyone of something they themselves would not consent to be persuaded of" [5]. Kaptein et al. extended their framework to encompass adaptive persuasive systems, [20] which is useful to describe the ethics related to behavioral advertising. Adapted to different contexts, these frameworks have been central for the ethical aspects of sub-sequent research. However, in a literature review of 51 persuasive technology studies produced between 2006–2008, Tørning and Oinas-Kukkonen identified that more research was urgently needed on ethics, going so far as to say that the sheer lack of studies about ethics could in itself be an unethical act! In addition, they questioned whether persuasive technologies cause voluntary cognitive change and emphasized that persuasive technology researchers' responsibilities extend far beyond the software systems they study and design [28]. From the perspective of design research, the ethics of *persuasive design* have been the subject of several studies defining the ethical qualities of features, products and services. As a reaction to the perceived lack of methods for translating the theoretical principles cited above, to actual software and hardware features, design researchers Davis and Nathan introduced updated design methods for ethical design of persuasive technologies, including Participatory Design and Value Sensitive Design for integrating user input in the design process and in doing so, making the end products embody more ethical and moral values [10]. Subsequently, Spahn developed ethical guidelines for software development and usage of persuasive technologies. With applied discourse ethics, he explores the fine line between manipulating and convincing someone, using the linguistic lens. *"Technology is no longer a neutral tool (if it ever was one), but helps to achieve moral goals like health, safety, sustainability and the like."* [27].

A notable addition to the ethical discussion in persuasive technology research was the establishment of a thorough theory of moral mediation of technological systems, a concept which was presented by Oinas-Kukkonen et al. [30] in 2008 and developed further by Verbeek [33], providing a valuable lens for persuasive technology designers. Verbeek challenged the traditional view that technological systems are neutral, instead highlighting the influence of technological mediation and technology's ability to shape human behavior and actions by their system design and architecture. In his book *Moralizing technology*, Verbeek also promoted the theory that technological systems could have an intentionality of their own. As pointed out by the author, this has far-reaching consequences - if a system can have an intentionality of its own, it can also be seen as a moral actor and thus be responsible for its actions. Spahn raised an important point regarding the ensuing risk for technological paternalism, stating that *"Critiques argue [...] that this way of 'moralizing' technology raises many ethical concerns. It might even be argued that PT can be regarded as the implementation of a techno-logical paternalism, which conflicts with the ideal of a free and autonomous choice of the individual."* [27]. Atkinson presented similar critique against persuasive technologies and emphasized that ethical qualities can be ensured if a persuasive system's macrosuasive intent is clear to the user. Timmer et al. described the challenges when persuasive technologies are integrated in smart environments. The authors also point out the governance problem with persuasive technologies in collective settings, such as when applied by the *UK behavioural insights team* (a government nudge unit), or by employers at workplaces [29]. In addition to the above-mentioned works, there are professional ethical codes such as the ACM Code of Ethics, which aim to 'inspire and guide the ethical conduct of all computing professionals' [2]. This code provides some high-level advice but does not give guidance for specific cases and as our case study shows, it can be questioned how orthodoxly these written codes are followed in practice.

2.5   Summarizing the Knowledge Gap

As we have discussed, the nature of persuasive technology landscape is rapidly shifting and there are signs that persuasive technologies are causing people harm when used in pervasive industry platforms. There is a vibrant ethical discussion in the persuasive technology community and knowledge about persuasive technology ethics which needs to be considered by executive functions in organizations and governments. In our view, the ethical perspectives found in persuasive technology literature are extremely relevant for executive decision makers and policy makers. However, there has been little research into how the ethical guidelines of persuasive technologies are used by managers when they make decisions about persuasive technologies in practice. As Shao et al. points out, there is also a need to understand how these can be integrated with theories of management [26]. We believe that important knowledge about the capabilities and threats from persuasive technologies should be translated faster from theory to practice, so that decision-makers who regulate or manage platforms can faster sense changes in the environment and proactively address problems before they turn awry. With an applied, interdisciplinary approach, persuasive technology research could *actively*, rather than *passively* shape their decisions regarding persuasive platforms, for the benefit of society. Despite a stronger focus on ethics in persuasive technology theory and design, both on feature level and system level, the *governance* and *management* perspectives on persuasive technology ethics are growing in importance and have largely been overlooked in persuasive technology literature to date.

3   Illustrative Case Study: Facebook's Governance Problem

To further argue for our viewpoint, we illustrate the need for a faster translation of persuasive technology research to practice, using the case of Facebook as an example. We recognize that Facebook is an extreme example, clearly, not all platforms have the influence and impact of Facebook. However, it is a pervasive industry platform that uses persuasive technologies, and which has been the subject of several studies in persuasive technology research over the years. Since Facebook was founded in February 2004, Facebook has grown to 2,2 billion users worldwide and is arguably the world's most influential social network. Facebook is an industry platform which allows for users, individuals, companies and organizations, to register and interact with each other in an online 'community' setting. The Founder and CEO of Facebook, Mark Zuckerberg, is also the company's Chairman [12]. In recent years, the platform has been the subject of multi-faceted criticism and despite the many positive values the platform create, there is mounting evidence that the platform has failed to protect its users against negative effects from using the platform. Facebook has been accused of breaching user privacy on several occasions and the company's role in the US and UK elections is now the subject of academic research and legal scrutiny. In addition to these problems, as mentioned earlier, it is hotly debated whether social media (such as Facebook) makes people depressed if the use of the platform is addictive and stealing our attention away from more important things [19, 37]. In a testimony to the US Congress on June 29, 2018, Mark Zuckerberg states:

"Facebook is an idealistic and optimistic company. For most of our existence, we focused on all the good that connecting people can bring. As Facebook has grown, people everywhere have gotten a powerful new tool to stay connected to the people they love, make their voices heard, and build communities and businesses. [...] But it's clear now that we didn't do enough to prevent these tools from being used for harm as well. That goes for fake news, foreign interference in elections, and hate speech, as well as developers and data privacy. We didn't take a broad enough view of our responsibility, and that was a big mistake. It was my mistake, and I'm sorry". [32].

While some see Facebook's troubles as the result of too rapid growth, others see it as a failure of governance and control. In a press call on November 15, 2018, Mark Zuckerberg initiated an effort to enforce community standards and stated that:

"I'm going to publish a note laying out how we're approaching content governance and enforcement of our Community Standards. This is something we've been working on for a couple months now. This is an important topic. It's about finding the right balance between two very important principles – giving people a voice and keeping people safe." [13].

The governance strategies presented were (1) moving from reactive to proactive enforcement of community standards using AI systems to identify potentially harmful content, (2) reducing the spread of sensational and provocative content, (3) give people more control over what they see, (4) build a more robust appeal process and (5) establishing an independent body to oversee content and make publishing decisions and (6) increasing transparency by issuing transparency and enforcement reports [12]. These actions are a welcome step in the right direction, but they are clearly added as an afterthought, to address some of the platform's long-standing problems. Our interpretation of this situation is that Facebook has had a *governance problem*, and *related management challenges* resulting from a rapidly growing platform and from a patchwork of management and design decisions made over the course of roughly 15 years. However unpredictable or unintended, the consequences of pervasive platforms influencing people's behaviors are real. In the words of the French philosopher Paul Virilio, 'the invention of any new technology is simultaneously the invention of a new accident' [36]. According to Fogg, persuasive technologies should only deal with planned persuasive effects of technology [7]. In this case however, the 'accidents' may have had negative impact on millions of people's lives. We therefore argue that it is not ethical for persuasive technology researchers to disregard the unintended effects of their work.

3.1 What Would Better Knowledge About Persuasive Technologies Have Contributed?

As we can see from the review in Sect. 2.4, ethical guidelines or design methods were readily available in the persuasive technology research community at the time of Facebook's inception in 2004 [5, 7]. More research is needed to understand why these guidelines were not followed or enforced when the earliest signs of problems surfaced, given that Facebook quickly absorbed the influence tactics that came out of the world's persuasive technology labs, but seemingly failed to implement the ethical guidelines. We do not believe that Facebook's problems are Facebook's alone. All fast-growing platforms experience similar pains, where 'unintended consequences' cause pains for users. Neither do we believe that the intentions of Facebook's owners, board members or management team are to deliberately cause people harm. However, we do recognize the ongoing challenge of balancing the sometimes-conflicting goals of public and private interests. By properly integrating knowledge about persuasive technologies into systems for checks and balances at an early stage, perhaps some of these problems could have been mitigated.

4   Discussion and Research Directions

In the previous sections, we have identified a need for new knowledge in governing and managing rapidly growing industry platforms. In this section, we propose three research directions which would stimulate further interdisciplinary research in the intersection between persuasive technology research and research on governance and management.

4.1   Research Direction #1 – Interdisciplinary Research into 'Good Governance' of Persuasive Systems

The term 'good governance' is regularly applied in the study of politics and international development. It is broadly defined as how 'well' countries or authorities manage public affairs. Governance implies that there is *power*, and *control* involved and 'good governance' that there is a *qualitative measurement* involved. It also means that there is also an antithesis which we here refer to as 'bad' governance. There are several frameworks for governance which could benefit from knowledge from persuasive technology research. As evident from the criticism described above, organizations, companies, regulators and citizens are still struggling with understanding how to manage and regulate platforms whose core business models and competitive advantages are based on industrial-scale persuasion. For comparison, civil law has emerged over thousands of years and been refined to relatively stable and predictable judicial systems. Digital platforms, however, emerge in a matter of years, sometimes even months, which requires new, ethical and dynamic systems to govern platforms in a rapidly shifting geopolitical landscape. Bratton suggests that political geography nowadays should be understood differently in the light of planetary-scale computation and that the border between a 'user' and a formal 'citizen' is blurring [6]. There is now an opportunity for the persuasive technology community to be a part of shaping these new governance processes and translate its knowledge directly into the strategic processes of policy makers and managers.

4.2   Research Direction #2 – Further Integration of Persuasive Technology Ethics in Management and Strategy Theory and Practice

The second proposed direction is an expansion of the proposal by Shao et al. [26]. It includes developing a more detailed roadmap for an integrated research agenda for persuasive technologies and organizational strategy, which include areas such as strategic planning, strategic thinking, management theory and organizational theory. This is the analytical level 'below' governance, however, the border between governance and management is not a hard line. Richer understanding of how knowledge about persuasive technology can be communicated and disseminated to owners, board members, managers and stewards of companies and other organizations, could lead to new methods for helping managers to understand persuasive systems and make more beneficial strategic decisions.

4.3   Research Direction #3 – Using Service Design to Translate Ethical Guidelines from Persuasive Technology Research to Practical Tools for Regulators, Owners, Board Members and Managers

A recent literature review by Alves et al. of software ecosystem governance concluded that *"the governance of software ecosystems is currently one of the largest challenges software companies need to deal with for the sake of their survival"* [3]. In this study, the authors explicitly pointed to the need for practical and strategic guidance, such as dashboards and analytic tools to help people to better understand the health of a software ecosystem. As described above, there is no lack of prescriptive ethical codes, however, the response time to integrate new knowledge about persuasive technologies such as design and ethical guidelines needs to increase, and it would be beneficial to explore how to better integrate these codes into governance and management structures. An old wisdom is that what gets measured gets done. In that spirit, a starting point could be to analyze the role of *management information systems* and *performance measurements*, such as Key Performance Indicators (KPI's), balanced scorecards etc. *Service design* is an emerging field in design which is uniquely positioned to guide the development of these tools. Design researchers should investigate the possibility of shaping the practical and communicative tools which are used by decision makers to help them shift their behavior towards 'good governance' of the industry platforms they manage. When analyzing industry platforms, the extensive work of Gawer and Cusumano on industry platforms and ecosystem innovation is a helpful theoretical base [16, 17].

5   Conclusion

This article has identified the need for better governance of pervasive industry platforms which are using persuasive technologies. We have reviewed relevant persuasive technology literature and proposed that new, interdisciplinary knowledge is needed about ways to work together with governance and management theorists and practitioners to develop new theories and tools for owners, board members, executive managers, regulators and other stakeholders who oversee industry platforms which use persuasive technologies. This would ensure that their emergent properties are beneficial for its users and for society. To conclude, we presented three research directions that would contribute to realizing this ambition.

References

1. Aagaard, A., Lindgren, P.: The opportunities and challenges of persuasive technology in creating sustainable innovation and business model innovation. Wirel. Pers. Comm. **81**, 1511–1529 (2015)
2. ACM.org.: ACM Code of Ethics and Professional Conduct (2018). http://www.acm.org/about-acm/acm-code-of-ethics-and-professional-conduct. Accessed 28 Jan 2019
3. Alves, C., Oliveira, J., Jansen, S.: Software ecosystems governance - a systematic literature review and research agenda. In: Proceedings of the 19th International Conference on Enterprise Information Systems, vol. 3, pp. 215–226 (2017)

4. Atkinson, B.M.C.: Captology: a critical review. In: IJsselsteijn, W.A., de Kort, Y.A.W., Midden, C., Eggen, B., van den Hoven, E. (eds.) PERSUASIVE 2006. LNCS, vol. 3962, pp. 171–182. Springer, Heidelberg (2006). https://doi.org/10.1007/11755494_25

5. Berdichevsky, D., Neuenschwander, E.: Toward an ethics of persuasive technology. Commun. ACM **42**, 51–58 (1999)

6. Bratton, B.H.: The Stack: On Software and Sovereignty. MIT Press, Cambridge (2016)

7. Fogg, B.J.: Persuasive technology: using computers to change what we think and do. Ubiquity (2002)

8. Cambridge University Press: Cambridge online dictionary: governance, Cambridge Dictionary online. Accessed 25 Nov 2018

9. Caraban, A., Karapanos, E., Teixeira, V., Munson, S.A., Campos, P.: On the design of *Subly*: instilling behavior change during web surfing through subliminal priming. In: de Vries, P., Oinas-Kukkonen, H., Siemons, L., Beerlage-de, J.N., van Gemert-Pijnen, L. (eds.) Persuasive Technology: Development and Implementation of Personalized Technologies to Change Attitudes and Behaviors. LNCS, vol. 10171, pp. 163–174. Springer, Cham (2017). https://doi.org/10.1007/978-3-319-55134-0_13

10. Davis, J., Nathan, L.P.: Value sensitive design: applications, adaptations, and critiques. In: van den Hoven, J., Vermaas, P., van de Poel, I. (eds.) Handbook of Ethics, Values, and Technological Design, pp. 11–40. Springer, Dordrecht (2015). https://doi.org/10.1007/978-94-007-6970-0_3

11. Epstein, R., Robertson, R.E.: The search engine manipulation effect (SEME) and its possible impact on the outcomes of elections. Proc. Natl. Acad. Sci. USA **112**, E4512–E4521 (2015)

12. Facebook Newsroom. https://newsroom.fb.com/company-info/. Accessed 25 Nov 2018

13. Facebook Newsroom. https://fbnewsroomus.files.wordpress.com/2018/11/call-transcript-11_15_2018.pdf/. Accessed 25 Nov 2018

14. Friedman, B., Kahn, P.H.: Human agency and responsible computing: Implications for computer system design. J. Syst. Softw. **17**, 7–14 (1992)

15. Fortune 500 Website. http://fortune.com/fortune500/list/filtered?sortBy=mktval. Accessed 25 Nov 2018

16. Gawer, A., Cusumano, M.A.: Platform leadership: How Intel, Microsoft, and Cisco Drive Industry Innovation, vol. 5. Harvard Business School Press, Boston (2002)

17. Gawer, A., Cusumano, M.A.: Industry platforms and ecosystem innovation. J. Prod. Innov. Manag. **31**, 417–433 (2014)

18. Ham, J., Midden, C., Beute, F.: Can ambient persuasive technology persuade unconsciously?: Using subliminal feedback to influence energy consumption ratings of household appliances. In: Proceedings of the 4th International Conference on Persuasive Technology. ACM (2009)

19. Hunt, M.G., Marx, R., Lipson, C., Young, J.: No more FOMO: limiting social media decreases loneliness and depression. J. Soc. Clin. Psychol. **37**, 751–768 (2018)

20. Kaptein, M., Eckles, D.: Selecting effective means to any end: futures and ethics of persuasion profiling. In: Ploug, T., Hasle, P., Oinas-Kukkonen, H. (eds.) PERSUASIVE 2010. LNCS, vol. 6137, pp. 82–93. Springer, Heidelberg (2010). https://doi.org/10.1007/978-3-642-13226-1_10

21. Lindgren, P.: Multi business model innovation in a world of 5G: what will persuasive business models look like in a world of 5G? Wirel. Pers. Comm. **88**, 79–84 (2016)

22. Matz, S.C., Kosinski, M., Nave, G., Stillwell, D.J.: Psychological targeting as an effective approach to digital mass persuasion. Proc. Natl. Acad. Sci. USA **114**, 12714–12719 (2017)

23. Oinas-Kukkonen, H., Harjumaa, M.: A Systematic Framework for Designing and Evaluating Persuasive Systems. In: Oinas-Kukkonen, H., Hasle, P., Harjumaa, M., Segerståhl, K., Øhrstrøm, P. (eds.) Persuasive Technology. LNCS, vol. 5033, pp. 164–176. Springer, Berlin (2008). https://doi.org/10.1007/978-3-540-68504-3_15

24. Primack, B.A., et al.: The association between valence of social media experiences and depressive symptoms. Depress. Anxiety **35**, 784–794 (2018)
25. Ruijten, P.A.M., Midden, C.J.H., Ham, J.: Unconscious persuasion needs goal-striving: the effect of goal activation on the persuasive power of subliminal feedback (2011)
26. Shao, X., Oinas-Kukkonen, H.: Thinking about persuasive technology from the strategic business perspective: a call for research on cost-based competitive advantage. In: Ham, J., Karapanos, E., Morita, P., Burns, C. (eds.) Persuasive Technology. LNCS, vol. 10809, pp. 3–15. Springer, Cham (2018). https://doi.org/10.1007/978-3-319-78978-1_1
27. Spahn, A.: And lead us (not) into persuasion…? Persuasive technology and the ethics of communication. Sci. Eng. Ethics **18**, 633–650 (2012)
28. Tørning, K., Oinas-Kukkonen, H.: Persuasive system design: state of the art and future directions. In: Proceedings of the 4th International Conference on Persuasive Technology (2009)
29. Timmer, J., Kool, L., van Est, R.: Ethical challenges in emerging applications of persuasive technology. In: MacTavish, T., Basapur, S. (eds.) PERSUASIVE 2015. LNCS, vol. 9072, pp. 196–201. Springer, Cham (2015). https://doi.org/10.1007/978-3-319-20306-5_18
30. UK Information Commissioner's Office (ICO), Democracy Disrupted? https://ico.org.uk/media/action-weve-taken/2259369/democracy-disrupted-110718.pdf. Accessed 25 Nov 2018
31. US Federal Trade Commission (FTC), Statement by the Acting Director of FTC's Bureau of Consumer Protection Regarding Reported Concerns about Facebook Privacy Practices. https://www.ftc.gov/news-events/press-releases/2018/03/statement-acting-director-ftcs-bureau-consumer-protection. Accessed 25 Nov 2018
32. US Senate Judiciary Committee. Mark Zuckerberg Hearing on April 10 2018. https://www.judiciary.senate.gov/imo/media/doc/04-10-18%20Zuckerberg%20Testimony.pdf. Accessed 25 Nov 2018
33. Verbeek, P.-P.: Moralizing Technology: Understanding and Designing the Morality of Things. University of Chicago Press, Chicago (2011)
34. Verbeek, P.-P.: Ambient intelligence and persuasive technology: the blurring boundaries between human and technology. Nanoethics **3**, 231–242 (2009)
35. Wiener, N.: The Human Use of Human Beings: Cybernetics and Society. Doubleday, Garden City (1954)
36. Virilio, P.: The Original Accident. Polity Press, Cambridge (2007)
37. Williams, J.: Stand Out of Our Light: Freedom and Resistance in the Attention Economy. Cambridge University Press, Cambridge (2018)
38. Wolfensohn, J.D.: A battle for corporate honesty, the economist: the world in 1999. Financial Times, p. 38 (1998)

How Does GDPR (General Data Protection Regulation) Affect Persuasive System Design: Design Requirements and Cost Implications

Xiuyan Shao[✉][iD] and Harri Oinas-Kukkonen

Oulu Advanced Research on Service and Information Systems,
University of Oulu, P.O. Box 3000, 90014 Oulu, Finland
{xiuyan.shao,harri.oinas-kukkonen}@oulu.fi

Abstract. In May 2018, GDPR came into effect in the European Union, placing additional requirements for data sensitive companies on data protection. For persuasive systems which deal with users' data, taking GDPR into consideration in the design phase is necessary. This paper analyzes and summarizes the requirements by GDPR and discusses how they affect persuasive systems design in terms of design requirements and cost implications.

Keywords: GDPR · Data protection · Persuasive systems design · Cost

1 Introduction

The European GDPR is new legislation on data protection in the European Union (EU). The GDPR strengthens the protection of personal data of individuals in the EU and improves the level of harmonization across the EU. The impact of the GDPR on European and non-European organizations is significant. However, many organizations are still unaware of the new legislation and its complexity, while others are still focusing on the first implementation stage. Non-compliance may expose these organizations to newly introduced high sanctions. Persuasive and behavior-change support systems, which aim to promote change in different domains (including health, safety and security, environmental sustainability, energy conservation, marketing, and education), are data-sensitive by definition [1]. For this reason, the GDPR should be taken into account in organizations which develop persuasive systems. This paper discusses the GDPR from the viewpoint of systems design and costs, and it suggests how development of persuasive systems should tackle these new challenges.

2 Data Protection and Essentials of GDPR

To harmonize data protection, Data Protection Directive 95/46/EC (hereafter DIR95) has been a central legislative instrument for personal data protection in the EU. DIR95 regulates the protection of individuals with regard to personal data processing and free movement within the EU. In 2002, Privacy and Electronic Communications (EC Directive 2002/58/EC) [2] was introduced to DIR95, adding new concerns of the

© Springer Nature Switzerland AG 2019
H. Oinas-Kukkonen et al. (Eds.): PERSUASIVE 2019, LNCS 11433, pp. 168–173, 2019.
https://doi.org/10.1007/978-3-030-17287-9_14

processing of personal data and the protection of privacy in the electronic communications sector. For example, the directive regulates confidentiality, unsolicited communications, and processing of billing, traffic, and location data [2].

After more than two decades, DIR95 no longer provided the degree of harmonization that is required among the EU member states or the efficiency to ensure the right to personal data protection in the present-day digital environment [3]. The inadequate harmonization put Europe at a disadvantage in the global competition with other countries, such as the United States and China [4]. The EU's data protection framework had a fundamental reform. The reform consisted of two instruments: the GDPR and the directive on protecting personal data processed for the purposes of prevention, detection, investigation, or prosecution of criminal offences and related judicial activities. The GDPR points out the role of the FIP (Fair Information Practices)-based Privacy by Design (PbD) principles [5] and obliges companies to integrate these principles into their business processes [6].

A major departure from current practices is embodied in the GDPR. The GDPR gives primacy to purpose: Data may be collected and stored only when (1) end-users have consented, often explicitly, to the purposes for which that data is collected and (2) the collected data is necessary for achieving these purposes, and the data must be deleted when those purposes are no longer applicable [7]. To highlight this, the GDPR emphases these requirements in its notions of purpose limitation and data minimization, its treatment of consent, and the right to be forgotten.

3 Impact of GDPR on Persuasive Systems Design

The implementation of the GDPR indicates the needs for various actions, planning and assignment of new responsibilities, which may have significant impacts on companies in using their resources and may demand the acquisition of new expertise. Eleven requirements can be recognized and specified for persuasive systems design, and they can be categorized into: (1) design requirements, (2) cost implications (See Table 1).

Table 1. Impact of GDPR on persuasive system design

Impact categories	Explanation
Impact on design requirements	1. Privacy by design and default
	2. Providing information to data subjects
	3. Ensuring individuals' right to be forgotten
	4. Ensuring individuals' right to data portability
Impact on costs	1. Data minimization
	2. Obtaining consent
	3. Data processing in international contexts
	4. Demonstrating compliance
	5. Obligation to report breaches within 72 h
	6. Profession of Data Protection Officer (DPO)
	7. Documentation of processing activities

3.1 Design Requirements

(1) Privacy by design and default. To ensure compliance with the GDPR and protection of data subjects' rights, companies are obliged to implement technical and organizational measures and procedures. Privacy should be considered not only in the business processes, but also throughout systems development. The influence on persuasive systems design would be the implementation of technical measures to ensure compliance with the GDPR. Yet, the definition of technical measures is not fully clear in this context. It would be best to consider such technical measures already in the systems planning phase, rather than after the fact. Thus, in order to satisfy the "privacy by design and default" requirement, privacy-related software features may have to be carefully designed into the persuasive system under development.

(2) Providing information to data subjects. The information that companies need to provide to data subjects includes processing operations, data security measures, the legal basis for processing, the data subjects' rights, and the companies' legitimate interests. The way of providing such data should be transparent, easily accessible, and understandable, especially when the data subject is a child. Procedures and mechanisms for exercising the data subjects' rights are also required, i.e. companies have to arrange for the means of responding to information requests according to GDPR requirements. There can be two ways to meet this requirement. First, information provision can be embedded in the information system, i.e. introducing a new software feature that communicates with data subjects about processing operations, data security measures, and so on. Another option is to have other channels (such as emails) to communicate with data subjects about the required items. Adding a software feature requires more planning in the design phase, while the email or other extra communication channel option are likely to cost more in the long run.

(3) Ensuring individuals' right to be forgotten. Companies are obliged to delete data subjects' personal data anytime they request it, which demands implementing processes and technical means for the deletion within time limits. These include ways of informing third parties about the deletion request, while processing personal data. Ensuring the right to be forgotten requires documentation of the data, how it is stored and with which parties it is shared. A software feature embedded in the system, which erases users' data per user request, could be developed. If the data has been shared with third party, making sure that third party deletes the data would require communication and coordination, which takes time and expense.

(4) Ensuring individuals' right to data portability. Companies are obliged to provide data subjects with an electronic copy of their data upon request. They must ensure that the personal data collected for processing is in a consistent format to facilitate its further use by the data subject and its transmission to other service providers' processing systems. A software functionality could be developed that would be embedded in the persuasive system. This could be implemented in such a way that when data subjects request to have an electronic copy of their data, the persuasive system generates the copy so that data subjects can download it by themselves. The format of data ought to match existing standards.

3.2   Cost Implications

(1) Data minimization. The principle of limiting data usage requires limiting personal data processing to the absolute minimum necessary. Profiling customers' needs to inform data subjects about the reasons and the need for profiling would add more documentation and communication work with customers, which would not necessarily influence persuasive systems design. However, this influences the cost of developing persuasive systems. New obligations may also be introduced when planning data collection and processing. For example, collecting data from children needs verification of age and consent from parents or custodians.

(2) Obtaining consent. The data subject's consent is required for utilizing personal data. Demonstrating that the data subject has consented to the processing is important. All relevant information about the processing should be contained and presented clearly when requesting for consent. The request should be clearly distinguishable from other information, such as contracts. To obtain consent, a software functionality could be developed so that when users start to use the system, the system pops out a consent letter on which users must choose "yes" or "no." To have this functionality doesn't increase the cost much, but handling the consent will increase the cost. Namely, at any given time, a service provider has to be informed when someone has withdrawn their consent and thus not utilize their data.

(3) Data processing in international contexts. With cloud service and other modern software infrastructures, personal data may transfer to a third country or an international organization. Companies need to make sure that their current safeguards for personal data transfers comply with the GDPR conditions and, when necessary, put into practice new safeguards. Companies outside the EU must comply with both their own national legislation and the GDPR when handling EU residents' personal data or monitoring data subjects' behavior within the EU. A non-EU established controller will need a representative in the EU. This is about understanding other organizations' practices; therefore, it is not directly linked to persuasive software features. But this involves personnel designation and communication, and these will end up with more costs.

(4) Demonstrating compliance. The GDPR obliges controllers to be able to demonstrate that their personal data processing complies with the regulation. To show compliance with GDPR requirements, getting data protection certifications, seals, and marks is recommended, which increases the cost.

(5) Obligation to report breaches within 72 h. Controllers should notify data protection authorities and data subjects about data breaches as early as possible. A possible software feature could be an automatic notification or warning for data subjects about possible data breaches. This has already been manifested in persuasive systems design through reminder features [8], which can take care of automatic notifications and/or warnings. In general, clearly defined and well-practiced procedures (because of the requirement to act within a very limited time) are needed in organizations to deal with possible breaches and related reporting. These support activities increase costs.

(6) Profession of Data Protection Officer (DPO). In some cases, an organization must designate a DPO of the organization. Conditions for organizations that must have a DPO are as follows: if they are a public authority (except for courts acting in their judicial capacity); if they carry out large-scale processing of special categories of data or data relating to criminal convictions and offences; and last but not least, if they carry out large-scale systematic monitoring of individuals (for example, online behavior tracking). Those organizations may need to obtain new experts who understand both the GDPR and the persuasive systems design. Obtaining new expertise is directly linked with the cost of persuasive systems development.

(7) Documentation of processing activities. Processing activities need to be recorded and made available to the supervising authority upon request. Data-protection impact assessments are also required prior to possible risky processing operations. Maintaining the required documentation involves more work time and therefore increases costs.

4 Discussion and Conclusion

Information provided by an information system will be more persuasive if it matches with the needs, interests, personal use and user context, and other factors relevant to a user or a user's group [8]. A critical question for persuasive systems design is: Could some persuasive software features be affected by the GDPR to such an extent they will not be able to function as planned, and therefore they would decrease the system's persuasive power?

The GDPR requires that the data subjects have the right to obtain from the controller the erasure of their personal data without undue delay. Suppose the following scenario: a personal trainer website provides different content for different user groups, e.g. beginners and professionals. When a user decides to erase data about one's user history or personal interests, the coaching system may end up providing general information and suggestions rather than personalized or tailored information.

Let's look at another example. Social learning is dependent on the fact that a person can observe others performing the same behavior. Social comparison is based on the fact that a person can compare his/her performance with the performance of others, and social facilitation is based on the idea that a system user can discern that others are performing the behavior along with them [8]. Principles under the social support category are based on the fact that the system has access to other users' data. Similar to personalization and tailoring, when users have no access to other users' data (since the GDPR provides the right to data subjects to erase their data), social support functionality could end up not working as planned because of users' erasure of data.

While the GDPR brings new design requirements and cost implications, naturally it also provides the field of persuasive system design with new research directions. A key question that will remain is, while system features may be affected, will this decrease the system's persuasive power? Future research could also study to what extent the GDPR would affect the selection of persuasive software features and to what extent those very features would influence users' actual behavioral change. As previously proposed by Shao and Oinas-Kukkonen [9], the cost of developing persuasive systems would also need more attention. For companies, compliance with GDPR requirements is costly. Thus, the essential question is, to what extent does the compliance with the GDPR influence the costs of persuasive system development? Future research should also seek to help companies assess the cost of persuasive systems development under the requirements of the GDPR.

To conclude, this paper recognized two impact categories for how the GDPR affects persuasive systems design: design requirements and cost implications. The GDPR requires organizations to treat privacy by design and as default, especially when providing information for users and ensuring both their right to be forgotten and their right to data portability. Complying with the GDPR also implies costs with minimizing data, obtaining consent, data processing in international contexts, demonstrating GDPR compliance, reporting breaches quickly, starting a new position of Data Protection Officer, and documenting processing activities carefully. Future research on these design requirements and cost implications is needed.

References

1. Oinas-Kukkonen, H.: A foundation for the study of behavior change support systems. Pers. Ubiquit. Comput. **17**(6), 1223–1235 (2013)
2. EuropeanCommission: Directive 2002/58/EC of the European Parliament and of the Council of 12 July 2002 concerning the processing of personal data and the protection of privacy in the electronic communications sector (directive on privacy and electronic communications). Off. J. L **201**, 0037–0047 (2002)
3. European Commission: Communication from the Commission to the European Parliament, the Council, the European Economic and Social Committee and the Committee of the regions – Safeguarding privacy in a connected world. A European data protection framework for the 21st century. COM (2012). 09 final (2012a)
4. Dix, A.: The commission's data protection reform after Snowden's summer. Intereconomics **48**(5), 268–271 (2013)
5. Cavoukian, A.: Privacy by design: the 7 foundational principles. Information and Privacy Commissioner of Ontario, Ontario, Canada (2009). (Revised version published in 2013)
6. European Commission: Proposal for a regulation of the European Parliament and of the Council on the protection of individuals with regard to the processing of personal data and on the free movement of such data (General Data Protection Regulation). COM (2012). 11 final (2012b)
7. Basin, D., Debois, S., Hildebrandt, T.: On purpose and by necessity: compliance under the GDPR. In: 22nd International Conference on Financial Cryptography and Data Security (2018)
8. Oinas-Kukkonen, H., Harjumaa, M.: Persuasive systems design: key issues, process model, and system features. Commun. Assoc. Inf. Syst. **24**, 485–500 (2009)
9. Shao, X., Oinas-Kukkonen, H.: Thinking about persuasive technology from the strategic business perspective: a call for research on cost-based competitive advantage. In: Ham, J., Karapanos, E., Morita, P.P., Burns, C.M. (eds.) PERSUASIVE 2018. LNCS, vol. 10809, pp. 3–15. Springer, Cham (2018). https://doi.org/10.1007/978-3-319-78978-1_1

Special Application Domains

Long-Term User Experience and Persuasion on 3DFysio, A Mobile Rehabilitation Application

Aino Ahtinen[1](✉), Anu Lehtiö[1], and Marion Boberg[2]

[1] Tampere University, Tampere, Finland
{aino.ahtinen,anu.lehtio}@tuni.fi
[2] Kineso OY, Kangasala, Finland
marion.boberg@kineso.fi

Abstract. This paper presents a field study of a persuasive mobile application, 3DFysio, to support patients' motivation in rheumatoid arthritis rehabilitation. The study was conducted with 10 patients over the period of 9 months, to study the user experience of the application and its persuasive features. The research data was collected with interviews and questionnaires in several phases of the trial. The findings show that the patients perceived the application as a motivational tool to support their rehabilitation process. The main persuasive and motivational aspects for patients were the interactive rehabilitation program, accurate and easily available physiotherapy exercises presented by 3D avatar, and the connection to the personal physiotherapist. 3DFysio seemed to motivate through a combination of persuasive elements on the application and real life. It also supported the establishment of an exercise routine. This paper provides new knowledge of persuasive design to support long-term rehabilitation process by means of mobile applications.

Keywords: Mobile rehabilitation · Persuasive design · User experience · Mobile health apps

1 Introduction

Mobile applications (apps) are ubiquitous and they are widely used to support well-being and health e.g. [2, 9, 12]. In *mobile rehabilitation* or *telerehabilitation*, i.e. rehabilitation that is delivered to patient's home [5], mobile apps can be beneficial by supporting and motivating the patients in everyday life. Telerehabilitation is a functional method for the patients especially because it enables the integration of prescribed exercises to daily life without being physically in the rehabilitation center [13]. Interactive technologies can play a strong role in persuading patients to exercise due to e.g. stimulation [20] and self-monitoring [2, 24].

Rheumatoid arthritis (RA) is a long-term autoimmune disorder that belongs to *chronic arthritis* (CA), an umbrella term for inflammatory rheumatic and other musculoskeletal diseases [7]. RA primarily affects joints and potentially other parts of the body. RA is not healable, and the treatment usually focuses on slowing down the progression of the disease. In addition to medication, active physical exercise of the

© Springer Nature Switzerland AG 2019
H. Oinas-Kukkonen et al. (Eds.): PERSUASIVE 2019, LNCS 11433, pp. 177–188, 2019.
https://doi.org/10.1007/978-3-030-17287-9_15

patient forms a key component in the rehabilitation of RA. As with other chronic or long-term conditions, the majority of the rehabilitation work is done at home.

Traditionally, RA patients have been provided with numerous paper-based instructions for conducting the exercises prescribed by the physiotherapist (PT). Adherence to conducting physical exercises is often very low [7]. The paper instructions do not include such motivational features that can easily be designed for the interactive digital rehabilitation programs utilizing persuasive design. *Persuasive technologies* aim at changing people's thinking and behavior; a great amount of *persuasion techniques* exists to support behavior change [e.g. 14]. Persuasive technologies have a great potential to motivate and support rehabilitation activities and behavior change in mobile rehabilitation as they can provide support and motivation on everyday basis [e.g. 7].

The aim of our research is to examine *the user experiences* of a *persuasive, mobile rehabilitation app called 3DFysio*, concentrating on the *app's motivational factors to support the patients' rehabilitation in everyday life*. We present the findings from the long-term (9 months) RA rehabilitation pilot study. To our knowledge, the field is still lacking in-depth long-term studies that explore the user experience (UX) of mobile rehabilitation of RA in everyday context. As Pickrell et al. [15] state, it is important to study patients' motivation towards rehabilitation in home environment, where the face-to-face support from the rehabilitation team is not available. Revenäs et al. [17, 18] emphasize that despite the evidence that exercising brings great health benefits, life-long adherence to health-enhancing physical activity (PA) is a major challenge for people with RA. *This paper deepens the knowledge of the design of mobile rehabilitation apps by (1) describing the long-term UX findings related to the mobile rehabilitation app and (2) discussing the role of several persuasive design elements to support long-term motivation in rehabilitation.*

2   Related Work

2.1   User Experience on Rehabilitation Apps

Grainger et al. [8] have examined the quality of available mobile RA apps. They found in total 14 apps, but noticed a lack of high-quality, attractive, engaging, easy-to-use apps, which would include suitable functions for RA management. Next, we present findings on studies related to the patients' expectations and user needs towards RA apps. Revenäs et al. [17] report results of a study on co-designing a web-based and mobile app concept to support physical activity in individuals with RA. They discovered the importance of two components to the maintenance of physical activity: *(1) a calendar feature for goal setting, planning, and recording of physical activity performance and progress,* and *(2) a small community feature for positive feedback and support from peers*. In their study about patients' attitude towards smartphone apps for RA, Azevedo et al. [4] emphasized the importance of *the self-management aspect* provided by the app. They further report on a cross-sectional study that revealed that the most requested feature in RA smartphone apps was *information in a simple format*. Though these studies provide interesting knowledge about patients' expectations and user needs, they do not explore the actual user experience evoked by the authentic use of any actual app.

Although the UX research of RA apps is still quite rare, many user studies have been conducted for mobile apps to support the rehabilitation process related to other conditions. Anderson et al. [2] examined how mobile health apps could sustain self-care in chronic conditions, especially via *self-monitoring*. The results indicate that these apps could provide a valid tool to practice self-monitoring and thus regain a *sense of autonomy*. The apps' ability to *adapt to changes in users' needs* and to *maintain desired behaviors* were key elements for their long-term use. Whitehead et al. [24] reviewed 9 papers that reported the results of interventions lasting from 6 weeks to one year. They noted that *involving health care professionals in the process*, specifically to monitor symptoms and exchange information with users, promoted *partnership in care*. Synnott et al. [22] introduced the ReApp for rehabilitation of ankle sprains. The app provided a 4-stage rehabilitation program, including text instructions and 21 animated exercises displayed on a mobile device. The users reviewed the app positively after the one-week trial. They emphasized *the importance of the look and feel* and *learning to use* the app. Stütz et al. [21] reported findings on a three-week study of an interactive smartphone app for frozen shoulder. The app proposed an avatar created from motion captured 3D animation. The results suggested that the app supported *correct exercise performance* and *compliance* in home-based physiotherapy. All participants *rotated the avatar performing the exercises* in order to get a better view of the movement for correct execution. Some patients read *the written instructions* and found *the audio instructions* helpful. Motion capture technology has become a more common component in recent telerehabilitation systems. The use of such systems with motion capture and related avatars has proven to increase the intensity of rehabilitation and further enhance user experience [3]. The presented studies show that e.g. self-monitoring, adaptation, easiness-of-use and 3D animations are important features on rehabilitation apps, but the field is missing long-term studies about their long-term UX.

2.2   The Role of Persuasion in Rehabilitation Apps

Persuasive technologies aim at changing people's thinking and behavior. There are several models of persuasive design principles. For example, Oinas-Kukkonen and Harjumaa [14] describe 28 principles for persuasive technologies. Examples of these include *self-monitoring, personalization, reminders, rehearsal, suggestions, rewards* and *social facilitation*. Persuasive techniques have been utilized broadly in technologies related to health and wellbeing [e.g. 12, 7]. Matthews et al. [12] discovered that the persuasive technologies that promote physical activity most commonly utilize *self-monitoring, social comparison* and *suggestion*.

Persuasive techniques have also been explored specifically in the area of rehabilitation technologies. In their stroke rehabilitation study, Pickrell et al. [16], recommend the following design guidelines: *relevant goals, feedback about short-term and long-term improvements, creation of community and collaboration*, and *informing about the purpose of each exercise*. In addition, their earlier work [15] mentions *easy setup* and *personalization* as important aspects for motivational rehabilitation technology.

Lopez-Jaquero et al. [11], present a set of guidelines for designing rehabilitation systems. First, the system should *avoid awareness overload*, i.e. only relevant information for the user and situation should be provided as an overload can cause them to overlook important parts. Second, the technology needs to *provide regular feedback* on the progress and achievements to improve motivation. Third, as a motivational factor, the system should *utilize collaboration* rather than competition between users. In addition to the support given to the patient, she *should be allowed some room* to take personal responsibility on achievements. The patient should also *become aware of the rewards* that she will receive when a goal is met, and the rules for getting the rewards should be clear. The system should *provide right tools and support* for the patient, suitable for her resources and skills. Last, the system needs to help the patients to *feel competent* and able by acknowledging their achievements. They constructed their design guidelines based on several theories of motivation, e.g. Theory of Influence [6]. Theory of Influence lists six principles for motivation. *Reciprocity* means that people feel in debt with someone who gave them something and *scarcity* refers to the preference for the things that are scarce. *Authority* principle states that people respect authority, *consistency* states that it is easier to make commitments if they are voluntary and made public. *Liking* means that it is easier to perform tasks that alike people do, and *consensus* is that it is usual to do what other people do.

According to the review by Geuens et al. [7] the current Chronic Arthritis (CA) apps do not utilize persuasive design properly, and those apps would benefit from adding more social support and rewarding techniques. In our long-term field study, we investigate the rehabilitation experience and motivation that is supported by a mobile app, 3DFysio, which utilizes several persuasive elements including exercise goals and program, 3D avatar and social support. In Discussion, we reflect our findings on the persuasive design principles presented in this section.

3 Methodology

3.1 Description of 3DFysio Applications

3DFysio[1] mobile health application has been co-designed with PTs and their patients. The app has been built as a tool to support physiotherapy treatment, and it works in two interlinked parts: *3DFysio pro*, and *3DFysio patient*. The app includes 3D animations of the physiotherapy exercises that are created using state of the art motion capture studio, where the physiotherapist performs the movements. For this study, 30 suitable exercises were created, e.g. squat and pectoral muscle stretch. In *3DFysio pro*, PTs can generate tailored rehabilitation programs. First, a patient profile is created, the length of the program using the calendar is predefined, and suitable exercises are selected. The number of sets and repetitions is added under every exercise. The PT can also prescribe "a rest day" and add "notes". Once the program is created, it is saved to the database and sent to the patient. The program can be updated at any time by the PT.

---

[1] https://www.kineso.co.uk.

Fig. 1. Screenshots of 3DFysio app showing, from left to right, (1) the exercises prescribed for the patient on the selected day, and (2) the exercise played as a 3D animation with the avatar.

In 3DFysio patient (see Fig. 1) patients can access their personalized rehabilitation program. By pressing, "Start" (Aloita) the patient accesses a 3D animated video of the first exercise. The exercises include instructions. Additional text description can be accessed from the left side of the screen (i). While playing the video, the avatar can be rotated 360 degree as well as zoomed in and out using touchscreen. After the exercise, the patient can check it as "Done". When the set of prescribed exercises are checked, patient is invited to give feedback (*Anna palautetta*) by selecting an emoticon (fairly happy to fairly unhappy) to describe their current state of mind. Patients can also send a message to their PT by using the communication channel (bubble icon on top right corner) if they wish.

3.2 Study Procedure, Data Collecting Methods and Data Analysis

3DFysio app was *trialed for 9 months in a field study*, in collaboration with a RA rehabilitation center in Finland. Long-term field studies about UX are conducted quite rarely due to their challenging nature and resources needed. However, it is essential to explore long-term UX of technologies that aim at motivating and supporting patients in health challenges over time. Short studies for such technologies do not reveal the motivational factors or issues related to the long-term period. Our study was conducted in authentic setting in the context of participants' everyday life. Field studies can reveal important information about the contextual UX factors, which cannot be explored in controlled or laboratory settings [10].

Together with the PTs of the rehabilitation center, the app was integrated to the RA rehabilitation to support the process and replace traditional A4 paper instructions. Initially, 10 patients with RA signed up for the pilot. The first patients started their rehabilitation in summer 2017, and the last ones ended in summer 2018. The statement from the ethical committee of the local hospital was received prior to starting the study. Tablets were given to patients for the duration of the trial.

The UX data related to 3DFysio was collected from the patients through questionnaires and interviews. The rehabilitation model for the RA patient and the research data collection procedure was the following (see Table 1):

Table 1. The rehabilitation model and research activities for the participating patients.

Phase of rehabilitation	Rehabilitation activities	Research activities
First week in rehabilitation center (one week)	Target setting for the rehabilitation, health checkups and hands on guidance related to the disease. Selection of exercises to the rehabilitation program in app	Offering a tablet with 3DFysio app installed, PTs instructions of 3DFysio. Online questionnaire about patients' expectations of 3DFysio
First home period (about 4 months)	3DFysio app in use to support rehabilitation	Online questionnaire about initial UX (after 1 months of use) of 3DFysio
Second week in rehabilitation center (one week)	Updating the rehabilitation program if needed. Health checkups	Online questionnaire and theme interview about the mid-term UX of 3DFysio
Second home period (about 4 months)	3DFysio app use continues	
Third week in rehabilitation center (one week)	Ending the rehabilitation. Health checkups	Online questionnaire and theme interview about the long-term UX of 3DFysio

The *online questionnaires* (4 rounds) included the SUXES UX questionnaire [23] and additional open-ended questions related to the suitability of 3DFysio for rehabilitation. Most of the questions were statements where the response was given on 7-point Likert scale, ranging from 1 (totally disagree) to 7 (totally agree). A link to the online questionnaire was sent by email to participants. Two rounds of *theme interviews* were conducted to get in-depth understanding of the UX and persuasion of 3DFysio. The interviews were conducted by phone and lasted 30–45 min/interview.

The qualitative data from the theme interviews and the open-ended questions of the online questionnaires was analyzed by the means of *qualitative content analysis*. The data was first anonymized, transcribed and then classified in Excel under pre-defined themes and new themes that emerged during the analysis. The analysis resulted in 26 themes, out of which all contained elements related to UX, persuasion and motivation. The quantitative data from the online questionnaires was analyzed by utilizing basic descriptive statistical methods.

3.3   Participants

10 RA patients (F = 6, M = 4) in the RA rehabilitation program took part in the study. Two patients dropped-out during the study. All were Finnish natives living in different parts of Finland. Participation to the study was voluntary. PTs introduced the study to the patients and the volunteers signed a consent form. Their average age was 47 years and their educational and professional backgrounds were diverse. Six participants were on a long-term sick leave or retired. All patients had a RA diagnosis - three had received the diagnosis recently (during last four years), while the oldest diagnosis was done 40 years ago. On average, they had used a PC and mobile phone for 20 years, and a tablet for four years. Seven of them had a smartphone (while 3 having a basic mobile phone) and six owned a tablet.

4   Findings

On this section, we present the user experiences of a mobile rehabilitation app 3DFysio that was studied on a 9-month field study. We focus on the findings related to the motivational and persuasive elements of the app.

4.1   General User Experiences of 3DFysio on Mobile Rehabilitation

3DFysio app was perceived to positively support rehabilitation. In the interviews, all participants described it as easy-to-use, clear, and motivational. Based on the interviews, the most preferred and useful features on the app were, in addition to its *generally motivational nature* (8/8), *the accurate rehabilitation program* (8/8) and *the connection to the physiotherapist* (6/8). The usefulness of the 3D exercise program was emphasized as all 8 participants reported having used it to support their rehabilitation throughout the trial. Most participants were satisfied with the appearance of the avatar and the way it presented the exercises (6/8). At the end of the trial, the participants were ready to recommend 3DFysio for other RA patients and agreed that "3DFysio app acts as a good tool in mobile rehabilitation", as well as that "the app motivates to carry out the exercises in everyday life". They would have been willing to continue to use the app as well (8/8). Out of the SUXES questionnaire statements, the app got highest ratings on its *learnability* (6,7/7) and *usefulness* (6,2/7), and lowest ratings on *error-freeness* (2,7/7) and *effortlessness* (3,7/7). Despite of some technical problems, mainly in signing in, the participants did not report any significant setbacks related to this issue.

4.2   Persuasion Through Accurate and Interactive Rehabilitation
Program Always at Hand

As described already, 3DFysio provided a personalized rehabilitation program for the patient. The physiotherapist modified predefined program based on each patient's rehabilitation situation and personal goals. The program was shown on app's calendar and the patient could view the exercises of each day as 3D animations. The patients considered the personal exercise program, presented by the 3D avatar, as very important (8/8) and motivational (6/8): *"It is important to see how these exercises are done correctly. I assume that I wouldn't do the exercises if I had a paper version. It's very nice to see concretely how they should be done, in 3D. Before, it's been very difficult to know if I am doing the exercises right."* (Female, 38 years).

The rotating and zooming of the 3D animation were used especially at the beginning of the trial for *learning the exercises* (6/8), and later on for *reminding and checking* the correct way of doing the movement (5/8). By rotating and zooming, the patient could see the movement *more accurately*. The *trust towards own performance* increased as the patient learned the correct way to do the exercises. Towards the end of the trial, checking the correct posture was typical (5/8) and four participants reported that they still used the 3D animation to guide them through the exercises every time. The written exercise instructions acted as an additional reassurance for the correct execution of movements, and they were considered important (6/8).

According to the interviews, the avatar was not viewed merely as an anonymous character on the display. Three participants commented that they felt that the *avatar acted as their training partner, accompanying and instructing* them throughout the rehabilitation. Two participants referred to the avatar by the first name of their PT who had performed the movements for the app: *"Sometimes I'd just watch what our (name of the PT) was doing there (in the animation). Like when taking a break between exercises."* (Male, 57 years). For these participants, having the trusted and known PT incorporated into the app via the avatar, and thus indirectly linked to conducting the exercises, provided motivation.

The exercises marked for the specific days by the PT acted as a backbone for exercising (7/8). The *readymade timetable and exercise program* containing the precise number of repetitions were easily available on the application. This decreased the threshold for exercising at home and helped the participants to *establish a routine* (4/8). Two patients used the *marking of conducted exercises* as "done" to support their memory about what exercises they had already done and what was left.

In addition to this, the feedback on conducted exercises could be used for self-monitoring in a form of rehabilitation diary (3/8). The patients could keep track on how they had felt on a particular day, doing a particular exercise. This allowed them to form *an overall picture of their progress*, which was considered motivational.

The app succeeded to sustain patients' motivation towards rehabilitation even in the long-term. 5/8 participants reported that they *experienced positive results* in their physical condition during the rehabilitation, i.e. they noticed improvements in their physical capability. They could *concretely feel the benefits* of conducting the exercises, and that acted as a motivational factor to continue to use the app and maintain the exercise routine. Thus, the app seemed to have *a strong role in establishing a routine* for exercising and taking care of oneself – all participants reported positive effects on forming a routine (8/8). 3/8 patients perceived the use of the app and doing the exercises as being for their own benefit, "like putting money in the bank".

4.3   Persuasion Through the Trusted Connection Between the Patient and Physiotherapist

The other significant motivational factor on the app was *the direct connection* between the patient and her *personal* physiotherapist (6/8). In practice, the connection was supported by three different app features: the communication channel, patients' feedback about the exercises and checking the exercises as "done". The interview data confirmed that by using these features of the app, a sort of *an unspoken agreement* formed between the patient and the physiotherapist: the physiotherapist *followed* the patient's situation (conducting the exercises, proceeding with the rehabilitation) and was *available to the patient*, while the patient *conducted her exercises, gave feedback* on them, and *checked them as done*. Three patients reported feeling reassured by the knowledge that the PT would actually receive and read their feedback. This type of social support, where the PT was available and shared the experience with the patient would not have been easily established without the interactive app. However, an important aspect on forming the connection was *getting to know the PT in real life* – this took place in the first rehabilitation center week. Knowing the therapist in real life increased trust, further maintained by the use of the app. According to the participants, another important aspect was that the physiotherapist was *a real person*, not for example a chatbot. Communication with a human physiotherapist increased the *trust*, perception of *being really cared by someone*, and that someone was interested in the patient's rehabilitation.

The connection between the PT and the patient had concrete implications on patient behavior. For example, four participants reported that even if they did not feel like doing their exercises, they nonetheless did because of the obligation they felt. The PT contributed her time and expertise and the participants, in return, provided their best effort, resulting *a fair trade-off situation*. Six patients commented on the importance of *the feedback from PT*. The nature of feedback was the key. It needed to be context-sensitive, to address the patient's current concerns. This was best established by direct messaging between the PT and the patient. Consequently, *the communication channel* was the most positively perceived feature out of the above-mentioned three features of connection (6/8). All patients used the communication channel but the number of messages varied a lot between them (range: 3–32 during the trial). All patients appreciated the *possibility to be in touch with a professional physiotherapist*, who was familiar with their personal situation. The communication channel was mainly used for asking advice, e.g. in case of pain caused by the exercises. In addition, it was used for more general interaction, e.g. discussing everyday challenges possibly affecting the patient's ability to exercise. Two patients were especially active in the use of the channel. They discussed how the rehabilitation was going and sought support. The incorporation of communication into the app lowered the threshold for patients to utilize it as part of the rehabilitation. Even the patients who did not use the communication channel actively perceived its high value – the knowledge that a familiar physiotherapist was following in the background was sometimes enough: *"The communication channel is nice. You know that you can send a message if... even if you never did. You have the permission to do that. There's a feeling of safety in having someone in the background. Your physiotherapist hasn't forgotten you."* (Female, 55 years).

5   Discussion and Conclusion

Pickrell et al. [15] notify the need for the support of the rehabilitation team to be brought at home. Based on our UX research findings, it seems that 3DFysio, a persuasive mobile rehabilitation app, managed to respond to that need well. During the 9-month field study with 10 participants (8 in the end as 2 dropped out) the 3DFysio app provided support utilizing several persuasive techniques: personalized exercise program and goals, 3D avatar for movements' accuracy, as well as social connection between the patient and PT. During the long rehabilitation period, the patients seemed to **build a relationship with the app**, which also included the knowledge of the real life PT support being available through the app, as well as the noticeable improvements on their physical condition during the rehabilitation. Initially, the app acted as an instructor for the patients (exercise program on calendar, regular viewing of 3D movements for learning them, asking for help if needed) while later it became to be seen more as a companion, being available when needed. 3DFysio seems to motivate through **a combination of persuasive elements on the app and real life,** similarly to what was already discussed by Ahtinen et al. [1]: *"The combination of the digital and non-digital persuasion may provide the most powerful setting towards the long-term intrinsic motivation"* (p. 9). Furthermore, **autonomy** [19] was a successful persuasive factor in the app. Lopez-Jaquero et al. [11] point the importance of giving the patients enough room to be responsible for their achievements to enable them to feel competent. 3DFysio seemed to provide enough support to keep up motivation without being too restrictive. As pointed out by the persuasive design guidelines [11], **the system should avoid awareness overload.** 3DFysio's amount of features and requested tasks was moderate, which made it easy to learn and manage, thus proving the user the experience of **being in control**, thereby increasing the usage motivation. The rehabilitation program created by the PT for the patient covered three more persuasive design principles: **goal setting, personalization** and **rehearsal** [e.g. 14–16]. The exercise goals of 3DFysio were challenging enough and suitable for each patient [16], and the personalized instructions were further considered as an important motivational factor [16]. 3D avatar acted as a motivational and accurate character for rehearsal of movements at home [14, 21]. 3DFysio did not provide any digital **rewards**, which is one of the basic persuasive design principles [e.g. 14]. Instead, it provided the possibility to get personal **feedback and praise** from the PT through the communication channel, which was perceived to be rewarding and motivational. In addition, the strong rewarding factor of 3DFysio was **the concrete results gained** by using it and through that, **the establishment of an exercise routine**. Most patients experienced improvements in their physical condition. Furthermore, 3DFysio provided **a collaboration space** for the patient and PT. According to Cialdini [6] **reciprocity** means that people feel to be in debt with someone who gave them something. This was visible in the use of 3DFysio – both the patient and PT participated to the rehabilitation process in a **collaborative** [11] way. With 3DFysio, **social support**, which is often missing from Chronic Arthritis apps [7], was provided for the patients, and even the knowledge of the availability of the trusted PT acted as a strong motivational factor. Some patients even regarded the avatar as their motivational **training partner**.

To conclude, as also discussed previously [1], **not all persuasion needs to be designed digitally in the app, but the best way to persuade is the combination of digital and real world persuasion.** Therefore, the app works best as a tool to support the PTs work, not as a replacement. The rehabilitation **app needs to include persuasive design elements** to support motivation towards the rehabilitation process, but at the same time, it can act **as a mediator of the real life persuasion,** such as support from the PT and recognizing the improvements in one's condition. Our study has limitations, which leave room for future research. The mostly qualitative nature of the study produced insights and knowledge on the area of persuasive rehabilitation apps design. However, more research with larger sample is needed to investigate the evidence-based effectiveness of the above described persuasive principles on mobile rehabilitation. It would also be beneficial to study the motivational nature of the application with patients that would belong to younger or higher age groups. This paper focuses on patients' perspective – in the future work we will investigate also the physiotherapists' viewpoint on persuasive rehabilitation apps.

Acknowledgments. This study was conducted as part of the 3DFysio project in a larger project about the development of telerehabilitation (Etäkuntoutus-hanke) financed by Kela, The Social Insurance Institution of Finland. We would like to express our gratitude to Kela, the project partners and the study participants.

References

1. Ahtinen, A., Andrejeff, E., Harris, C., Väänänen, K.: Let's walk at work: persuasion through the brainwolk walking meeting app. In: Proceedings of the 21st International Academic Mindtrek Conference, pp. 73–82. ACM (2017)
2. Anderson, K., Burford, O., Emmerton, L.: Mobile health apps to facilitate self-care: a qualitative study of user experiences. PLoS One 11(5), e0156164 (2016)
3. Antón, D., Berges, I., Bermúdez, J., Goñi, A., Illarramendi, A.: Knowledge-based telerehabilitation monitoring. In: Chbeir, R., Manolopoulos, Y., Maglogiannis, I., Alhajj, R. (eds.) AIAI 2015. IAICT, vol. 458, pp. 237–249. Springer, Cham (2015). https://doi.org/10.1007/978-3-319-23868-5_17
4. Azevedo, R., Bernardes, M., Fonseca, J., et al.: Smartphone application for rheumatoid arthritis self-management: cross-sectional study revealed the usefulness, willingness to use and patients' needs. Rheumatol. Int. 35(10), 1675–1685 (2015)
5. Botsis, T., Demiris, G., Pedersen, S., Hartvigsen, G.: Home telecare technologies for the elderly. J. Telemed. Telecare 14(7), 333–337 (2008)
6. Cialdini, R.B.: Harnessing the science of persuasion. Harvard Bus. Rev. 79(9), 72–81 (2001)
7. Geuens, J., Swinnen, T.W., Westhovens, R., de Vlam, K., Geurts, L., Vanden Abeele, V.: A review of persuasive principles in mobile apps for chronic arthritis patients: opportunities for improvement. JMIR mHealth uHealth 4(4), e118 (2016)
8. Grainger, R., Townsley, H., White, B., Langlotz, T., Taylor, W.J.: Apps for people with rheumatoid arthritis to monitor their disease activity: a review of apps for best practice and quality. JMIR mHealth uHealth 5(2), e7 (2017)
9. Hailey, D., Roine, R., Ohinmaa, A., Dennett, L.: Evidence on the effectiveness of telerehabilitation applications. Institute of Health Economics and Finnish Office for Health Technology Assessment, Edmonton and Helsinki, Canada (2010)

10. Klasnja, P., Consolvo, S., Pratt, W.: How to evaluate technologies for health behavior change in HCI research. In: Proceedings of the SIGCHI Conference on Human Factors in Computing Systems, pp. 3063–3072. ACM, May 2011
11. López-Jaquero, V., Montero, F., Teruel, M.A.: Influence awareness: considering motivation in computer-assisted rehabilitation. J. Ambient Intell. Humaniz. Comput. 1–13 (2017)
12. Matthews, J., Win, K.T., Oinas-Kukkonen, H., Freeman, M.: Persuasive technology in mobile applications promoting physical activity: a systematic review. J. Med. Syst. 40(3), 72 (2016)
13. Minet, L.R., Hansen, L.W., Pedersen, C.D., et al.: Early telemedicine training and counselling after hospitalization in patients with severe chronic obstructive pulmonary disease: a feasibility study. BMC Med. Inform. Decis. Making 15(1), 3 (2015)
14. Oinas-Kukkonen, H., Harjumaa, M.: Persuasive systems design: key issues, process model, and system features. Commun. Assoc. Inf. Syst. 24(28), 484–501 (2009)
15. Pickrell, M., Bongers, B., van den Hoven, E.: Understanding persuasion and motivation in interactive stroke rehabilitation. In: MacTavish, T., Basapur, S. (eds.) Persuasive Technology. LNCS, vol. 9072, pp. 15–26. Springer, Cham (2015). https://doi.org/10.1007/978-3-319-20306-5_2
16. Pickrell, M., Bongers, B., van den Hoven, E.: Understanding changes in the motivation of stroke patients undergoing rehabilitation in hospital. In: Meschtscherjakov, A., De Ruyter, B., Fuchsberger, V., Murer, M., Tscheligi, M. (eds.) International Conference on Persuasive Technology. LNCS, vol. 9638, pp. 251–262. Springer, Cham (2016). https://doi.org/10.1007/978-3-319-31510-2_22
17. Revenäs, Å., Opava, C.H., Martin, C., et al.: Development of a web-based and mobile app to support physical activity in individuals with rheumatoid arthritis: results from the second step of a co-design process. JMIR Res. Protoc. 4(1), e22 (2015)
18. Revenäs, Å., Opava, C.H., Ahlén, H., et al.: Mobile internet service for self-management of physical activity in people with rheumatoid arthritis: evaluation of a test version. RMD Open 2, e000214 (2016)
19. Ryan, R.M., Deci, E.L.: Self-determination theory and the facilitation of intrinsic motivation, social development, and well-being. Am. Psychol. 55(1), 68 (2000)
20. Smith, S.T., Schoene, D.: The use of exercise-based videogames for training and rehabilitation of physical function in older adults: current practice and guidelines for future research. Aging Health 8(3), 243–252 (2012)
21. Stütz, T., Domhardt, M., Emsenhuber, G., et al.: An interactive 3D health app with multimodal information representation for frozen shoulder: co-creation and evaluation with patients. In: Proceedings of the 19th International Conference on Human-Computer Interaction with Mobile Devices and Services, p. 3. ACM, September 2017
22. Synnott, J., et al.: ReApp – a mobile app for the rehabilitation of Ankle sprains. In: Bravo, J., Hervás, R., Villarreal, V. (eds.) AmIHEALTH 2015. LNCS, vol. 9456, pp. 61–67. Springer, Cham (2015). https://doi.org/10.1007/978-3-319-26508-7_6
23. Turunen, M., Hakulinen, J., Melto, A., et al.: SUXES – user experience evaluation method for spoken and multimodal interaction. In Proceedings of the 10th Annual Conference of the International Speech Communication Association (Interspeech), pp. 2567–2570 (2009)
24. Whitehead, L., Seaton, P.: The effectiveness of self-management mobile phone and tablet apps in long-term condition management: a systematic review. J. Med. Internet Res. 18(5), e97 (2016)

Evaluation of Breastfeeding Mobile Health Applications Based on the Persuasive System Design Model

Shahla Meedya[1(✉)], Muhamad Kashif Sheikh[1,2], Khin Than Win[1],
and Elizabeth Halcomb[1]

[1] University of Wollongong, Wollongong, NSW 2522, Australia
smeedya@uow.edu.au
[2] Gippsland Primary Health Network, Traralgon, VIC 3844, Australia

Abstract. The rapid and ongoing growth in information technology has created many applications for health and wellbeing, including breastfeeding. However, due to a lack of rigorous evaluation of these applications, midwives and other health professionals are unable to recommend any specific breastfeeding application in supporting women towards long-term breastfeeding as a global challenge. Only half of women in developed countries continue any form of breastfeeding for six months. The aim of this study was to evaluate the existing breastfeeding applications based on the Persuasive System Design model. An online search was conducted of the Apple Store in May 2017. The search strategy included the following keywords: breastfeeding, lactation and breast milk. After being checked against the inclusion criteria, each application was assessed based on the four Persuasive System Design Principles. Data from each application was then compared for each element of the design model. Eleven applications met the inclusion criteria and were included in the review. Primary task support and system credibility support principles were addressed at acceptable level in all of the included apps. However, dialogue support and social support principles and their features like praise, reward and social networking were not identified in many of the applications. This review demonstrates the lack of dialogue support and social support principles that could augment human to computer dialogue. There is a need for designing a breastfeeding app that can persuade women to engage and continue breastfeeding based on a full Persuasive System Design model, thus promoting long term breastfeeding.

Keywords: Breastfeeding · Persuasive Systems Design · Evaluation

1 Introduction

The rapid and ongoing growth in mobile health applications is creating new opportunities to assist people to change their behavior [1]. Concurrently, it has created some concerns for midwives and other health care professionals about the quality of the applications and the information provided to women and their families on this platform. A mobile health application (mHealth app) refers to a standalone software application

© Springer Nature Switzerland AG 2019
H. Oinas-Kukkonen et al. (Eds.): PERSUASIVE 2019, LNCS 11433, pp. 189–201, 2019.
https://doi.org/10.1007/978-3-030-17287-9_16

that can deliver healthcare or health related services through the use of portable devices like smartphones and tablets [2]. Over 97,000 mHealth apps including breastfeeding applications are available to smartphone users [3]. By 2020, the number of smartphone users will reach 2.87 billion [4] and more than 1000 mHealth apps will be created every month [3]. Women who are pregnant for the first time seek information related to the pregnancy, delivery, health conditions, and breastfeeding [5]. Breastfeeding is a long-term social behavior and can be influenced by women's intention, confidence and social support [6]. These factors can potentially be influenced by the information that women and support people receive from health care providers and social media through online networks and the internet [7, 8]. However, for successful long-term breastfeeding, women need education and support that can start from early pregnancy and continue after birth [9]. Therefore, the best breastfeeding apps would be the ones that have a reliable source of information with persuasive features in the design where a pregnant woman could develop personal connections with her device and connect to a larger social support system anytime that she requires. The Persuasive system design model that was developed by Oinas-Kukkonen and Harjumaa in 2009 provides the best evidence based, structured and scientific framework to evaluate breastfeeding apps against their credibility and persuasive system features where human to human interaction has been replaced with a computer to human interaction [10]. Persuasive systems are computerized software or information systems that have been designed to reinforce, modify or form attitudes and/or behaviors without using coercion or dishonesty [10]. This model has demonstrated effective results to motivate and persuade people to engage in physical activities [11–13]; being compliant in metabolic syndrome management [14], and adherence to medical regimes [15] and treatment plans [16]. Moreover, information, motivation, and behavior skill model has been adopted in health intervention studies and it has been beneficial in health behavior change [17–20]. The model indicated that information and motivation have direct effect on health behavior. Information plays a crucial role and is the prerequisite for the required health behavior [18]. Therefore, relevant knowledge is a prerequisite for motivation to change behavior [21]. Therefore, a breastfeeding application must include important breastfeeding information and motivational perspectives which consumers can adapt to achieve their targeted behavior by understanding the importance of adopting the behavior and being prepared for any unexpected event. In this study, the Persuasive Systems Design model as a suitable and evidence based framework was used to evaluate the breastfeeding applications and identify any persuasive features that have been incorporated into the applications to persuade women to initiate and continue breastfeeding long-term.

2 Method

In May 2017, an online search on iPhone (App Store) was conducted using the following key terms: breastfeeding, lactation, and breast milk. Only the apps that were available in English language, targeted on breastfeeding education, and able to be installed on iOS version 9.3.5 were included in the study. Any apps that were: (a) in a language other than English; (b) feeding trackers; (c) baby's activity trackers for food, sleep, diaper changes, growth measurements and medical appointments; (d) games;

(e) targeted towards health professionals; and (f) music, stickers and breastfeeding related products, pregnancy and social apps were excluded. Feeding trackers were excluded as they are against WHO's breastfeeding recommendation where women are encouraged to focus on the baby's demand feeding without any time restraints or limitations on the frequency of feed [22].

Only free apps were included and evaluated in this study as these are the apps that would reach to all the consumers. The second author (MKS) first downloaded and installed all the apps and they were reviewed by the other two authors (KTW, and SM) who had extensive experience in this research field. The apps were installed and evaluated from May to July to ensure features and communications presented from these apps. The evaluators were from both the medical field and persuasive technology field. Two evaluators (MKS, KTW) had extensive experience in health information technology, medicine (medical doctors) and persuasive technology and one evaluator (SM) had significant clinical and academic background on breastfeeding. The included apps were mapped out to generate a preliminary coding system to analyze the content and main purpose of the eligible apps. The general information was extracted based on the app category, year of release, year of update, affiliation (commercial, non-profit, tertiary institute, or private health professional company), type of information (benefits of breastfeeding and tips for common breastfeeding problems), and use of multimedia in delivering the content and multilingual support. Then each app was assessed against four main principles in the PSD model: primary task support, dialogue support, credibility support and social support. Considering that each principle has different forms of features, each app was evaluated based on the design features. Any kind of disagreement was discussed in a face to face meeting to clarify the specific features of the PSD model. In some cases the coding system for the features was revised to minimize any overlapping features.

3   Results

The search yielded 400 applications (Fig. 1). After review of title and basic information, 342 apps were excluded as they did not meet the inclusion criteria. A further 19 applications were identified as duplicate and removed. The final 39 applications were downloaded for full review. Twenty eight of these applications were excluded as they did not meet the inclusion criteria. The final review included 11 applications (2.75% of total 400 apps) in the study.

All the apps were assessed for general features including app category, last update, link to healthcare professional, using multimedia in delivering the content, tips for common breastfeeding issues, sponsorship, and multilingual support. Seven out of 11 provided some links for the health professionals or breastfeeding support services. Ten out of 11 apps used multimedia features like text, images, audio and video media to deliver the content. All the apps provided breastfeeding tips and information for common breastfeeding issues. In terms of sponsorship, five apps were sponsored by commercial resource and the rest were sponsored either by governmental or non-governmental organizations. There was only one app that provided multilingual support (Info for Nursing mum) (Table 1).

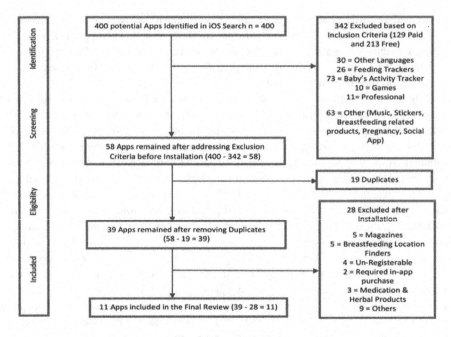

Fig. 1. Search results

The included breastfeeding applications were analyzed based on the Persuasive Systems Design model. Table 2 provides a summary of the evaluation of included applications against the Persuasive System Design principles and their specific features. Whilst the crossed boxes indicate whether the feature was observed, the quantity of the features is not reflected in the table.

3.1 Primary Task Support

All included applications used primary task support principle. The main features were on: (a) reducing effort needed in searching breastfeeding information by using text, images, audio and videos (reduction, n = 11), (b) allowing color scheme selection or uploading personal images and personal data input (personalization, n = 4); (c) tracking nursing/feeding behavior, diaper change (self-monitoring, n = 5); and (d) providing information for cause & effect such as "How to increase milk supply?" (simulation, n = 10). For instance, WebMD Baby application used video illustration to represent issues faced during breastfeeding. However, the "Info for Nursing Mum" application provided too many audio options which can confuse the user and can detract them from finding a quick answer. The app provided a lot of information, thus users need to know which information would be relevant to them. Tailoring feature was observed in two apps where there was a specific section for dads group and the breastfeeding content was in Chinese language as well as English language. Other features like tunneling and rehearsal were not found in any of the included breastfeeding applications (Table 3).

Table 1. General Information

App name	App category	Last update	App website	Link to health care professional	Sponsorship
1. My Medela Breastfeeding Companion	Health & Fitness	4 Apr 2017	https://appsto.re/au/6dNm2.i	Lactation consultants	Commercial organisation (Medela Store)
2. Glow Baby	Medical	13 Mar 2017	https://appsto.re/au/WXgnab.i	Nil	Commercial organisation (Hard Valuable Fun company)
3. Guide to Breastfeeding	Reference	29 Jan 2017	https://appsto.re/au/FLB5_.i	Lactation consultants & breastfeeding clinic	Individual organisation
4. WebMD Baby	Health & Fitness	21 Dec 2016	https://appsto.re/au/dk9lD.i	Nil	Commercial organisation (Multiple private Sponsorships)
5. Feed Safe	Health & Fitness	12 Apr 2016	https://appsto.re/au/qz9OV.i	Australian Breastfeeding Association & Alcohol and Drug Information Service	None profit organisation (Australiana Breastfeeding Association and Curtin University)
6. Breastfeeding Helper	Reference	27 Jan 2016	https://appsto.re/au/kcskab.i	Nil	Individual organisation
7. WYNI Breastfeeding Information	Health & Fitness	24 Oct 2015	https://appsto.re/au/dne74.i	Telehealth Ontario Breastfeeding Support	None profit organisation (Health Nexus)
8. Info for Nursing Mum	Education	29 Mar 2016	https://appsto.re/au/NgXs9.i	Hong Kong Department of Health	Governmental organisation (Family Health Service, Department of Health)
9. Breast Start	Health & Fitness	28 Aug 2015	https://appsto.re/au/KltAF.i	National Health Service of the united Kingdome	Governmental organisation (Wirral Community NHS Trust)
10. Flourish	Health & Fitness	25 Aug 2015	https://appsto.re/au/wvbB0.i	Nil	Commercial organisation (Summa Foundation Circle)
11. NSH Baby Bump*	Health & Fitness	-	https://appsto.re/au/qM6d7.i	North Side Hospital	Commercial organisation (North Side Hospital)

*The following apps used the same prototype from the same vendor: Melrose Wakefield Baby Bundle, Baby Beginning, CWH Baby, SFMC 4 Moms, NHCL Arrivals, Sharp Baby, Childbirth101, Memorial Mommy, NCH Baby, LVHN Baby, Aurora Baby

Table 2. Persuasive System Design features observed in the evaluated mobile applications

APP NAME	PRIMARY TASK SUPPORT							DIALOGUE SUPPORT							CREDIBILITY SUPPORT							SOCIAL SUPPORT						
	REDUCTION	TUNNELLING	TAILORING	PERSONALIZATION	SELF MONITORING	SIMULATION	REHEARSAL	PRAISE	REWARDS	REMINDERS	SUGGESTION	SIMILARITY	LIKING	SOCIAL ROLE	TRUSTWORTHINESS	EXPERTISE	SURFACE CREDIBILITY	REAL WORLD FEEL	AUTHORITY	THIRD PARTY ENDORSEMENT	VERIFIABILITY	SOCIAL LEARNING	SOCIAL COMPARISON	NORMATIVE INFLUENCE	SOCIAL FACILITATION	COOPERATION	COMPETITION	RECOGNITION
My Medela Breastfeeding Companion	x			x	x	x					x					x	x	x	x		x							
Glow Baby	x			x	x	x					x					x	x	x	x		x	x	x	x				
Guide to Breastfeeding	x					x					x	x				x	x	x	x		x	x						
WebMD Baby	x		x	x	x	x					x	x	x			x	x	x	x		x			x			x	
Feed Safe	x	x									x	x	x		x	x	x	x	x		x						x	
Breastfeeding Helper	x					x					x		x		x	x		x	x		x	x						
WYNI Breastfeeding Information	x			x	x						x				x	x	x	x	x		x			x			x	
Info for Nursing Mum	x					x					x	x			x	x	x	x	x		x	x		x			x	
Breast Start	x					x						x	x		x	x	x	x	x		x						x	
Flourish	x					x						x	x		x				x		x							
NSH Baby Bump	x			x	x	x		x		x	x	x				x	x	x	x		x	x		x				

Table 3. Primary Task Support features

Feature	Example used in Apps
Reduction (n = 11)	Reduced effort in searching for breastfeeding information using text, images, audio and video content focused on breastfeeding. For example simple images of breastfeeding positions were used in "Guide to Breastfeeding" app; audio illustration was used in "Info for Nursing Mum" app, and video illustration was used in "WebMD Baby in providing the information on breastfeeding problems
Tunnelling (n = 0)	– Nil
Tailoring (n = 2)	– Tailored information based on the gender of the parents and language of the users. For example, WebMD Baby application tailored the breastfeeding information under Just for Moms and Just for Dads sections. Info for Nursing mum application included the breastfeeding content in Chinese language as well as English language
Personalisation (n = 4)	– Allowed different color scheme selection, uploading personal images & personal data input "WebMD Baby", "Glow Baby", "MyMedela" & "NSH Baby Bump" apps
Self-Monitoring (n = 5)	– Tracked nursing, feeding behaviour & diaper change in "WebMD Baby", "Glow Baby", "MyMedela", "WYNI Breastfeeding Information" & "NSH Baby Bump" applications
Simulation (n = 10)	– Provided information for cause & effect e.g. How to increase milk supply in "Guide to Breastfeeding" application
Rehearsal (n = 0)	– Nil

3.2   Dialogue Support

Half of the suggested features for dialogue support were more or less neglected by the app designers. For example, no applications included any feature for praise, reward and social role. The main strategies were: (a) sending text messages or alarms as reminders for appointments/tasks (reminders, n = 1); (b) providing information on increasing milk supply or diet during breastfeeding (suggestions, n = 9); (c) reflecting breast-feeding information available on the app (similarity, n = 6); and (d) using multimedia content that appeals to the app user (linking, n = 6) (Table 4).

Table 4. Dialogue Support features and examples

Feature	Example used in Apps
Praise (n = 0)	Nil
Reward (n = 0)	Nil
Reminders (n = 1)	– Reminder for the suggestions in "NSH Baby Bump" app only
Suggestion (n = 9)	– Provided information on Healthy eating for pregnant & Lactating mothers in "Info for Nursing Mum" app
Similarity (n = 6)	– User can reflect from breastfeeding information available on the app e.g. videos on breastfeeding in "Info for Nursing Mum", WebMD Baby", "NSH Baby Bump" apps where the women can feel similarities in their breastfeeding
Liking (n = 6)	– Good look and feel of the app interface, user friendliness & multimedia content e.g. High-quality videos and images in "WebMD Baby" & "NSH Baby Bump" app
Social role (n = 0)	Nil

3.3   System Credibility Support

All included applications demonstrated some level of system credibility to the users. The app designers used women's trusted sources like the Australian Breastfeeding Association; and pediatric or child and family experts' opinions. Trustworthiness of apps that were sponsored by a commercial or individual organization like Medela was questionable. It can be seen that some of the apps are from trustworthy sources like government organization or endorsed by Health on the Net Foundation and URAC (Utilization Review Accreditation Commission (Table 5).

Table 5. System Credibility Support features and examples

Feature	Example used in Apps
Trustworthiness (n = 5)	Information provided by trusted sources for example the Australian Breastfeeding Association & Curtin University is the "Feed Safe" app
Expertise (n = 11)	Having videos & information provided by experts in the field for example, Dr Jack Newman, a Physician & Rose Le Blanc, an international board-certified lactation consultant are behind the "Guide to Breastfeeding" app, information provided by trusted sources for example the Australian Breastfeeding Association & Curtin University is behind the "Feed Safe" app and "Breast Start" by NHS, UK
Surface Credibility (n = 9)	Incorporation of a pleasant color theme, usage, and font size in "WebMD Baby" & "WYNI Breastfeeding" apps among others
Real World Feel (n = 10)	Providing information about the organization behind the app including email addresses, web address, phone numbers etc. in all apps except "Flourish" app
Authority (n = 11)	Quoting an authority such as the department of health, child and family health centers or healthcare professionals e.g. information provided in "Info for Nursing Mum" is by Family Health Service, Department of Health, Hong Kong Special Administrative Region Government (HKSARG), Dr Jack Newman, a Physician & Rose Le Blanc, an International Board-Certified Lactation Consultant are behind the "Guide to Breastfeeding" app, the Australian Breastfeeding Association & Curtin University are behind the "Feed Safe" app and "Breast Start" app is by NHS, UK
Third Party Endorsements (n = 0)	Nil
Verifiability (n = 11)	Information & video illustrations by health professionals with their names and titles & references to other sources in content e.g. "WebMD Baby", "Guide to Breastfeeding", "Info for Nursing Mum" apps among others

3.4 Social Support

The social support principle was underdeveloped in many of the applications. None of the apps used any feature for social facilitation, competition and recognition features. However, social learning (n = 5), normative influence (n = 6) and cooperation features (n = 5) were provided by showing social meeting group timetables, contact information and location maps. Only one application used social comparison by comparing other women's breastfeeding situations with other app users through linking the women to online breastfeeding communities through blogs, forums and Facebook (Table 6).

Table 6. Social Support features and examples

Feature	Example used in apps
Social Learning (n = 5)	– Breastfeeding Peer Support Scheme in "Info for Nursing Mum" app
Social Comparison (n = 1)	– Using online breastfeeding communities forums in "Glow Baby" app
Normative Influence (n = 6)	– Using online breastfeeding communities in "Glow Baby" app and information on social meeting groups with times, days and location addressed in "Breast Start" app
Social facilitation (n = 0)	– Nil
Co-operation (n = 5)	– Increased communication among breastfeeding women by using online breastfeeding communities in "Glow Baby" app, providing Support Group Contact information and location including Maps in "Breast Start" app
Competition (n = 0)	– Nil
Recognition (n = 0)	– Nil

4 Discussion

This study is the first review that evaluated the mHealth breastfeeding applications based on the Persuasive System Design model [10]. The Persuasive System Design model was an acceptable guide to evaluate the features of the breastfeeding applications because breastfeeding is a long-term health behavior and needs a persuasive system to engage the women easily with their personal devices where they have access to reliable information accompanied with social and professional support. Evidence demonstrated that other mHealth applications with Persuasive System Design model have positive clinical outcomes in long-term health behavior issues such as managing diabetes [16, 23], having a healthy diet, encouraging physical activity, and increasing a compliance rate in taking medication [12, 15].

This review demonstrates that there were only a few professional breastfeeding applications available that provided evidence based information. This result is aligned with a systematic review of 600 websites and 2884 apps on infant feeding where the authors found only two university based apps in iOS and Google play for android phones [24]. Evaluation of the applications against PSD demonstrated that WebMD Baby app had comprehensive information that was accredited by a credible organization. However, the information was available in 32 different screens which could have confused the users. The reduction feature in the primary task support principle was the main feature in all of the applications. For example many of the applications used multimedia illustrations to reduce the effort of the users to reach the information. Tunneling, tailoring and rehearsal were found to be under developed among the applications. These three features seem to be neglected in other mHealth applications [1]. This could be due to technical issues or lack of attention of the designers into the need of different groups of people like young mothers or women from diverse cultural and ethnical backgrounds.

Praise, reward, reminder, and social support features are important features in augmenting human to computer dialogue [1]. However, they were not observed in many of the applications. This could be the shortcoming in being able to maintain the users' involvement in interacting with their devices. Once the user loses interest in using the application, the target behavior may not be achieved [8].. Considering that people perceive their interaction with their devices as a social interaction [1], there is a need to improve these features.

Social support features were not observed in many of the selected breastfeeding applications. Only one of the applications used blogs, forums and groups where the application had multiple commercial sponsors. Although, the results are comparable to other studies such as persuasive lifestyle modification in physical activity and other mHealth applications [1, 13, 23], this is an important issue in any breastfeeding app; because social support is a major influencing factor for breastfeeding women. Systematic reviews of effective interventions on breastfeeding outcomes have demonstrated the significant impact of support on breastfeeding initiation and duration [9]. The results of a study on evaluating the role of app users, demonstrated that when the users interact in social networking, they engaged more in the discussion forums, read blogs and watch multimedia which can improve self-monitoring and achieving target behavior [25].

Overall, this review revealed that despite many other studies in different specialties [2, 26–29], the information in the selected breastfeeding applications (n = 11) showed some level of system credibility to the users. For instance, the applications earned the users' trust by using well-known brands and logos. They demonstrated reliability by using reliable information from health professionals and personalized content [30]. However, the underlying issue is that many of the applications were sponsored by different commercial organizations and there was no evidence of external peer review or support from regulatory bodies to ensure evidence base and quality of the applications. Therefore, the applications may be trusted by the users but they may not be reliable at all. That could also be reflected with the Health on the Net foundation code of conduct for quality of health information as online health information provided should be trusted and not biased [25]. Considering that credibility of information has the potential to critically affect health outcomes for many users [31, 32], there is a need for credible regulatory bodies to review the applications and certify the products for the safety of the users for mHealth applications. This study is not the first to highlight the lack of regulatory system to assist the end users to identify the best available mHealth applications for them [2, 26–29].

The Persuasive System Design model can potentially increase the quality check of the breastfeeding applications, because one of the major principles of the Persuasive System Design model is system credibility. However, due to the lack of attention to the dialogue support and social support systems in designing the breastfeeding app, it is very hard to recommend any app that could have a potential impact on initiation and continuation of breastfeeding. Women need to make informed decisions for themselves and their babies' health and wellbeing. Having a trusted resource would empower women to make their own choices in breastfeeding. However, none of the included apps in this study were identified as a gold standard breastfeeding app that could support women who intend to breastfeed.

A notable limitation of this review was the conduct of the search in the Apple app store with free downloads and only in the English language which could impact the results. Therefore the results of this study cannot be generalized to paid applications, other platforms and languages. One reason for limiting the search was that the free apps are within the reach of more consumers. Additionally, downloading all the apps required time and payment for installation which was out of scope of this unfunded study. Regardless of the limitations, we argue that this study is valuable for midwives and health professionals because it provides evidence based methodology to evaluate, analyze and criticize breastfeeding or any other mHealth application that aims to initiate, alter or reinforce health behavior through persuasive technology. This study introduces a new perspective for clinicians to consider when they evaluate and design mHealth applications for women and children, specifically on breastfeeding.

5   Conclusion

This review demonstrates the use of some features from the Persuasive System Design model in the included breastfeeding apps. However, dialogue support and social support principles and their features like praise, reward and social networking that could augment human to computer dialogue were missing in many of the applications. The Persuasive System Design model can be a valuable reference for health professionals, app designers, and policy makers to evaluate the available breastfeeding applications to support women in initiating and continuing breastfeeding. However, further studies are required to develop breastfeeding applications based on the Persuasive System Design model and evaluate the effectiveness of them among the women who choose to use the application.

References

1. Langrial, S., Lehto, T., Oinas-Kukkonen, H., Harjumaa, M., Karrippnen, P.: Native mobile applications for personal wellbeing: a persuasive system design evaluation. In: Pacific Asia Conference on Information Systems (2012)
2. Mobasheri, M.H., Johnston, M., King, D., Leff, D., Thiruchelvam, P., Darzi, A.: Smartphone breast applications–what's the evidence? Breast **23**, 683–689 (2014)
3. Becker, S., Miron Shatz, T., Schumacher, N., Krocza, J., Diamantidis, C., Albrecht, U.-V.: mHealth: experiences, possibilities, and perspectives. JMIR mHealth uHealth **2** (2014)
4. https://www.statista.com/statistics/330695/number-of-smartphone-users-worldwide/
5. García-Gómez, J.M., De La Torre-Díez, I., Vicente, J., Robles, M., López-Coronado, M., Rodrigues, J.J.: Analysis of mobile health applications for a broad spectrum of consumers: a user experience approach. Health Inform. J. **20**, 74–84 (2014)
6. Meedya, S., Fahy, K., Kable, A.: Factors that positively influence breastfeeding duration to 6 months: a literature review. Women Birth **23**, 135–145 (2010)
7. Krishnamurti, T., Davis, A., Wong-Parodi, G., Fischhoff, B., Sadovsky, Y., Simhan, H.: Development and testing of the MyHealthyPregnancy app: a behavioural decision research-based tool for assessing and communicating pregnancy risk. JMIR mHealth uHealth **10**, e42 (2017)

8. Asiodu, I.V., Waters, C.M., Dailey, D.E., Lee, K.A., Lyndon, A.: Breastfeeding and use of social media among first-time African American mothers. JOGNN – J. Obstet. Gynecol. Neonatal Nurs. **44**, 268–278 (2015)
9. Meedya, S., Fernandez, R., Fahy, K.: Effect of educational and support interventions to increase long-term breastfeeding rates in primiparous women: a systematic review and meta-analysis. JBI Database Syst. Rev. Implementation Rep. **15**, 2307–2332 (2017)
10. Oinas-Kukkonen, H., Harjumaa, M.: Persuasive systems design: key issues, process model, and system features. Commun. Assoc. Inf. Syst. **24**, 28 (2009)
11. Matthews, J., Win, K.T., Oinas-Kukkonen, H., Freeman, M.: Persuasive technology in mobile applications promoting physical activity: a systematic review. J. Med. Syst. **40**, 72 (2016)
12. Lau, E.Y., Lau, P.W., Chung, P.K., Ransdell, L., Archer, E.: Evaluation of an internet-short message service-based intervention for promoting physical activity in Hong Kong chinese adolescent school children: a pilot study. Cyberpsychol. Behav. Soc. Netw. **15**, 425–434 (2012)
13. Win, K., Roberts, M., Oinas-Kukkonen, H.: Persuasive system features in computer mediated lifestyle modification interventions for physical activity. Inform. Health Soc. Care 1–19 (2018)
14. Karppinen, P., Oinas-Kukkonen, H., Alahäivälä, T., Jokelainen, T., Keränen, A., Salonurmi, T., Savolainen, M.: Persuasive user experiences of a health behavior change support system: a 12-month study for prevention of metabolic syndrome. Int. J. Med. Inform. **96**, 51–61 (2016)
15. Migneault, J.P., et al.: A culturally adapted telecommunication system to improve physical activity, diet quality, and medication adherence among hypertensive African-Americans: a randomized controlled trial. Ann. Behav. Med. **43**, 62–73 (2012)
16. Kelders, S.M., Kok, R.N., Ossebaard, H.C., Van Gemert-Pijnen, J.E.: Persuasive system design does matter: a systematic review of adherence to web-based interventions. J. Med. Internet Res. **14**, e152 (2012)
17. Amico, K.R., et al.: The information-motivation-behavioral skills model of ART adherence in a deep south HIV+ clinic sample. AIDS Behav. **13**, 66–75 (2009)
18. Osborn, C.Y., Amico, K.R., Fisher, W.A., Egede, L.E., Fisher, J.D.: An information—motivation—behavioral skills analysis of diet and exercise behavior in Puerto Ricans with diabetes. J. Health Psychol. **15**, 1201–1213 (2010)
19. Shrestha, R., Altice, F.L., Huedo-Medina, T.B., Karki, P., Copenhaver, M.: Willingness to use pre-exposure prophylaxis (PrEP): an empirical test of the information-motivation-behavioral skills (IMB) model among high-risk drug users in treatment. AIDS Behav. **21**, 1299–1308 (2017)
20. Fisher, C.M.: Adapting the information-motivation-behavioral skills model: predicting HIV-related sexual risk among sexual minority youth. Health Educ. Behav. **39**, 290–302 (2012)
21. Vlahu-Gjorgievska, E., Mulakaparambil Unnikrishnan, S., Win, K.T.: mHealth applications: a tool for behaviour change in weight management. Stud. Health Technol. Inform. **252**, 158–163 (2018)
22. World Health Organization: Ten steps to successful breastfeeding, Revised 2018. https://www.who.int/nutrition/bfhi/ten-steps/en/. Accessed 28 Jan 2019
23. Chomutare, T., Fernandez-Luque, L., Årsand, E., Hartvigsen, G.: Features of mobile diabetes applications: review of the literature and analysis of current applications compared against evidence-based guidelines. J. Med. Internet Res. **13**, e65 (2011)
24. Taki, S., Campbell, K., Russell, C., Elliott, R., Laws, R., Denney-Wilson, E.: Infant feeding websites and apps: a systematic assessment of quality and content. Interact. J. Med. Res. **4**, e18 (2015)

25. Preece, J., Shneiderman, B.: The reader-to-leader framework: motivating technology-mediated social participation. AIS Trans. Hum.-Comput. Interact. **1**, 13–32 (2009)
26. Carter, T., O'Neill, S., Johns, N., Brady, R.: Contemporary vascular smartphone medical applications. Ann. Vasc. Surg. **27**, 804–809 (2013)
27. Neithercott, T.: Health apps. 12 on-the-go diabetes tools for your smartphone. Diab. Forecast **66**, 34–37 (2013)
28. Rosser, B.A., Eccleston, C.: Smartphone applications for pain management. J. Telemed. Telecare **17**, 308–312 (2011)
29. Stevens, D.J., Jackson, J.A., Howes, N., Morgan, J.: Obesity surgery smartphone apps: a review. Obes. Surg. **24**, 32–36 (2014)
30. Sillence, E., Briggs, P., Harris, P.: A framework for understanding trust factors in web-based health advice. Int. J. Hum.-Comput. Stud. **64**, 697–713 (2006)
31. Hansen, J.: Stillbirth: Pregnant Women Warned to Avoid Smartphone App with Two Babies Recently Dying. The Daily Telegraph News Corp., Surry Hills (2016)
32. Wolf, J.A., et al.: Diagnostic inaccuracy of smartphone applications for melanoma detection. JAMA Dermatol. **149**, 422–426 (2013)

Engaging Bystanders Using Persuasive Technology: A Meta-analysis of Influencing Factors on Moral Courage

Kathrin Röderer[✉], Julia Himmelsbach, Stephanie Schwarz,
and Manfred Tscheligi

Austrian Institute of Technology, Vienna, Austria
{kathrin.roederer, julia.himmelsbach,
stephanie.schwarz, manfred.tscheligi}@ait.ac.at

Abstract. Interventions in emergency situations with an aggressor are characterized by potentially high costs but no or very little direct reward for an intervening person. In such moral courage situations, the willingness to act is critical for the safety and well-being of others. Persuasive technology has a high potential for changing attitudes and behavior and thus, supporting such a behavior for the greater good. Aiming at identifying promising persuasive strategies, a meta-analysis to identify factors relevant for moral courage was conducted. Findings highlight seven attitude and competence factors with high potential for attitude and behavior change towards morally courageous behavior. By that, the process model of helping behavior as well as social and motivational psychology results can inform evidence-based persuasive design for technology for moral courage.

Keywords: Moral courage · Evidence-based persuasion strategies ·
Meta-analysis

1 Introduction

Persuasive technology has the potential to change behavior in various situations (e.g., [1]). Willingness and skills to act are critical in situations in which the safety and well-being of people are threatened by other persons. To act morally courageous, individuals have to overcome several steps: they have to recognize the incident, interpret it as an emergency, decide on taking the responsibility and decide when and how to help [2]. Moreover, moral courage is characterized by high potential personal and social costs, i.e. negative consequences, as well as no or very little direct reward for the actor [3].

As most people state moral courage as a favorable behavior [4], researchers have long been trying to answer the question of why people often do not help. The bystander effect [5] is a well-known phenomenon that leads to inaction: The more people are present at the occurrence of an incident, the less likely one of them will intervene. While this callous behavior cannot be conclusively explained, it is assumed to depend on various factors, such as diffusion of responsibility. Furthermore, culture, social and moral norms, mood, negative social consequences, emotions, and tendencies toward heroism and altruism have been suggested as factors of influence [3].

© Springer Nature Switzerland AG 2019
H. Oinas-Kukkonen et al. (Eds.): PERSUASIVE 2019, LNCS 11433, pp. 202–209, 2019.
https://doi.org/10.1007/978-3-030-17287-9_17

Persuasive technologies can help overcome behavioral barriers and constraints by training and automating helpful behavior patterns [6]. To be effective, technologies must be based on relevant barriers and promoting conditions. But which are the factors that drive moral courage? Although empirical studies on moral courage - due to their difficulty in realization - are limited in number, a synthesis of these results that allows prioritization of the factors along their persuasive potential is still lacking. In this meta-analysis, we identify relevant factors and give insights into the design of persuasive technologies that build upon these factors to allow evidence-based persuasive design.

2 Related Work

Only rare knowledge regarding persuasive design for moral courage is given, but the interest is arousing. For instance, only recently the MIT Media Lab called to design a platform for kindness and prosocial behavior [7]; studies investigate fostering prosocial behavior among strangers with wearables [8], or explore effects of prosocial video games on helping behavior and moral courage [9].

However, even though moral courage is a form of prosocial behavior, there are critical differences to helping behavior. Most importantly, whereas for helping behavior actors can expect immediate social rewards, moral courage is usually accompanied by negative social consequences [10]. Yet, such behavior is always beneficial for a social group or for society [4]. This fact makes it particularly complex as well as interesting for persuasive design. Users must be persuaded to take personal risks [3], such as being endangered or experiencing negative reactions from other bystanders, to uphold social norms [11], and have to be trained to intervene in a safe way. Moreover, they themselves often must act against values, such as privacy of the disputants when interfering in a fight, to uphold prosocial values [11]. In line, moral courage is defined by "the expression of personal views and values in the face of dissension and rejection" and "when an individual stands up to someone with power over him or her […] for the greater good" [12]. Moral courage is influenced by various factors, such as anger [13], social responsibility and openness [14]. However, it remains unclear, which factors are most influential and thus promising in terms of persuasive design.

Up to now, moral courage training rarely takes up the advantages of technology. Such approaches would allow reaching a wider number of people (e.g. in regions where no training is offered). In HCI, moral courage is most often associated with intervention against cyberbullying (e.g. [15, 16]) with a high potential for persuasive design: [15], for example, show that persuasive training can be effective in fostering interventions against cyberbullying. Experimental examinations in technology-supported interventions have proven that playing games with prosocial content to increase short-term helping behavior and moral courage [9]. Our meta-analysis aims at identifying the most promising evidence based persuasive design factors for moral courage.

3 Research Methodology: Meta-analysis

We carried out a meta-analysis following the instructions by Cooper [17] to give a systematic and comprehensive research overview on which factors drive moral courage.

3.1 Material

We included empirical studies that collected data on moral courage as the dependent variable. Studies were only considered if moral courage was operationalized as social control behavior, entailed a high risk for the intervening person, and if there was a perpetrator present. No restrictions regarding publishing date, sample, study design, or geographic region were made[1].

The literature research began by collecting papers containing the term "moral courage" and additional keywords, such as "experiment", "norms", and "social control". First, we searched in Elsevier Scopus, the largest abstract and citation database of peer-reviewed literature[2]. The search resulted in 562 papers. Removing duplicates revealed 355 papers, where the abstracts were screened. Next, we extended the search[3] and checked the references of papers published after 2015 for additions. We conducted a detailed screening based on the moral courage definition and the reporting of quantitative effects. As a result, 20 papers were included in the analysis (see Appendix).

3.2 Coding of Effects and Effect Sizes and Analysis

Extraction of effects was based on detailed guidelines that also recorded information on publication year, peer review, reliability criteria, and sample. Quality of studies was rated according to validity and reliability measures as well as plausibility. Except for one often cited dissertation, all papers were published in peer-reviewed journals.

The body of material was coded by four researchers experienced in quantitative social sciences research. The coding focused on main effects from group comparisons, correlational analyses, and chi-square tests. No interaction effects were included. Effect sizes β were not included in the analysis due to their dependency on the respective statistical model. Missing sample data was estimated, assuming equal sample sizes and gender ratios ratio after the exclusion of subjects or for each experimental condition.

Following [17], all effect sizes were z-transformed into correlation coefficients, weighted according to sample size, averaged within the respective measurement unit, and retransformed to correlation coefficients. Confidence intervals of $\alpha = .05$ were calculated. Next, weighted effect sizes were averaged to avoid distortion biases due to the overrepresentation of dependent effects. Variables were inductively aggregated to codes and groups based on theoretical concepts.

---

[1] In order to ensure that the coders understand all content in detail, the publication languages had to be limited to English and German.

[2] http://www.scopus.com.

[3] https://scholar.google.com; http://apps.webofknowledge.com.

4   Results and Discussion

In sum, the meta-analysis includes data of 4,361 study participants and 248 effect sizes. Most studies (70.0%) were carried out in a university context. 57.5% of all participants were female, 39.5% were male. Mean ages ranged from 18.8 to 70.9 years with all mean ages under 30 years except in one study [18]. Studies included interviews using scenarios or vignettes, empirical (quasi-)experiments and observational studies, as well as interviews on past behavior.

In relation to morally courageous behavior, 56 influencing factors were identified. We clustered the factors to the groups *situational factors, attitudes, competencies, emotions, personality traits,* and *socio-demographics & biography.* In terms of altering behavior using persuasive design, we argue that *attitude* and *competence* are the most promising factor groups since effects of persuasive technologies on attitudes change (e.g. [19]) and effects of competence training (e.g. [20, 21]) are well established.

After controlling for confidence intervals to be within a significant range ($\alpha < .05$), the factors with the highest influence on moral courage were extracted. These factors either (1) had the highest effect size r or (2) more conservatively estimated - had a confidence interval farthest from 0. As a result, we present seven promising factors which fulfill at least one of these criteria (see Table 1).

Table 1. Overview of the seven most conducive personal factors

Category	Independent variable	Effect size r	Confidence interval		n	Fail-safe N
Attitude	Social responsibility	.712	.552	.873	152	43
Attitude	Altruistic moral reasoning	.702	.542	.863	152	41
Competence	Attention & emergency awareness	.480	.393	.567	256	101
Attitude	Attitude towards civil disobedience	.379	.141	.617	71	3
Competence	Intervention skills	.376	.252	.499	256	14
Competence	Resistance to group pressure	.343	.105	.581	71	3
Competence	Empathy	.322	.237	.406	554	73

With two exceptions (*attitude towards civil disobedience* and *resistance to group pressure*), all factors displayed in Table 1 have a high fail-safe N, indicating the number of studies needed to falsify the findings.

The two factors with the largest effect sizes are *social responsibility* and *altruistic moral reasoning*, both being *attitudes*, both showing remarkable large effect sizes [22]. These are followed in effect size by the *competencies attention & emergency awareness, attitude towards civil disobedience, intervention skills, resistance to group pressure,* and *empathy*. The effect sizes can be described as medium [22].

Both, *attitudes* as well as *competencies*, can be altered or trained relatively easily. Thus, they have a high potential for behavioral change as conveyed by persuasive technologies (cf. [19]). We suggest combining the strengths of the process model of help behavior [2] with social and motivational psychology models: With persuasive training, certain behavioral options for specific situations can be learned and automated [23]. Training competencies can thus help to reduce barriers towards action, accelerate this process and ensure safe intervention. Designers and researchers should focus on habitualizing *attention and emergency awareness, intervention skills* and *empathy*, especially the competence of perspective taking. Trainings that practice automatic processes such as *attention and emergency awareness*, e.g. by practicing moral courage in situations as realistic as possible, are assumed to be the most effective [24]. Simulating emergency situations in virtual environments or using immersive persuasive games for training purposes seems to be the logical continuation of these considerations.

Drawing back on social and motivational psychology models, we recommend developing persuasive design strategies based on the attitude factors, which have been shown to have large potential: *social responsibility, altruistic moral reasoning* and *the attitude towards civil disobedience*. Enduring and resistant attitude change, as one of the core businesses of persuasive technologies, will predict behavior [19] and should be focused on in persuasive designs aiming at increasing interventions.

5 Conclusion

A meta-analysis on persuasive design factors relevant for moral courage was conducted. Results show seven conducive factors that have a high potential for attitude and behavior change as conveyed by persuasive technologies and therefore should be focused on when designing persuasive strategies and technologies supporting moral courage. Future work should concentrate on research and persuasive design based on these factors and evaluate implementation and applicability in persuasive technologies.

Appendix: List of Publications Included in the Meta-analysis

1. Baumert, A., Halmburger, A., Schmitt, M.: Interventions Against Norm Violations: Dispositional Determinants of Self-Reported and Real Moral Courage. Personal. Soc. Psychol. Bull. 39, 1053–1068 (2013).
2. Brauer, M., Chaurand, N.: Descriptive norms, prescriptive norms, and social control: An intercultural comparison of people's reactions to uncivil behaviors. Eur. J. Soc. Psychol. 40, 490–499 (2010).
3. Bronstein, P., Fox, B.J., Kamon, J.L., Knolls, M.L.: Parenting and gender as predictors of moral courage in late adolescence: A longitudinal study. Sex Roles A J. Res. 56, 661–674 (2007).
4. Dost, M.: Techniken der Neutralisierung: eine empirische Analyse von Werten beim Handeln unter Risiko. In: Rehberg, K.-S., Deutsche Gesellschaft für Soziologie (eds.) Die Natur der Gesellschaft: Verhandlungen des 33. Kongresses der Deutschen Gesellschaft für Soziologie in Kassel 2006, pp. 2059–2073. Campus Verlag, Frankfurt am Main (2008).
5. Fagin-Jones, S., Midlarsky, E.: Courageous altruism: Personal and situation correlates of rescue during the Holocaust. J. Posit. Psychol. 2, 136–147 (2007).

6. Fischer, P., Greitemeyer, T., Pollozek, F., Frey, D.: The unresponsive bystander: Are bystanders more responsive in dangerous emergencies? Eur. J. Soc. Psychol. 36, 267–278 (2006).
7. Greitemeyer, T., Fischer, P., Kastenmüller, A., Frey, D.: Civil courage and helping behavior differences and similarities. Eur. Psychol. 11, 90–98 (2006).
8. Greitemeyer, T., Osswald, S.: Effects of prosocial video games on prosocial behavior. J. Pers. Soc. Psychol. 98, 211–221 (2010).
9. Halmburger, A., Baumert, A., Schmitt, M.: Anger as driving factor of moral courage in comparison with guilt and global mood: A multimethod approach. Eur. J. Soc. Psychol. 45, 39–51 (2015).
10. Hannah, S.T., Avolio, B.J., Walumbwa, F.O.: Relationships between Authentic Leadership, Moral Courage, and Ethical and Pro-Social Behaviors. Bus. Ethics Q. 21, 555–578 (2011).
11. Hannah, S.T., Avolio, B.J., Walumbwa, F.O.: Addendum to "Relationships between Authentic Leadership, Moral Courage, and Ethical and Pro-Social Behaviors." Bus. Ethics Q. 24, 277–279 (2014).
12. Kayser, D.N., Greitemeyer, T., Fischer, P., Frey, D.: Why mood affects help giving, but not moral courage: Comparing two types of prosocial behavior. Eur. J. Soc. Psychol. 40, 1136–1157 (2010).
13. Kinnunen, S.P., Windmann, S.: Dual-Processing Altruism. Front. Psychol. 4, 1–8 (2013).
14. Kinnunen, S.P., Lindeman, M., Verkasalo, M.: Help-giving and moral courage on the internet. Cyberpsychology. 10, (2016).
15. Laner, M.R., Benin, M.H., Ventrone, N.A.: Bystander attitudes toward victims of violence: Who's worth helping? Deviant Behav. 22, 23–42 (2001).
16. May, D.R., Luth, M.T.: The Effectiveness of Ethics Education: A Quasi-Experimental Field Study. Sci. Eng. Ethics. 19, 545–568 (2013).
17. May, D.R., Luth, M.T., Schwoerer, C.E.: The Influence of Business Ethics Education on Moral Efficacy, Moral Meaningfulness, and Moral Courage: A Quasi-experimental Study. J. Bus. Ethics. 124, 67–80 (2014).
18. Schwartz, S.H., Gottlieb, A.: Bystander Reactions to a Violent Theft: Crime in Jerusalem. J. Personal. Soc. Psychol. 34, 1188–1199 (1976).
19. Sonnentag, T.L., Wadian, T.W., Barnett, M.A., Gretz, M.R., Bailey, S.M.: Characteristics Associated With Individuals' Caring, Just, and Brave Expressions of the Tendency to Be a Moral Rebel. Ethics Behav. 0, 1–18 (2017).
20. Voigtländer, D.: Hilfeverhalten und Zivilcourage: Ein Vergleich von antizipiertem und realem Verhalten, http://webdoc.sub.gwdg.de/diss/2009/voigtlaender/, (2008).

References

1. Fogg, B.J.: Persuasive Technology: Using Computers to Change What We Think and Do. Morgan Kaufmann, Burlington (2003)
2. Latané, B., Darley, J.M.: Help in a Crisis: Bystander Response to an Emergency. General Learning Press, Morristown (1976)
3. Osswald, S., Greitemeyer, T., Fischer, P., Frey, D.: What is moral courage? Definition, explication and classification of a complex construct. In: Pury, C., Lopez, S. (eds.) Psychology of Courage, pp. 149–164. APA, Washington (2010)
4. Penner, L.A., Dovidio, J.F., Piliavin, J.A., Schroeder, D.A.: Prosocial behavior: multilevel perspectives. Annu. Rev. Psychol. **56**, 365–392 (2005)
5. Darley, J.M., Latané, B.: Bystander intervention in emergencies: diffusion of responsibility. J. Pers. Soc. Psychol. **8**, 377–383 (1968)
6. Fogg, B.: A behavior model for persuasive design. In: Proceedings of the 4th International Conference on Persuasive Technology - Persuasive 2009, p. 1. ACM Press, New York (2009)
7. Ananthabhotla, I., Rieger, A., Greenberg, D., Picard, R.: MIT community challenge: designing a platform to promote kindness and prosocial behavior. In: Proceedings of the 2017 CHI Conference Extended Abstracts on Human Factors in Computing Systems - CHI EA 2017, pp. 2352–2358. ACM Press, New York (2017)
8. Lee, S., Chung, W.Y., Ip, E., Schiphorst, T.: The laughing dress. In: Proceedings of the Extended Abstracts of the 32nd Annual ACM Conference on Human Factors in Computing Systems - CHI EA 2014, pp. 2143–2148. ACM Press, New York (2014)
9. Greitemeyer, T., Osswald, S.: Effects of prosocial video games on prosocial behavior. J. Pers. Soc. Psychol. **98**, 211–221 (2010)
10. Osswald, S., Frey, D., Streicher, B.: Moral courage. In: Kals, E., Maes, J. (eds.) Justice and Conflicts, pp. 391–405. Springer, Heidelberg (2012). https://doi.org/10.1007/978-3-642-19035-3_24
11. Jonas, K.J., Brandstätter, V.: Zivilcourage. Zeitschrift für Sozialpsychologie. **35**, 185–200 (2004)
12. Lopez, S.J., O'Byrne, K.K., Petersen, S.: Profiling courage. In: Positive Psychological Assessment: A Handbook of Models and Measures, pp. 185–197. American Psychological Association, Washington, DC (2003)
13. Halmburger, A., Baumert, A., Schmitt, M.: Anger as driving factor of moral courage in comparison with guilt and global mood: a multimethod approach. Eur. J. Soc. Psychol. **45**, 39–51 (2015)
14. Kayser, D.N., Greitemeyer, T., Fischer, P., Frey, D.: Why mood affects help giving, but not moral courage: comparing two types of prosocial behavior. Eur. J. Soc. Psychol. **40**, 1136–1157 (2010)
15. Difranzo, D., Taylor, S.H., Bazarova, N.N.: Upstanding by design: bystander intervention in cyberbullying. In: Proc. SIGCHI Conference on Human Factors in Computing Systems - CHI 2018, pp. 1–12 (2018)
16. van der Zwaan, J.M., Dignum, V., Jonker, C.M., van der Hof, S.: On technology against cyberbullying. In: van der Hof, S., van den Berg, B.S. (eds.) Minding Minors Wandering the Web: Regulating Online Child Safety, pp. 211–228. TMC Asser Press, The Hague (2014)
17. Cooper, H.M.: Research Synthesis and Meta-analysis: a Step-by-Step Approach. SAGE Publications, Thousand Oaks (2010)
18. Fagin-Jones, S., Midlarsky, E.: Courageous altruism: personal and situation correlates of rescue during the Holocaust. J. Posit. Psychol. **2**, 136–147 (2007)

19. Oinas-Kukkonen, H., Harjumaa, M.: Towards deeper understanding of persuasion in software and information systems. In: Proceedings of the 1st International Conference on Advances in Computer-Human Interaction, ACHI 2008, pp. 200–205 (2008)
20. Chang, T.-R., Kaasinen, E., Kaipainen, K.: Persuasive design in mobile applications for mental well-being: multidisciplinary expert review. Wirel. Mob. Commun. Healthc. **61**, 154–162 (2015)
21. Wais-Zechmann, B., Gattol, V., Neureiter, K., Orji, R., Tscheligi, M.: Persuasive technology to support chronic health conditions: investigating the optimal persuasive strategies for persons with COPD. In: Ham, J., Karapanos, E., Morita, P.P., Burns, C.M. (eds.) PERSUASIVE 2018. LNCS, vol. 10809, pp. 255–266. Springer, Cham (2018). https://doi.org/10.1007/978-3-319-78978-1_21
22. Cohen, J.: Statistical Power Analysis for the Behavioral Sciences. Academic Press, New York (1988)
23. Fogg, B.J.: A behavior model for persuasive design. In: Proceedings of 4th International Conference on Persuasive Technology - Persuasive 2009, vol. 1 (2009)
24. Baumert, A., Halmburger, A., Schmitt, M.: Interventions against norm violations: dispositional determinants of self-reported and real moral courage. Personal. Soc. Psychol. Bull. **39**, 1053–1068 (2013)

Motivation and Goal Setting

I Focus on Improvement: Effects of Type of Mastery Feedback on Motivational Experiences

Evy L. Ansems, Elçin Hanci, Peter A. M. Ruijten[✉],
and Wijnand A. IJsselsteijn

Eindhoven University of Technology, Eindhoven, The Netherlands
p.a.m.ruijten@tue.nl

Abstract. Measurement technologies provide persuasive feedback to elicit motivation. However, little is known about whether different types of standards in progress feedback yield different motivational experiences. The current study investigates effects of mastery goals with either a self-based or a task-based standard on motivational experiences. An interactive dance game was developed to provide persuasive progress feedback in the form of a self- versus task-based standard. Participants played the game and reported their experiences with it. Results showed that participants in the self-based condition responded more in terms of Improvement and less in terms of Performance compared to those in the task-based condition. This finding implies that the type of standard in progress feedback can yield different motivational experiences.

Keywords: Persuasive feedback · Mastery goals ·
Self-based standard · Task-based standard · Motivational experiences

1 Introduction

Advances in measurement technologies provide opportunities for stimulating health related behaviour change. A promising way to let users of these technologies reach their health goals is by providing immediate, persuasive feedback about their progress towards a certain standard. Such feedback aims to elicit motivational experiences for continued engagement with the health activity.

When people begin with an activity, they may think about the goals they want to achieve (e.g. improving their skills, or achieving a certain score). People can have different types of achievement goals, or they can be triggered by the achievement goals that are suggested by measurement technologies. For example, 10.000 steps is a default daily goal that is suggested by the majority of activity trackers that are currently on the market. However, different types of achievement goals can have different effects on people's motivation.

According to the Dichotomous Achievement Goal Model, a distinction can be made between mastery and performance goals [2]. Mastery goals focus on the

© Springer Nature Switzerland AG 2019
H. Oinas-Kukkonen et al. (Eds.): PERSUASIVE 2019, LNCS 11433, pp. 213–224, 2019.
https://doi.org/10.1007/978-3-030-17287-9_18

development of competence and mastering a task, whereas performance goals focus on the demonstration of competence and outperforming others [3]. Mastery and performance goals are applicable to various achievement-relevant domains such as school, sports, work, games and so on [2,3,12].

1.1 Different Standards of Competence

Within mastery goals, a distinction can be made between the standards of competence of achievement goals [6]. The standard of competence is a reference point that is used in evaluating one's competence [5]. According to the 3×2 Achievement Goal Model, the standard of competence in mastery goals is either self-based or task-based, while the standard of competence in performance goals is other-based [6]. An example of a self-based mastery goal is trying to do better than before. An example of a task-based mastery goal is doing the task well relative to an absolute demand of the task. An example of an other-based performance goal is doing better than others.

Based on the 3×2 Achievement Goal Model, progress feedback can contain self-based standards (e.g. scores of your previous self), task-based standards (e.g. minimum/maximum scores) or other-based standards (e.g. scores of others). Earlier work showed that mastery goals consistently lead to a wide range of positive processes and outcomes such as high intrinsic motivation [4,11], showing the potential benefits of having self-based standards.

1.2 The Value of Self-based Progress Feedback

Behaviour change technologies seem to focus mostly on task-based goals. Devices such as Fitbit provide daily, default or self-set goals such as an amount of steps, an amount of stairs climbed or an amount of active minutes. These predetermined goals emphasize task-based standards instead of self-based standards. Likewise, in games for health such as the Wii Fit U that turns exercise into a game, people set weight and time-frame goals after which the device provides an amount of calories to burn every day. While these devices do provide some information about one's highest scores that allows them to compare themselves with previous performance, the default goals are task-based and do not focus on self-improvement.

In the field of academic performance, studies consistently show that self-based goals are associated with higher motivation and engagement [10,17]. In addition, earlier work in the context of video games showed an increased focus on self-improvement when providing information about past performance [13]. These findings may be relevant in the field of personal informatics as well. When technologies provide feedback about an individual's achievement, it is important to know the extent to which a task-based or a self-based focus influences achievement- and motivation-relevant processes. After all, the manner in which progress feedback is presented to the user may influence motivational experiences and subsequent active behaviour. It is unclear, however, which type of mastery goal (self-based or task-based) is more effective in providing progress feedback.

1.3   Research Aims

In order to investigate whether task-based or self-based standards are more effective in providing progress feedback, a study was designed in which people's motivational experiences were measured. Based on earlier work on effects of providing self-based progress feedback, we expect that self-based goals are more likely to make people focused on self-improvement than task-based goals. This expectation is tested with an interactive dance game that provides immediate progress feedback on physical activity with a self-based or task-based standard.

2   Method

2.1   Participants and Design

Forty-four participants, 20 females and 24 males ($M_{age} = 25.6$, $SD_{age} = 3.8$, Range $= 18$ to 34) were recruited using a participant database open to students and employees of Eindhoven University of Technology. The study had two between-subjects conditions: Task-based vs. Self-based progress feedback. Four participants communicated with each other about the study and therefore may have been aware of the goal of the study. For this reason they were excluded from any analyses, leaving 40 participants (20 females and 20 males).

Each participant played several rounds in an activity game that will be explained in the next section. They received progress feedback on their performance in the game that was based on either their own previous performance (Self-based) or the percentage of the maximum score they reached (Task-based). The experiment took about 30 min to complete for which participants were compensated with either course credits or €5.

2.2   Game and Feedback Design

In order to investigate people's motivational experiences with Self-based versus Task-based standards in progress feedback, an interactive dance game was developed in Adobe Flash™. The game was inspired by Dance Revolution, in which a player stands on a dance mat with different arrows. During the game, a music track is played while arrows of various orientations move from the bottom of the screen to the top. Players need to step on the corresponding arrow on the dance pad at the correct time to receive points. A visualization of the game in action is provided in Fig. 1.

Each participant could play a maximum of five game rounds, where one round took approximately 2 min. A very large numerical score consisting of seven digits was shown during the rounds. This number grew with participants' performance. With such large numbers we could make sure to manipulate the scores without causing any suspicion among participants. As such, final scores that were presented were similar across the whole sample.

After each round, a progress bar was shown that indicated performance. This bar was programmed to be approximately filled for 25% after the first round,

Fig. 1. Visualization of the game in action. The game is displayed on a Digi board, connected to a laptop, and the player stands on a dance mat.

35% after the second, 50% after the third, 66% after the fourth and 75% after the fifth and final round. These scores were experimentally controlled to avoid confounding factors and to ensure increasing progress in each round.

The feedback that was coupled with the progress bar depended on the experimental condition the participants were in, and was based on earlier work on gaming goals [12]. The Self-based feedback was based on 'doing better than before', and thus represented past performance. Hence, the achieved score was visualized as a comparison with the participants' previous score. The Task-based feedback was based on 'beating the game', and thus represented a predefined endpoint. This score was visualized as a comparison to the maximum dance score. The two types of feedback are shown in Fig. 2.

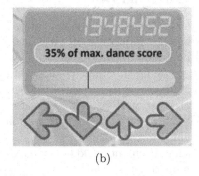

        (a)   (b)

Fig. 2. Visualization of the feedback participants received after one of the game rounds in the (a) self-based and (b) task-based conditions.

In the final screen, a message was provided to emphasize the reference point. In the Self-based condition, this message was "Well done, you did better than your previous dance score". In the Task-based condition, this message was "Well done, you did better than 35% of the maximum dance score".

2.3 Materials and Procedure

At the start of the experiment, participants read and signed an informed consent form that informed them about their rights and the procedure of the experiment. Next, they were asked to hand over their phones and take off their watch if they were wearing one. The first round of the game was a trial round for participants to get used to the game. After each round, the game asked participants whether they wanted to play the next round or not. They could step on one of the buttons of the dance pad to indicate whether they wanted to continue.

All participants were required to play the trial round and two game rounds. After this, the experimenter left the room with some papers to "make a copy". Participants were now free to choose whether they continued playing or not. Due to technical issues, however, we were not able to use any data from this free-choice period. After 4 min the experimenter returned back in the room and asked participants to complete a questionnaire consisting of open questions about participants' motivational experiences. These questions asked (1) how participants felt when receiving the feedback on their dance score, (2) how they interpreted this feedback, (3) why the feedback made them feel in a certain way, and (4) what their main goals were during the game.

Participants also completed the Situational Motivation Scale [8] (16 items, $\alpha = 0.86$) and a Task Enjoyment scale [9] (5 items, $\alpha = 0.88$). Since the power of the study is too low to draw statistically valid conclusions from these scales, we decided to not include them in our analyses. Instead, we coded all responses into a description of one or a few words–two coders were used, showing an inter-coder reliability of 81%–, and categorized those codes into themes. We then counted how often each theme occurred in the Self-based and Task-based conditions, so we could get an understanding of participants' motivational experiences while playing the game. At the end of the experiment, participants were thanked for their participation, debriefed and compensated.

3 Results

Responses to the open questions were categorized into themes, leading to six different themes: (1) Motivation (related to enjoying the game and feelings of motivation), (2) Failure (related to making mistakes), (3) Performance (related to achieving high scores), (4) Improvement (related to improving oneself, (5) Physical exercise (related to being physically active), and (6) Self-orientation (that are self-involved, such as referring to 'my score' instead of 'the score').

For each open question, the frequency in which answers fell in the categories was compared between the two conditions, and Pearson adjusted residuals representing the difference between observed and expected values were calculated. A positive residual means that there are more observed responses than are expected, and a negative residual means that there are fewer observed responses than expected. Residual value that exceed ±2.00 indicate that there is a significant difference between observed and expected values [14]. The remainder of this section will present the findings on each of the four open questions.

3.1 How Participants Felt When Receiving the Feedback on Their Dance Score

This question provides insights into participants' feelings about the feedback in general. A Chi-square test indicated that the pattern of responses to this question differed significantly between the two conditions, $\chi^2(5) = 14.15$, $p < 0.05$. Table 1 shows that this effect is mainly caused by the differences in responses related to Performance.

Table 1. Contingency table of responses to Question 1. For each condition and each category, the table shows the observed response frequency, the expected frequency and the Pearson adjusted residual. Residuals greater or smaller than ±2 are bold printed.

Condition	Motivation	Failure	Performance	Improvement	Physical exercise	Self-orientation
Self-based	14	1	1	14	1	9
	14.0	3.0	5.0	11.5	0.5	6.0
	0.0	−1.7	**−2.7**	1.2	1.0	1.9
Task-based	14	5	9	9	0	3
	14.0	3.0	5.0	11.5	0.5	6.0
	0.0	1.7	**2.7**	−1.2	−1.0	−1.9

As can be seen in Fig. 3, feedback during the game was perceived as motivating in both conditions. This should not come as a surprise given that the game was designed in such a way that all participants improved their scores over time. Interestingly, participants in the Task-based condition were more concerned with their performance, as indicated by the high frequency of performance-related answers. Participants in the self-based condition were more concerned with improving themselves, as seen by the high frequency of improvement-related answers. These findings show that providing self-based feedback makes people more focused on improvement than providing task-based feedback.

3.2 How Participants Interpreted the Feedback

This question provides insights into how participants interpreted the feedback itself while they were playing the game. A Chi-square test indicated that the pattern of responses to this question differed significantly between the two conditions, $\chi^2(4) = 18.06$, $p < 0.05$. As can be seen in Table 2, this effect is mainly caused by the differences in responses related to Performance and Improvement.

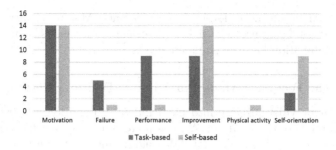

Fig. 3. Response frequencies per category and condition on Question 1.

Table 2. Contingency table of responses to Question 2. For each condition and each category, the table shows the observed response frequency, the expected frequency and the Pearson adjusted residual. Residuals greater or smaller than ±2 are bold printed.

Condition	Motivation	Failure	Performance	Improvement	Physical exercise	Self-orientation
Self-based	4	1	3	15	0	14
	3.6	1.2	10.2	11.3		10.7
	0.4	−0.3	**−4.2**	**2.1**		1.9
Task-based	2	1	14	4	0	4
	2.4	0.8	6.9	7.7		7.3
	−0.4	0.3	**4.2**	**−2.1**		−1.9

An interesting pattern or findings occurred. As can be seen in Fig. 4, the feedback was interpreted as highly performance-related in the task-based condition, showing that participants interpreted the feedback in such a way that it was designed to increase their performance in the game. Participants in the self-based condition, however, interpreted the feedback as improvement-related, showing that they were concerned more with improving themselves over time. This finding clearly shows how the type of feedback made people concerned

Fig. 4. Response frequencies per category and condition on Question 2.

with either demonstrating or developing competence. Moreover, participants in the Self-based condition provided many self-oriented answers, showing that the feedback manipulation had the intended effects.

3.3   Why the Feedback Made Participants Feel in a Certain Way

This question provides insights into participants' attributions regarding their affective responses to the feedback. A Chi-square test indicated that the pattern of responses to this question did not differ significantly between the two conditions, $\chi^2(5) = 9.23$, $p > 0.05$. As can be seen in Table 3, however, a significant difference did occur on Performance-related answers, showing that participants in the Task-based condition mentioned performance more often than expected, while those in the Self-based condition mentioned performance less often than expected.

Table 3. Contingency table of responses to Question 3. For each condition and each category, the table shows the observed response frequency, the expected frequency and the Pearson adjusted residual. Residuals greater or smaller than ±2 are bold printed.

Condition	Motivation	Failure	Performance	Improvement	Physical exercise	Self-orientation
Self-based	7	2	5	14	1	9
	5.4	2.7	10.2	11.2	1.1	7.5
	1.1	−0.6	**−2.8**	1.4	−0.1	0.9
Task-based	3	3	14	7	1	5
	4.7	2.3	8.8	9.8	0.9	6.5
	−1.1	0.6	**2.8**	−1.4	0.1	−0.9

As can be seen in Fig. 5, responses to this question in general are comparable with those to Question 2. That is, performance was mentioned more often by participants in the Task-based condition, while improvement was mentioned more often by those in the Self-based condition. Though the differences in frequencies are small, they do follow the same pattern in which feedback based on an absolute demand of the task makes people disregard their growth in competence and instead focus on their ability to correctly perform the task.

3.4   What Participants' Main Goals Were During the Game

This question provides insights into what participants regarded as their goals while playing the game. A Chi-square test indicated that the pattern of responses to this question did not differ significantly between the two conditions, $\chi^2(5) = 6.56$, $p > 0.05$. Moreover, no significant effects were found on any of the six categories of responses, see Table 4. This means that the frequencies of responses did not differ significantly from the expected frequencies.

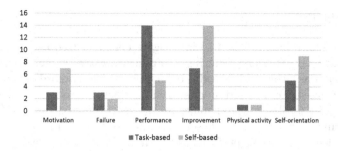

Fig. 5. Response frequencies per category and condition on Question 3.

Table 4. Contingency table of responses to Question 4. For each condition and each category, the table shows the observed response frequency, the expected frequency and the Pearson adjusted residual.

Condition	Motivation	Failure	Performance	Improvement	Physical exercise	Self-orientation
Self-based	14	2	10	14	10	10
	13.1	3.6	13.1	13.7	9.5	7.1
	0.5	−1.3	−1.5	0.2	0.3	1.8
Task-based	8	4	12	9	6	2
	8.9	2.4	8.9	9.3	6.5	4.9
	−0.5	1.3	1.5	−0.2	−0.3	−1.8

As can be seen in Fig. 6, many of the categories show relatively high response frequencies. This can be explained by the fact that the question specifically asked participants to list their three most important goals. Many participants therefore provided answers that were categorized into multiple categories. A participant could thus have provided three goals that fell into the categories Improvement, Motivation, and Performance. This is a consequence of the way in which the question was asked that we did not foresee beforehand, and is something that should be taken into account in future studies.

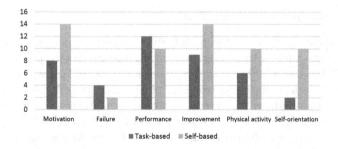

Fig. 6. Response frequencies per category and condition on Question 4.

4   Discussion

The current study was designed to investigate effects of feedback type on people's motivational experiences during a physically active game. Feedback was provided that was either task-based (i.e. focused on the absolute demands of the task) or self-based (i.e. focused on ones own past performance). It was expected that task-based feedback would make people more focused on demonstrating their performance on a task, while self-based feedback would make people more focused on developing their performance by improving themselves.

To test these expectations, an interactive dance game was designed that was able to display feedback on people's performance based on either a maximum reachable score or a player's past performance. People played the game and evaluated the feedback they received through answering open questions. Results confirmed our expectation that different types of mastery feedback yield different motivational experiences. More specifically, self-based feedback mainly elicited motivational experiences in terms of enjoyment, improving oneself, and being self-oriented, whereas task-based feedback mainly elicited motivational experiences in terms of performance and competition.

For the development of feedback systems such as self-tracking devices that are designed to motivate people to live healthier lives, this means that implementing self-based feedback could steer people's focus towards self-improvement. An inquiry in what motivates people to track their own health showed that all important factors are self-related [7], emphasizing the importance of self-knowledge for self-trackers. An important component that enhances the success of health apps is for the feedback or information provided by the app to be event-based [16]. Self-based feedback by default is event based, since it provides information about how one performs compared with an earlier event.

Results of this study could be used for designing and tailoring progress feedback in devices that collect personal information in such a way that it supports engagement and behaviour change. This means that for people who want to live healthier lives, the feedback of personal informatics devices should allow them to compare their current activity level with their previous activity level, instead of mainly allowing them to compare their current activity level with a task-based standard which is often the focus in current self-tracking devices.

4.1   Limitations and Future Work

Because of technical issues we were not able to compare people's motivational experiences with their actual behaviour during the free-choice period. It would be interesting to test whether people who are more focused on self-improvement than on mere performance also continue playing the game for a longer period of time. If this would be the case, this would strengthen our conclusion that progress feedback on activity behaviour should focus on a person's past performance rather than an absolute demand of a task. Future studies could investigate whether this relationship between motivational experiences and actual behaviour exists.

We did not include any measure for whether participants believed that the progress feedback was their true feedback. If participants did not believe that the scores were theirs, this could have influenced their answers to the open questions. However, when participants were asked what they thought the experiment was about, none of the participants who were included in the analysis showed any suspicion. Nevertheless, the credibility of feedback of self-tracking devices is an important issue, because they can evoke emotional responses [1,15]. Future studies that investigate effects of feedback type on people's motivational experience and behavior should include a measure for testing whether the feedback is believed to be true.

As this study is a first attempt of investigating effects of different types of mastery feedback on motivational experiences, more research in this field is needed to validate the results. For example, it could be investigated whether the mastery standards influence people's true performance or whether these effects also occur on health related behaviour (rather than in an activity game context). Future studies could also focus on more longitudinal designs to investigate effects of feedback on motivational experiences and apply combinations of task and self-based goals strategies.

4.2   Conclusions

The current study shows how different types of mastery feedback can influence people's motivational experiences while playing a physically active game. These findings are relevant for the design of self-tracking devices or behaviour change technologies in general, as they show that feedback based on past performances increase people's focus on self-improvement. We hope that these findings ultimately contribute to creating devices that truly motivate people to live healthier lives.

References

1. Ancker, J.S., Witteman, H.O., Hafeez, B., Provencher, T., Van de Graaf, M., Wei, E.: "You get reminded you're a sick person": personal data tracking and patients with multiple chronic conditions. J. Med. Internet Res. **17**(8), e202 (2015). https://www.ncbi.nlm.nih.gov/pmc/articles/PMC4642375/
2. Dweck, C.S.: Motivational processes affecting learning. Am. Psychol. **41**(10), 1040 (1986)
3. Elliot, A.J., Dweck, C.S.: Handbook of Competence and Motivation. Guilford Publications, New York (2013)
4. Elliot, A.J., Dweck, C.S., Yeager, D.S.: Handbook of Competence and Motivation: Theory and Application. Guilford Publications, New York (2017)
5. Elliot, A.J., McGregor, H.A.: A 2 × 2 achievement goal framework. J. Pers. Soc. Psychol. **80**(3), 501 (2001)
6. Elliot, A.J., Murayama, K., Pekrun, R.: A 3 × 2 achievement goal model. J. Educ. Psychol. **103**(3), 632 (2011)

7. Gimpel, H., Nissen, M., Görlitz, R.: Quantifying the quantified self: a study on the motivations of patients to track their own health. In: Thirty Fourth International Conference on Information Systems, pp. 1–16 (2013)
8. Guay, F., Vallerand, R.J., Blanchard, C.: On the assessment of situational intrinsic and extrinsic motivation: the situational motivation scale (SIMS). Motiv. Emot. **24**(3), 175–213 (2000)
9. Harackiewicz, J.M., Elliot, A.J.: Achievement goals and intrinsic motivation. J. Pers. Soc. Psychol. **65**(5), 904 (1993)
10. Martin, A.J., Elliot, A.J.: The role of personal best (PB) and dichotomous achievement goals in students' academic motivation and engagement: a longitudinal investigation. Educ. Psychol. **36**(7), 1285–1302 (2016)
11. Michou, A., Matos, L., Gargurevich, R., Gumus, B., Herrera, D.: Building on the enriched hierarchical model of achievement motivation: autonomous and controlling reasons underlying mastery goals. Psychol. Belg. **56**(3), 269–287 (2016)
12. Quick, J.M., Atkinson, R.K.: Modeling gameplay enjoyment, goal orientations, and individual characteristics. Int. J. Game-Based Learn. (IJGBL) **4**(2), 51–77 (2014)
13. Sailer, M., Hense, J.U., Mayr, S.K., Mandl, H.: How gamification motivates: an experimental study of the effects of specific game design elements on psychological need satisfaction. Comput. Hum. Behav. **69**, 371–380 (2017)
14. Sharpe, D.: Your chi-square test is statistically significant: now what? Pract. Assess. Res. Eval. **20**(8), 2–10 (2015)
15. Sjöklint, M., Constantiou, I.D., Trier, M.: The complexities of self-tracking - an inquiry into user reactions and goal attainment. In: Twenty-Third European Conference on Information Systems (ECIS), pp. 1–15 (2015)
16. Stawarz, K., Cox, A.L., Blandford, A.: Beyond self-tracking and reminders: designing smartphone apps that support habit formation. In: Proceedings of the 33rd Annual ACM Conference on Human Factors in Computing Systems, pp. 2653–2662. ACM (2015)
17. Yu, K., Martin, A.J.: Personal best (PB) and 'classic' achievement goals in the Chinese context: their role in predicting academic motivation, engagement and buoyancy. Educ. Psychol. **34**(5), 635–658 (2014)

Recovering from Work-Related Strain and Stress with the Help of a Persuasive Mobile Application: Interview-Based Thematic Analysis of Micro-entrepreneurs

Markku Kekkonen[1](✉), Harri Oinas-Kukkonen[1],
Eveliina Korkiakangas[2], and Jaana Laitinen[2]

[1] Faculty of Information Technology and Electrical Engineering,
Oulu Advanced Research on Service and Information Systems,
University of Oulu, 90570 Oulu, Finland
{markku.kekkonen,harri.oinas-kukkonen}@oulu.fi
[2] Finnish Institute of Occupational Health (Työterveyslaitos),
P.O. Box 40, 00032 Helsinki, Finland
{eveliina.korkiakangas,jaana.laitinen}@ttl.fi

Abstract. People often have long-term personal goals regarding health behavior change. Recently, the processes for achieving these goals have begun to be supported through behavior change support systems and especially through their persuasive software features. In a multidisciplinary research project focused on helping micro-entrepreneurs to recover from work-related strain and stress, a persuasive mobile application was developed. For gaining insights about the workings of the system and its persuasive features, we conducted 29 interviews with the system users. We used thematic analysis method with a deductive emphasis for analyzing the interviews. For some, concurrent usage of wearables or other applications led to discarding our application. Users thought that the application was relatively persuasive, but technical issues reduced its persuasiveness noticeably. When functioning properly, self-monitoring and reminders were found to be supportive for users to achieve their goals. Unobtrusiveness was found to increase the persuasiveness of reminders, while self-monitoring always seems to be dependent on the user's personal needs.

Keywords: Health · Behavior change · Recovery from work · Goal setting ·
Mobile application · Persuasive Systems Design · Self-monitoring ·
Reminders · Thematic analysis

1 Introduction

Modern health information technologies can provide cost-effective solutions for improved healthcare [1]. Such technologies can be successfully adopted into use by healthcare providers and professionals even for seeking to change old routines into new and more efficient ones [2]. The digital transformation of healthcare is not a silver bullet void of challenges, however [1]. For example, health behavior interventions utilizing information technology can be less effective if they do not incorporate

© Springer Nature Switzerland AG 2019
H. Oinas-Kukkonen et al. (Eds.): PERSUASIVE 2019, LNCS 11433, pp. 225–236, 2019.
https://doi.org/10.1007/978-3-030-17287-9_19

evidence-based approaches and behavior change theories effectively [3]. Technologically delivered health solutions, especially mobile-based, can also potentially change healthcare for those, who currently have poor access to it [4]. Mobile health solutions can influence health behaviors of large population segments [3].

In Promo@Work research project, a Health Behavior Change Support System (HBCSS) [5], known as 'Recover!' was developed. The aim of the system was to help entrepreneurs to recover from work-related strain and stress. The system was implemented as a native mobile application for Android operating system. The target users, micro-entrepreneurs, are a special group of entrepreneurs who employ less than 10 persons while having an annual turnover less than 2 million EUR [6]. Micro-entrepreneurs, a large segment of population, may often lack proper occupational healthcare.

The application was developed in collaboration with a multidisciplinary team including entrepreneurship researchers, social psychologists and occupational healthcare professionals. Persuasive Systems Design (PSD) model [7], Self-determination theory (SDT) [8] and an adaptation of the Transtheoretical model (TTM) [9] were utilized in the design and development process.

A randomized controlled trial was successfully conducted. After two-month intervention period, we sought out to interview the intervention group participants about the usage of the application, their experiences and achieving of goals.

The research question for this paper is as follows: *In the case of goal setting, how and to what extent did the users' goals change during the usage period and whether the PSD features supported the users in achieving their goals?*

The outline for the paper is as follows. The system and research method will be described in the 'Study setting' section. The findings will be presented and interpreted in 'Results'. In 'Discussion', the practical and theoretical implications will be discussed, in addition to limitations. The final section will be 'Conclusions'.

2   Study Setting

2.1   The HBCSS

The developed HBCSS was theory-based. SDT was chosen as the theoretical model based on the reported effectiveness regarding behavior change interventions [10]. TTM was adopted for goal setting because of the pragmatism of the 'stages-of-change' approach. Additionally, it was suited for research in this case, as there was no need for complex approaches, thus a simplified adaption of TTM was sufficient. In addition to personal goals the users might have had, the application offered support for individual goal setting via tasks set for the user. Before undertaking any tasks within the app, users had to choose one of the three goals adapted from TTM: *Thinking and observing, Acting and doing*, or *Maintaining*. The tasks in each goal could be undertaken on the spot e.g. reading a short text about a health topic while answering self-reflective questions; or were ones that required activities during a longer period while requiring the usage of self-monitoring tools of the HBCSS.

The persuasive features of the system were carefully analyzed and decided together by the research consortium by using the PSD model. The persuasive features included goal setting and the principles of *self-monitoring, rehearsal, praise, reminders, suggestion, liking, trustworthiness* and *social comparison* [7]. In the PSD model, both *self-monitoring* (primary task support) and *reminders* (dialogue support) are specifically tied to achieving goals. In addition to these, all features in the primary task support category are to varying extents linked to goal setting and achieving set goals.

The HBCSS under investigation contained seven health problem domain modules. Each module contained one or more *self-monitoring* tools (see Table 1). The main role of the tools was to allow the users to measure and monitor their self-perceived situation in relation to health behaviors. Additionally, the tools were also meant to be self-reflective, thus allowing the users to reflect on the behaviors that may lead to health choices [11]. Some of the self-monitoring tools might be considered as having additional functions, in addition to self-monitoring. For example, the posture change reminder not only reminded the users to change posture, but also allowed the users to reflect whether they had not moved for 30 or 60 min.

Table 1. Health problem domains and self-monitoring tools in the application.

Self-monitoring software feature	Health problem domain
Stress statistics	Stress management
Pedometer	Exercising
Recovery statistics	Recovery from work
Posture change reminder	Sedentary behavior
Dietary rhythm rehearsal	Nutrition (dietary behavior)
Diet planning	Nutrition (dietary behavior)
Circadian rhythm	Sleep, Efficient working hours (time management), Recovery from work

Both tools at the nutrition category (dietary rhythm rehearsal and diet planning) were inherently about virtual *rehearsal*, but as one could check the plans for both diet and rhythm, they served also as self-monitoring tools. Regarding the statistic tools, both were self-reflective in nature, as you could monitor your daily or weekly level of self-perceived stress/recovery. Additionally, both also incorporated aspects of *social comparison,* as users could also compare their own level to the average level of the user base. Circadian rhythm tool allowed users to monitor the proportion of work, free time, and sleep within 24-h timeframe.

The second goal setting related persuasive software feature studied here, *reminders,* had two main roles in the application: (1) Once a week the users received a push notification reminding them to fill a quick weekly survey, thus also reminding them to use the application. (2) Whenever users chose tasks requiring longer periods for completion, a push notification was send after a day (or few days, depending on the goal and task), thus reminding the users that they had a task pending.

2.2   Research Method

We decided to take a closer look at the goals of the participants, and the premises, validity and role of the two aforementioned principles in achieving goals. Therefore, we conducted a deductive thematic analysis from the transcribed interviews. Among qualitative research, interviews are the most common method for collecting data [12].

According to Braun and Clarke [13], "Thematic analysis is a method for identifying, analyzing and reporting patterns (themes) within data. It minimally organizes and describes your data set in (rich) detail". We chose a deductive approach for this thematic analysis, because we aimed to test the PSD principles of *self-monitoring* and *reminders* in this particular case [14]. Deductive thematic analysis, however, tends to produce less rich overall description of the data set, but is suited for answering theory-bound research questions, as it is analyst-driven, i.e. driven by analytical or theoretical interest; and the analysis can be more detailed for some aspects of the data [13].

Data Collection. The interviews were conducted as semi-structured, with a predefined set of open-ended questions. When deemed necessary, the interviewer could ask follow-up questions for in-depth answers. Question sets had been used in a previous intervention study [15], in which the team had participated, and the questions were piloted with two pilot participants for this intervention study.

When piloting the application, it was discovered that recruiting interviewees via email could be difficult, as most pilot users never answered our emails. Therefore, we decided to ask for a voluntary pre-agreement for interview in the enrollment phase of the intervention, which required those interested to fill in their phone numbers. Some other researchers in the research consortium were also interviewing other participants from a different point of view. All those who had expressed consent to be interviewed, were randomized and split into two lists, one for each group of researchers. The list for our team consisted of 50 randomized participant names and contact info.

Each participant on the list was tried to be reached by a phone call three times, while dividing the calls into several days and potentially suitable times. In case a participant did not answer these calls, we send an email or mobile text message explaining why we had called, which led to some calling back to us. Total of 32 participants were recruited for our study to be interviewed about their experiences regarding the application. Three interviewees canceled for personal reasons; therefore, we conducted 29 interviews. As we also collected log data about the actual usage of the application, we checked that all invited interviewees had logged into the application.

The main platform used for the interviews was Skype, a Voice over Internet Protocol (VoIP) software. Only the audio connection was enabled and thus recorded. The interviewees were asked for their final consent in the beginning of the interviews and each had received the information about the research beforehand. In case the interviewees shunned using Skype, recorded telephone calls were used instead.

The recorded interviews were transcribed into textual form for analysis purposes. The content of the interviews were not altered in any way for the transcriptions, e.g. dialects were transcribed precisely, but the transcriptions were not precise phonetically, meaning that for example not all coughs or sneezes were marked down explicitly.

Data Analysis. In the first phase of thematic analysis, researchers should familiarize themselves with the data, while in the second phase, initial coding of the data takes place [13, 16], potentially with the help of computer program software [17] suited for the process. The third phase consists of searching for themes within the coded data and once themes are devised, the themes are reviewed in the fourth phase [13, 16]. Definition and naming takes place in the fifth phase [13, 16], while making sure that all text relevant for the research question are included in the themes, but avoiding the pitfall of refining the themes forever [17]. In the sixth phase, a final thematic analysis is written [13, 16], while using direct quotes from the participants as examples in the report [17]. Making notes and/or marking ideas for coding in the first phase of analysis can be beneficial later on [13]. Keeping a reflexivity journal during the process increases the trustworthiness of the research [16].

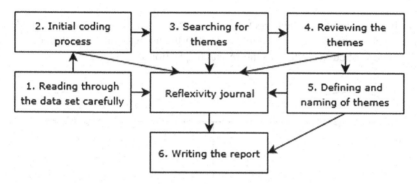

Fig. 1. The data analysis process

At first, the transcribed interviews were read through carefully, while paying attention to information, such as names and places of living, which could be used to recognize the interviewees, thus needing to be shrouded in order to grant the interviewees anonymousness. A reflexivity journal was initiated concurrently. Next, the interviews were carefully re-read twice. After the data set familiarization phase, the interviews were printed on paper and initial codes were generated. At this point, the coding was done manually by using colored highlighter pens and by writing notes [13].

After the initial coding, we decided to use computer software program NVivo version 11 (by QSR International) for the next phase. Therefore, the transcribed interview files were exported into NVivo and the prints were used for guidance for transferring the initial codes into the program. Because we had chosen a deductive approach, we formed the main themes (parent nodes in NVivo) based on the research question. Memos linked to each main theme were created in NVivo at this point. Sub-themes were formed in similar way and presented as child nodes in NVivo.

The themes were reviewed, which involved deleting unnecessary codes as well as those overlapping with other codes. In the next phase, the themes were defined and named. In the final phase, a report of the findings and a final analysis was written, which will be presented in the 'results' section. The reflexivity journal in the form of memos and notes was helpful for presenting and interpreting the results (see Fig. 1).

3 Results

Reactions to the application were mostly positive, although many complained about technical difficulties hindering their usage. Total of 21 interviewees reported that the application was persuasive (believable and convincing) for them, whereas eight interviewees thought that it was not that persuasive in their case. Nevertheless, the application was deemed persuasive by over two thirds of the interviewees, including many of those complaining about the technical difficulties, as they expressed that it would be even more persuasive if it would function correctly. As regarding persuasiveness, the aspect was brought up in two different questions in the interviews, and few interviewees asked for a clarification, which was given for them. Most of the interviewees expressed interest in an updated and bug-free version of the application, giving further evidence that the application was found useful and engaging, thus also persuasive.

During the interviews, the users were asked about their personal goals and had their personal goal changed or remained the same after the usage period. The themes for goal setting were formed according to the research question (see Fig. 2).

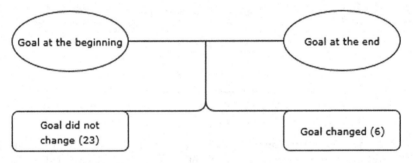

Fig. 2. Themes for goal setting

We planned to ask the interviewees about *reminders*, but the subject actually came up in most of the interviews, regardless whether we would have asked the prepared question or not. Only with the case of one user, we did not ask about reminders due to low usage of the app and neither did the subject come up by the interviewee.

We did not ask any specific questions about *self-monitoring*, but the subject came up frequently. The themes for persuasive features investigated here (*self-monitoring* and *reminders*, see Fig. 3) were formed according to the research question.

The only exception was one subtheme (*customization*), which was formed inductively. Combining deductive and inductive approaches is not an uncommon phenomenon in thematic analysis [16, 18, 19].

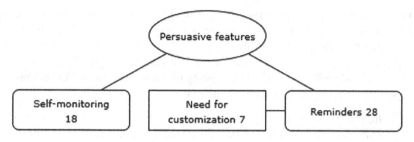

Fig. 3. Themes for persuasive features tested

3.1 Personal Goal

Goal at the Beginning of Usage. A recurring pattern could be spotted from the interviews: all participants either had problems with their well-being or concerns about their health. Both issues were intertwining with the core of the intervention, which was recovery from work-related strain and stress. The motivation for enrollment might have differed, as for some it was curiosity:

"Well, mostly I came along because of interest, as I should do something about my own well-being and occupational well-being, so it hit the spot. When thinking about having enough strength to keep on working, mostly the goal was that working life and spare time would be in some sort of balance, so maybe having more free time and gaining tools for balancing it" (Interview 16).

For others, there might have been more severe need for help, but everyone had obviously realized that they had to do something about their situation eventually:

"I had an idea about somehow getting something new, which would help me to get by, because at the moment I'm working on the brink of exhaustion" (Interview 13).

Personal Goal at the End of Usage. It should be noted that several interviewees used the application for shorter than two months due to various reasons, which led them to not use the application regularly. Five users stopped using the application altogether almost immediately after the beginning of the intervention. The early abandonment of the application was mostly due to technical issues experienced or from being too busy due to work. Nonetheless, 15 users reported that the application had clearly supported or affected their personal goal in one way or another:

"My goals are the same as before, so the app has not changed them, but it has been a part of supporting the orientation to achieving the goals with time" (Interview 17).

Goal Did Not Change. For 23 interviewees, the goal remained practically the same at the end of usage. Nevertheless, even if remaining the same, the goal or idea of the goal had been strengthened for some users:

"The application, it also fortifies the confirmation that I just have to take the time for exercising. All those fancy goals regarding exercising in the app those might not never truly be reality for me as such, but if adapted, then they might" (Interview 15).

Achieving personal goals might be hard and take a lot of time, especially if one tries to change a behavior that has been going on for years. Even with the support and coaching of a persuasive application, it could be difficult, if one does not want to take any time off from work. Being addicted to work bears down to such fundamental issues that no application alone could resolve:

"The goals are more or less the same, because it is hard [to achieve them], when one is a so-called workaholic, which has been going on for many years as an entrepreneur. Therefore, changing habits is not easy" (Interview 9).

Goal Changed. For six interviewees, the goal appeared to have changed beyond the point of fortification up to expansion or refinement. Achieving personal health-related goals might take years, so we held no misconception about the application miraculously curing all sort of ailments during a two-month usage period. Nevertheless, self-reflection [11] was one of the key issues in the application, therefore it comes as no surprise that people who take the time to reflect their own behavior might have their goals at least refined or expanded, if not achieved:

"I now have a [new] goal as I have to get my sleep [quality and quantity] in order and here [in the application] is help for that" (Interview 3).

For many interviewees, the reason for enrolling into the intervention was the need to do something about their health, so they might have been pondering their personal health issues for years. In that sense, even starting to use or trying out the application might have been an important factor in the long road to better health behavior:

"Therefore, if my goal has changed, it has only been to the better direction, because when I was busy and stressed, which I had been for many years, I thought that eventually I would die. I thought that now I just have to start taking better care of myself and that has only increased. Whether the application had a part in that, it certainly did not decrease my need, so yes, it was a small part in the process" (Interview 19).

3.2   Self-monitoring

As described in the PSD model [7], "A system that keeps track of one's own performance or status supports the user in achieving goals". The application was a system that enabled *self-monitoring*; therefore, the application should have supported the users in achieving goals. In this case, it could be said that the self-monitoring tools were there to help the users in the three-level TTM-based task related goals, rather than directly with their personal goals. Nevertheless, this did not exclude the tools being used by the users for supporting their personal goals:

"Well now, that pedometer is by definition a good thing, because I became aware of the fact that as I am doing [sedentary] work at the office, I get really too few steps during the day. At least to that it has helped, so maybe because of it I have paid more attention now when following the amount of steps" (Interview 16).

Some of the interviewees reported using wearables (for self-monitoring) concurrently with the application, or even abandoning the application in favor of wearables or other health applications with sensor-based real-time self-monitoring functions. Previous experiences with health applications seemed to have molded the expectations for them, which might have led to disappointments, as the app did not have various sensor-based measuring functions. Few had started using wearables or another application more or less after the intervention period begun. Some thought that it would have been nice to be able to connect their wearables into the 'Recover!'-application, but as they could not, they continued to use both:

"Now I have actually been testing this bracelet or watch, which follows my heartbeat and sleep and so on automatically. I don't have to mark those up myself, so I have used it for about a month now, but it doesn't mean that I wouldn't use the application, because there was that other stuff in there" (Interview 26).

It seemed that the interviewees chose whether to use the self-monitoring tools of the app, or those provided by other applications or wearable devices, based on their personal needs or situations. Lack of comprehensive set of sensor-based self-monitoring tools did not bother everyone, as they were more or less satisfied with the tools provided by the application. This was likely because the tools, such as the circadian rhythm, suited their needs. Nevertheless, the app had an automatic, sensor-based pedometer, which was used by many interviewees. All the other tools were interactive and required actions from the user. Rather than being merely *self-monitoring*, the tools were also intended to be *self-reflective*:

"In a way, I had this conception of how these things are, but when you really start marking them and following them, it might be that the truth really is not what you thought it to be" (Interview 26).

One interviewee complained that the application and the circadian rhythm tool were too persuasive in the sense that the user felt like being a slave to the phone, constantly interacting with it. This led to the user abandoning the app due to stress, so apparently the self-monitoring tool did not suit the user's current health problem that well, as the user also complained about being busy and stressed otherwise. However, the afore-mentioned user also thought that the application was still partially responsible for changing the personal goal in a positive way. Few others complained about minor issues with the self-monitoring tools, mostly with pedometer, of which one issue was a major bug (app crashing when turning phone sideways):

"There were good systems, pedometer and such, but if I went for a jog and the phone turned sideways [while jogging], it rather became an obstacle" (Interview 11).

It could be said that in the case of the application, the premises were true if the user had a need for the types of tools provided by the application and the tools functioned technically. Therefore, if the premises were true, then the argument was also solid, thus the application could be said supporting the users, whether they achieved their goals during the usage or not.

3.3 Reminders

As described in the PSD model [7], "If a system reminds users of their target behavior, the users will more likely achieve their goals". The application was a system that utilized reminders, so therefore the users of the application should have been more likely to achieve their goals. It should be noted that many users had some technical difficulties with the reminders, although it should also be mentioned that some of the difficulties reported might rather have been misconceptions by the users (than actual bugs). For example, one user thought that the reminders regarding tasks were mal-functioning for not getting any. The user for some reason had assumed that tasks would be given for the users automatically, which was not the case. Nevertheless, when functioning properly, the reminders were seen as helpful for achieving the goals set:

"[Reminders] were good, because otherwise those [tasks] would be left undone, so it is very good that there comes reminders [from the application], because if there are not reminders, then you just will not remember" (Interview 15).

However, there were other opinions, as not all users were keen on having reminders, at least not very often. If not using the application actively, the reminders might have been felt as annoying. Even if the user knew and admitted that reminders were useful and supportive, they might still have been felt as annoying. One solution to dissolving potential annoyance of reminders could very well be *customization*:

"When you know that I've set this reminder myself, just like you put alarms in a calendar, I must say that those aren't annoying at all when they are something that I've set there myself, so that would be a good idea" (Interview 17).

Some users felt that the reminders occasionally arrived at improper times, such as when they had meetings with customers. Therefore, it was difficult for them to react to reminders at due times. According to the sixth postulate of the PSD model [7], persuasive features at improper moments may lead to undesirable outcomes and in the case of reminders, ending up ignored. Customization could also be a solution for avoiding the possible obtrusiveness of reminders:

"I cannot have any reminders beeping in those situations [with customers], so for example it would be proper only on those days that I am at the office, which are limited. I noticed, that I could not set a [customized] reminder in this app" (Interview 6).

It could be said that in the case of the application, the premises were true if: (1) the reminders were not annoying, or obtrusive, and (2) the reminders functioned technically. Therefore, if the premises were true, then the argument was also solid, thus the users could have been said to be more likely to achieve their goals, whether they achieved them during the usage or not.

4 Discussion

The long-term personal goals of participants might have been under the way for a while. Fifteen users reported that the application had clearly supported or affected their personal goal, of which six users thought that their goal had changed during the relatively short usage period. Hence, it could be seen as quite a positive thing that over a half of the users felt that their personal goals were fortified and perhaps even refined or expanded during the usage process.

Commercial systems supporting behavior change might nowadays be depending heavily on sensor based self-monitoring tools, as well as on external wearable devices. This seemed to have molded the expectations of some of the interviewed participants, which evidently affected the usage. Pedometer was the only sensor based self-monitoring tool in the application, which for some was enough, but for others insufficient as they were clearly expecting more. Nevertheless, those using the self-monitoring tools of the application, whether the pedometer or the non-sensor based options e.g. circadian rhythm tool, seemed to benefit from the self-reflective side of the tools. On the other hand, if the users could not find tools suitable for their specific needs, they could still use the application by going through the contents and completing the tasks. They seemed to switch to using the tools of other applications or wearable devices for self-monitoring purposes in the aforementioned case, which in turn seemed to decrease the overall interest for the 'Recover!'-application for those users.

As regarding reminders, *customization* could be a solution for avoiding annoying the users, as well as avoiding obtrusiveness. Even if push notifications at improper times would not be bothersome for all, they seemed to disturb some. Implementing full customization (times and dates) for reminders (push notifications) could consume resources. At minimum, it might be wise to allow the option of turning the reminders off altogether.

The contents of the application were planned specifically for micro-entrepreneurs, but as they were derived from general evidence-based health and well-being recommendations, they were also largely applicable for other entrepreneurs as well as for the general population.

As regarding the limitations, this study was about one application in one context. Additional limitations of this study include that the results were based on the interviews, which were more or less subjective opinions of the users, although important as portrayals of personal experiences. Analyzing application's actual usage by using log data could add value to analyses such as the one carried out here.

5 Conclusions

Interviews can be fruitful for gaining insights about users' goals, system's persuasiveness, and its persuasive features. Users may have long-term goals, which persuasive technologies can offer support. Nevertheless, it is a challenge for design that some users may perceive a persuasive feature as fine, whereas others may find it irritating or useless. This is especially challenging when designing for very heterogeneous target groups. In any case, software bugs tend to decrease the persuasiveness and overall trustworthiness dramatically.

For designers, this study offers user-based insights and perceptions about self-monitoring tools and customization of reminders. For researchers, this study offers further evidence that self-monitoring and reminders can indeed support users, as long as the premises are true.

Acknowledgements. We wish to thank our colleagues at Promo@Work research project, funded by the Strategic Research Council at the Academy of Finland, contract no. 303430 (Finnish Institute of Occupational Health) and contract no. 303431 (University of Oulu, OASIS).

References

1. Agarwal, R., Gao, G., DesRoches, C., Jha, A.: Research commentary—the digital transformation of healthcare: current status and the road ahead. Inf. Syst. Res. **21**(4), 796–809 (2010)
2. Goh, J.M., Gao, G., Agarwal, R.: Evolving work routines: adaptive routinization of information technology in healthcare. Inf. Syst. Res. **22**(3), 565–585 (2011)
3. Borrelli, B., Ritterband, L.M.: Special issue on eHealth and mHealth: challenges and future directions for assessment, treatment, and dissemination. Health Psychol. **34**(S), 1205 (2015)
4. Meier, C.A., Fitzgerald, M.C., Smith, J.M.: eHealth: extending, enhancing, and evolving health care. Annu. Rev. Biomed. Eng. **15**, 359–382 (2013)
5. Oinas-Kukkonen, H.: A foundation for the study of behavior change support systems. Pers. Ubiquit. Comput. **17**(6), 1223–1235 (2013)
6. European Commission: Commission Recommendation of 6 May 2003 concerning the definition of micro, small and medium-sized enterprises. Official J. Eur. Union **46** (2003)
7. Oinas-Kukkonen, H., Harjumaa, M.: Persuasive systems design: key issues, process model, and system features. Commun. Assoc. Inf. Syst. **24**(1), 28 (2009)
8. Ryan, R.M., Deci, E.L.: Self-determination theory and the facilitation of intrinsic motivation, social development, and well-being. Am. Psychol. **55**(1), 68 (2000)
9. Prochaska, J.O., DiClemente, C.C.: The transtheoretical approach. Handb. Psychother. Integr. **2**, 147–171 (2005)
10. Ng, J.Y., et al.: Self-determination theory applied to health contexts: a meta-analysis. Perspect. Psychol. Sci. **7**, 325–340 (2012)
11. Halttu, K., Oinas-Kukkonen, H.: Persuading to reflect: role of reflection and insight in persuasive systems design for physical health. Hum.–Comput. Interact. **32**(5–6), 381–412 (2017)
12. King, N.: Using interviews in qualitative research. In: Cassel, C., Gillian, S. (eds.) Essential Guide to Qualitative Methods in Organizational Research. SAGE, London (2004)
13. Braun, V., Clarke, V.: Using thematic analysis in psychology. Qual. Res. Psychol. **3**(2), 77–101 (2006)
14. Vaismoradi, M., Turunen, H., Bondas, T.: Content analysis and thematic analysis: implications for conducting a qualitative descriptive study. Nurs. Health Sci. **15**(3), 398–405 (2013)
15. Karppinen, P., et al.: Persuasive user experience in health behavior change support system: a 12-month study for prevention of metabolic syndrome. Int. J. Med. Inform. **96**, 51–61 (2016)
16. Nowell, L.S., Norris, J.M., White, D.E., Moules, N.J.: Thematic analysis: striving to meet the trustworthiness criteria. Int. J. Qual. Meth. **16**(1) (2017). https://doi.org/10.1177/1609406917733847
17. King, N.: Using templates in the thematic analysis of text. In: Cassel, C., Gillian, S. (eds.) Essential Guide to Qualitative Methods in Organizational Research. SAGE, London (2004)
18. Fereday, J., Muir-Cochrane, E.: Demonstrating rigor using thematic analysis: a hybrid approach of inductive and deductive coding and theme development. Int. J. Qual. Meth. **5**(1), 80–92 (2006)
19. Gregory, R., Muntermann, J.: Theorizing in design science research: inductive versus deductive approaches. In: ICIS 2011 Proceedings (2011)

Goal Setting for Persuasive Information Systems: Five Reference Checklists

Sainabou Cham[✉], Abdullah Algashami, John McAlaney,
Angelos Stefanidis, Keith Phalp, and Raian Ali

Bournemouth University, Poole, UK
{scham,aalghashami,jmcalaney,astefanidis,
kphalp,rali}@bournemouth.ac.uk

Abstract. The concept of goals is prominent in information systems and also artificial intelligence literature such as goal-oriented requirements engineering and self-adaptive systems. Digital motivation systems, e.g. gamification and persuasive technology, utilise the concept of behavioural goals which require a different mind-set on how to elicit and set them up, how to monitor deviation from such goals and how to ensure their completion. Behavioural goals are characterised by a range of factors which are not the main focus in classic information systems and AI literature such as self-efficacy, perceived usefulness. To engineer software supporting goal setting, a concretised taxonomy of goals would help a better-managed analysis and design process. In this paper, we provide a detailed classification of behavioural goals and their associated properties and elements (types, sources, monitoring, feedback, deviation and countermeasures). As a method, we review the literature on goal setting theory and its application in different disciplines. We subsequently develop five reference checklists which would act as a reference point for researchers and practitioners in persuasive and motivational systems.

Keywords: Goal setting · Persuasive systems · Behavioural goals

1 Introduction

Goal Setting Theory relates to the relationship between people and goals. It includes how people set up goals, how they react to them, and how they use them to attain behavioural change [1]. Goal setting research is informed by cognitive psychological theories, which demonstrate how a person's perception of their skills, and the usefulness and ease of achieving a specific goal, play a vital role in being successful in meeting that goal [2]. Goal setting is a core element of various persuasive information system paradigms, such as gamification [3] and persuasive technology [4, 5]. A persuasive system is an information system intended to strengthen, change or shape states of mind or behaviour or both without utilising pressure, this might delay or avoid the onset of a range of medical problems, and enhance the quality of life [6, 7].

Goal setting is a core element of various techniques and principles within persuasive technology. In terms of Fogg's mechanisms [8], goal setting relates to reduction and tunnelling where smaller steps lead to a bigger goal; self-monitoring, where goal

© Springer Nature Switzerland AG 2019
H. Oinas-Kukkonen et al. (Eds.): PERSUASIVE 2019, LNCS 11433, pp. 237–253, 2019.
https://doi.org/10.1007/978-3-030-17287-9_20

achievement is tracked and enforced; surveillance where peers monitoring can put pressure towards goal achievement and, conditioning, where failure or success in meeting goals is rewarded accordingly. Regarding Cialdini's principle of influence [9], goal setting correlates well with the commitment and consistency principle, where people remain motivated to sustain a behaviour that helps or has helped them to achieve a behaviour change goal. In particular, self-set or agreed goals require a commitment that then boosts the degree of adherence to the goal [10].

Research on goal setting can be found across a wide range of disciplines. This includes the domain of management and business administration where the emphasis is on productivity and supporting business achievement of tactic and strategic goals [11], and the domain of social psychology, e.g. the use of goal setting within groups in which social relationships become an integral part of goal definition and achievement [12]. Similarly, targeted behaviour in theories of reasoned action [13] and planned behaviour [14] can be defined as a goal. These theories highlight that the self-perception of the ability to meet a goal affects the commitment and adherence to plans to reach it.

In this paper, we present five reference checklists developed based on reviewing the literature on goal setting theory and its application in various domains. Producing reference checklists for goal setting that concretise the concept and depict its common and variable components will help to achieve better software and automation of behavioural goals support.

At the start of the research, we made a proposition that behavioural change goals introduce the need for a new mindset when dealt with as requirements in persuasive systems. Informed by goal-setting theory [1] and the literature on goal-oriented requirements engineering [15], we defined five main pillars of behavioural goals to guide our investigation. These pillars are *sources of behavioural goals, goal identifiers, goal elicitation, monitor and feedback, deviation and countermeasures*. After setting the initial template, we reviewed the relevant literature to inform our approach to constructing the five goal setting reference checklists. We reviewed the research on goal setting in various communities, including behavioural economics, persuasive technology, and health and environmental sciences. We only considered papers which adopted goal-setting as their primary research strategy and provided a description of how it was used. Search criteria used to obtain the relevant work included variations and combinations of keywords, incorporating terms such as goal setting, behavioural goals, persuasive systems, and behavioural change. We used snowballing approach [16], starting with influential papers in the field which led to further references.

2   Behavioural Goals: Five Reference Checklists

2.1   Sources of Behavioural Goals

The source of goals represents the party who sets the goal. Based on the literature review findings, we identified five sources of goals; Table 1 provides a brief description of each source of behavioural goals. By *experts*, we mean a behavioural change expert. By *subjects*, we mean the people who are to achieve goals.

Table 1. Sources of behavioural goals

Source	Description
Self-set	Goals are designed and chosen solely by subjects
Assigned	The experts designed goals with no subjects input
Participatory	Goals are designed jointly by subjects and experts
Guided	Subjects are given directions by experts on how to choose a goal, but the choice is left for them to make
Group-set	Goals are designed and chosen within a group, typically facilitated by an expert

There are some factors to consider when deciding the suitability of each source of goal in the behavioural change process. These include:

Problem Origin plays a vital role in the decision about the subjects' level of involvement in the behavioural goal specification process. A subject's behaviour could be influenced by factors relating to social and individual context [17]. The social context refers to the social influence of and peer pressure on a subject's behaviour, and the individual factors refer to the beliefs, values and state of mind of the subject. Any intention to change the subject's behaviour should, therefore, take into account such influencing factors. If the social context is the origin of the problem, then the behavioural goals would need to be set collaboratively, agreed upon and committed to by the subjects, with help from an expert. If the problem originates from individual factors, such as the subject's personality, or the pleasure derived from performing the behaviour, consideration would be necessary for assessing variables such as personality, the stage of change and treatment levels before selecting a source for the goals.

Self-efficacy refers to one's belief that one has the skills and abilities required to attain the goals. Subjects with a higher self-efficacy, tend to be more committed to their goals, as they are likely to come up with better strategies and put in more effort towards goal attainment [18]. When goals are to be set collaboratively, the selection of subjects should be based on their skills and abilities to attain the goals. Subjects self-efficacy can be increased by employing specific persuasion techniques, such as providing information about the require approaches for goal-related tasks.

Behavioural change state affects the ability of subjects to set goals and their receptiveness to external goal sources. For users in the contemplation stage, self-set goals could be avoided as the users may be defensive about their behaviour and may be in denial or biased when expressing goals [19]. When this is the case, we might consider choosing participatory, guided, group-set or even assigned goals. Self-set goals would fit those in the advanced stages of change, i.e. users who have already started to implement the behavioural change.

2.2   Behavioural Goal Identifiers

Various properties describe goals. The goals can be influenced by specific moderating variables relating to the person or their group context. Table 2 provides a summary.

Table 2. Behavioural goals identifiers

Goal properties	Description
Proximity	The time by which the goals is to be achieved; Distal (goals set on a long-term basis) or Proximal (goals based on short-term goals)
Goal specificity	The precision and granularity of what is to be achieved
Goal difficulty	The effort required from a subject for goal attainment
Goal moderators	Description
Commitment	The importance of goal attainment and an individual's determination to achieve the goal defined by subjects': • Self-efficacy or believing in one's ability to achieve the goal • Perception of usefulness, and the significance of achieving the goal
Feedback	The knowledge of performance progress in relation to attaining goals
Task complexity	The complex nature of a task defines the level of effort, skills, and also the strategy required to attend the goal

Proximity refers to how far into the future goals are set. Setting proximal goals, in addition to distal goals, could enhance performance [1] and self-efficacy [20], because they provide a relatively quick sense of achievement in the short-term, leading to sustained performance. For example, a distal goal to spend less time online this month could be attained by setting proximal goals such as to reduce the time spent online by 20 min a week. Also, goal proximity could help lessen the loss of goal interest, increase motivation and confidence toward goal attainment. In persuasive systems, users could be motivated to set proximal goals by awarding gamification elements such as points to a user when goals are self-set or collectively when the behavioural change goals are set in a group.

Commitment refers to the status of a person dedicated to a goal. In [1], two factors are found to influence commitment; (1) the importance of goal attainment, and (2) self-efficacy. Elsewhere in [21], external influences (peer influence, authority), interactive influences (participation and competitiveness), and internal factors (expectancy and internal rewards) are outlined as elements which could define commitment. To improve commitment, when goal setting is performed collaboratively, the individuals involved could make a collective commitment to attaining the goals. When the goal is assigned, the subject's commitment tends to reflect their self-efficacy levels; therefore, assessing self-efficacy before assigning goals could be essential in gauging the subject's commitment to the goals.

2.3   Behavioural Goal Elicitation

The main techniques to elicit behavioural change goals are listed in Table 3. We comment on the main types in the following. *Interviewing* as an elicitation method could be used at the initial stages of implementing the system. The technique can capture in-depth information relating to a subject's behaviour. During the interview process, subjects could be encouraged to reflect on their emotional state, the behaviour which needs to change and how they plan to change such behaviour. The findings from this activity could then be used to determine the correct behavioural change goals, but also assess the eligibility of subjects pursuing a behavioural change goal as employed in [22]. *Diaries* could enable the capturing of events as they happen. This information may be used to help identify adverse behavioural issues and possible techniques to act as countermeasures. In [23], diary entries were used to gather student motivation strategies, employed for improving their school work, demonstrating a self-regulatory process for managing learning.

Table 3. Behavioural goal elicitation methods

Elicitation method	Description
Interview	Used when in-depth understanding is required
Diary study	Used for capturing events as they happen
Group discussion	Used for discussing barriers and strategies for alleviating them
Counselling	Used for helping subjects understand their behavioural change needs
Brainstorming	Used for discovering bespoke strategies for reaching the goal
Observation	Used for assessing behaviours in a natural setting
Algorithms	Used for understanding a subject's behaviour from their historical data

When goals are set collaboratively, *group discussion* could be more useful as it enables a debate amongst the subjects to help understand their behaviour, and consequently, the setting of goals. Furthermore, obstacles to goal attainment and strategies for overcoming such obstacles could be addressed more efficiently in such a group-therapy style [24]. The social element of a group discussion could lead to better goal performance, as a result of peer influence and the ability to make a collective commitment to the goals of a group [25]. *Algorithms* could be used to learn and understand the behaviour and behaviour pattern of subjects, by performing behaviour analysis on their historical activity data.

2.4   Behavioural Goals Monitoring and Feedback

Our fourth checklist is related to the monitoring and feedback strategies used to assess and enhance behavioural goal attainment. Table 4 provides a summary.

Table 4. Behavioural goals monitoring & feedback

Monitor and feedback	
Monitor	Self-monitoring; Peer monitoring; Automated
Feedback content	Motivational feedback; Learning feedback; Outcome feedback; Performance feedback; Comparative feedback (Self-comparisons; Social comparisons)
Feedback timing	Reflection during the behaviour; Reflection after the behaviour
Feedback framing	Gain frame; Loss frame; Formal; Informal

Monitor refers to the agent who collects behavioural metrics and progress status. Monitoring can be performed by the subjects, by peers or be computerised.

- *Self-monitoring* refers to the responsibility of a subject to observe and reflect on their behaviour and goals. Self-monitoring is performed by recording and tracking goal-related activity, and by evaluating the progress made. Reminders and journaling, in the form of a progress bar or timers, could help individuals perform self-monitoring and increase their awareness of their behaviour [26].
- *Peer-monitoring* refers to other individuals observing a subject's behaviour, possibly on mutual understanding. Peer-to-peer monitoring could lead to social relationship breakdown if the feedback method implemented is not carefully designed, as it may be viewed as spying [27]. Peer monitoring could be useful in relation to behavioural change when goal setting is performed collaboratively. Hence, the surveillance is seen positively as part of behaviour awareness and change.
- *Automated monitoring* is based on the use of sensors and communication technology, e.g. geographic location and heart rate monitoring via a smartwatch. The accuracy and intensity of monitoring could empower individuals to gain insight into their behaviour or pattern of behaviour. However, the lack of privacy and anxiety could have negative consequences. Also, automated monitoring may fail to capture the intention and context of the behaviour. This may necessitate a blended approach putting together self-monitoring or peer monitoring with an automated one.

Feedback content refers to the central theme in the feedback informational content.

- *Motivational feedback* informs subjects how well they perform towards their goals and encourages them to continue in the same way or perform better. Performance could be rewarded by employing gamification elements such as points, badges and avatars. Competitive rewards and game mechanics, such as the leader-board, need to be avoided as they may distract from the primary goal or the spirit of the ultimate behavioural change goal, especially when goals are set collaboratively.

- *Learning feedback* helps subjects to learn the consequences of specific committed or avoided behaviours [22]. This feedback needs a clear rationale. For example, in regulating printing behaviour, when a subject prints ten articles daily while the goal is not to exceed four articles a day, the feedback should clarify how the deviation from goal occurs, and show the subject how this was manifested in their printing behaviour.

- *Performance feedback* shows a subject's performance toward their goal and could be used to help determine the chances of attaining behavioural goals. This feedback could help persuade the subjects who are committed, motivated, and have the right ability, to put in more effort and time when a discrepancy is detected between the feedback provided and their behavioural goal.

- *Outcome feedback* represents the knowledge of results; subjects should be able to have the skills required to evaluate whether the outcome feedback represents a good or poor performance toward the goal.

- *Comparative feedback* compares subjects to their past goal performance (self-comparison) or to the performance of their peers when the collaborative goal setting is adopted (social comparison). *Self-comparison* may work better when self-monitoring is employed and may fit well those subjects with lower self-esteem. *Social-comparison* works by comparing goal performance within a social circle to motivate individuals to attain their goals. It may also lead to competition and conflict between subjects within the same group or between groups if an inter-group comparison is adopted. This could negatively impact self-esteem and self-efficacy.

Feedback timing is concerned with the right timing of feedback message so that it is seen as a motivational tool and its acceptance is increased. Feedback can be delivered while the behaviour is taking place (reflection during usage) for real-time awareness or afterwards (reflection after usage) for off-line learning and future planning.

Framing refers to the language used in the message content of the feedback in style and orientation. The feedback may not have the desired effect when the subjects view it as strict or consisting of threatening messages [28]. The language used relates to what extent the feedback is consistent with the subjects' attitudes and preferences, e.g. whether the message is a gain or a loss frame, strict, precise, or personal. Loss frame refers to feedback which shows a negative impact, e.g. smoking can cause cancer, whereas gain frame relates to feedback which indicates a positive impact of healthy behaviour, e.g. quitting smoking makes sleep quality better.

2.5   Deviation and Countermeasures

Deviation refers to the difference between the desired behaviour of a person and their actual behaviour [29]. Deviation consists of different types, and various facilitators can trigger it. Reducing or preventing deviation is achieved by employing a series of countermeasures, as summarised in Table 5. Due to space limitation and given that most of these deviation facilitators and countermeasures are self-explanatory; we will only elaborate on main and more complex elements from each category.

Table 5. Deviation from behavioural goals: types, facilitators and countermeasures

Type	Time-related; Frequency-related; Communication-related
Facilitators	Goals that combined, conflict or compete with other goals; Source of the behavioural goal; Social influence or peer pressure on the subject pursuing the goals; Setting ambiguous goals with limited skills or time to attain the goals; Lack of commitment to the set goals; Lack of proper timing of the goals; Setting complex goals that do not match subjects' ability to attain them; Lack of self-efficacy to achieve the goal; Environmental influence; Lack of a structured method for goal setting; Inaccessibility to resources to aid goal attainment; Not understanding users' needs for the goals; Over-estimating participants' self-efficacy level to achieve goals; Lack of understanding of barrier to gain attainment; Timing of the behavioural goals; Frequency of executing the set goals
Countermeasures	Detect and resolve goal conflict; Discuss barriers to goal attainment and ensure subjects could adequately handle them; State clear goal outcome; Assess subjects commitment and self-efficacy levels; Assess complexity of goal and analyse complex goals into series of sub-goals; Review goals, re-strategise and analyse complex goals into series of sub-goals; Monitor goal-related activities; Provide summary feedback in relation to goal performance; Reminders; Perform manipulation checks to assess whether subjects understand the goal or task; A proper explanation of the goal-related task; Task familiarisation by asking subjects to try out a task similar to the goal; Persuade subjects to verbally commit to the goal; Set unambiguous goals, Rewards

Deviation Facilitators. These capture the various factors that can facilitate deviation.

- *The timing of the goal* refers to when goals are improperly time which could lead to conflicting, combined or competing goals. For instance, a smoking cessation goal may conflict with other goals, such as a weight loss goal or stress coping goal [30]. Similarly, individuals who have a heavy workload in conjunction with their goals could easily deviate due to their busy lifestyle [5]. It is, hence, vital to set goals so that their timing does not coincide with other personal activities.
- *The frequency of executing the goal* is essential for ensuring that the execution of goal-related actions does not overwhelm the subjects. If the rate of goal execution is not ideal for the subjects, they may lose interest in pursuing their goal.
- *Inaccessibility to resources* needed to achieve a goal, even temporarily, may affect the attainment of the goal. Examples of such resources include devices such as mobile phones and personal computers, or software application. To illustrate this point, a study by Gasser et al. [31], showed the difference in application usage between mobile phone application users and web application users which may be based on the lack of internet access and the restriction of mobile phone usage in the workplace, both been resources needed to accomplish the given goal.

- *A complex task* perception depends on the subject's self-efficacy, i.e. their perception of their ability to come up with the right strategies to achieve the task [1]. When the goals are set collaboratively, the experts could help subjects overcome the challenges that come as a barrier to attain the goal. They can also help them develop the required skills needed to continue pursuing their goals.

- *Not understanding users' needs* when setting a goal is a primary deviation facilitator and can be avoided by supporting users to comprehend their current behavioural patterns firstly. The ideation technique used in [32] could be adopted in the initial stages of the goal-setting process, to help understand the users and their needs.

- *Source of behavioural goals* whether goals are group-set, guided or participatory set, deviation could be attributed in part to insufficient communication between the subjects and experts involved in the process. As a result, the experts may not understand the subjects and their needs, and subsequently, may set goals that cannot be attainable. Also, when goals are assigned, the subjects' lack of participation in the process could affect their interest, commitment or motivation towards the goals, and this could lead to goal deviation or complete goal abandonment.

- *Social influence and peer pressure* occur when a person's feelings, emotional state and behaviour are affected by others' actions or behaviours [33]. When the behavioural change goals are set collaboratively, social influence could either have a positive effect, for instance, group members motivating each other toward goal attainment or a negative effect where people deviate from their goals, particularly those with low self-esteem. In a social setting, the individuals' actions are driven by the group norms which are most often than not agreed upon by the group members. When goal setting is performed collaboratively, it is essential that the group's, commitment and motivation are at the same or similar level to avoid social loafing and social compensation.

Deviation Countermeasures. The applicability of the countermeasures largely depends on the deviation type and their facilitator. Some of the identified countermeasures are discussed here.

- *Review goal, re-strategise and analyse complex goals into a series of sub-goals.* When goal performance is lower than expected; then the goal could be reviewed to develop better attainment strategies. Poor performance could be the result of task complexity, low skills and ability levels, and not tackling other barriers to goal attainment. A complex task could be broken down into a series of subtasks that could relate to individuals' self-efficacy level which could help improve goal progress. Performance could be enhanced by adopting techniques such as barrier counselling, skill development approaches [34], and persuasion by providing subjects information concerning the approaches to use to attain their goals.

- *Monitor goal-related activities.* This technique involves monitoring and tracking the difference between the desired and actual behaviour which could be facilitated by an action-oriented approach, where subjects document their actions in pursuit of the goal. This process would enable the subjects to review their actions and identify the source of the deviation which may be related to some contextual or emotional factors and find the best plan for countering the deviation. Action planning is considered necessary during the early stages of behavioural change, while coping planning is assumed to be useful in the advanced stages of behaviour change, i.e. the action or maintenance stage [35].

- *Obtain verbal commitment to goals.* Verbal expression of commitment, and also the confidence to attain the behavioural goals may be obtained through persuasion. When subjects commit verbally to the setting of goals, this could help prevent deviation, especially when goals are set collaboratively. Subjects tend to adhere to the group goal once a verbal commitment is obtained due to fear of being socially excluded which may lead to loss of group identity, negative judgement, and blame for the group's failure to attain their behavioural change goals.

- *Detect and resolve goal conflict.* Conflicting goals should be identified and managed so that the subjects can progress toward attaining their goal. The environment could influence conflicting goals, i.e. the social setting of subjects, and also the source of the goals, i.e. when goals are assigned or set collaboratively. Goals could be prioritised to help resolve the conflicts among them. Also, the expert involved could facilitate negotiation with the subjects by applying, for example, logic and emotion negotiation approaches and help subjects understand that such conflict if not resolve may lead to deviation and lack of goal attainment in the long term.

- *Assess individual self-efficacy and commitment.* A subject's self-efficacy levels may influence their goal performance. Therefore, it is important to evaluate self-efficacy before setting the goals, to ensure that the right goals are chosen, in terms of difficulty and complexity levels. When goals are set collaboratively, subjects could be asked to confirm their goal commitment level verbally. To ensure that some of the subjects' responses are not influenced by the answers given by others in the group, all responses regarding goal commitment levels could be anonymised. Hence, reassuring subjects that given a lower response compare to others in the group will not lead to any negative reinforcement.

- *Conduct manipulation checks.* These checks are conducted to detect whether the subjects are paying attention to the set goals and goal-related tasks. Conducting manipulation checks could help assess the eligibility and credibility of the users in pursuing and attaining the goals. Persuasive techniques, such as tunnelling and conditioning, could be employed to aid subjects through these checks to help persuade them and improve their behaviour and commitment towards the set goals. Providing positive reinforcement and guidance through the process may help improve the outcome of such checks.

- *Task explanation and task familiarisation.* Regarding task explanation, before executing the goal-related task, a session could be conducted to explain to the subjects the task that they are expected to perform, ensuring that they understand what is expected of them. This process could be regarded as the induction phase of the goal setting process. Establishing an understanding of the task at an early stage could help prevent goal deviation which results from a lack of understanding of the goal-related task. Also, for familiarisation purposes, subjects could be asked to perform a task that is similar to the goal task before executing their goal related task.
- *Goal summary feedback.* Providing summary feedback may help motivate subjects to continue pursuing their goals and help them make an informed decision regarding the goals. Getting the feedback timing right, presenting it using an appropriate language and messaging style could help prevent deviation from goal. In a group setting, making the performance feedback visible to everyone may demotivate some subjects, therefore, eliciting the subjects' preferences is vital. Summary feedback may be provided in the form of a progress bar or an avatar.
- *Rewards.* Rewarding subjects positively, e.g. for goal attainment or significant goal progress, may help prevent deviation from the goal. The rewards could be provided personally or collectively based on the source of the goal and the subjects' preferences. When the rewards are to be displayed collectively, the individual differences within the group, i.e. personality, motivation, skills and confidence levels, should be carefully considered to ensure that reactance towards the rewards would not negatively affect their future goal performances.

3   Conclusion and Future Work

Our literature reviewed around goal setting led to the development of five reference checklists. We presented the reference checklists and elaborated on the various analysis and design considerations for persuasive systems and explained some of the conventional countermeasures for dealing with the deviation from goals. The five checklists are meant to provide a much easier reference point for researchers and practitioners using the strategy across different disciplines and build foundations for engineering goals embedded in persuasive information systems. Our future work will build on these initial results and further investigate the reference checklists in relation to behavioural change goals with the aim of providing a specification method for these goals. We will explore the set of stakeholders and their roles in the goal-setting process and also elicitation methods for behavioural goals and their socio-technical processes, e.g. in the reporting and adapting to behavioural change and progress.

Acknowledgement. This work has been partially supported by the EROGamb project funded jointly by GambleAware and Bournemouth University.

Appendix 1. References for Reference Checklists

Reference checklists	Papers which where included in the literature review
Sources of behavioural goals	Bickmore et al. (2005), Herrmanny et al. (2016), Kim and Hamner (1976), Landers et al. (2015), Mangos and Steele-Johnson (2001), Oettingen et al. (2000), Schunk (1996), Smith et al. (1990), Sobell et al. (1992), Van Hoye et al. (2012)
Behavioural goal identifiers	Bandura and Simon (1977), Curtin et al. (2001), Damon (1989), Emir and Judge (2001), Fanta et al. (2005), Mahfud et al. (2011), Michelle et al. (2016), Miriam et al. (1990), Nahrgang et al. (2013), Nothwehr and Yang (2007), Schweitzer et al. (2004)
Behavioural goal elicitation methods	Boekaerts and Corno (2005), Butler (1997), Consolvo et al. (2006), DeWalt et al. (2009), Enggasser et al. (2015), Erez and Arad (1986), Litchfield et al. (2011), Ussher et al. (2003), Zhu et al. (2012)
Behavioural goals monitoring and feedback	Abrahamse (2007), Alitto et al. (2016), Hamner and Harnett (1974), Johnson et al. (1997), Koskosas and Asimopoulos (2011), Lin et al. (2006), Loock et al. (2013), Munson and Consolvo (2012), Ries et al. (2014), Schunk (1983), Schunk and Swartz (1993), Seijts and Latham (2001), Vance and Colella (1990), Wijsman et al. (2013), Zimmerman et al. (1992)
Deviation from behavioural goals and countermeasures	Annesi (2002), Asmus et al. (2015), Aunurrafiq et al. (2015), Bergen et al. (1992), Bodenheimer and Handley (2009), Brusso and Orvis (2013), Burke and Settles (2011), Consolvo et al. (2009), Croteau (2004), Erez and Zidon (1984), Gasser et al. (2006), Glasgow et al. (1996), Hansen and Wills (2014), Koskosas (2009), Latham and Seijts (1999), McCalley and Midden (2002), Oettingen et al. (2001), Saini and Lacroix (2009), Shilts et al. (2004), van Houwelingen and van Raaij (1989)

Appendix 2: References for Reference Checklists in Alphabetical Order

Abrahamse, W., Steg, L., Vlek, C., Rothengatter, T.: The effect of tailored information, goal setting, and tailored feedback on household energy use, energy-related behaviours, and behavioural antecedents. Journal of Environmental Psychology 27(4), 265–276 (2007).

Alitto, J., Malecki, C., Coyle, S., Santuzzi, A.: Examining the effects of adult and peer mediated goal setting and feedback interventions for writing: Two studies. J of School Psychology 56, 89-109 (2016).

Annesi, J.J.: Goal-setting protocol in adherence to exercise by Italian adults. Perceptual Motor Skills 94(2), 453-8 (2002).

Asmus, S., Karl, F., Mohnen, A., Reinhart, G.: The impact of goal-setting on worker performance empirical evidence from a real-effort production experiment. Procedia CIRP 26, 127-132 (2015).

Aunurrafiq, Sari, R.N., Basri, Y.M.: The Moderating Effect of Goal Setting on Performance Measurement System-managerial Performance Relationship. Procedia Economics and Finance 31, 876–884 (2015).

Bandura, A., Simon, K.M.: The role of proximal intentions in self-regulation of refractory behavior. Cognitive Therapy and Research 1(3), 177–193 (1977).

Bergen, C.W.V., Barlow, S, Rosenthal, G.T.: The moderating effects of self-esteem and goal difficulty level on performance. College student journal 30(2), 262-268, (1992).

Bickmore, T., Caruso, L., Clough-Gorr, K.: Acceptance and Usability of a Relational Agent Interface by Urban Older Adults. In: CHI EA, pp.1212-1215. ACM, New York, NY (2005).

Bodenheimer, T., Handley, M.A.: Goal-setting for behavior change in primary care: An exploration and status report. Patient Educ. Coun 76(2), 174–180 (2009).

Boekaerts, M., Corno, L.: Self-regulation in the classroom: A perspective on assessment and intervention. Applied Psychology 54(2), 199–231 (2005).

Brusso, R.C., Orvis, K.A.: The impeding roles of initial unrealistic goal-setting on videogame-based training performance: identifying underpinning processes and a solution. Computer in Human behaviour 29(4), 1686-1694 (2013).

Burke, M., Settles, B.: Plugged into the Community: Social Motivators in Online Goal-Setting Groups. In: C&T, pp. 1-10. ACM, Brisbane, (2011).

Butler, D. L.: The role of goal setting and self-monitoring in students self-regulated engagement in tasks. Paper presented at the annual meeting of the American Education Research Association, Chicago. ERIC Document Reprinting Services No. ED 409 323 (1997).

Consolvo, S., Everitt, K., Smith, I. E., Landay, J. A.: April. Design requirements for technologies that encourage physical activity. In: Proceedings of the SIGCHI Conference on Human Factors in Computing Systems, pp. 457– 466. ACM, New York, Montréal, Québec, Canada, (2006).

Consolvo, S., Klasnja, P.V., McDonald, D.W., Landay, J.A.: Goal-setting considerations for persuasive technologies that encourage physical activity. In: 4th international conference on Persuasive Technology, ACM, New York (2009).

Croteau, K.: A preliminary study on the impact of a pedometer-based intervention on daily steps, American Journal of Health Promotion 18, 217-220 (2004).

Curtin, L. Stephen, R. S., Bonenberger, J.L.: Goal setting and feedback in the reduction of heavy drinking in female college students. Journal of college student psychotherapy 15(3), 17-37 (2001).

Damon. B.: The Impact of goal specificity and task complexity on basketball skill development. Human Kinetics Journals 3(1), 34-47 (1989).

DeWalt, D.A., Davis, T.C., Wallace, A.S. Seligman, H.K., Bryant-Shilliday, B., Arnold, C. L., Freburger, J., Schillinger, D.: Goal setting in diabetes self-management: Taking the baby steps to success. Patient Education and Counselling 77(2), 218–223 (2009).

Emir, E., Judge, T.A.: Relationship of Core Self-Evaluations to Goal Setting, Motivation, and Performance. J. of App. Psychology 86(6), 1270-1279 (2001).

Enggasser, J.L., Hermos, J.A., Rubin, A., Lachowicz, M., Rybin, D., Brief, D. J., Roy, M., Helmuth, E., Rosenbloom, D., Keane, T.M.: Drinking goal choice and outcomes in a Web-based alcohol intervention: Results from Vet Change. Addictive Behaviours 42, 63–68 (2015).

Erez, M., Arad, R.: Participative goal-setting: Social, motivational, and cognitive factors. Journal of Applied Psychology 71(4), 591–597 (1986).

Erez, M., Zidon, I.: Effects of goal acceptance on the relationship of goal difficulty to performance. Journal of Applied Psychology 58, 69-78 (1984)

Fanta, E., Evansb, K.R., Zoub, S.: The moderating effect of goal-setting characteristics on the sales control systems-job performance relationship. Journal of business research. 58, 1214-1222 (2005).

Gasser, R., Brodbeck, D., Degen, M., Luthiger, J., Wyss, R., Reichlin, S.: Persuasiveness of a Mobile Lifestyle Coaching Application Using Social Facilitation. In: IJsselsteijn W.A., de Kort Y.A.W., Midden

C., Eggen B., van den Hoven E. (eds.) Persuasive technology for human well-being 2006, LNCS, vol. 3962, pp. 27-38. Springer, Berlin, Heidelberg (2006).

Glasgow, R.E., Toobert, D.J., Hampson, S.E.: Effects of a Brief Office-Based Intervention to Facilitate Diabetes Dietary Self- Management. Diabetes Care 19(8), 835-842 (1996).

Hamner, W., Harnett, D.: Goal setting, performance and satisfaction in an interdependent task. Organizational Behaviour and Human Performance 12(2), 217-230 (1974).

Hansen, B., Wills, H.: The effects of goal setting, contingent reward, and instruction on writing skills. Journal of Applied Behaviour Analysis 47(1), 171-175 (2014).

Herrmanny, K., Ziegler, J., Dogangün, A.: Supporting Users in Setting Effective Goals in Activity Tracking, in Using Activity Theory to Model Context Awareness. Social Informatics 9638 (2), 15–26 (2016).

Johnson, L., Graham, S., Harris, K.R.: The Effects of Goal Setting and Self-Instruction on Learning a Reading Comprehension Strategy: A Study of Students with Learning Disabilities. Journal of learning disability 30(1), 80-91 (1997).

Kim, J.S., Hamner, W.C.: Effect of performance feedback and goal setting on productivity and satisfaction in an organizational setting. Journal of Applied Psychology 61(1), 48-57 (1976).

Koskosas, I.V., Asimopoulos, N.: Information systems security goals. International Journal of Advanced Science and Technology 27, 15-26 (2011).

Koskosas, I. V.: Communicating information systems goals - A case in internet banking security. ComSIS. 6(1), 71–92 (2009).

Landers, R.N., Bauer, K.N., Callan, R.C.: Gamification of task performance with leaderboards: A goal setting experiment. Computers in Human Behavior 71, 508-515 (2015).

Latham, G.P., Seijts, G.H.: The effects of proximal and distal goals on performance on a moderately complex task. Journal of Organizational Behavior 20 (4), 421–429 (1999).

Lin J.J., Mamykina, L., Lindtner S., Delajoux G., Strub H.B.: Fish'n'Steps: Encouraging Physical Activity with an Interactive Computer Game. In: Dourish P., Friday A. (eds.) 8th international conference on Ubiquitous Computing 2006, LNCS, vol. 4206, pp. 261-278. Springer, Verlag Berlin Heidelberg (2006).

Litchfield, R.C., Fan, J., Brown, V. R.: Directing idea generation using brainstorming with specific novelty goals. Motivation and Emotion 35(2), 135-143 (2011).

Loock, C.M., Staake, T., Thiesse, F.: Motivating energy-efficient behaviour with green is an investigation of goal setting and the role of defaults. MIS Quarterly 37(4), 1313-1332 (2013).

Mahfud, S., Pike, R., Mangena, M., Li, J.: Goal-setting participation and goal commitment: Examining the mediate roles of procedural fairness and interpersonal trust in a UK financial services organisation. The British Accounting Review 43 (2), 135-146 (2011).

Mangos, P.M., Steele-Johnson, D.: The Role of Subjective Task Complexity in Goal Orientation, Self-Efficacy, and Performance Relations. Human performance 14(2), 1532-7043 (2001).

McCalley, L.T., Midden, C.J.H.: Energy conservation through product-integrated feedback: The roles of goal-setting and social orientation. Journal of Economic Psychology 23(5), 589-603 (2002).

Michelle, D., Collen, F., Jayne, F.: An example of how to supplement goal setting to promote behavior change for families using motivational interviewing. Health communication 31(10), 1276-1283 (2016).

Miriam, E., Daniel, G., Nira, A.: Effects of goal difficulty, self-set goals, and monetary rewards on dual task performance. Organizational behavior and human decision processes 47(2), 247-269 (1990).

Munson, S., Consolvo, S.: Exploring Goal-setting, Rewards, Self-monitoring, and Sharing to Motivate Physical Activity. In: 6th International conference on pervasive computing technologies for Healthcare, pp. 25-32. IEEE, San Diego, CA, USA (2012).

Nahrgang, J.D., DeRue, S., Hollenbeck, J.R., Spitzmuller, M., Jundt, D.K., Llgen, D.R.: Goal setting in teams: The impact of learning and performance goals on process and performance. Organisational Behaviour and Human Decision Processes 122(1), 12-21 (2013).

Nothwehr, F., Yang, J.: Goal setting frequency and the use of behavioural strategies related to diet and physical activity. Health Education Research 22(4), 532-532 (2007).

Oettingen, G., Honig, G., Gollwitzer, P.M.: Effective self-regulation of goal attainment. International Journal of Educational Research 33 (7-8), 705-732 (2000).

Oettingen, G., Pak, h., Schnetter, k.: Self-regulation of goal setting: turning free fantasies about the future into binding goals. Journal of Personality and Social Psychology 80(5), 736–753 (2001).

Ries, A. V., Blackman, L. T., Page, R. A., Gizlice, Z., Benedict, S., Barnes, K., Kelsey, K., Carter-Edwards, L.: Goal setting for health behaviour change: evidence from an obesity intervention for rural low-income women. Rural and Remote Health 14(2), (2014).

Saini. P., Lacroix, J.: Self-setting of physical activity goals and effects on perceived difficulty, importance and competence. In: 4th International Conference on Persuasive Technology. ACM, New York, Claremont, California (2009).

Schunk, D. H.: Developing children's self-efficacy and skills: The roles of social comparative information and goal setting. Contemporary Educational Psychology 8, 76-86 (1983).

Schunk, D.H., Swartz, C.: Goals and progress feedback: effects of self-efficacy and writing achievement. Contemporary education psychology 18(3), 337-354 (1993).

Schunk, D.H.: Goals and self-evaluative influences during children's cognitive skill learning. Educational Research Journal 33, 359 – 382 (1996).

Schweitzer, M.E., Ordonez, L., Douma, B.: Goals setting as a motivator of unethical behaviour. The Academy of Management Journal 47(3), 422-453 (2004).

Seijts, G.H., Latham, G.P.: The effect of distal learning outcome, and proximal goals on a moderately complex task. Journal of Organizational Behavior 22(3), 291–307 (2001).

Shilts, M, K., Horowitz, M.S., Townsend, M, S.: An innovative approach to goal setting for adolescents: guided goal setting. Journal Nutrition Education Behaviour 36 (3), 155-156 (2004).

Smith, K.G., Locke, E.A., Barry, D.: Goal Setting, Planning, and Organizational Performance: An experimental simulation. Organizational Behaviour and Human Decision Processes 46(1),118-134 (1990).

Sobell, M., Sobell, L., Bogardis, J., Leo, G., Skinner, W.: Problem drinkers' perceptions of whether treatment goals should be self-selected or therapist-selected. Behaviour Therapy 23(1), 43-52 (1992).

Ussher, M., West, R., McEwen, A., Taylor, A., Steptoe. A.: Efficacy of exercise counselling as an aid for smoking cessation: a randomized controlled trial. Addiction 98(4), 523-32 (2003).

van Houwelingen, J.H., van Raaij, W.F.: The Effect of Goal-Setting and Daily Electronic Feedback on In-Home Energy Use. Journal of Consumer Research 16(1), 98–9 (1989).

Vance, J.R., Colella, A.: Effects of two types of feedback on goal acceptance and personal goals. Journal of Applied Psychology 75(1), 68-76 (1990).

Van Hoye, K., Boen, F., Lefevre, J.: The Effects of Physical Activity Feedback on Behavior and Awareness in Employees: Study Protocol for a Randomized Controlled Trial. Journal of telemedicine and applications 1-9 (2012).

Wijsman, C.A., Westendorp, R.G., Verhagen, E.A., Catt, M., Slagboom, P.E., de Craen, A.J., Broekhuizen, K., van Mechelen, W., van Heemst, D., van der Ouderaa, F., Mooijaart, S.P.: Effects of a Web-Based Intervention on Physical Activity and Metabolism in Older Adults: Randomized Controlled Trail. J Med Internet Res 15(11), (2013).

Zhu, H., Kraut R., Kittur, A.: Organizing without formal organization: group identification, goal setting and social modelling in directing the online production. In: Proceedings of the conference on computer supported cooperative work, pp. 935 – 944. ACM, New York, Seattle, WA, USA, (2012).

Zimmerman, B.J., Bandura, A., Martinez-Pons, M.: Self-Motivation for Academic Attainment: The Role of Self-Efficacy Beliefs and Personal Goal Setting. American Educational Research Journal 29(3), 663-676 (1992).

References

1. Locke, E.A., Latham, G.P.: Building a practically useful theory of goal setting and task motivation: a 35-year odyssey. Am. Psychol. **57**(9), 705–717 (2002)

2. Bandura, A., Simon, K.M.: The role of proximal intentions in self-regulation of refractory behavior. Cogn. Therapy Res. **1**(3), 177–193 (1977)

3. Landers, R.N., Bauer, K.N., Callan, R.C.: Gamification of task performance with leaderboards: a goal setting experiment. Comput. Hum. Behav. **71**, 508–515 (2015)

4. Consolvo, S., Klasnja, P.V., McDonald, D.W., Landay, J.A.: Goal-setting considerations for persuasive technologies that encourage physical activity. In: 4th International Conference on Persuasive Technology. ACM, New York (2009)

5. Lin, J.J., Mamykina, L., Lindtner, S., Delajoux, G., Strub, H.B.: Fish'n'Steps: encouraging physical activity with an interactive computer game. In: Dourish, P., Friday, A. (eds.) UbiComp 2006. LNCS, vol. 4206, pp. 261–278. Springer, Heidelberg (2006). https://doi.org/10.1007/11853565_16

6. Oinas-Kukkonen, H., Harjumaa, M.: Towards deeper understanding of persuasion in software and information systems. In: ACHI 2008, Proceedings of the First International Conference on Advances in Human-Computer Interaction, pp. 200–205. IEEE, Washington, DC (2008)

7. IJsselsteijn, W., de Kort, Y., Midden, C., Eggen, B., van den Hoven, E.: Persuasive technology for human well-being: setting the scene. In: IJsselsteijn, W.A., de Kort, Y.A.W., Midden, C., Eggen, B., van den Hoven, E. (eds.) PERSUASIVE 2006. LNCS, vol. 3962, pp. 1–5. Springer, Heidelberg (2006). https://doi.org/10.1007/11755494_1
8. Fogg, B.J.: Persuasive Technology: Using Computers to Change What We Think and Do. Kaufmann Publishers, Inc., San Francisco (2003)
9. Cialdini, R.B.: Influence (1984)
10. Klein, H.J., Wesson, M.J., Hollenbeck, J.R., Wright, P.M., DeShon, R.P.: The assessment of goal commitment: a measurement model meta-analysis. Org. Behav. Hum. Decis. Process. 85(1), 32–55 (2009)
11. Steers, R.: Task-goal attributes, n achievement, and supervisory performance. Org. Behav. Hum. Perform. 13(3), 392–403 (1975)
12. Oettingen, G., Pak, H., Schnetter, K.: Self-regulation of goal setting: turning free fantasies about the future into binding goals. J. Pers. Soc. Psychol. 80(5), 736–753 (2001)
13. Fishbein, M.: A theory of reasoned action: some applications and implications. Nebr. Symp. Motiv. 27, 65–116 (1980)
14. Ajzen, I.: The theory of planned behaviour. Org. Behav. Hum. Decis. Process. 50, 179–211 (1991)
15. van Lamsweerde, A.: Goal-oriented requirements engineering: a guided tour. In: 5th IEEE International Symposium on Requirements Engineering, pp. 1–14. IEEE Computing Society, Toronto (2001)
16. Jalali, S., Wohlin, C.: Systematic literature studies: database searches vs. backward snowballing. In: Proceedings of the ACM-IEEE International Symposium on Empirical Software Engineering and Measurement, pp. 29–38. IEEE, Lund (2013)
17. Farahat, T.: Applying the technology acceptance model to online learning in the Egyptian universities. Procedia Soc. Behav. Sci. 64, 95–104 (2012)
18. Latham, G.P., Seijts, G.H.: The effects of proximal and distal goals on performance on a moderately complex task. J. Org. Behav. 20(4), 421–429 (1999)
19. Prochaska, J.O., DiClemente, C.C.: Stages and processes of self-change of smoking: toward an integrative model of change. J. Consult. Clin. Psychol. 51(3), 390–395 (1983)
20. Seijts, G.H., Latham, G.P.: The effect of distal learning, outcome, and proximal goals on a moderately complex task. J. Org. Behav. 22(3), 291–307 (2001)
21. Aunurrafiq, Sari, R.N., Basri, Y.M.: The moderating effect of goal setting on performance measurement system-managerial performance relationship. Procedia Econ. Finance 31, 876–884 (2015)
22. van Houwelingen, J.H., van Raaij, W.F.: The effect of goal-setting and daily electronic feedback on in-home energy use. J. Consum. Res. 16(1), 98–105 (1989)
23. Boekaerts, M., Corno, L.: Self-regulation in the classroom: a perspective on assessment and intervention. Appl. Psychol. 54(2), 199–231 (2005)
24. Locke, E.A., Latham, G.P.: New directions in goal-setting theory. Curr. Dir. Psychol. Sci. 15(5), 265–268 (2006)
25. Erez, M., Arad, R.: Participative goal-setting: social, motivational, and cognitive factors. J. Appl. Psychol. 71(4), 591–597 (1986)
26. Munson, S., Consolvo, S.: Exploring goal-setting, rewards, self-monitoring, and sharing to motivate physical activity. In: 6th International Conference on Pervasive Computing Technologies for Healthcare, pp. 25–32. IEEE, San Diego (2012)
27. Alrobai, A., McAlaney, J., Dogan, H., Phalp, K., Ali, R.: Exploring the requirements and design of persuasive intervention technology to combat digital addiction. In: Bogdan, C., et al. (eds.) HCSE/HESSD -2016. LNCS, vol. 9856, pp. 130–150. Springer, Cham (2016). https://doi.org/10.1007/978-3-319-44902-9_9

28. Locke, E.A., Latham, G.P., Erez, M.: The determinants of goal commitment. Acad. Manag. Rev. **13**(1), 23–39 (1988)
29. Reese, J.D., Leveson, N.G.: Software deviation analysis. In: ICSE 1997, Proceedings of the 19th International Conference on Software Engineering, pp. 250–260. ACM, New York (1997)
30. Bodenheimer, T., Handley, M.A.: Goal-setting for behavior change in primary care: an exploration and status report. Patient Educ. Counc. **76**(2), 174–180 (2009)
31. Gasser, R., Brodbeck, D., Degen, M., Luthiger, J., Wyss, R., Reichlin, S.: Persuasiveness of a mobile lifestyle coaching application using social facilitation. In: IJsselsteijn, W.A., de Kort, Y.A.W., Midden, C., Eggen, B., van den Hoven, E. (eds.) PERSUASIVE 2006. LNCS, vol. 3962, pp. 27–38. Springer, Heidelberg (2006). https://doi.org/10.1007/11755494_5
32. Morschheuser, B., Hassan, L., Werder, K., Hamari, J.: How to design gamification? A method for engineering gamified software. Inf. Softw. Technol. **95**, 219–237 (2018)
33. Bandura, A.: Social Foundations of Thought and Action: A Social Cognitive Theory. Prentice-Hall Series in Social Learning Theory. Prentice-Hall, Upper Saddle River (1986)
34. Strecher, V.J., et al.: Goal setting as a strategy for health behavior change. Health Educ. Behav. **22**(2), 190–200 (1995)
35. Sniehotta, F.F., Scholz, U., Schwarzer, R.: Bridging the intention-behaviour gap: planning, self-efficacy, and action control in the adoption and maintenance of physical exercise. Psychol. Health **20**(2), 143–160 (2005)

Personality, Age and Gender

A Study on Effect of Big Five Personality Traits on Ad Targeting and Creative Design

Akihiro Kobayashi[(✉)], Yuichi Ishikawa[(✉)],
and Atsunori Minamikawa[(✉)]

KDDI Research, Inc., 2-1-15 Ohara, Fujimino-shi, Saitama 356-8502, Japan
{ak-kobayashi,yi-ishikawa,
at-minamikawa}@kddi-research.jp

Abstract. This paper examines two personalization approaches to web advertisements focusing on the Big Five personality traits: (i) personality-based ad targeting, which predicts users' receptiveness to ads from their Big Five personality and delivers ads to those with high receptiveness, and (ii) personality-based ad creative design, which specifies target Big Five personalities and tailors ad creative design for each personality. Previous research on (i) has not sufficiently verified whether it works for various ad products/services and ad creatives. To address this, we examined correlation between individuals' Big Five and their general receptiveness to ads across various ad products/services and ad creatives. Regarding (ii), though its effectiveness has already been demonstrated, what to tailor in the ad creative and how to tailor it have not been clarified in previous research. We focused on cognitive bias, of which various kinds are commonly used in ad creatives today, and, assumed that using different cognitive bias depending on Big Five personality improves ad reaction (e.g., click through rate). Conducting a questionnaire survey, which included over 3,000 subjects and 20 ad creatives, we confirmed that Big Five personality can be significant predictor of receptiveness to ads and verified the potential of (i) to work for various products/services and creatives. On the other hand, regarding (ii), survey results did not support our assumption, the reason for which we consider is that there is no/little interaction effect between Big Five and cognitive bias on ad reaction.

Keywords: Personalization · Big Five · Advertisement · Cognitive bias

1 Introduction

Recently, user's psychographic attributes have been attracting considerable attention as the basis for personalization of web advertisements [17] in addition to demographic, geographic and behavioral attributes. Many researchers have studied personality-based ad personalization from various perspectives, among which two of the main aspects are (i) ad targeting and (ii) ad creatives design. For example, [6] studied an approach for (i), which predicts users' receptiveness to ads from their Big Five personality traits (Openness, Conscientiousness, Extraversion, Agreeableness and Neuroticism [11]), and delivers ads to those with high receptiveness. Regarding (ii), [14, 19] specified multiple target personalities by using the Big Five personality model (e.g., highly

© Springer Nature Switzerland AG 2019
H. Oinas-Kukkonen et al. (Eds.): PERSUASIVE 2019, LNCS 11433, pp. 257–269, 2019.
https://doi.org/10.1007/978-3-030-17287-9_21

extravert, highly introvert, highly neurotic, etc.) and tailored ad creatives design to each personality. These studies observed performance improvement (e.g., CTR/CVR lift, CTR: Click Through Rate, CVR: Conversion Rate) under certain conditions.

However, they conducted their evaluation under only a limited condition, and have not sufficiently verified whether (i) and (ii) work effectively under various conditions including for different ad products/services, different skill levels of the ad designers and different ad distribution media (e.g., Facebook, Twitter, web-banner etc.). In [6], (i) was evaluated for only one specific ad service, a few specific ad creatives and one specific ad distribution media. As for (ii), though ad creatives consist of various kinds of components such as keywords, photos, color usage, fonts, and layout, [14, 19] did not clarify which components contribute to ad performance improvement and how they should be designed for a particular target personality. Almost all of the above have been decided by ad designers based on their implicit knowledge, making it difficult for (ii) to work effectively when the designer's skill level is not high enough.

Given the above, this paper examines the potential of (i) and (ii); whether they work effectively in various conditions. As for (i), we examined correlation between Big Five personality and general receptiveness to ads of various ad products/services and ad creatives, and evaluated whether ad targeting model using Big Five personality work effectively regardless of ad products/services and ad creatives. Regarding (ii), we focused on cognitive bias, of which various kinds such as the Zeigarnik effect [28], Bandwagon effect [4] and Barnum effect [10] are commonly used in ad creatives today. We assumed that using different cognitive biases depending on target Big Five personalities contributes to ad performance improvement, and examined the assumption. The motivation of the assumption was to reduce dependence on a designer and make (ii) to work independently of the designer's skill by predicting which cognitive bias is effective for particular target personality and recommending it to designers.

We conducted a questionnaire survey, where the key findings were as follows:

- Big Five personality can be significant predictor of general receptiveness to ads. Although the degree of effectiveness differed on a case by case, ad targeting model using Big Five personality works effectively and outperforms demographic targeting across various ad products/services and ad creatives (CTR lift: avg – 1.26, max – 1.70).
- Using different cognitive bias depending on the target's Big Five personality did not improve ad performance. Although we prepared ad creatives with different cognitive biases in the survey, preference for ad creatives did not differ significantly by subjects' personality in the same ad product/service.

2 Related Work

2.1 Personality-Based Ad Targeting

Chen et al. [6] conducted an experiment using Twitter to examine whether personality-based ad-targeting improves ad performance. Since their Twitter ad was an unsolicited advertisement from newly created unknown brand, they assumed that people with high

Openness, which includes the facet of "curiosity", will be more willing to give their service a try. They also assumed that people with high Neuroticism will be less trusting of the Twitter ad and thus be less likely to respond positively. In the experiment, they estimated Twitter users' Big Five personality from their tweets, and demonstrated that Openness was a significant positive predictor of click and follow, and Neuroticism was a significant negative predictor.

However, their assumption on correlation between Big Five personality and receptiveness to ads depended heavily on the characteristics of advertising media i.e. an unsolicited advertisement tweet. In addition, only a single ad product/service ("TravelersLikeMe") and only three ad creatives were used in their experiment. Thus, it is still an open question whether personality-based ad targeting improves ad performance for various ad products/services, ad creatives and ad distribution media.

2.2   Personality-Based Ad Creatives Design

Hirsh et al. [14] and Matz et al. [19] conducted experiments to demonstrate ad performance improvement by personality-based ad creatives design. First, they selected ad products/services and specified multiple target personalities using Big Five personality model. Next, they consulted with professional ad designers to design ad creatives for each target personality. They provided ad designers with information about the target personality, based on which the designers designed ad creatives by their own implicit knowledge. In [14], mobile phone ads were prepared for five different personalities which were high for each of the Big Five traits. In [19], prepared were cosmetic ads for targets whose Extraversion was either high or low and crossword puzzle ads for targets whose Openness was either high or low. Finally, they investigated users' reactions to each ad creative. Their results showed that users reacted to ad creatives more positively when exposed to creatives which matched their personality.

Since their experiments were conducted using multiple different ad products/ services and ad creatives, it is expected that ad performance improvement can be reproduced for other ad products/services and ad creatives. However, it was not examined which components in their ad creatives elicited a positive reaction from a targeted personality. In addition, how the components should be designed was still dependent on the implicit knowledge of the designers. Thus, it is quite uncertain whether the ad performance improvement can be reproduced when skillful designers are not available.

3   Hypotheses

To examine the potential of (i) and (ii), we formulated two hypotheses about the correlation between the Big Five personality and reactions to ads:

- (H1) People's Big Five personality is correlated with their general receptiveness to web advertisement regardless of ad products/services and ad creatives.
- (H2) People with different Big Five personalities prefer ad creatives with different cognitive biases.

(H1) is the basis for the potential of (i) to work effectively in various ad products/services and ad creatives. If (H1) is true, it is possible to predict people's general receptiveness to web ads from Big Five personality.

(H2) is for (ii). A cognitive bias is "a systematic pattern of deviation from the norm or rationality in judgment" [13]. Table 1 shows examples of cognitive biases. Previous research has confirmed that there is a correlation between Big Five personality and effectiveness of cognitive bias. For example, the Barnum effect positively correlates with Neuroticism and negatively correlates with Conscientiousness [3]. Agreeableness increases the bandwagon effect [25]. Agreeableness, Extraversion, and Openness regress reactance [26]. These correlations suggest that people's Big Five personality can be a predictor of the degree to which they are influenced by a given cognitive bias. Thus, if (H2) is true, we can reduce dependence on a designers' implicit knowledge for ad creative design by recommending a cognitive bias which has been predicted to be effective for a particular target personality.

Table 1. List of cognitive biases

Cognitive bias	Description
Zeigarnik effect	People remember uncompleted or interrupted tasks better than completed tasks [28]
Barnum effect	Individuals give high accuracy ratings to descriptions of their personality that supposedly are tailored specifically to them [10]
Reactance	An unpleasant motivational arousal (reaction) to offers, persons, rules, or regulations that threaten or eliminate specific behavioral freedoms [5]
Prospect theory	The way people choose between probabilistic alternatives that involve risk, where the probabilities of outcomes are uncertain [15]
Bandwagon effect	The rate of uptake of beliefs, ideas, fads and trends increases the more that they have already been adopted by others [4]
False consensus	People tend to overestimate the extent to which their opinions, beliefs, preferences, values, and habits are normal and typical of those of others [18]
Size–weight illusion	The illusion occurs when a person underestimates the weight of a larger object (e.g. a box) when compared to a smaller object of the same mass [23]
Cocktail party effect	The brain's ability to focus one's auditory attention on a particular stimulus while filtering out a range of other stimuli, as when a partygoer can focus on a single conversation in a noisy room [20]

4 Questionnaire Survey

We conducted a questionnaire survey that included 3,365 subjects and 20 ad creatives across six different ad products/services. The questionnaire enabled us to collect data on participants Big Five scores and their expected reactions to ad creatives.

4.1 Subjects

We recruited 4,122 Japanese subjects and measured their Big Five scores. Table 2 and Fig. 1 show the demographic and psychographic distribution of the subjects, respectively. To measure the Big Five scores, we used a Big Five personality inventory which consists of 70 questions with 2-point scale (yes/no) [21]. In Fig. 1, squares show random sampling in Japan (N = 1,166) [22], and circles show distribution in our survey. There is no marked difference in the distribution shape between our subjects and random sampling in Japan. In the measurement, 757 outliers were detected as non-collaborative participants by scores defined the inventory [21] and these individuals were subsequently excluded from the analysis.

Table 2. Demographic distribution of subjects

Age	15-	20-	25-	30-	35-	40-	45-	50-	55-	60-	65-	All
Male	108	195	315	263	355	282	336	231	181	209	152	2,627
Female	71	144	249	200	161	169	140	179	79	66	37	1,495
All	179	339	564	463	516	451	476	410	260	275	189	4,122

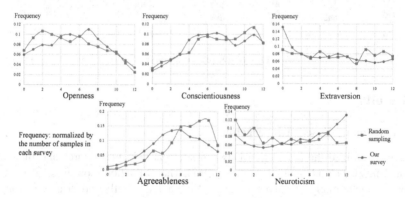

Fig. 1. Psychographic distribution of subjects

4.2 Creatives

Figure 2 shows ad creatives used in the survey. Among six ad products/services, three were fictional products/services used only for this survey (A ~ C in Fig. 2) and the other three were real ones which were available commercially (D ~ F in Fig. 2). For the former, we created the ad creatives from scratch; that is, we consulted with professional ad designers and asked them to design the ad creatives so that only the cognitive biases differ among the ad creatives and the same design policy was applied to the rest of the materials (product/service name, logo design, color usage, photos/illustrations, etc.) in the same ad products/services. For the latter, we selected ad creatives from the web according to the same policy used for the fictional ones.

4.3   Questionnaire

For each ad creative, subjects were asked to evaluate it by answering the following 5 questions (4-point scale answer: agree strongly, agree slightly, disagree slightly, and disagree strongly): Q1: The creative is interesting, Q2: I want to click it, Q3: I want to search it, Q4: I want to go to the store or inquire the store, and Q5: I want to buy it.

As for Q2, in the subsequent analysis, we regarded the answer "agree strongly" as a click on the ad creative.

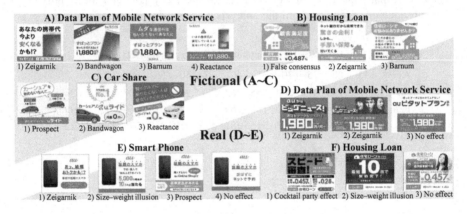

Fig. 2.   Displayed creatives

5   Results

5.1   Personality-Based Ad Targeting

First, we examined the correlation between subjects' Big Five scores and their evaluation scores for all ad creatives to verify (H1). The evaluation score was calculated as follows: agree strongly - 2, agree slightly - 1, disagree slightly and disagree strongly - 0. Table 3 shows the results. It can be seen that all Big Five traits positively correlated with evaluation scores. Among the traits, Openness and Extraversion have a relatively strong correlation with ad evaluation. The same correlation is shown more explicitly in Fig. 3, where CTR (calculated by Q2 answers) averaged across all creatives are plotted for each personality segment (High/Mid/Low for 5 traits. Criteria for High/Mid and Mid/Low were set at $\mu + \sigma$ and $\mu - \sigma$, respectively). For segments of high Openness and high Extraversion, CTR lift from the average of all personality segments is 1.54 and 1.37, respectively. All these results support (H1).

Table 3. Correlations between Big Five scores and creative evaluation score

Big Five	Openness	Conscientiousness	Extraversion	Agreeableness	Neuroticism
Attract	0.1457 ‡	0.0123	0.1506 ‡	0.0625 ‡	0.0874 ‡
Click	0.1435 ‡	0.0455 †	0.1400 ‡	0.0835 ‡	0.0895 ‡
Search	0.1611 ‡	0.0535 †	0.1508 ‡	0.0748 ‡	0.0871 ‡
Store	0.1570 ‡	0.0339 *	0.1528 ‡	0.0451 †	0.0816 ‡
Buy	0.1520 ‡	0.0308	0.1448 ‡	0.0482 †	0.0814 ‡

$N = 3{,}364$, *$p < 0.05$, †$p < 0.01$, ‡$p < 0.001$

Given the validity of (H1), we proceeded to build and evaluate the ad targeting model which predicts clicks on ad creatives from subjects' scores for Big Five traits. Specifically, we evaluated the model by conducting cross validation as follows; we divided subjects into five equal groups, four of which were used for training the model, with the remaining group used for testing. When training the model, we excluded the click data of the ad product/service to be tested. For example, when predicting clicks on A-* by Group-1, data about clicks on B-1 ~ F-3 by Group-2 ~ 4 were used for training. We used logistic regression to train and test the model, which calculates click probability for each subject on the ad creative being tested. For comparison, we also evaluated the targeting model which uses subjects' demographic attributes (i.e., gender and age). We evaluated the CTR when the models target at subjects in top 20% click probability.

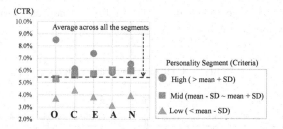

Fig. 3. CTR by each personality segment

Figure 4 shows the results for the CTR lift of ad targeting by model compared to random ad distribution and demographic ad targeting. Though the degree of improvement varies with ad creatives, our model significantly lifted CTR for all ad creatives compared to random distribution (CTR lift: avg. − 1.82, max − 2.12) and also outperformed demographic targeting in almost all cases (CTR lift: avg. − 1.26, max − 1.70), confirming that personality-based ad targeting works effectively for various ad products/services and ad creatives.

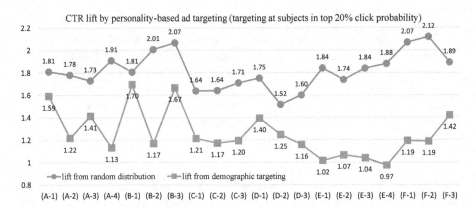

Fig. 4. CTR lift for each ad creative

5.2 Personality-Based Ad Creative Design

To verify (H2), we checked whether reaction to ad creatives with different cognitive biases differs in relation to Big Five personality. Tables 4 and 5 show CTR of each creative for each personality segment (High/Mid/Low for Big Five traits). The bold font indicates the highest CTR for each ad product/service for each personality segment (i.e., best creative in the same ad product/service for a given segment), and the meshed cell denotes that the best creative for a given segment is different from that for all segments (e.g., A-1 is the best creative for O-Low among A-1 ~ 4, while A-3 is the best creative for all segments (refer to the "All" row in the table)). For meshed cells, we conducted t-tests to examine whether CTR of the meshed cells were significantly different from the best creatives for all segments.

Table 4. CTR of fictional ad creatives

	Ad Creative	A-1	A-2	A-3	A-4	B-1	B-2	B-3	C-1	C-2	C-3
	Cognitive Bias	Zeigarnik	Bandwagon	Barnum	Reactance	False Consensus	Zeigarnik	Barnum	Prospect	Bandwagon	Reactance
	High	0.097	0.092	**0.115**	0.086	0.081	0.069	**0.083**	**0.090**	0.078	0.074
O	Mid	0.072	0.055	**0.074**	0.059	**0.041**	0.041	0.039	**0.072**	0.059	0.058
	Low	**0.064**	0.047	0.059	0.034	**0.027**	0.027	0.022	**0.047**	0.043	0.040
	High	0.082	0.072	**0.106**	0.064	0.045	**0.052**	0.049	**0.082**	0.072	0.062
C	Mid	**0.077**	0.061	0.075	0.062	**0.049**	0.043	0.047	**0.068**	0.054	0.056
	Low	0.061	0.048	**0.065**	0.042	0.036	**0.038**	0.028	**0.071**	0.069	0.059
	High	**0.108**	0.073	0.093	0.073	**0.058**	0.055	**0.058**	0.080	**0.088**	0.082
E	Mid	0.074	0.063	**0.082**	0.064	**0.049**	0.044	0.048	**0.075**	0.054	0.052
	Low	0.049	0.045	**0.060**	0.037	0.030	**0.032**	0.026	**0.053**	0.046	0.046
	High	**0.086**	0.084	**0.086**	0.065	**0.059**	0.042	0.050	**0.071**	0.057	0.061
A	Mid	0.079	0.063	**0.085**	0.066	0.048	**0.050**	0.047	**0.075**	0.065	0.062
	Low	**0.053**	0.031	0.049	0.025	0.027	0.020	**0.029**	**0.051**	0.040	0.036
	High	0.093	0.075	**0.099**	0.069	0.048	0.044	**0.051**	**0.088**	0.073	0.073
N	Mid	**0.082**	0.061	0.079	0.062	**0.054**	0.051	0.051	**0.070**	0.057	0.055
	Low	0.044	0.046	**0.060**	0.043	**0.027**	0.027	0.026	**0.055**	0.053	0.048
	All	0.075	0.061	**0.079**	0.059	**0.046**	0.044	0.045	**0.071**	0.060	0.057

Table 5. CTR of real ad creatives

Personality Segment	Ad Creative Cognitive Bias	D-1 Zeigarnik	D-2 Zeigarnik	D-3 No Effect	E-1 Zeigarnik	E-2 Size-weight Illusion	E-3 Prospect	E-4 No Effect	F-1 Cocktail Party	F-2 Size-weight Illusion	F-3 No Effect
O	High	**0.115**	0.103	0.096	**0.089**	0.081	0.081	0.062	0.064	**0.075**	0.068
	Mid	0.069	**0.071**	0.055	0.045	**0.054**	0.050	0.039	0.038	0.031	**0.041**
	Low	0.050	**0.062**	0.041	0.030	**0.035**	0.027	0.031	0.013	0.016	**0.030**
C	High	0.082	**0.091**	0.069	0.059	**0.059**	0.052	0.045	0.029	0.035	**0.042**
	Mid	**0.076**	0.074	0.063	0.052	**0.058**	0.056	0.042	0.043	0.042	**0.048**
	Low	0.057	**0.063**	0.040	0.036	**0.042**	0.034	0.038	0.026	0.018	**0.028**
E	High	**0.107**	0.106	0.082	**0.076**	0.068	0.062	0.049	0.052	0.048	**0.058**
	Mid	**0.073**	0.071	0.060	0.049	**0.061**	0.056	0.049	0.040	0.039	**0.043**
	Low	0.049	**0.058**	0.040	0.032	**0.033**	0.033	0.020	0.021	0.024	**0.033**
A	High	**0.109**	0.107	0.059	0.050	**0.052**	0.040	0.025	0.038	0.034	**0.040**
	Mid	0.073	**0.078**	0.070	0.057	**0.062**	0.058	0.050	0.043	0.043	**0.050**
	Low	**0.051**	0.038	0.020	0.025	0.031	**0.034**	0.022	0.018	0.016	**0.020**
N	High	0.075	**0.096**	0.064	0.057	0.057	**0.069**	0.049	0.040	0.035	**0.051**
	Mid	**0.082**	0.071	0.064	0.055	**0.062**	0.055	0.048	0.043	0.048	**0.049**
	Low	0.057	**0.063**	0.048	0.037	**0.040**	0.028	0.022	0.026	0.017	**0.027**
	All	0.075	**0.075**	0.060	0.051	**0.056**	0.052	0.042	0.038	0.037	**0.044**

The results did not support (H2). For all meshed cells, results of t-tests did not show significant differences (i.e., $p \gg 0.05$ for all meshed cells). That is, reaction to ad creatives with different cognitive biases did not differ in relation to Big Five personality.

6 Discussion

We consider that following are the possible reasons why (H2) was not verified by the survey results:

(1) The cognitive biases we chose were not sufficiently incorporated into the ad creatives.
(2) There is no/little interaction effect between Big Five personality and cognitive bias on reaction to web ads.

The likelihood of (1) being the reason is low because our ad creatives were reviewed by another designer other than one who designed the creatives to check whether the chosen cognitive biases were reflected.

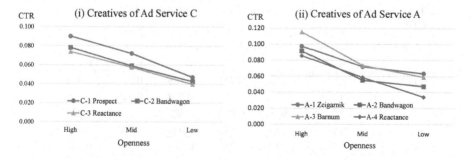

Fig. 5. CTR of C-1 ~ 3 and A-1 ~ 4 by Openness score segments

We consider (2) is more possible reason. Figure 5 shows examples of CTR comparisons between ad creatives by different personality segments. In Fig. 5 (i), preference order of ad creatives in each personality segment is the same, which typically exemplifies (2). On the other hand, preference orders differ between personality segments in Fig. 5-(ii) (e.g., 1st and 2nd best creatives differ between O-High and O-Low, and 3rd and 4th best creatives differ between O-High and O-Mid), which appears there is the interaction effect. However, it was not statistically significant according to the test results described below. Table 6 shows the results of interaction tests between ad creatives and personality segments on CTR by two-way analysis of variance (ANOVA). In almost all cases, the interaction effects are not significant ($p \gg 0.05$). The only exception was D, in which the best ads varied in relation to the Agreeableness score (The best creative for high and low is D-1, whereas the best for mid is D-2 in Table 5) and ANOVA result shows the existence of the interaction effect ($p < 0.05$). However, the effect did not originate from cognitive bias (both D-1 and D-2 used Zeigarnik effect), but from other components of ad creatives, one of which we consider is with/without a picture of famous people.

Previous studies on persuasive strategies have found the similar relations between Big Five personality and persuasion principles. They showed that the most effective persuasion principle did not differ regardless of the Big Five personality. Alkış et al. [1] estimated the correlations between Big Five personality and Susceptibility to Persuasion Scale (STPS) [16], an inventory that measures the persuasiveness of Cialdini's six principles [7]. Thomas et al. [27] implemented four of Cialdini's principles into a healthy eating message application and compared performance between the principles for each personality. Halko et al. [12] personalized the original factors for health-promoting mobile applications, and Anagnostopoulou et al. [2] personalized eight of the Persuasive Systems Design (PSD) principles [24] for changing the public's transport habits. These works show a trend that is similar to our experiment. In the experiment conducted by Thomas [27], the Big Five affected the persuasiveness of each principle, but the most effective principle was not changed by Big Five scores. While Anagnostopoulou et al. [2] found several significant correlations between the Big Five and persuasion principles, the order of effectiveness of principles does not differ significantly by Big Five personality, i.e. The most effective principle for a high Neuroticism user is the same as that for a low Neuroticism user.

Table 6. Tests for interaction between ad creatives and personality segments on CTR

Personality	P-value of ANOVA (Ad Products/Services)					
	A	B	C	D	E	F
O	0.822	0.783	0.981	0.829	0.627	0.410
C	0.708	0.792	0.905	0.928	0.929	0.916
E	0.564	0.955	0.282	0.823	0.522	0.939
A	0.882	0.713	0.995	**0.048**	0.882	0.987
N	0.705	0.979	0.946	0.280	0.720	0.644

Given the above, we consider that using different cognitive bias depending on Big Five personality contributes little to increasing effectiveness of personality-based ad creatives design. Other ad creative components, such as keywords, pictures, color usage and layout, require further study. For example, as for pictures, previous studies have found a correlation between Big Five personality and the features of a favorite picture [8, 9] (e.g., Extraverts showed a preference for pictures portraying people and colorful pictures while the preference of introverts was the reverse). We consider that, by leveraging these findings, appropriate kinds of pictures and other components to be used for a particular target personality can be predicted and recommended to ad designers, reducing dependence on their implicit knowledge in ad creative design.

7 Conclusion

We studied two personalization approaches for web advertisements with a focus on the Big Five personality: (i) personality-based ad targeting and (ii) personality-based ad creative design. By administering a questionnaire survey to over 3,000 subjects and including 20 ad creatives across six different ad products/services, we investigated the correlation between the Big Five personality traits and receptiveness to web advertisements and effectiveness of cognitive bias in ads, and examined whether (i) and (ii) have potential to work effectively under various conditions.

In summary, the contribution of this paper is threefold:

1. Confirmed that the Big Five can be a predictor of general receptiveness to web advertisements regardless of ad products/services and creatives, and, thus, personality-based ad targeting is effective across various ad products/services and ad creatives.
2. Confirmed that using different cognitive biases in ad creatives contributes little to increasing effectiveness in personality-based ad creative design.
3. Identified the most likely reason for ii, namely, interaction effects on reaction to web ads do not exist between Big Five and cognitive bias. People are most heavily influenced by the same cognitive bias regardless of their Big Five personality traits when exposed to ads for the same ad products/services.

References

1. Alkış, N., Taşkaya Temizel, T.: The impact of individual differences on influence strategies. Pers. Individ. Differ. **87**, 147–152 (2015). https://doi.org/10.1016/J.PAID.2015.07.037
2. Anagnostopoulou, E., Magoutas, B., Bothos, E., Schrammel, J., Orji, R., Mentzas, G.: Exploring the links between persuasion, personality and mobility types in personalized mobility applications. In: de Vries, P.W., Oinas-Kukkonen, H., Siemons, L., Beerlage-de Jong, N., van Gemert-Pijnen, L. (eds.) PERSUASIVE 2017. LNCS, vol. 10171, pp. 107–118. Springer, Cham (2017). https://doi.org/10.1007/978-3-319-55134-0_9
3. Andersen, P., Nordvik, H.: Possible Barnum effect in the five factor model: do respondents accept random neo personality inventory-revised scores as their actual trait profile? Psychol. Rep. **90**, 539–545 (2002). https://doi.org/10.2466/pr0.2002.90.2.539

4. Asch, S.E.: Opinions and social pressure. Sci. Am. **193**, 31–35 (1955). https://doi.org/10.1038/scientificamerican1155-31

5. Brehm, J.W.: A Theory of Psychological Reactance. Academic Press, Oxford (1966)

6. Chen, J., Haber, E., Kang, R., Hsieh, G., Mahmud, J.: Making use of derived personality: the case of social media ad targeting. In: Ninth International AAAI Conference on Web and Social Media, pp. 51–60 (2015)

7. Cialdini, R.: Harnessing the science of persuasion. Harv. Bus. Rev. **79**, 72–81 (2001)

8. Cristani, M., Vinciarelli, A., Segalin, C., Perina, A.: Unveiling the multimedia unconscious: implicit cognitive processes and multimedia content analysis. In: Proceedings of the 21st ACM International Conference on Multimedia, pp. 213–222. ACM, New York (2013)

9. Ferwerda, B., Tkalcic, M.: Predicting users' personality from Instagram pictures. In: Proceedings of the 26th Conference on User Modeling, Adaptation and Personalization - UMAP 2018, pp. 157–161. ACM Press, New York (2018)

10. Forer, B.R.: The fallacy of personal validation; a classroom demonstration of gullibility. J. Abnorm. Psychol. **44**, 118–123 (1949)

11. Goldberg, L.R.: The development of markers for the big five factor structure. Psychol. Assess. **4**, 26–42 (1992). https://doi.org/10.1037/1040-3590.4.1.26

12. Halko, S., Kientz, J.A.: Personality and persuasive technology: an exploratory study on health-promoting mobile applications. In: Ploug, T., Hasle, P., Oinas-Kukkonen, H. (eds.) PERSUASIVE 2010. LNCS, vol. 6137, pp. 150–161. Springer, Heidelberg (2010). https://doi.org/10.1007/978-3-642-13226-1_16

13. Haselton, M.G., Nettle, D., Andrews, P.W.: The evolution of cognitive bias. In: The Handbook of Evolutionary Psychology, pp. 724–746. Wiley, Hoboken (2005)

14. Hirsh, J.B., Kang, S.K., Bodenhausen, G.V.: Personalized persuasion. Psychol. Sci. **23**, 578–581 (2012). https://doi.org/10.1177/0956797611436349

15. Kahneman, D., Tversky, A.: Prospect theory: an analysis of decision under risk. Econometrica **47**, 263–291 (1979). https://doi.org/10.2307/1914185

16. Kaptein, M.C.: Personalized persuasion in ambient intelligence. Technische Universiteit Eindhoven (2012)

17. Lin, C.: Segmenting customer brand preference: demographic or psychographic. J. Prod. Brand Manag. **11**, 249–268 (2002). https://doi.org/10.1108/10610420210435443

18. Marks, G., Miller, N.: Ten years of research on the false-consensus effect: an empirical and theoretical review (1987)

19. Matz, S.C., Kosinski, M., Nave, G., Stillwell, D.J.: Psychological targeting as an effective approach to digital mass persuasion. Proc. Natl. Acad. Sci. USA **114**, 12714–12719 (2017). https://doi.org/10.1073/pnas.1710966114

20. Moray, N.: Attention in dichotic listening: affective cues and the influence of instructions. Q. J. Exp. Psychol. **11**, 56–60 (1959). https://doi.org/10.1080/17470215908416289

21. Murakami, Y., Murakami, C.: Scale construction of a "Big Five" personality inventory. Jpn. J. Personal. **6**, 29–39 (1997). (in Japanese). https://doi.org/10.2132/jjpjspp.6.1_29

22. Murakami, Y., Murakami, C.: The standardization of a Big Five personality inventory for separate generations. Jpn. J. Personal. **8**, 32–42 (1999)

23. Murray, D.J., Ellis, R.R., Bandomir, C.A., Ross, H.E.: Charpentier (1891) on the size—weight illusion. Percept. Psychophys. **61**, 1681–1685 (1999). https://doi.org/10.3758/BF03213127

24. Oinas-Kukkonen, H., Harjumaa, M.: Persuasive systems design: key issues, process model, and system features. Commun. Assoc. Inf. Syst. **24**, 485–500 (2009). https://doi.org/10.4324/9781351252928-14

25. van Schalkwyk, C.L.: Consumer personality and bandwagon consumption behaviour. Auckland University of Technology (2014)

26. Seemann, E., Buboltz, W., Thomas, A., Soper, B., Wilkinson, L.: Normal personality variables and their relationship to psychological reactance (2005)
27. Josekutty Thomas, R., Masthoff, J., Oren, N.: Adapting healthy eating messages to personality. In: de Vries, P.W., Oinas-Kukkonen, H., Siemons, L., Beerlage-de Jong, N., van Gemert-Pijnen, L. (eds.) PERSUASIVE 2017. LNCS, vol. 10171, pp. 119–132. Springer, Cham (2017). https://doi.org/10.1007/978-3-319-55134-0_10
28. Zeigarnik, B.: On finished and unfinished tasks. In: A Source Book of Gestalt Psychology, pp. 300–314. Kegan Paul, Trench, Trubner & Company, London (1938)

Effect of Shopping Value on the Susceptibility of E-Commerce Shoppers to Persuasive Strategies and the Role of Gender

Ifeoma Adaji[(⊠)], Kiemute Oyibo, and Julita Vassileva

University of Saskatchewan, Saskatoon, Canada
{ifeoma.adaji,kiemute.oyibo,
julita.vassileva}@usask.ca

Abstract. Research has shown that persuasive strategies are more effective when personalized to an individual or group of similar individuals. However, there is little knowledge of how the value derived from consumers' online shopping can be used for group-based tailoring of persuasive strategies. To contribute to research in this area, we conducted a study of 244 e-commerce shoppers to investigate how the value they derive from shopping online (hedonic or utilitarian value) can be used to tailor the persuasive strategies: reciprocation, commitment and consistency, social proof, liking, authority and scarcity. In addition, we investigate the susceptibility of the participants to these strategies based on their gender. Our results suggest that people that derive hedonic shopping value online are influenced by scarcity, while those that derive utilitarian shopping value are influenced by consensus. In addition, male shoppers who derive hedonic value from online shopping are influenced by commitment. The results presented here can inform e-commerce developers and stakeholders on how to tailor influence strategies to consumers based on the value the consumers derive from online shopping.

Keywords: Persuasive strategies · E-commerce · Hedonic value · Utilitarian value

1 Introduction

Research has shown that one of the reasons consumers return to a retailer is because of the value they get from the retailer [26]. A shopping experience can be valuable or valueless [10]. There are two common dimensions of value proposition: hedonic and utilitarian values. Research has shown that people with high hedonic shopping value tend to shop for the pleasure or happiness they derive from the shopping experience and not necessarily for the utility or service the product offers [12, 26]. These shoppers are typically motivated to approach pleasure and avoid pain and they can be spontaneous [10, 23]. On the other hand, shoppers with high utilitarian shopping value shop for the functional benefits; they are typically goal-focused, see no need for commitment and see shopping as a task that has to be carried out consciously [12]. Because persuasive strategies are more effective when tailored to individuals or groups of similar individual [1–3, 7], identifying how consumers who belong to each of these

© Springer Nature Switzerland AG 2019
H. Oinas-Kukkonen et al. (Eds.): PERSUASIVE 2019, LNCS 11433, pp. 270–282, 2019.
https://doi.org/10.1007/978-3-030-17287-9_22

dimensions of value proposition are influenced by persuasive strategies can lead to a more personalized experience for shoppers. For example, if consumers with hedonic values are susceptible to a particular influence strategy, implementing that strategy when such consumers come online could lead to a desired behavior or attitude change in the consumer.

E-commerce companies implement persuasive strategies (also referred to as influence strategies) to change the behavior and attitude of their consumers [4, 5, 14]. The change in behavior could be to influence shoppers to buy more products or to buy specific products. Research has shown that persuasive strategies are more effective when they are tailored to individuals or groups of *similar individuals* [6, 13, 25]. Using the right factors in grouping *similar users* is therefore important to the success of group-based tailoring of persuasive strategies. To contribute to ongoing research in the area of group-based personalization in e-commerce, we investigated the use of consumers' shopping value in identifying *similarity* of users. In particular, we aim to answer two main research questions:

(1) Are there any significant differences in the susceptibility of e-commerce shoppers to persuasive strategies based on their shopping value (hedonic or utilitarian)?
(2) What are the moderating effects (if any) of gender on the results from the first research question?

To answer these questions, we carried out a survey of 244 e-commerce shoppers. Using the result from the survey, we developed and tested a global model using partial least squares structural equation modeling. Our result suggests that while online consumers with hedonic shopping value are susceptible to scarcity, those with utilitarian shopping value are influenced by consensus. The result of a multi-group analysis between males and females suggests that utilitarian males are significantly influenced by commitment compared to females who are not.

This paper contributes significantly in three ways to the field of e-commerce and personalized persuasion. First, we validate the results of other researchers who suggest that it is important to tailor persuasive strategies to groups of similar individuals by showing that people of different value propositions are influenced differently. Second, we show what influence strategies could be implemented for the different shopping values derived by e-commerce shoppers and suggest design guidelines that can be adopted when developing systems or presenting products to shoppers of the different value propositions: hedonic or utilitarian. Finally, we show that people of different genders are influenced differently.

2   Related Work

2.1   Hedonic and Utilitarian Shopping Value

Hedonic and utilitarian shopping motivations have been explored in e-commerce. Overby and Lee [27] studied the effect of utilitarian and hedonic shopping motivation on consumer preference and intentions in e-commerce. The authors suggest that the hedonic and shopping motivations of e-shoppers are positively related to their preference for the retailer, however, the preference towards the retailer was stronger for shoppers with utilitarian value compared to shoppers with hedonic shopping value. The authors concluded that the consumers who shop for the functional benefits derive more value shopping online compared to those who shop for pleasure.

2.2 Persuasive Strategies

Research suggests that the use of persuasion can result in behavior change in e-commerce, such as consumers' desire to buy more products or buy certain products as influenced by the system [4, 22]. For example, according to Kaptein [22], *"The average sales of an e-commerce website increases by the use of persuasion"*. Persuasion is defined by Simons and Jones [28] as "human communication designed to influence the autonomous judgments and actions of others".

There are many persuasive strategies that could be used to influence behavior change. The Persuasive Systems Design framework defines twenty four strategies which can be used in systems' design [24]. Cialdini's six principles of persuasion [15] comprises of six persuasive strategies: *reciprocation, commitment and consistency, social proof, liking, authority* and *scarcity*. Cialdini argues that each category targets human behavior and is based on basic psychological principles. Cialdini's six principles were developed in the context of marketing, to get people to buy things. Thus, we used these strategies in this paper.

Reciprocation is based on the psychological behavior of most humans who feel obligated to return a favor. The principle of commitment and consistency is based on the theory of Cognitive Consistency which states that when faced with internal inconsistencies among their interpersonal relations, beliefs, feelings or actions, people tend to behave in ways that reduce these inconsistencies because internal inconsistencies produce a state of tension in individuals. Hence, humans are consistent in nature [17]. When people are uncertain, they look up to others (social proof or consensus) for hints on how to behave and act. Thus providing people with specific information about what others are doing, can evoke similar behavior in them [14]. Humans are trained to believe in obedience of authority figures, hence in deciding what action to take in any situation, information from people in authority could help humans make decisions. According to the liking strategy, people are more persuaded by something/someone they like. Scarcity is referred to by Cialdini as "the rule of the few". This principle, according to him, is based on man's seemingly desire for things that are scare, less readily available or limited in number.

There have been research on the use of these six influence strategies in e-commerce. Kaptein and Eckles [21] used three of the six influence principles in their study of heterogeneity in the effect of online persuasion. Their study set out to identify the difference in peoples' responses to the effects of the influence principles in product evaluations. In other words, to determine to what extent people responded to the various principles. This could help marketers and online businesses determine if a one-size-fits-all approach would be better in influencing users or a more adaptive approach. The authors concluded that implementing the wrong influence strategy for individuals could lead to negative effects compared to implementing no strategy at all and that implementing the best influence principle for an individual could lead to positive change in behavior compared to implementing the strategy that performed best on the average.

Because of the extensive use of Cialdini's six principles of persuasion in various domains, we used it in this study.

3   Research Design and Methodology

In this paper, we set out to investigate the susceptibility of online shoppers to the influence strategies *reciprocation, scarcity, authority, commitment, consensus* and *liking*, based on the shopping value of the shopper. We also investigated the influence of gender on these results. To achieve this, we developed and tested a hypothetical path model described in Fig. 1 using structural equation modeling. Our research model is made up of four constructs: hedonic shopping value, utilitarian shopping value, the persuasive strategies (which comprise of *reciprocation, scarcity, authority, commitment, consensus* and *liking*), use continuance and four hypotheses.

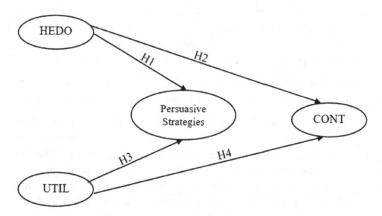

Fig. 1. Research model. HEDO = Hedonic shopping motivation, UTIL = Utilitarian shopping motivation, CONT = Continuance intention, Persuasive strategies = *reciprocation, scarcity, authority, commitment, consensus* and *liking*

3.1   Development of Hypotheses

Research has identified six main motivations of shoppers with hedonic value: *adventure shopping, social shopping, gratification shopping, idea shopping, role shopping* and *value shopping* [8]. Adventure shopping is when people shop for the thrill and adventure that comes with shopping while social shopping is when people see shopping as an opportunity to socialize with others. Gratification shopping is shopping as a means to "alleviate a negative mood", while idea shopping is a means of keeping up with trends and the latest fashions. Role shopping is when people derive pleasure from shopping for others, while value shopping is when consumers shop for sales; hedonic shoppers in this category enjoy the hunt for bargains and discounts [8].

Because consumers with hedonic shopping value see shopping as a social event (social shopping) and an opportunity to bond and interact with others (that they possibly like) such as family and friends [8], we hypothesize that consumers with hedonic shopping value will be influenced by the persuasive strategy *liking*.

Hedonic consumers enjoy shopping for sales, discounts and bargains *(value shopping)*. These shoppers are known to enjoy the thrill of seeking bargains and they see bargain hunting as a challenge to be won [8]. Since limited edition products or scarce products are not typically bargain products, we hypothesize that hedonic consumers will not be influenced by the persuasive strategy *scarcity*.

Consumers with hedonic shopping value are also motivated by *role shopping;* they enjoy shopping for others and are known to feel excited when they find the perfect product for others [8]. For these consumers, shopping for people in their social circle is important to them and they derive pleasure from carrying out this activity. Since hedonic shoppers enjoy shopping for others in their social circle and see shopping as a social event *(social shopping)*, we hypothesize that consumers with hedonic shopping motivation will be influenced by the persuasive strategy *social proof*, also known as *consensus*. We also hypothesize that these shoppers will be influenced by the persuasive strategy *commitment* because if they enjoy shopping for those in their social circle, if they commit to shopping for these people, they will likely keep to their word. In other words, they will likely keep to their commitment of shopping because they derive pleasure from the shopping experience. Based on these, we propose hypothesis 1:

H1: Consumers with hedonic shopping value will be influenced by the persuasive strategies *liking, commitment, consensus and reciprocity* and not by *scarcity*

Consumers with hedonic shopping value derive pleasure from adventure shopping and social shopping; they enjoy the thrill of shopping and see it as an adventure and a social activity. They also enjoy value shopping for deals and bargains [8]. We hypothesize that though value shopping can be accomplished online, these shoppers might not derive the social experience they expect while shopping online. We thus hypothesize that consumers with hedonic shopping value might not be influenced to continue shopping online. We thus propose the following hypothesis:

H2: Consumers with hedonic shopping value will not be influenced to continue shopping online

Shoppers who derive utilitarian value from shopping have no requirement for commitment [12]. We thus propose that they will not be influenced by the persuasive strategy *commitment*.

H3: Consumers with utilitarian shopping value will not be influenced by the persuasive strategy *commitment*

Consumers with utilitarian shopping value see shopping as a task that has to be carried out consciously [12]. They are goal-focused and prefer convenience, accessibility, selection, and availability of information [12]. We hypothesize that these shoppers will likely be influenced to continue shopping online because of the ease of online shopping and the availability of a lot of information online. We therefore propose the following:

H4: Consumers with utilitarian shopping value will be influenced to continue shopping online

3.2   Measurement Model

We developed an online survey to measure the constructs described above. We adopted the previously validated scale of Babin et al. [9] to measure hedonic and utilitarian shopping values, while we adopted the scale of Anol [11] to measure continuance intention. Persuasive strategies were measured using the scale of Kaptein [16]. All items were measured on a seven-point Likert scale (1 = strongly disagree, 7 = strongly agree). Due to space restrictions, we did not include the questionnaire in this paper.

3.3   Participants

We recruited 244 e-commerce shoppers for this study through Amazon Mechanical Turk, social media platforms and news boards. Overall, 66% of the participants were female while 34% were male. 63% were aged 30 years or less while 37% were older than 30 years. Participation was voluntary and approved by the ethics board of the University of Saskatchewan. Table 1 summarizes some of the demographics.

Table 1. Demographics of participants

	Value	(%)
Age	Less than or 30 years	63
	Greater than	37
Gender	Female	66
	Male	34
House hold size	1 to 3 persons	65
	More than 4 persons	35

4   Data Analysis and Results

The data collected was analyzed using Partial Least Squares Structural Equation Modeling (PLS-SEM) with the SmartPls tool. In the following section, we present the results of our analysis.

4.1   Evaluation of Global Measurements

Before considering the relationship between constructs in a model, it is important to evaluate the relationships between the indicators and constructs of the model [20]. This is typically done by assessing the internal consistency, indicator reliability, convergent and discriminant validity of the model [20]. We present the result of these in the following sections.

4.1.1   Internal Consistency

Composite reliability has been suggested as a better alternative to the popular Cronbach's alpha in measuring internal consistency [20, 29]. This is because Cronbach's alpha assumes that all indicators are equally reliable. However, this is not the case as not all indicators usually have equal outer loadings on the construct. In addition, Cronbach's alpha is sensitive to the number of items on the scale [20]. The composite reliability values for all latent variables were higher than the acceptable threshold of 0.6 [20], hence high levels of internal consistency reliability were established among all latent variables.

4.1.2   Indicator Reliability

Indicator reliability indicates how much the outer loading and the associated indicators have in common. In our model, all constructs have outer loadings of at least 0.70, the acceptable minimum [20].

4.1.3   Convergent Validity

Convergent validity describes the extent to which the indicators of a construct correlate positively with the construct [20]. The average variance extracted (AVE) is an accepted method of determining the convergent validity of a model in structural equation modeling [29]. The constructs in our model had AVE values of at least 0.5, the minimum acceptable threshold [20, 29].

4.1.4   Discriminant Validity

Discriminant validity describes the extent to which a construct is unique and captures phenomena that are not captured by other constructs in the model [20]. For each construct in our model, the square root of AVE is greater than the other correlation variables. Hence, discriminant validity was well established [20].

4.2   Structural Model

Table 2 shows the results of our structural model. In particular, it shows the path coefficients (β value) between the various constructs. The path coefficient explains how strong the effect of the exogenous variables are on the endogenous variables. In addition, the model indicates how much the variance of the endogenous variables are explained by the exogenous variables [29]. Finally, the number of asterisks indicates the significance of each direct effect. The number of asterisks ranges from 1 to 4, and this corresponds with the p-value of <0.05, <0.01, <0.001 and <0.0001 respectively.

Table 2. Results of structural equation modeling. HEDO = Hedonic shopping value, UTIL = Utilitarian shopping value, RECI = Reciprocation, SCAR = Scarcity, AUTH = Authority, COMM = Commitment, CONS = Consensus, LIKE = Liking, CONT = Continuance intention

	RECI	SCAR	AUTH	COMM	CONS	LIKE	CONT
HEDO	0.166*	**0.346******	0.212**	0.063	0.183*	0.227*	0.124
UTIL	0.024	0.085	0.213*	0.105	**0.300***	0.170	0.087

From the results of our structural equation modeling shown in Table 2, hedonic shopping value has the strongest effect on scarcity. The path HEDO → SCAR has the highest β value of 0.346 and the strongest significance of <0.0001. This suggests that shoppers with hedonic shopping value are more susceptible to scarcity compared to the other persuasive strategies. Thus, while presenting products to hedonic shoppers, (people who see shopping as a fun activity), using strategies that emphasize scarce or limited goods could bring about the desired behavior change in these category of consumers. On the other hand, utilitarian shopping value has the strongest effect on consensus compared to the other persuasive strategies, which suggests that utilitarian shoppers are more influenced by the consensus strategy compared to the other strategies. According to the consensus strategy [14], people look up to similar others when they are making decisions. Thus, utilitarian shoppers will likely look up to others when making buying decisions online.

4.3   Validation of Hypotheses

We hypothesized in H1 that "Consumers with hedonic shopping value will be influenced by the persuasive strategies *liking, commitment, consensus and reciprocity* and not by *scarcity*". This was however not the case. As shown in Table 2, consumers with hedonic value were influenced by all six persuasive strategies (including *scarcity*) except *commitment*. In addition, we hypothesized in H2 that "Consumers with hedonic shopping value will not be influenced to continue shopping online". This hypothesis was valid as consumers with hedonic shopping value were not significantly influenced to continue shopping online as shown in Table 2.

We hypothesized in H3 that "Consumers with utilitarian shopping value will not be influenced by the persuasive strategy *commitment*". This hypothesis was validated; as shown in Table 2, consumers with utilitarian shopping motivation were not significantly influenced by *commitment*. On the other hand, we hypothesized in H4 that "Consumers with utilitarian shopping value will be influenced to continue shopping online" because of the convenience. As shown in Table 2, this was not the case as these group of shoppers were not significantly influenced to continue shopping online.

4.4   Moderating Effect of Gender

Research has shown that people of different genders behave differently and are thus influenced differently [3, 7, 25]. We therefore investigated the moderating effect of gender on the susceptibility of e-commerce shoppers to persuasive strategies based on their shopping values. The result of the multi-group analysis carried out between males and females is presented in Table 3.

As shown in Table 3, men with utilitarian shopping value are significantly more influenced by commitment compared to females. This appears to be the only significant difference between females and males as suggested by the results of our multi-group analysis in Table 4. This implies that when the gender of utilitarian shoppers is known, applying the commitment strategy on them could bring about the desired behavior change in e-commerce.

Table 3. Result of structural model for males and females. HEDO = Hedonic shopping value, UTIL = Utilitarian shopping value, RECI = Reciprocation, SCAR = Scarcity, AUTH = Authority, COMM = Commitment, CONS = Consensus, LIKE = Liking, CONT = Continuance intention, F = Female participants, M = Male participants. Red rectangle indicates significant difference

	RECI	SCAR	AUTH	COMM	CONS	LIKE	CONT
HEDO (F)	0.161	0.377****	0.242*	0.026	0.190	0.221*	0.123
HEDO (M)	0.144	0.211	0.334**	0.018	0.214	0.395	0.193
UTIL (F)	−0.031	−0.028	0.211	−0.141	0.187	0.080	0.051
UTIL (M)	0.240	0.323	0.251	0.251*	0.433*	0.143	0.124

Table 4. Results of multi-group analysis between males and females showing that the only significant difference is between UTIL → COMM. Red rectangle indicates significant difference

Path	Path Coefficient difference |male-female|	p-value (male vs female)
HEDO→RECI	0.018	0.544
HEDO→SCAR	0.166	0.767
HEDO→AUTH	0.093	0.288
HEDO→COMM	0.009	0.512
HEDO→CONS	0.024	0.449
HEDO→LIKE	0.175	0.214
HEDO→CONT	0.071	0.355
UTIL→RECI	0.271	0.170
UTIL→SCAR	0.351	0.101
UTIL→AUTH	0.040	0.462
UTIL→COMM	**0.392**	**0.048***
UTIL→CONS	0.245	0.199
UTIL→LIKE	0.063	0.395
UTIL→CONT	0.074	0.422

5   Discussion

In this section, we discuss the findings presented earlier and the implications for e-commerce stakeholders.

5.1   Susceptibility of E-Shoppers to Persuasive Strategies

Shoppers who derive hedonic value from their shopping experience are those who purchase items because of the pleasure and enjoyment they derive from such goods [19]. They typically shop for the entertainment the shopping experience brings and for the out-of-routine experience the shopping trip affords them [26]. Results from our global model as shown in Table 2 suggest that shoppers with hedonic value are more influenced by *scarcity* compared to the other persuasive strategies. This result is similar to previous research [18] that suggests that scarcity threatens consumers' shopping freedom, thereby influencing people that are high in hedonic shopping motivation to become competitive and go after scarce products. The implication of this to e-commerce stakeholders is to emphasize the scarcity principle when products are being presented to shoppers of hedonic shopping value. One-way e-commerce stores such as Laura[1] implement scarcity is by using phrases such as *"Hurry! 1 item left in stock"*. Amazon uses a similar phrase *"Only 9 left in stock"*.

Shoppers who derive utilitarian shopping value are goal-focused and see shopping as a task that has to be carried out. They shop for the functional benefits, see no need for commitment and they see shopping as a task that has to be carried out consciously [12]. Our results in Table 2 suggest that this category of shoppers are more influenced by consensus compared to other strategies. The consensus strategy suggests that people look up to similar others when they are uncertain of how to act [14]. Similarity in e-commerce can be based on products; people are similar because they have purchased the same products. One way consensus is implemented by Amazon.com is by suggesting products that are often bought together based on one's current shopping cart. By so doing, shoppers can be influenced to buy other products that similar shoppers bought. By using phrases such as *"customers who viewed this item also viewed"*, Amazon.com shows the user the products that other similar shoppers have viewed. This could influence the shopper into buying those products. Amazon also uses phrases such as *"frequently bought together"* to emphasize consensus. The result from this study is not surprising; people with utilitarian shopping value see shopping as a "task" that has to be carried out [12]. Therefore, having suggestions presented to them from similar others makes it easier and quicker for them to carry out the "task" of shopping. Thus, it is within reason that people with utilitarian shopping value will be influenced by the persuasive strategy *consensus*.

One surprising result is that neither consumers with hedonic nor utilitarian shopping value were influenced to continue shopping online. This suggests that shoppers that are high in both hedonic and utilitarian value do not find value shopping online. This was surprising for the shoppers with utilitarian shopping value because online

---

[1] https://www.laura.ca/.

shopping provides an easy way of searching for products and carrying out the "task" of shopping quickly. For the shoppers with hedonic shopping value, we attribute this result to the fact that the online shopping experience might not be as pleasant to the shopper as that available in physical stores where shoppers can touch, feel and even try on products before purchasing them; thereby adding more pleasurable value to their shopping experience. This hypothesis will be explored in our future work.

5.2 Moderating Role of Gender

Because people of different genders act differently and are persuaded differently, we investigated the influence of the persuasive strategies on shoppers based on their gender [25]. The results of a multi-group analysis in Tables 3 and 4 show that the only significant difference between females and males is between those who derive utilitarian shopping value online; the male participants who derive utilitarian shopping value online were significantly influenced by commitment while the females were not. There were no other differences between females and males. This result was unexpected because previous studies suggest that females and males are influenced differently and there are significant differences in their susceptibility to most of Cialdini's six principles of persuasion [18]. We attributed our results to the domain that we investigated which is e-commerce and the fact that we included the shopping value of consumers in determining their susceptibility to the influence strategies.

The implication of our results to stakeholders of e-commerce include the following: (1) Shopping value **can be used in group-based tailoring** of persuasive strategies; our results suggest significant differences in the influence of persuasive strategies on shoppers based on their shopping value - hedonic or utilitarian. (2) While presenting products to shoppers who derive hedonic value from online shopping, **the persuasive strategy that could likely bring about the desired behavior change is *scarcity***. (3) While presenting products to shoppers who derive utilitarian value from online shopping, the persuasive strategy that could likely bring about the desired behavior change is *consensus*. **If however the gender of the utilitarian shopper is known to be male, the persuasive strategy that should be used is *commitment*.**

5.3 Limitations

Our research has a few limitations. First, our study presents the self-reported persuasiveness of the six persuasive strategies that were used in this study; the actual persuasiveness of the strategies could differ when observed and is not self-reported. Therefore, we plan to explore the persuasiveness of these strategies by observing shoppers in an actual e-commerce platform on a larger scale. Second, the ratio of males to females is not equal. We are in the process of collecting more data from specific genders so that we can have an equal or close to an equal number of females and males in the future. Finally, our research was conducted in the domain of e-commerce. The results presented here may not generalize to other forms of commerce such as brick-and-mortar commerce.

6   Conclusion and Future Work

Persuasive strategies are more effective when personalized to an individual or group of similar individuals. There is ongoing research to improve e-commerce personalization by identifying the factors can be used for group-based personalization. There is little knowledge of how the value derived from consumers' online shopping can be used for group-based tailoring of persuasive strategies. To contribute to research in this area, we conducted a study of 244 e-commerce shoppers to investigate how the value derived from shopping online (*hedonic* or *utilitarian value*) can be used to tailor the persuasive strategies: *reciprocation, commitment and consistency, social proof, liking, authority* and *scarcity*. We developed and tested a global model using structural equation modeling. In addition, we investigated the susceptibility of our participants to these strategies based on their gender. Our results suggest that people that derive hedonic shopping value online are influenced by scarcity more than the other strategies, while those that derive utilitarian shopping value are influenced by consensus more than the other strategies. In addition, the male shoppers who derive hedonic-value from online shopping are influenced by commitment compared to the female shoppers. In the future, we will like to explore the influence of other demographic data on our global model. Of interest is the influence of age; to determine if younger and older adults are influenced by the same strategies.

References

1. Adaji, I., Oyibo, K., Vassileva, J.: Consumers' need for uniqueness and the influence of persuasive strategies in E-commerce. In: International Conference on Persuasive Technology, Waterloo, pp. 279–284 (2018)
2. Adaji, I., Oyibo, K., Vassileva, J.: Shopper types and the influence of persuasive strategies in e-commerce. In: International Workshop on Personalized Persuasive Technology, Waterloo, pp. 58–65 (2018)
3. Adaji, I., Oyibo, K., Vassileva, J.: The effect of gender and age on the factors that influence healthy shopping habits in e-commerce. In: Proceedings of the 26th Conference on User Modeling, Adaptation and Personalization - UMAP 2018, Singapore, pp. 251–255 (2018)
4. Adaji, I., Vassileva, J.: Evaluating personalization and persuasion in e-commerce. In: International Workshop on Personalized Persuasive Technology, Salzburg, pp. 107–113 (2016)
5. Adaji, I., Vassileva, J.: Perceived effectiveness, credibility and continuance intention in e-commerce. A study of Amazon. In: Proceedings of 12th International Conference on Persuasive Technology, Amsterdam, pp. 293–306 (2017)
6. Adaji, I., Vassileva, J.: Tailoring persuasive strategies in e-commerce. In: International Workshop on Personalized Persuasive Technology, Amsterdam, pp. 57–63 (2017)
7. Adaji, I., Vassileva, J.: The impact of age, gender and level of education on the persuasiveness of influence strategies in e-commerce. In: Adjunct Proceedings of the 12th International Conference on Persuasive Technology, April 2017, p. 10 (2017)
8. Arnold, M.J., Reynolds, K.E.: Hedonic shopping motivations. J. Retail. **79**(2), 77–95 (2003)
9. Babin, B.J., Darden, W.R.: Consumer self-regulation in a retail environment. J. Retail. **71**(1), 47–70 (1995)

10. Babin, B.J., Darden, W.R., Griffin, M.: Work and/or fun: measuring hedonic and utilitarian shopping value. J. Consum. Res. **20**(4), 644–656 (1994)
11. Bhattacherjee, A.: Understanding information systems continuance: an expectation-confirmation model. MIS Q. **25**(3), 351 (2001)
12. Bridges, E., Renée, F.: Hedonic and utilitarian shopping goals: the online experience. J. Bus. Res. **61**(4), 309–314 (2008)
13. Busch, M., et al.: Personalization in serious and persuasive games and gamified interactions. In: Proceedings of the 2015 Annual Symposium on Computer-Human Interaction in Play - CHI PLAY 2015, New York, pp. 811–816 (2015)
14. Cialdini, R.: The science of persuasion. Sci. Am. **284**, 76–81 (2001)
15. Cialdini, R.B.: Influence: Science and Practice. Pearson Education, Boston (2009)
16. Kaptein, M.: Adaptive persuasive messages in an e-commerce setting: the use of persuasion profiles. ECIS (2011). aisel.aisnet.org
17. Feldman, S.: Cognitive Consistency: Motivational Antecedents and Behavioral Consequents (2013)
18. Gupta, S.: The psychological effects of perceived scarcity on consumers' buying behavior. Dissertations, Thesis, and Student Research from the College of Business, July 2013
19. Gupta, S., Kim, H.-W.: Value-driven internet shopping: the mental accounting theory perspective. Psychol. Mark. **27**(1), 13–35 (2010)
20. Hair Jr., J., Hult, T., Ringle, C., Sarstedt, M.: A Primer on Partial Least Squares Structural Equation Modeling (PLS-SEM). Sage Publications, Thousand Oaks (2016)
21. Kaptein, M., Eckles, D.: Heterogeneity in the effects of online persuasion. J. Interact. Mark. **26**(3), 176–188 (2012)
22. Kaptein, M.: Personalized Persuasion in Ambient Intelligence. IOS Press, Amsterdam (2012)
23. O'Shaughnessy, J., Jackson O'Shaughnessy, N.: Marketing, the consumer society and hedonism. Eur. J. Mark. **36**(5/6), 524–547 (2002)
24. Oinas-Kukkonen, H., Harjumaa, M.: A systematic framework for designing and evaluating persuasive systems. In: Oinas-Kukkonen, H., Hasle, P., Harjumaa, M., Segerståhl, K., Øhrstrøm, P. (eds.) PERSUASIVE 2008. LNCS, vol. 5033, pp. 164–176. Springer, Heidelberg (2008). https://doi.org/10.1007/978-3-540-68504-3_15
25. Orji, R., Mandryk, R.L., Vassileva, J.: Gender, age, and responsiveness to Cialdini's persuasion strategies. In: MacTavish, T., Basapur, S. (eds.) PERSUASIVE 2015. LNCS, vol. 9072, pp. 147–159. Springer, Cham (2015). https://doi.org/10.1007/978-3-319-20306-5_14
26. Overby, J.W., et al.: The effects of utilitarian and hedonic online shopping value on consumer preference and intentions (2006). Elsevier
27. Overby, J.W., Lee, E.-J.: The effects of utilitarian and hedonic online shopping value on consumer preference and intentions. J. Bus. Res. **59**(10–11), 1160–1166 (2006)
28. Simons, H.H.W., Jones, J.: Persuasion in Society. Taylor & Francis, New York (2011)
29. Wong, K.: Partial least squares structural equation modeling (PLS-SEM) techniques using SmartPLS. Mark. Bull. **24**(1), 1–32 (2013)

Actual Persuasiveness: Impact of Personality, Age and Gender on Message Type Susceptibility

Ana Ciocarlan[1][(✉)], Judith Masthoff[1,2], and Nir Oren[1]

[1] University of Aberdeen, Aberdeen, UK
{ana.ciocarlan,j.masthoff,n.oren}@abdn.ac.uk
[2] Utrecht University, Utrecht, The Netherlands

Abstract. Persuasive technologies use a variety of strategies and principles to encourage people to adopt and maintain beneficial behaviours and attitudes. In this paper we investigate the influence of Cialdini's seven persuasive principles on people's choices, actions and behaviour. In contrast to related work investigating perceived persusaion, this study analyses actual persuasion. We also investigate the impact of personality, age and gender on people's susceptibility to different message types. Furthermore, we investigate if people's susceptibility to different persuasive messages is consistent over time. The findings suggest that certain persuasive principles have a greater influence on a person's actions than others, with Reciprocity and Liking being the most effective. Our results differ from work investigating perceived persuasiveness, suggesting that what people perceive to be more persuasive is not necessarily what will persuade them to perform an action. Moreover, the study showed that people's susceptibility to different principles is dependent on their personality traits, and it remains constant with time. The findings from this study have implications for future work on personalising persuasive strategies and designing digital behaviour change interventions.

1 Background

Persuasive technologies and interventions motivate, shape and reinforce beneficial behaviours and attitudes through the use of a wide range of strategies. Some of the most commonly employed strategies in the design of behaviour change interventions have been identified by Cialdini [1,2], Fogg [6], Michie et al. [16], and Oinas-Kukkonen and Harjumaa [18].

While digital behaviour change interventions can be delivered using various approaches, persuasive games have attracted attention in recent research work, due to their strong motivational pull [22]. Persuasive games are very interactive and require active engagement from participants, which can increase the emotional quality of the intervention [17] and act as an incentive to keep users engaged with the intervention [13].

Recent work has shown that persuasive interventions are more effective if they are personalised [9,14] and an increasing number of persuasive games have been

© Springer Nature Switzerland AG 2019
H. Oinas-Kukkonen et al. (Eds.): PERSUASIVE 2019, LNCS 11433, pp. 283–294, 2019.
https://doi.org/10.1007/978-3-030-17287-9_23

developed in recent years as novel solutions for motivating healthier behaviours, such as encouraging physical activity and balanced nutrition [11,12,24]. For example, the game by [24] encourages healthy eating and physical activity to prevent diabetes and obesity among adolescents, the *Re-Mission* game improves self-efficacy in young adults undergoing cancer treatment [11], and the work of Orji [19] investigated personalisation to gamer types to motivate healthy eating.

With a growing interest in tailoring persuasive technologies and games, many studies investigate people's *perceived* persuasiveness of different strategies [20,21, 23,25]. Some studies have focused on investigating whether persuasive messages have an effect on behaviour, such as [10] who showed that using persuasive cues can increase compliance to a perform request. However, there remains a need to further analyse *actual* persuasiveness, or the direct influence different persuasive strategies and principles have on people's actions and behaviour. Furthermore, we need to investigate whether people's susceptibility to these strategies and principles is consistent over a longer period of time.

In this paper, we present the results of a study which investigates the influence of different persuasive principles on people's direct actions and behaviour. Moreover, we analyse the relationship between people's characteristics and their susceptibility to different principles. We also investigate whether people's susceptibility to Cialdini's persuasive principles varies with time. The findings from our study will allow us to develop personalisation algorithms for further experiments and will inform the design of effective persuasive interventions for wellbeing.

2   Study Design

The aim of this study was to investigate how choices, actions and behaviour are influenced by messages using different persuasive principles. We wanted to investigate if certain persuasive principles have a greater impact than others and which persuasive principles are most suited for people of different personality types, age and gender. Additionally, we investigated if people's susceptibility to persuasive principles is consistent over time.

2.1   Research Questions

The study was designed to investigate the following research questions:

1. How effective are different persuasive principles in influencing people's behaviour and actions?
2. What is the effect of age, gender and personality on people's susceptibility to different persuasive principles?
3. Is susceptibility to different persuasive principles consistent over time?

2.2   Participants

We recruited a total of 130 unique participants to take part in the experiment (79 females and 51 males, age ranges between 18 and 70 years old). A subset of

55 participants (29 females and 26 males, age ranges between 18 and 53 years old) agreed to return one week later for a second session. The second session was intended to investigate whether people's susceptibility to different persuasive principles is consistent over time, but participants were not aware of this. Participants were recruited using email lists and social media platforms. Participants reported that they generally played games a few times per year (19 participants), a few times per month (20 participants), a few times per week (22 participants), every day (45 participants) and almost never (24 participants). Participants were not offered any monetary payment or reward to take part in this study. Table 1 shows participants' demographics.

Table 1. Participants' demographics

Study session	Participants			Age range
	Total	Males	Females	
Session A	130	51	79	18–70
Session A and B	55	29	26	18–53

2.3 Procedure

Participants were told that the purpose of this experiment is to investigate how persuasion principles influence people's behaviour and actions. Consent forms and information sheets were provided and participants were informed that taking part in the study was voluntary and that they could withdraw at any time and for any reason. All materials produced by the participants were stored securely. Ethical consent for our experiments was obtained from the Physical Sciences and Engineering ethics board of the University of Aberdeen.

Participants completed a brief demographics questionnaire, as well as the Ten Item Personality Inventory [7] to determine their personality traits. Additionally, participants were asked to play a short text adventure game in which they were shown a scenario and a list of quests displayed in a randomised order. The quests required participants to help various fictional characters and each quest reflected one of Cialdini's seven principles of persuasion. Table 2 shows the mapping of Cialdini's persuasive principles to the quests in the adventure text game.

Participants were told that they could only help one of the characters and they must choose one of the seven quest options. They were informed that they would receive the same reward, independent of the quest they choose to complete. We asked participants not to roleplay when taking decisions in the game, but instead, consider the choices as they would in real life. Figure 1 shows an example with the first game scenario and quests displayed in a randomised order.

After selecting a quest, participants received a randomly generated amount of gold and experience points. They were also given feedback about their progress through the game. A new round would start in which participants were shown a new list of quests to choose from, excluding any they selected in previous rounds,

Table 2. Mapping of Cialdini's persuasive principles to adventure game quests

Persuasive principle	Quest
Authority	The king of these lands would really like you to help this character
Liking	You have always admired this character and you enjoy their company
Scarcity	This character is a traveling merchant who will be leaving tomorrow, so this is your only chance to help them
Reciprocity	This character has done a favour for you in the past, so now you can help them too
Commitment	You have already agreed to help this character with another task, so you could help them with this one too
Social proof	The majority of those living in this village would like you to help this character
Unity	This character is originally from the same village as you

You are an adventurer, arriving in a small village on the edge of the forest. While resting at the inn, you find out that the village is often attacked by various creatures. Before you leave, you decide to offer some help.

Your total XP: 0
Your gold: 0

You must choose which quest to go on next. There are 7 different characters in the village who want your help. All quests are of the same difficulty and you will receive the same reward for completing them. If you could only help one character, which quest would you choose to go on?

You have always admired this character and you enjoy their company.

This character is a traveling merchant who will be leaving tomorrow, so this is your only chance to help them.

This character has done a favour for you in the past, so now you can help them too.

The king of these lands would really like you to help this character.

This character is originally from the same village as you.

You have already agreed to help this character with another task, so you could help them with this one too.

The majority of those living in this village would like you to help this character.

Continue...

Fig. 1. Example of the first scenario in the text adventure game, followed by a list of quests displayed in a randomised order, reflecting Cialdini's principles of persuasion.

until only two choices remained. Thus, participants made a quest selection over a total of seven rounds. To maintain the influence of scarcity throughout the game, the quest would refer to a different character requiring help for a limited period of time during each round. Through this method, we were able to observe the action paths taken by participants in the adventure game. The order in which they selected quests resulted in a ranking for each persuasive principle, thus showing the direct influence the messages have on behaviour. Figure 2 shows an example of the scenario in the fourth round when participants are left with four quest choices to select from.

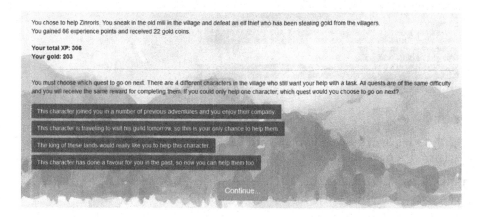

You chose to help Zinroris. You sneak in the old mill in the village and defeat an elf thief who has been stealing gold from the villagers. You gained 86 experience points and received 22 gold coins.

Your total XP: 306
Your gold: 203

You must choose which quest to go on next. There are 4 different characters in the village who still want your help with a task. All quests are of the same difficulty and you will receive the same reward for completing them. If you could only help one character, which quest would you choose to go on next?

This character joined you in a number of previous adventures and you enjoy their company.

This character is traveling to visit his guild tomorrow, so this is your only chance to help them.

The king of these lands would really like you to help this character.

This character has done a favour for you in the past, so now you can help them too

Continue...

Fig. 2. The fourth scenario in the text adventure game showing feedback and rewards received, as well as a new list of quests displayed in a randomised order

After one week, 55 of the participants took part in the second session of the adventure game. We wanted to investigate whether the selections they make in the game after some time has passed are similar to their previous ones. Participants' progress was saved from the first session, so they kept any gold and experience points they earned in the previous week. The scenario and quests were slightly changed to provide continuity to the story in the game. Figure 3 shows an example of a scenario from the second session of the study. The quests were displayed in a randomised order.

3   Results

3.1   Influence of Persuasive Principles on Behaviour

Overall, we identified that people are more susceptible to certain persuasive principles than others. Table 3 shows the frequency and percentages of what participants selected in each round of the game during the first session of the study. The highest proportion of participants chose to complete the quest reflecting the Reciprocity principle (32.8%) in the first round. They also preferred to complete the quests representing either the Reciprocity or Liking principles (29.9%) in the second round, followed by the Scarcity principle (24.6%) in the third round. This suggests that people are more persuaded by Reciprocity, Liking and Scarcity

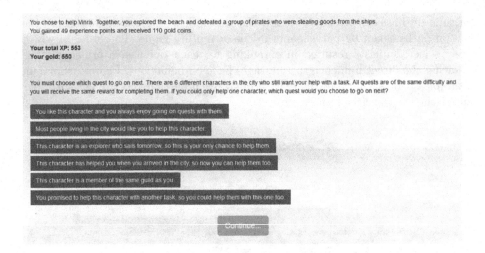

You chose to help Vinris. Together, you explored the beach and defeated a group of pirates who were stealing goods from the ships.
You gained 49 experience points and received 110 gold coins.

Your total XP: 553
Your gold: 550

You must choose which quest to go on next. There are 6 different characters in the city who still want your help with a task. All quests are of the same difficulty and you will receive the same reward for completing them. If you could only help one character, which quest would you choose to go on next?

You like this character and you always enjoy going on quests with them.

Most people living in the city would like you to help this character.

This character is an explorer who sails tomorrow, so this is your only chance to help them.

This character has helped you when you arrived in the city, so now you can help them too.

This character is a member of the same guild as you.

You promised to help this character with another task, so you could help them with this one too.

Continue...

Fig. 3. Example of scenario in the second session of the study and the list of quests displayed in a randomised order

Table 3. Frequency and percentages of selections of quests reflecting persuasive principles across rounds R1 to R7 in Session A (N = 130)

	Liking	Scarcity	Authority	Reciprocity	Unity	Commitment	Consensus
R1	30 (22.4%)	11 (8.2%)	7 (5.2%)	**44 (32.8%)**	4 (3%)	10 (7.5%)	24 (17.9%)
R2	**40 (29.9%)**	11 (8.2%)	7 (5.2%)	**40 (29.9%)**	7 (5.2%)	9 (6.7%)	16 (11.9%)
R3	18 (13.4%)	**33 (24.6%)**	10 (7.5%)	14 (10.4%)	16 (11.9%)	19 (14.2%)	20 (14.9%)
R4	17 (12.7%)	16 (11.9%)	20 (14.9%)	17 (12.7%)	18 (13.4%)	20 (14.9%)	**22 (16.4%)**
R5	14 (10.4%)	17 (12.7%)	25 (18.7%)	5 (3.7%)	**30 (22.4%)**	19 (14.2%)	20 (14.9%)
R6	7 (5.2%)	21 (15.7%)	23 (17.2%)	6 (4.5%)	**31 (23.1%)**	25 (18.7%)	17 (12.7%)
R7	4 (3%)	21 (15.7%)	**38 (28.4%)**	4 (3%)	24 (17.9%)	28 (20.9%)	11 (8.2%)

when they must make a choice regarding their next action. The least selected persuasive principle was Authority, with 28.4% of participants completing this quest last.

A Chi-Square Test showed that there is a significant overall difference between people's susceptibility to the various principles ($\chi^2(36) = 260.938$, $p < 0.001$). Pairwise comparisons (with Bonferroni corrected p-values to account for the 21 comparisons made) showed that Liking and Reciprocity were significantly different from all other principles ($p < 0.05$), but not from each other. Authority was significantly different from all other principles ($p < 0.05$) except from Unity and Commitment. Unity was significantly different from Consensus ($p < 0.05$). Other comparisons were not significant. Combining the results with Table 3, this seems to indicate that people were most susceptible to Liking and Reciprocity principles, and least susceptible to Authority, Unity and Commitment principles. Analysing whether the principles were used differently over different rounds, there is a significant difference for each principle

(Liking $\chi^2(6) = 51.677$, p < 0.001; Scarcity $\chi^2(6) = 18.508$, p < 0.01; Authority $\chi^2(6) = 42.092$, p < 0.001; Reciprocity $\chi^2(6) = 90.662$, p < 0.001; Unity $\chi^2(6) = 35.954$, p < 0.001; Commitment $\chi^2(6) = 16.031$, p < 0.05), with the exception of Consensus ($\chi^2(6) = 6.015$, p = 0.421).

3.2 Influence of Age, Gender and Personality on Susceptibility to Persuasive Principles

To analyse the influence of different characteristics on susceptibility, we investigated the relationship between age, gender, personality traits, and the ranking of principles which resulted from participants' actions. We found a weak positive correlation between participant age and the ranking of the Authority principle (r = 0.278, p < 0.01), as well as a weak negative correlation between participant age and the ranking of the Commitment principle (r = −0.240, p < 0.01). This suggests that people's susceptibility to the Authority principle increases with age, while their susceptibility to the Commitment principle decreases as they grow older.

An Independent t-test was used to evaluate differences in susceptibility to different persuasive principles between female and male participants. We found that female participants had statistically significantly lower susceptibility (3.96 ± 1.8) to the Scarcity principle compared to male participants (4.73 ± 1.8), t(128) = −2.295, p = 0.023. This suggests that gender does not generally influence susceptibility to principles, but Scarcity could persuade male participants more than female participants.

To observe the effect of personality, we investigated the relationship between the five personality traits of the Five Factor Model [15] and the rankings obtained for each persuasive principle. We identified several significant correlations, shown in Table 4. For Extraversion, we found two weak negative correlations with Liking and Authority, as well as two weak positive correlations with Reciprocity and Commitment. A weak negative correlation was found for Agreeableness and Scarcity, as well as a weak positive correlation for Conscientiousness and Authority. Emotional Stability was positively correlated with Scarcity and Commitment principles, but negatively correlated with the Consensus principle. For Openness

Table 4. Correlations between personality traits and rankings of principles in Session A (N = 130; * = p < 0.01; ** = p < 0.001)

	Liking	Scarcity	Authority	Reciprocity	Unity	Commitment	Consensus
Extraversion	−.180*	−.052	−.242**	.183*	−.081	.178*	.170
Agreeableness	.064	−.232**	.072	.019	.082	0.57	−.036
Conscientiousness	.018	−.060	.216*	.015	−.127	.110	−.171
Emotional stability	−.092	.173*	.054	−.097	−.068	.175*	−.173*
Openness	−.070	−.063	−.193*	0.008	−.010	.249**	.059

we found a weak negative correlation with Authority and a weak positive correlation with Commitment. These findings suggest that people's personality traits have an impact on their susceptibility to different persuasive principles.

3.3 Consistency in Susceptibility to Persuasive Principles

Our findings show that people's susceptibility to different persuasive principles does not vary over time. In general, participants who completed both sessions of the experiment were consistent in their choices and followed similar paths of action in the second session of the adventure game. A Paired Samples t-test was used to compare participants' rankings from the first session and the second session of the experiment. As shown in Table 5, we found no significant average difference between the scores of the two sessions, with the exception of the Commitment principle[1]. Table 6 shows that all the pair scores were significantly positively correlated. This suggests that people's susceptibility to different messages remains consistent over time.

Table 7 compares the mean and standard deviation for the rankings in the first and second sessions of the adventure game. We found that percentages of selections of quests reflecting different persuasive principles were similar in sessions A and B. Figure 4 show the percentages for the first three rounds of the adventure game. The majority of participants selected Reciprocity, Liking and Scarcity during the first round for both sessions, while only a small proportion of participants chose Authority or Unity.

Table 5. Paired differences between rankings of persuasive principles in sessions A and B (N = 55; df = 54; * = p < 0.05)

	Liking	Scarcity	Authority	Reciprocity	Unity	Commitment	Consensus
Mean (SD)	−.400 (1.5)	.109 (1.7)	.200 (1.7)	.145 (1.7)	−.164 (1.4)	.436 (1.5)	−.327 (1.6)
t score	−1.903	.457	.870	.629	.852	2.058*	−1.496
p-value	.062	.650	.388	.532	.398	.044	.140

Table 6. Paired Samples correlations between rankings of persuasive principles in sessions A and B (N = 55; * = p < 0.01; ** = p < 0.001)

Liking	Scarcity	Authority	Reciprocity	Unity	Commitment	Consensus
.599**	.653**	.458**	.348*	.582**	.655**	.614**

Table 7. Mean and standard deviation of rankings for Sessions A and B (N = 55)

	Liking	Scarcity	Authority	Reciprocity	Unity	Commitment	Consensus
Session A	2.82 (1.7)	4.07 (1.9)	4.89 (1.6)	2.33 (1.5)	5.11 (1.5)	4.82 (1.9)	3.96 (1.7)
Session B	3.22 (1.7)	3.96 (2.2)	4.69 (1.6)	2.18 (1.3)	5.27 (1.5)	4.38 (1.8)	4.29 (1.8)

---

[1] This was only borderline significant (p = 0.044), so, if a Bonferroni correction was applied given the number of statistical tests performed, it would not be significant.

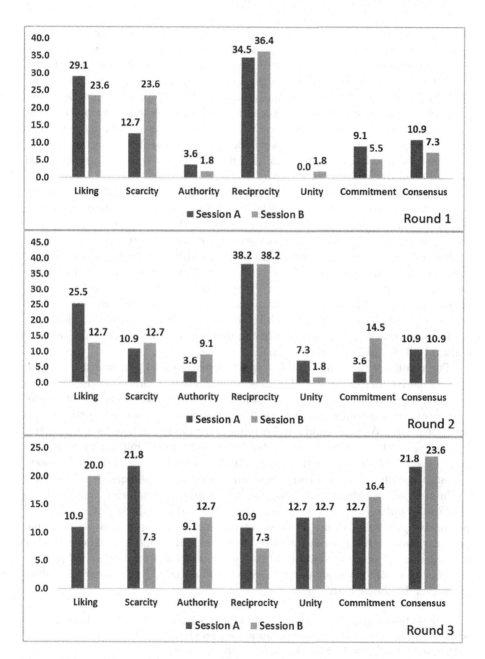

Fig. 4. Percentages for selections of quests reflecting different persuasive principles in the first three rounds of sessions A and B (N = 55)

4   Conclusions and Future Work

Our findings in this study lead us to conclude that people are influenced to take an action due to certain persuasive principles more than others. In general, Reciprocity and Liking were the most effective persuasion principles, while Authority and Unity are the least effective persuasion principles. The findings differ from work investigating perceived persuasiveness, such as [23] who found that people perceived messages using the Authority or Liking principles to be the most persuasive. This is an indication that what people perceive to be more persuasive is not necessarily what will persuade them to complete a certain action. Further investigation is required to identify differences between *percieved* and *actual* persuasiveness.

Recent work has shown that perceived persuasiveness to different message types is influenced by personality [8,20,21]. While our study focused on investigating actual persuasion, our results also show that personality influences people's susceptibility to different principles, while gender and age seem to have a small effect. Furthermore, we found that susceptibility to persuasive principles remains stable over time. This could be explained by the fact that people's personality does not change and, therefore the level of influence different persuasive principles has on them remains constant. In this study we investigated consistency over time with one week in between the two sessions. An additional study could investigate if susceptibility to different persuasive messages remains constant after a longer period of time.

The results of the study could support future work in personalising persuasive strategies and designing digital behaviour change interventions. We have done some initial research on how a gamified digital behaviour intervention can be adapted to encourage people of different personality types to perform kind activities [3,5]. We also conducted a qualitative study on how to adapt activity complexity to personality, stress level and attitude [4]. Further investigation is necessary to find out whether other attributes such as an individual's mood states or need for cognition can impact susceptibility to persuasive principles.

In this study, participants did not have the choice to select no quest, so the results only show relative behaviour when individuals are exposed to all persuasive principles. Hence, it does not provide an absolute measure of actual persuasiveness, but a relative measure. A future study could investigate whether participants are persuaded at all. Future work could also explore actual persuasiveness in a different domain, such as persuading people to engage in healthy or sustainable behaviours.

Acknowledgements. The authors would like to acknowledge and thank all the volunteers who participated in the experiment and provided helpful comments. The first author is funded by an EPSRC doctoral training grant.

References

1. Cialdini, R.: The Psychology of Influence and Persuasion. NY Quill, New York (1991)
2. Cialdini, R.: Pre-Suasion: A Revolutionary Way to Influence and Persuade. Simon & Schuster, New York (2016)
3. Ciocarlan, A., Masthoff, J., Oren, N.: Kindness is contagious: exploring engagement in a gamified persuasive intervention for wellbeing. In: Proceedings of Positive Gaming: Workshop on Gamification and Games for Wellbeing, ACM SIGCHI Annual Symposium on Computer-Human Interaction in Play (CHI PLAY 2017). CEUR Workshop Proceedings, vol. 2055. CEUR-WS.org (2017)
4. Ciocarlan, A., Masthoff, J., Oren, N.: Qualitative study into adapting persuasive games for mental wellbeing to personality, stressors and attitudes. In: Adjunct Publication of the 25th Conference on User Modeling, Adaptation and Personalization, UMAP 2017, pp. 402–407. ACM, New York (2017)
5. Ciocarlan, A., Masthoff, J., Oren, N.: Kindness is contagious: study into exploring engagement and adapting persuasive games for wellbeing. In: Proceedings of the 26th Conference on User Modeling, Adaptation and Personalization, UMAP 2018, pp. 311–319. ACM, New York (2018)
6. Fogg, B.J.: Persuasive Technology: Using Computers to Change What We Think and Do. Morgan Kaufmann, San Francisco (2003)
7. Gosling, S.D., Rentfrow, P.J., Swann, W.B.J.: A very brief measure of the big five personality domains. J. Res. Pers. **37**, 504–528 (2003)
8. Josekutty Thomas, R., Masthoff, J., Oren, N.: Adapting healthy eating messages to personality. In: de Vries, P.W., Oinas-Kukkonen, H., Siemons, L., Beerlage-de Jong, N., van Gemert-Pijnen, L. (eds.) PERSUASIVE 2017. LNCS, vol. 10171, pp. 119–132. Springer, Cham (2017). https://doi.org/10.1007/978-3-319-55134-0_10
9. Kaptein, M., De Ruyter, B., Markopoulos, P., Aarts, E.: Adaptive persuasive systems. ACM TIIS **2**(2), 10:1–10:25 (2012)
10. Kaptein, M., Markopoulos, P., de Ruyter, B., Aarts, E.: Can you be persuaded? Individual differences in susceptibility to persuasion. In: Gross, T., et al. (eds.) INTERACT 2009. LNCS, vol. 5726, pp. 115–118. Springer, Heidelberg (2009). https://doi.org/10.1007/978-3-642-03655-2_13
11. Kato, P.M., Cole, S.W., Bradlyn, A.S., Pollock, B.H.: A video game improves behavioral outcomes in adolescents and young adults with cancer: a randomized trial. Pediatrics **122**(2), e305–e317 (2008)
12. Khaled, R., Barr, P., Noble, J., Fischer, R., Biddle, R.: Fine Tuning the persuasion in persuasive games. In: de Kort, Y., IJsselsteijn, W., Midden, C., Eggen, B., Fogg, B.J. (eds.) PERSUASIVE 2007. LNCS, vol. 4744, pp. 36–47. Springer, Heidelberg (2007). https://doi.org/10.1007/978-3-540-77006-0_5
13. Kraft, P., Drozd, F., Olsen, E.: ePsychology: designing theory-based health promotion interventions. Commun. Assoc. Inf. Syst. **24**, 24 (2009)
14. Masthoff, J., Grasso, F., Ham, J.: Preface to the special issue on personalization and behavior change. UMUAI **24**(5), 345–350 (2014)
15. McCrae, R.R., John, O.P.: An introduction to the five-factor model and its applications. J. Pers. **60**(2), 175–215 (1992)
16. Michie, S., et al.: The behavior change technique taxonomy (v1) of 93 hierarchically clustered techniques: building an international consensus for the reporting of behavior change interventions. Behav. Med. **46**(1), 81–95 (2013)
17. Norman, D.A.: Emotional Design: Why We Love (or Hate) Everyday Things (2003)

18. Oinas-Kukkonen, H., Harjumaa, M.: A systematic framework for designing and evaluating persuasive systems. In: Oinas-Kukkonen, H., Hasle, P., Harjumaa, M., Segerståhl, K., Øhrstrøm, P. (eds.) PERSUASIVE 2008. LNCS, vol. 5033, pp. 164–176. Springer, Heidelberg (2008). https://doi.org/10.1007/978-3-540-68504-3_15

19. Orji, R.: Design for behaviour change: a model-driven approach for tailoring persuasive technologies. Ph.D. thesis, University of Saskatchewan, Canada (2014)

20. Orji, R., Mandryk, R.L., Vassileva, J.: Gender, age, and responsiveness to Cialdini's persuasion strategies. In: MacTavish, T., Basapur, S. (eds.) PERSUASIVE 2015. LNCS, vol. 9072, pp. 147–159. Springer, Cham (2015). https://doi.org/10.1007/978-3-319-20306-5_14

21. Oyibo, K., Orji, R., Vassileva, J.: Investigation of the influence of personality traits on Cialdini's persuasive strategies. In: PPT@PERSUASIVE (2017)

22. Rigby, S., Ryan, R.M.: Glued to Games: How Video Games Draw Us in and Hold Us Spellbound (2011)

23. Smith, K.A., Dennis, M., Masthoff, J.: Personalizing reminders to personality for melanoma self-checking. In: Proceedings of the 2016 Conference on User Modeling Adaptation and Personalization, pp. 85–93. ACM (2016)

24. Thompson, D., Baranowski, T., Buday, R., et al.: Serious video games for health how behavioral science guided the development of a serious video game. Simul. Gaming 41(4), 587–606 (2010)

25. Vargheese, J., Sripada, G., Masthoff, J., Oren, N.: Persuasive strategies for encouraging social interaction for older adults. Int. J. Hum.-Comput. Interact. 32(3), 190–214 (2016)

Social Support

Exploring the Effectiveness
of Socially-Oriented Persuasive
Strategies in Education

Fidelia A. Orji, Jim Greer[✉], and Julita Vassileva[✉]

Department of Computer Science, University of Saskatchewan,
Saskatoon, Canada
{fidelia.orji,jim.greer}@usask.ca, jiv@cs.usask.ca

Abstract. Persuasive technology (PT) has been shown to be effective at motivating people to accomplish their behaviour goals in different areas, especially health. It can support students to improve their learning by increasing their motivation to engage deeply with their educational resources. Research on the use of persuasive systems to improve students' motivation to learn is still scarce. Thus, in this research, we examined whether three socially-oriented influence strategies (upward social comparison, social learning, and competition), implemented in a persuasive system, can motivate students to engage more in learning activities. Research has shown that the strategies can motivate people for attitude- or behaviour-change when employed in PT design. The strategies were operationalized in a persuasive system as three versions of visualization using students' assessment grades. The persuasive system was applied in a real university setting to determine whether it can encourage students to improve their learning activities in an introductory biology class. Three groups of students used the persuasive system versions, each group used one version. Among the groups, some students received a version of the persuasive system, tailored to their personal preference to the corresponding influence strategy. The results of this research analysis show that tailoring the persuasive system versions to students' strategy preference increases its effectiveness. Moreover, the results reveal that the three social influence strategies can be employed in educational software to influence students to achieve a positive goal in their learning.

Keywords: Persuasive technology · Social influence · Persuasion profile · Personalization · Social comparison · Social learning · Competition · Education

1 Introduction

An increasing number of universities are using computing technologies to enhance the process of teaching and learning in order to meet the needs of diverse learners. Interactive systems and internet technology allow effective distribution and delivery of educational resources to students. This gives students the opportunity to learn at their own pace and convenience. Despite the usefulness of these systems, students find it hard to engage for a long time with learning resources. There are many distractions which compete for students' attention, such as chatting, playing games, listening to

© Springer Nature Switzerland AG 2019
H. Oinas-Kukkonen et al. (Eds.): PERSUASIVE 2019, LNCS 11433, pp. 297–309, 2019.
https://doi.org/10.1007/978-3-030-17287-9_24

music, watching videos, etc. Thus, a wide gap exists in academic performance between successful and unsuccessful students (those that drop out of universities). Therefore, there is a need for research on how to increase students' motivation to learn and engage actively in learning activities. The level of motivation of students to learn and progress in their education determine the length of time they spend on learning-related activities.

Reading, understanding and remembering various learning materials in the quest for knowledge can be tedious and monotonous. Students make plans on how to succeed in their learning activities but find it difficult to motivate themselves to stick to their plans. Thus, this research investigates the use of persuasive technology (PT) in promoting students' learning activities to improve their academic performance. PT describes technological applications and software purposely designed to change users' attitudes or actions without using coercion or deception [5]. It achieves behaviour change through the use of various techniques (strategies) that promote a positive change of behaviour or attitude. The success of PT applications in encouraging users to adopt desirable behaviour has been established in various domains. For example, the ability of persuasive systems built on socially-oriented strategies to inspire people to achieve their goals has been established in e-commerce [16] and health [14]. This suggests that strategically designed PTs using social influence constructs can motivate for a desirable change of attitude or behaviour in other domains, for example, increasing engagement in learning activities.

Social influence persuasive strategies are a good candidate in this case because a wide gap exists in academic performance between successful students and unsuccessful ones (those that fail) in universities. To bridge this gap, there is a need to create performance awareness among students offering a course. It will help the students to measure and understand their academic progress in relation to their peers. Besides, it will encourage the students to improve their learning activities because according to the social influence theory [15], individual behaviours and actions are often influenced by those of other people. Therefore, this research explores the use of social influence strategies (upward social comparison, social learning, and competition) implemented in PT in motivating students for learning activities. The three strategies are operationalized as different versions of a social visualization in a persuasive system used by students. The effect of each individual strategy on students' learning activities is established in a controlled study.

This work has the following contributions: Firstly, we show that the three strategies can be implemented in a persuasive system and applied in a university setting without jeopardizing students' privacy and security. Secondly, we demonstrate how to make implementation of different strategies in a persuasive system easier. We implemented three strategies as three versions of a persuasive system. Next, this research establishes that the system versions which implemented the strategies are effective in motivating students for learning activities. This means that implementing one suitable strategy for a desirable goal will be effective to motivate users to achieve a target goal. Lastly, we show that personalizing the persuasive system versions by tailoring the strategies employed in their design makes them more effective.

2   Background and Related Work

The application area of persuasive technologies has been growing rapidly over the recent years [6, 10, 13]. The driving force for this has been its potential to intentionally change users' opinion and action towards a desired goal. The success of PT applications is based on the use of appropriate strategies for users that target a specific behaviour change domain and goal. In this research, we investigate the suitability of three social influence strategies of PT at changing students' learning behaviour positively.

According to Kelman' social influence theory [15], thoughts, attitudes, and behaviours of an individual are influenced by that of other people. He postulated that changes in behaviour and attitude are a result of social influence and are brought about by three processes: compliance, identification, and internalization.

Compliance - the individual changes to the desired behaviour to get a reward or evade chastisement.

Identification - adopting to the target behaviour or attitude is as a result of the individual trying to sustain his relationship to other people (conformity).

Internalization - the individual decides and accepts to change her belief and activities to that of other people because she thinks the change will be beneficial to her.

Hence, Kelman suggested that the processes used in implementing social influence cause differences in the level of changes in behaviour among individuals. In line with this, Fogg proposes that computers can act as a behaviour change support agent as they can influence users through the services built on them. And can manipulate different influence strategies for different users and still persist the influence as long as is needed. Based on Fogg's work [5], Oinas-Kukkonen et al. [9] established a design model called Persuasive Systems Design (PSD) model which describes the development and evaluation process for persuasive systems. Among Oinas-Kukkonen et al. [9] persuasive strategies are the social influence strategies. Social influence strategies change people's opinion or attitude by using other people who are performing the desired behaviour as a role model for the target behaviour change. This research investigated social comparison, social learning, and competition of the PSD model.

The *Social Comparison strategy* offers users the opportunity to view and compare their behaviour performance data with that of other user(s). The direction of social comparison could be upward or downward. The upward social comparison is normally used for self-improvement as people are motivated to improve in behaviour or task performance by comparing themselves to similar others who are performing well (or better than themselves) on the specified task. Social comparison in this research refers to an upward comparison; research [4] has established that students use upward comparison when comparing their performance. The *Social Learning* strategy assumes that people learn through observation, modelling and imitation of others performing the intended behaviour. It points to what many similar others have done or what they are already doing to induce observational learning. According to Bandura [1], observational learning can be achieved by watching an actual performance of a task, reading or visualizing behaviour performance description, and symbolic demonstration of behaviour performance. The *Competition Strategy* provides opportunities for users to compete with each other; getting ahead of others motivates them to perform the desired behaviour.

Research has established the efficacy of social influence strategies of PTs in motivating people to achieve certain goals in various domains [12, 16]. Christy and Fox [3] investigated the effects of social influence strategy (Social Comparison) on students' academic performance in a virtual classroom. They reveal that social comparison can influence women academic performance in Math. Stibe et al. [16] explored the use of social influence strategies: social comparison, social learning, normative influence, social facilitation, cooperation, competition, and recognition in encouraging customers to generate and share feedbacks. Based on the results of their analysis of the influence strategies, they indicate that the strategies motivated customers to improve the rate at which they generate and share feedbacks. Orji et al. [12] examined the influence of competition, social comparison, and cooperation in the health domain.

Based on our literature search, research has not shown how the three influence strategies can affect students' learning activities in a real university setting. However, the effectiveness of the strategies at encouraging users to achieve a desired goal in other domain has been demonstrated.

3   Study Design and Methods

Our study aims to investigate the persuasiveness of three versions of a persuasive system designed with social comparison, social learning, and competition in motivating students' learning activities in a real university course-based setting. We intend to answer the following research questions:

RQ 1:   How do the students perceive the three versions of the persuasive system?
RQ 2:   Is there a difference in the perceived persuasiveness of the three system versions overall?
RQ 3:   Does tailoring the persuasive system increase the perceived persuasiveness of the system?

To successfully implement a persuasive system and answer our research questions, we first determine the suitability of the strategies for our user group.

3.1   Determining Users' Susceptibility to the Three Social Influence Strategies

Determining the applicability of PT strategies to a particular user group is an important step prior to PT design. Hence, implementing appropriate strategies in PT design increases its efficacy to achieve the intended objective. We examined the susceptibility of our user group (Biol 120 students) to social comparison, social learning, and competition. According to existing research [2], understanding users' preferences for PT strategies assist designers in making informed decisions on the requirements and implications of their design. Some of the decisions are to determine whether specific strategies will be effective in motivating a particular user group for a task, and how to personalize PTs built with the strategies to users.

We used a tool developed by Busch et al. [2] for measuring susceptibility to social influence strategies called persuasive inventory (PI). A questionnaire implementing the

PI was slightly adapted to reflect the target domain, education. All questions were assessed using the participants' agreement to a 9-Likert scale ranging from "1 = Strongly Disagree" to "9 = Strongly Agree". According to Busch et al. [2], the persuadability inventory gives an estimation of people's susceptibility to a specific persuasive strategy which designers of persuasive technology can use in identifying the most effective persuasive strategy to use in designing PT for a particular user or user group.

The total number of participants was n = 220. The reliability test for participants' responses is $\alpha = 0.817$ and KMO sampling adequacy is 0.858 which means that the responses were reliable. Our repeated-measure ANOVA results show significant main effect of strategy type ($F_{1.63, 355.54} = 22.04$, p < .0001) on persuasiveness and pairwise comparison reveal that a significant difference exists between the persuasiveness of competition (M = 5.615) and social learning (M = 5.029) and also between social comparison (M = 5.560) and social learning, p < 0.05. There was no significant difference between the persuasiveness of competition and social comparison.

Based on the result of our analysis, all the strategies were perceived as persuasive, as each strategy has a mean rating which is greater than the neutral score of 4.5 (p < .001). Table 1 shows the susceptibility of the participants to the three strategies. According to the table, the majority (88%) of the students could be persuaded using the three social influence strategies of PT.

Table 1. Susceptibility of the participants to the three social influence strategies of PT

Strategies	Number of participants	Percentage of students (%)
Social comparison - social learning – competition	112	51
Social comparison - social learning	20	9
Social comparison – competition	34	15
Social learning – competition	9	4
Competition	10	5
Social comparison	6	3
Social learning	3	1
Non-susceptible	26	12

The results from the analysis demonstrate that the strategies are effective tools which can be employed to influence students' learning behaviour positively. Hence, most of the students rated some of the strategies as persuasive. It suggests that implementation of the strategies in persuasive applications will encourage students to improve their learning behaviour. In general, there is no significant effect of gender on the persuasiveness of strategies by the students. This implies that educational systems designed with these strategies will create the same persuasive effect in both male and female students. Therefore, in creating the students' persuasion profiles, we did not consider the gender of the student, but only considered the student's susceptibility to the three strategies. Following Busch et al. [13], *"participants having higher scores in one or more of the scales are expected to be more susceptible to these specific persuasive strategies (p. 36)."* However, some students are susceptible to all the three strategies, as shown in Table 1. This means that any of the three strategies can motivate them to achieve a specific goal. The level of motivation each strategy provides depends on the participant's preference for that strategy. Hence, we considered participants' highest preference for any of the strategies in their persuasion profile. According to their highest preference, 38% of the students had competition as their highest preferred strategy, 30% had social comparison, 20% had social learning, and 12% were not susceptible to any of the strategies. This result indicates that the preference for competition (38%) is the highest, followed by social comparison (30%), and social learning (20%) is the least.

Having established the appropriateness of the strategies for the students using this study, we moved to operationalize the strategies in an actual persuasive system to evaluate their effectiveness at motivating students to improve in learning activities.

3.2 Persuasive Intervention Experiment

We developed a web application for our persuasive system and operationalized each of the strategies as a system version in our application. In most PT designs, strategies are achieved as a design goal or based on system usage. For example, Stibe et al. [16] implemented the three strategies in their visualization. To facilitate social comparison, they display the number of tweets each user submitted. The number of tweets for each user changes colour as it increases to make comparison easy. For the competition, they ranked users based on their number of tweets. To allow for social learning, they displayed newsfeed from users so that others can observe and learn.

We considered the issue of security and students' privacy as we used individual students' information to develop the application for social comparison and competition. Social learning also uses students' information but in an aggregated form. The application was integrated with the learning management system (LMS) which the students access for most of their course information needs to make it easier for them to use the application. Students log in to the LMS with their student identification number (Id). To solve the privacy problem, we used a pseudonymized student Id to display students' grades and points except for the logged-in student. For the logged-in student (who views the visualization), the student's actual Id and name are shown so that he or she can identify his or her position in comparison with the others. Each version depicts one of the strategies using a persuasive visual display (visualization), as shown in Figs. 1, 2, and 3.

The visualization (in all three versions) updates dynamically when students perform new assessments and provides students with an opportunity to send feedback expressing their feeling about their grade by clicking on an emoticon, shown in Figs. 1, 2, and 3. The visualizations allow the students to view their class performance in a course so that they can compare, compete, or model their behaviour. This aligns with previous research showing that human actions and attitude could be influenced by that of others. People can change their behaviour to adopt or imitate the behaviour of other people which they think will be beneficial to them.

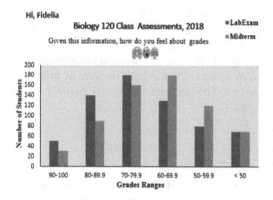

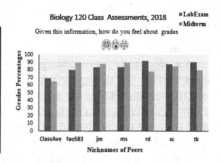

Fig. 1. A display of the logged-in student's grades and grades of five random students with anonymized id who have higher grades than the target student (upward social comparison)

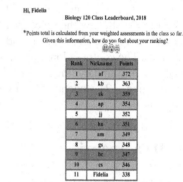

Fig. 2. A display of grade ranges and the number of students that has each range in a course (social learning)

Fig. 3. A display of students' ranks based on their performance (competition)

3.3 Measurement Instruments and Data Collection

Each student was assigned a version of the application. The persuasion profile of students who participated in the PI survey was used to tailor the versions to them. Students that did not participate in the PI survey described in Sect. 3.1 were randomly assigned. The students used the system for six (6) weeks.

To elicit feedback on the persuasiveness of the system versions in our application, we employed a validated tool for assessing the perceived persuasiveness of applications. The tool was adapted from Orji et al. [11] and other PT research works [13, 15] have used it. The tool consists of four questions: *(1) "The system would influence me." (2) "The system would be convincing." (3) "The system would be personally relevant for me." (4) "The system would make me reconsider my study habits."* The questions were measured using participant agreement with a 7-point Likert scale ranging from "1 = Strongly disagree" to "7 = Strongly agree". We designed a *system exit survey* with the questions and conducted the survey among the students after they have used our persuasive system for six weeks.

Data Collection

Participants for this study were undergraduate students of the University of Saskatchewan taking Biol 120 during the winter term 2018. All the participants (students) were at least 16 years old. Before the main study, we conducted a pilot study to test the validity of our persuasive system design. For the pilot study, we recruited nine random students from the same university and they used the system versions. We ascertain that our system versions were persuasive based on their feedback. For our main persuasive system experiment, a total of 643 students taking Biol 120 participated in the intervention. We received a total of 266 responses from our system exit survey conducted among the students that used the system. Among the 266 students that responded, 228 agreed that we should use their data for analysis. Among the 228 participants, 96 used a tailored version of the system, 11 used the contra-tailored version (i.e. the version based in the strategy they were least susceptible to), 35 were in the control group that didn't use or rate the system, and 86 were randomly assigned to the three different versions. The contra-tailored group was too small and therefore was not involved in the analysis. In summary, the sizes of the groups subjected to the analysis were as follows: competition – 21 students, social comparison – 105 students, and social learning – 67 students.

4 Data Analysis

To measure the persuasiveness of the three versions of the persuasive system and evaluate the effect of the tailored compared to the random assignment of students to versions, we employed some well-known analytical techniques and procedures. The following steps were followed to analyze the data.

1. Kaiser-Meyer-Olkin (KMO) sampling adequacies and the Bartlett Test of Sphericity were used to determine the suitability of the data for analysis.
2. After establishing the suitability of the data, we conducted a one-sample t-test on the data measuring the persuasiveness of each persuasive system version separately to establish their individual persuasiveness overall.
3. Next, to examine and compare the persuasiveness of the three system versions, we computed the average persuasiveness score for each strategy and performed a One-Way ANOVA after validating for ANOVA assumptions.
4. Finally, to compare the efficacy of the tailored and random assignment intervention types with respect to their ability to promote learning activities among students, we conducted an independent sample t-test.

The detailed results of the analysis are presented below.

5   Results of System Perceived Persuasiveness

The Kaiser-Meyer-Olkin (KMO) sampling adequacy was 0.764 and the Bartlett Test of Sphericity was statistically significant ($\chi 2$ (6) = 548.12, p < 0.0001). These results show that the data were suitable for further analysis [8].

5.1   The Persuasiveness of the Persuasive System Versions

Each version of the persuasive system was used by different groups of students and each group rate the version that they used.

In 7-point Likert scale, system persuasiveness score above 3.5 (median score of scale) is categorized as high. To determine if the persuasiveness of the system versions is high, each version persuasive score is compared to the scale median score. From the results of the one-sample t-test examining the persuasiveness of each system version using a confidence interval of 95, we established that the three persuasive system versions representing social comparison, social learning, and competition were rated as significantly persuasive with persuasiveness score higher than the neutral value (median rating) of 3.5 as shown Fig. 4, social comparison ($M = 4.64$, $SD = 1.42$, $t_{104} = 7.61$, $p = .0001$), social learning ($M = 4.39$, $SD = 1.64$, $t_{66} = 3.77$, $p = .0001$), and competition ($M = 4.28$, $SD = 1.35$, $t_{20} = 2.38$, $p = 0.03$). Overall, the system implementations of the three strategies were perceived as persuasive by the students.

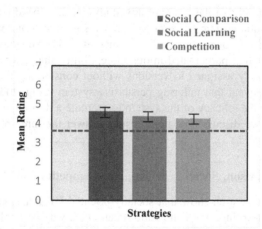

Fig. 4. A bar graph of the mean of the individual strategies showing their overall persuasiveness

5.2   Comparison of the Persuasiveness of the Three Persuasive System Versions

The results of one-way ANOVA show that there was no statistically significant difference between the three persuasive system versions with respect to their persuasiveness ($F_{2,190} = 0.711$, $p = .493$). This result indicates that the perceived persuasiveness of the three system versions did not differ significantly among the experimental condition (social comparison, social learning, and competition) of students even though they used different system versions.

5.3 Comparison of the Persuasiveness of the Tailored and Non-tailored Group

The independent sample t-test results between tailored and non-tailored students' groups show a statistically significant difference in the persuasiveness of the system, $t_{132.74} = 2.66$, $p = .009$. Specifically, the students in the tailored group that used their preferred persuasive system version rated the system as more persuasive than the students that were randomly assigned to use any of the system versions without considering their strategy preference.

6 Summary and Discussion

The results of our study of students' susceptibility to the strategies demonstrated that students can be motivated by all of the three social influence strategies and that the preferences of students to the strategies differ. Most students are motivated by competition, followed by social comparison and then social learning. Based on this we developed persuasion profiles for students that we used for tailoring a persuasive application.

To validate the results of the susceptibility study, we developed three versions of a persuasive visualization system to encourage students to engage in learning activities, using social comparison, social learning, and competition. The versions were tailored to some of the students that participated in our susceptibility study, while the rest of the students were randomly assigned to versions without considering their strategy preference. Our results reveal that tailoring persuasive system using students' persuasion profile will improve the efficacy of the system to promote a desired learning behaviour of students. Below we discuss how these results answer the three research questions formulated in Sect. 3.

6.1 Social Comparison, Social Learning, and Competition of PT

The findings in this research show that socially-oriented PT strategies (upward social comparison, social learning, and competition) can effectively be applied in university education to promote desirable learning behaviour among students. Although the three strategies differ in their operationalization in the system design, students acknowledged their potential in promoting learning behaviour (engagement) overall. Based on the system evaluation results, all the students that used the system perceived as persuasive the implementation of the three strategies with respect to their ability to motivate students to engage in their learning activities. Thus, the research question *RQ1* has been answered by showing that persuasive visualizations designed based on socially-oriented persuasive strategies (upward social comparison, social learning, and competition) are perceived by students as promoting learning and engagement.

6.2   The Persuasiveness of the Different System Versions

Without considering tailoring, our results indicate that the three versions of the persuasive system do not differ significantly in their perceived persuasiveness, suggesting that the strategies are not fundamentally different in their effectiveness overall. Thus, *RQ2* has been answered. However, tailoring the system versions to the individual susceptibility of the students showed a difference in their persuasiveness. This reveals that tailoring the persuasive system to students using their persuasion profile makes them perceive it as more persuasive as shown by the higher rating of the system persuasiveness by students in the tailored condition. This answers the third research question, *RQ3,* showing that the effectiveness of the strategies in education software can improve, if students receive tailored versions of the system that match their persuasion strategy preference.

6.3   Timing of Persuasive Intervention

It is hard in the education domain to manage the timing for persuasion so that it catches students' attention without causing a distraction to their learning. This work shows one possible way to achieve this. The persuasive system was integrated into a learning management system through which students access their course information. Our results demonstrate the success of this approach at apprehending and directing students' attention to the persuasive information, thereby making students reflect on their learning progress in general. Feedback from students to the system supports this conclusion, for example: *"I should be doing better, its just a poor effort on my part"*, *"I don't know how to study"*, and *"I usually do better, and I know I can, but I just don't have the time"*.

6.4   Design Implications of Our Study

The common practice in the design of persuasive systems is to incorporate multiple strategies in a single system. In this way, at least one of the strategies would be able to motivate some users. However, this approach makes it hard to evaluate the persuasiveness of the individual strategies and to improve the overall persuasiveness of the system. Our approach of applying different strategies, tailored to different user groups allows the evaluation of the persuasiveness of each deployed strategy.

Our evaluation results reveal that the use of a single strategy suitable for a particular user group is more effective at achieving the intended goal. Moreover, research [7] has shown that combining appropriate strategies in a single system may not increase the persuasion effect in motivating for the intended behaviour change. Thus, designers should aim to incorporate means to profile users according to their susceptibility to persuasive strategies and determine a single appropriate strategy for a particular user group for an intended goal.

Tailoring of persuasive systems to individual users can be costly if the designer has to develop different system version for each user. Our work has shown that specifically with persuasive visualizations and social influence strategies, this task is not so hard, as the three strategies can be implemented in a fairly straightforward way as tailored visualizations, generated from the same system data.

7 Conclusion

Previous research has established the efficacy of persuasive systems at encouraging users to achieve a specific objective in various domains. To contribute in advancing the field of persuasive technology research in the education domain, our work investigated the perceived persuasiveness of three strategies based on the Social Influence Theory in increasing students' engagement in learning activities. Our study in a large first-year University biology class shows that these strategies can be implemented as persuasive visualizations that are perceived as motivating by students in engaging them in their learning activities. Moreover, it shows that tailoring can enhance the effect of each persuasive strategy. Our work can help designers of learning management systems by providing an example of how three social-influence-based persuasive strategies can be implemented in persuasive visualizations of learning analytics data, and suggesting tools that can be used to profile students to allow for personalization based on students' persuasion preference.

Acknowledgement. This work has been supported by the NSERC Discovery Grant of the third author.

References

1. Bandura, A.: Social learning theory. Gen. Learn. Corp. **1971**, 1–46 (1971)
2. Busch, M., Schrammel, J., Tscheligi, M.: Personalized persuasive technology – development and validation of scales for measuring persuadability. In: Berkovsky, S., Freyne, J. (eds.) PERSUASIVE 2013. LNCS, vol. 7822, pp. 33–38. Springer, Heidelberg (2013). https://doi.org/10.1007/978-3-642-37157-8_6
3. Christy, K.R., Fox, J.: Leaderboards in a virtual classroom: a test of stereotype threat and social comparison explanations for women's math performance. Comput. Educ. **78**, 66–77 (2014)
4. Dijkstra, P., Kuyper, H., Van der Werf, G., Buunk, A.P., van der Zee, Y.G.: Social comparison in the classroom: a review. Rev. Educ. Res. **78**(4), 828–879 (2008)
5. Fogg, B.J.: Persuasive Technology: Using Computers to Change What We Think and Do. Morgan Kaufmann Publishers, Burlington (2002)
6. Kaptein, M.: Adaptive persuasive messages in an e-commerce setting: the use of persuasion profiles. In: European Conference on Information Systems (ECIS), p. 183 (2011)
7. Kaptein, M., De Ruyter, B., Markopoulos, P., Aarts, E.: Adaptive persuasive systems: a study of tailored persuasive text messages to reduce snacking. ACM Trans. Interact. Intell. Syst. **2**(2), 1–25 (2012)
8. Kupek, E.: Beyond logistic regression: structural equations modelling for binary variables and its application to investigating unobserved confounders. BMC Med. Res. Methodol. **6** (1), 13 (2006)
9. Oinas-Kukkonen, H., Harjumaa, M.: Persuasive systems design: key issues, process model and system features. Commun. Assoc. Inf. Syst. **24**, 485–500 (2009)

10. Orji, R., Mandryk, R.L., Vassileva, J.: Improving the efficacy of games for change using personalization models. ACM Trans. Comput.-Hum. Interact. **24**(5), 1–22 (2017)

11. Orji, R., Vassileva, J., Mandryk, R.L.: Modeling the efficacy of persuasive strategies for different gamer types in serious games for health. User Model. User-Adapt. Interact. **24**(5), 453–498 (2014)

12. Orji, R., Oyibo, K., Lomotey, R.K., Orji, F.A.: Socially-driven persuasive health intervention design: competition, social comparison, and cooperation. Health Inform. J. (2018). https://doi.org/10.1177/1460458218766570

13. Orji, R., Nacke, L.E., Di Marco, C.: Towards personality-driven persuasive health games and gamified systems. In: Proceedings of the 2017 CHI Conference on Human Factors in Computing Systems - CHI 2017, New York, USA, pp. 1015–1027 (2017)

14. Orji, R., Moffatt, K.: Persuasive technology for health and wellness: state-of-the-art and emerging trends. Health Inform. J. **24**(1), 66–91 (2018)

15. Social influence theory (2000). https://is.theorizeit.org/wiki/Social_Influence_Theory. Accessed 04 July 2018

16. Stibe, A., Oinas-Kukkonen, H.: Using social influence for motivating customers to generate and share feedback. In: Spagnolli, A., Chittaro, L., Gamberini, L. (eds.) PERSUASIVE 2014. LNCS, vol. 8462, pp. 224–235. Springer, Cham (2014). https://doi.org/10.1007/978-3-319-07127-5_19

Social Behaviors: A Social Topology and Interaction Pattern Affect the Properties of a Changed Behavior

Tatsuya Konishi[1]([✉]) [iD], Masatoshi Nagata[1] [iD], Masaru Honjo[1] [iD], Akio Yoneyama[1] [iD], Masayuki Kurokawa[2], and Koji Mishima[3]

[1] KDDI Research, Inc., Fujimino, Japan
{tt-konishi,ms-nagata,honjo,yoneyama}@kddi-research.jp
[2] Aichi University of Education, Kariya, Japan
kurokawa@auecc.aichi-edu.ac.jp
[3] Chubu University, Kasugai, Japan
bau340k@isc.chubu.ac.jp

Abstract. The current study is based on the assumption that social topology and its interaction pattern affect users' behavioral changes, especially continuity. To verify the hypothesis, several metrics have been introduced, and experiments have been conducted, resulting in interesting and quantitative findings. In the experiments, two conditional differences lead to statistic significance in continuity and other metrics; the first difference is the existence of feedback implementation, another one is information visibility. It has been experimentally confirmed that users who received more feedback from system bots (i.e., they did not know that they were controlled until the experiment ended) tend to also send more feedback themselves. Moreover, it has been found that only the fact that the others (i.e., bots), except the participant, sent feedback to each other made the person feel isolated, and the participant sent feedback him/herself to avoid being depressed with no interaction. On the other hand, information visibility had little effect on their continuity and no effect on their consciousness.

Keywords: Social behavior · Behavior change · Healthcare · Social network · Continuity

1 Introduction

Recently, the traditional research areas of psychology and behavioral economics have absorbed new Information and Communication Technology (ICT) and mobile devices, resulting in a movement towards persuasive technology in the world [5,17]. Previously, only a few studies have been reported where research knowledge can be accumulated. Persuasive systems design (PSD), proposed by Harri et al. [19], suggests a thinking framework by which people can be persuaded

© Springer Nature Switzerland AG 2019
H. Oinas-Kukkonen et al. (Eds.): PERSUASIVE 2019, LNCS 11433, pp. 310–321, 2019.
https://doi.org/10.1007/978-3-030-17287-9_25

effectively and naturally and a behavior change support systems (BCSS)[12] that proposes a way to implement ICT systems in accordance with the PSD.

Although short-term goals, such as temporary advertisements, are in a broad range of behavior change topics, a large number of social issues that should be associated with continuity of behavior still exist. Addictions to tobacco, drugs, or gambling, for instance, and night-life problems still require solutions [2,6,7, 10,14]. As mentioned above, the techniques that allow people to continue their behavior without coercion are incredibly important in the healthcare research areas.

Traditional psychology and sociopsychology have revealed that forming a support community of people can guide individuals to take sustainable action to some extent [11]. These studies, however, identified only offline relationships, and they have not mentioned whether social networking services with online strangers, which have been remarkably developed, have the potential to create the same effect. Although the effect of social influence has often been evaluated in the persuasive technology research domain, only a few studies deal with the continuity of a changed action. Software features named "social influence" are currently being investigated still more deeply. This area is crucial for the settlement of social issues and sustainable development and should be tackled.

Sherman et al. [18] raised the problem caused by information overload in the world that accessible information depends on the search engines, calling it "the invisible web." When considering Social Networking Service (SNS) via Internet communications, all the information is not necessarily seen by all participants. Participants who tend to be absorbed in SNS out of the sheer desire to get others' feedback cannot check all the feedback to others, except what they send, resulting in subjective persistence only in feedback to them. The communications in SNS are characterized by the strong working of a certain kind of confirmation bias. In order to grasp the property of SNS, the impact on the effect of behavior change given by "social influence" features should be validated not with binary presence or absence but in gradual steps. This paper aims to gradually inspect the utility of information visibility by handling experimental situations where ones are made aware of being seen by other participants and others are socially excluded or included [16]. No study has quantitatively investigated the effect caused by the difference in the structure of a social community or information visibility to the best of our knowledge.

In the following sections, we define information visibility and classify it in terms of the difference in social topology, then describe the behavioral change result of the experiment and our findings and contributions.

2 Related Work

The work done by Verduyn et al. [20] is one of the studies on the relationship between happiness and the use of online SNSs, such as Facebook, through the validating effects of forming a SNS community with many and unspecified persons. They concluded that the feeling of connectedness might have the potential to promote social capital and happiness. Moreover, social capital is roughly divided into two kinds; bridging social capital and bonded social capital [13,21]. Ellison et al. [4] found a positive correlation between bridging social capital in Facebook and the number of actual friends rather than acquaintances. Although this study, however, mentioned the engagement to communication, in other words, activities to retain communities, it has not tried to change behavior. This is, however, very important in the fact that it revealed the way to build SNS communities, namely social influence, which affects the sustainability of a community.

Ruijten et al. [16] used virtual agents to demonstrate that the two situations when participants were socially included or excluded, which led to the difference in the behavior change effect. The study reported by Hamari et al. [8] revealed experimentally that the existence of badges would increase interactions among users and indicated that the difference in SNS's functionality could influence users' actions while it dealt with nothing about continuity. Alluhaidan et al. [1] constructed an ICT empowerment model from the theoretical aspects to direct a spotlight on continuous behavior changes. However they did not verify whether it worked through experiments; therefore, it should be validated quantitatively.

3   Materials and Methods

The current study is based on the assumption that behavioral changes differ depending on information visibility. The structure of a community that varies with information visibility is defined as "Social Topology" (hereinafter called "ST"), and four types of STs (Table 1) are introduced. For simplicity, we consider only the case when three persons are in each ST. Additionally, we also introduced the "Social Topology Interaction Pattern" (called "STIP") as shown in Fig. 1, which means the existence of the orientation of feedback used in ST 3 and 4. In the figures, the black lines/circles and purple lines are invisible and visible for others, respectively, then the green arrows depict feedback such as "Like" used by Facebook. It is assumed that the difference in STIP (Fig. 1) may raise various psychological effects. To evaluate the hypothesis, we conducted an experiment by recruiting participants.

Table 1. Four patterns of Social Topologies (✓ means it can be seen by "you")

ST	Your posts	Others' posts	Feedback to you	Feedback to others
1	✓	-	-	-
2	✓	✓	-	-
3	✓	✓	✓	-
4	✓	✓	✓	✓

ST 1 (Fig. 1a) You can NOT see the others and you are NOT seen by the others.
ST 2 (Fig. 1b) You can see the others and you are seen by the others.

ST 3 (Fig. 1c) You can see the others and you are seen by the others. You can
   see ONLY feedback to you and feedback to you is NOT seen by the others.
ST 4 (Fig. 1d) You can see the others and you are seen by the others. You can
   see ALL feedback to the others and feedback to you is seen by the others.

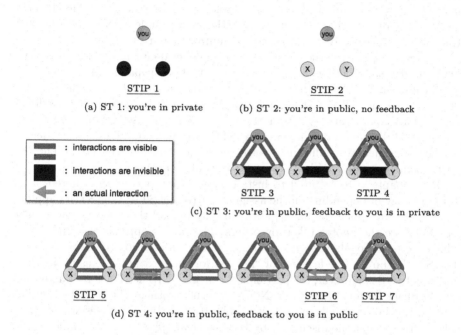

(a) ST 1: you're in private   (b) ST 2: you're in public, no feedback

(c) ST 3: you're in public, feedback to you is in private

(d) ST 4: you're in public, feedback to you is in public

Fig. 1. Social Topologies and Social Topology Interaction Patterns

4 Experiments

4.1 Experimental Design

It is crucial for the health management of people to understand not only exercises
but also meals. Especially for those who must manage and record every meal,
such as diabetic patients, there should be smartphone apps that help them do
so [15]. Although those apps have recently appeared and calories are calculated
automatically, taking a photo each mealtime requires a lot of attention [3]. Before
the trial, we asked 22 participants to take a photo of every meal. Participants
could see on the app how many times they had continuously completed the
tasks until then. They were told that if they missed the task three times in a
row they would not receive participation fees, resulting in the fact that only one
participant completed all the tasks without an once mistake.

   As the difficulty of this task was discovered, we adopted it as the experimental
task and evaluated the effect of ST and STIP through an experiment. A total of

560 participants were finally recruited by a research agency; female participants were about 60%, and the average age of all was about 38 years old (the detailed statistics are shown in Table 2). We extracted the participants who did not use a kind of meal management apps at that time and used daily SNS, such as Twitter, Facebook, and Instagram, with the use of posting their contents or liking others' posts. They were required to continue to upload photos of every meal for 18 days, and they were told that they would get the reward unless they miss the task three times successively with the same condition as our preliminary survey.

In order to control the effect of STIP and evaluate it quantitatively, we introduced system bots as actors, except the real participants (i.e., X and Y in Fig. 1) in each ST. All of the system bots always uploaded pre-defined photos of meals, and in STIP 4, 6, and 7, they were programmed to give feedback to real participants an hour after the uploaded photo. Although there are 11 kinds of STIPs in total (Fig. 1), only STIPs from 1 to 7 have been selected as the experimental condition because these are considered effective. The 560 participants were divided into seven patterns of 80 people.

Participants were required to install an Android app, which differed in its system behavior depending on the assigned pattern of STIP. The ST 1's app has the features by which the participant can only upload their photos and he/she can NOT see the photos taken by others. The ST 2's app has the features by which the participants can see the others' photos in addition to the ST 1's app. The ST 3's app has the features of "request for the next upload" as feedback in addition to ST 2; however, the participant can see ONLY feedback to him/herself and feedback to him/herself can NOT be seen by others. The ST 4's app has the features by which all feedback is visible to all participants. Besides, we have taken into account the discussion by Hamari et al. [9], so that we implemented these features carefully not to change the UI or ease of use. Moreover, the participants were told of the existence of system bots only after the experiment was completed.

The images and comments that the participants uploaded and in-app actions, such as a "Like" or a page transition, were saved in the server with its timestamp. On the beginning of the experiment, all the 560 participants were asked for a questionnaire about whether they give care to everyday meals and they want to apps to manage meals. After the experiment, the xxx participants who did not miss the tasks three times successively were asked again about an impression on using the experimental app in addition to the same as Pre questionnaire. These two questionnaires are described as "Pre" and "Post" in Table 3, respectively.

Table 2. The number of participants (sociodemographic characteristics)

Sex	Age			
	20–29	30–39	40–49	50–59
Male	18	54	90	58
Female	96	158	59	27

4.2 Metrics

Thirteen metrics (M-1, 2, $\cdots$, 13) were introduced as shown in Table 3 to evaluate the behavior change effect quantitatively. They include a "continuity", which depicts how long the participants continued the tasks. Also, seven research questions as shown in Table 4 were defined. We considered these questions as the keys to the psychological effect.

Table 3. Metrics

(a) Log data

No.	ST	Item	Definition
M-1	1–4	Continuity	Continuity(n) means the ratio of those who have continued the task without consecutive n times miss/misses ($n = 0, 1, 2$). When $n = 2$, this condition is as same as told to the participants
M-2	1–4	The # of sent feedback	The total number of feedback responses they sent to teammates during the whole experiment

(b) Questionnaire items

No.	ST	Item	Pre	Post	Choices
M-3	1–4	Do you give care to everyday meals?	✓	✓	Three-point scale[a]
M-4	1–4	Do you want apps to manage meals?	✓	✓	Five-point scale[b]
M-5	2–4	Did you feel a sense of intimacy to teammates?		✓	Five-point scale
M-6	2–4	Did you get encouraged by seeing teammates uploading photos?		✓	Five-point scale
M-7	2–4	Were you conscious that your photos can be seen?		✓	Five-point scale
M-8	2–4	Did you feel isolated on the team?		✓	Five-point scale
M-9	3, 4	Did you expect to receive requests?		✓	Five-point scale
M-10	3, 4	Did you get encouraged by receiving requests?		✓	Five-point scale
M-11	3, 4	Did you want boast to teammates that you received requests?		✓	Five-point scale
M-12	3, 4	Were you concerned whether teammates received requests?		✓	Five-point scale
M-13	4	Were you conscious that requests you received can be seen?		✓	Five-point scale

[a] Three-point scale of "I want to care about meals, and do well.", "I want to care about meals, but cannot do well.", and "I do not want to care about meals."
[b] Five-point scale of "Strongly agree", "Agree", "Neither agree nor disagree", "Disagree", and "Strongly disagree."

Table 4. Research questions and Metrics

No.	Factor that may be influential	A pair of STIP	Metric
RQ-1	The fact that your photos can be seen by teammates	{1, 2}	1, 3–4
RQ-2	The expectation of receiving feedback	{2, 3}	1, 3–8
Rq-3	The positive feeling when receiving private feedback	{3, 4}	1–12
RQ-4	The positive feeling when receiving public feedback	{5, 7}	1–13
RQ-5	The desire to boast of receiving public feedback	{4, 7}	1–12
RQ-6	The relief from the fact teammates received no feedback	{3, 5}	1–12
RQ-7	The sense of isolation under the condition that teammates send feedback to each other	{5, 6}	1–13

Table 5. Results summary

Metric	RQ-1 (STIP 1,2)	RQ-2 (STIP 2,3)	RQ-3 (STIP 3,4)	RQ-4 (STIP 5,7)	RQ-5 (STIP 4,7)	RQ-6 (STIP 3,5)	RQ-7 (STIP 5,6)
M-1; Continuity	n.s.	STIP 3 > 2	STIP 3 > 4	STIP 5 > 7	STIP 7 > 4	n.s.	n.s.
M-2; The # of sent feedback	-	-	STIP 4 > 3	STIP 7 > 5	n.s.	n.s.	STIP 6 > 5
M-3(diff); A will to care about meals	STIP 1 > 2	n.s.	n.s.	STIP 7 > 5	n.s.	n.s.	n.s.
M-4(diff); A will to use apps to manage meals	STIP 2 > 1	n.s.	n.s.	n.s.	n.s.	n.s.	n.s.
M-5; A sense of intimacy	-	n.s.	n.s.	STIP 7 > 5	n.s.	n.s.	STIP 5 > 6
M-6; Be encouraged by teammates' photos	-	n.s.	n.s.	n.s.	n.s.	n.s.	n.s.
M-7; Consciousness that your photos are seen	-	n.s.	n.s.	STIP 5 > 7	n.s.	n.s.	n.s.
M-8; To feel isolated	-	n.s.	n.s.	STIP 5 > 7	n.s.	n.s.	STIP 6 > 5
M-9; To expect feedback	-	-	STIP 4 > 3	STIP 7 > 5	n.s.	n.s.	n.s.
M-10; To be encouraged by feedback	-	-	STIP 3 > 4	STIP 5 > 7	n.s.	n.s.	n.s.
M-11; A will to boast that you received FB	-	-	n.s.	n.s.	n.s.	n.s.	n.s.
M-12; Consciousness that teammates' feedback is seen	-	-	n.s.	n.s.	n.s.	n.s.	n.s.
M-13; Consciousness that your feedback is seen	-	-	-	STIP 7 > 5	-	-	n.s.

4.3   Results

The results associated with each metric are shown in Figs. 2, 3, 4, and 5. Even though each STIP has 80 participants, not everyone started the tasks. The numbers of people who did the task even once, which is used to calculate M-1 (Continuity), are 31, 37, 35, 40, 41, 43, and 39 from STIP 1 to 7, respectively. On the other hand, the numbers of people who has completed all the tasks with less than three times misses in a row and answered the questionnaire, which is used to calculate M-2 to M-13, are 28, 30, 33, 34, 34, 38, and 37 from STIP 1 to 7, respectively. In the following, the results of the research questions are summarized in Table 5 with associated metrics. A chi-square test and a t-test were used to assess the statistical significance of M-1 and of the other metrics (i.e., from M-2 to M-13), respectively.

From the comparison between by RQ-1 (STIP 1, 2), no significant difference can be caused by whether the completion of the task can be seen by teammates or not. Observations associated with RQ-2 (STIP 2, 3) can lead to the assumption that the existence of the feedback feature enables people to continue the "primary task."

RQ-3 (STIP 3, 4) derived the receiving feedback may reduce users' continuity a little but has strong power to allow users to send feedback from them subjectively. It was so surprising that those who received a lot of feedback desired more feedback but were less encouraged by that feedback. The effect caused by the automatically received feedback can be observed also in RQ-4 (STIP 5, 7), so it can be said that this psychological effect is a universal truth. Moreover, the result of M-13 (shown in Fig. 5) tells us the automated mechanism plays a part in teaching users of the existence of the feature.

On the other hand, as shown in RQ-5 (STIP 4, 7), information visibility had no significance in this experiment; meanwhile, there is a little difference in continuity in Fig. 3. This insight is consistent with the one by RQ-6 (STIP 3, 5).

Additionally, RQ-7 (STIP 5, 6), where the key is a sense of isolation, revealed an interesting result. Those who are isolated tend to send feedback more than natural people (i.e., STIP 5) and feel less familiar with teammates (M-5) because they were feeling isolated (M-8). This result indicated they were willing to send feedback and expecting feedback from teammates for a present received, in other words to get familiar with them.

In conclusion, with the focus on the result of M-1, it can be said that the existence of the implementation of feedback is effective in making users continue the task, meanwhile too much feedback has the opposite effect.

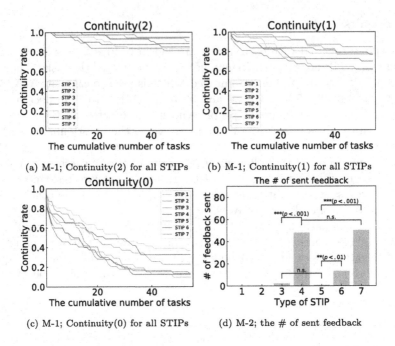

(a) M-1; Continuity(2) for all STIPs   (b) M-1; Continuity(1) for all STIPs

(c) M-1; Continuity(0) for all STIPs   (d) M-2; the # of sent feedback

Fig. 2. The results associated with M-1, M-2

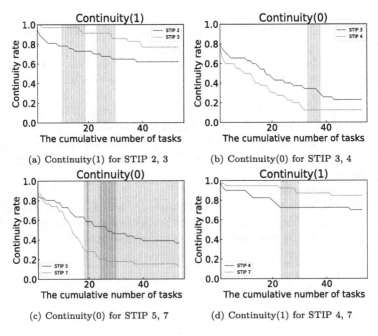

(a) Continuity(1) for STIP 2, 3   (b) Continuity(0) for STIP 3, 4

(c) Continuity(0) for STIP 5, 7   (d) Continuity(1) for STIP 4, 7

Fig. 3. Continuity (The yellow/red background means statistical significance, where $p < .05/p < .01$, respectively.) (Color figure online)

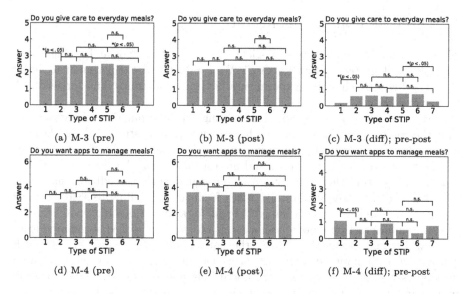

Fig. 4. The results associated with M-3, M-4

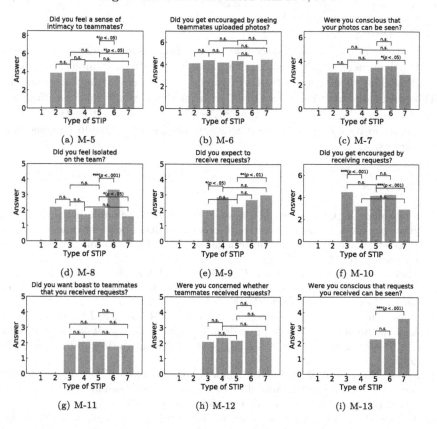

Fig. 5. The results associated with M-5 to M-13

5   Discussion and Conclusion

This paper focused on the psychological effect caused by "Social Topology" and "Social Topology Interaction Pattern". We conducted the experiment to verify the hypothesis by changing experimental settings and controlling for feedback with system bots.

The experiment revealed some interesting information. First, only the fact that the completion of tasks is seen by others had little statistical significance, nevertheless this feature has been implemented in many applications generally. If apps try to activate users more and improve user behavior, it is not satisfied only by this feature then further software features, such as feedback, should be installed. Second, those who receive much feedback are willing to send feedback themselves, as well as, and continued the task for a short time. If a system desires to maintain interaction among active users, this work validated automated feedback, which may be helpful. Third, the participants easily can feel isolated if others only communicate with each other as our system bots showed. System developers and designers must care about this phenomenon in order to avoid puncturing participants. What we contributed to the society is this quantitative findings since they are known only empirically. Even though we assumed that information visibility might lead to some differences in user behavior, that could not be proved in our experiment.

In this work, we adopted only positive feedback as interaction among users. Nevertheless there are also communications with negative meanings in real communities. The effect caused by them should be studied further. Additionally, although we designed the experiment with participants of equal position, real interaction can be affected by other properties, such as "authority" or "social role." The position or role of the person sending feedback should be considered in future work.

References

1. Alluhaidan, A., Chatterjee, S., Drew, D., Stibe, A.: Sustaining health behaviors through empowerment: a deductive theoretical model of behavior change based on information and communication technology (ICT). In: Proceedings of Persuasive Technology, pp. 28–41 (2018)
2. Alrobai, A., Dogan, H., Phalp, K., Ali, R.: Building online platforms for peer support groups as a persuasive behavior change technique. In: Proceedings of Persuasive Technology, pp. 70–83 (2018)
3. Casperson, S.L., Sieling, J., Moon, J., Johnson, L., Roemmich, J.N., Whigham, L.: A mobile phone food record app to digitally capture dietary intake for adolescents in a free-living environment: usability study. JMIR mHealth and uHealth, p. e30 (2015)
4. Ellison, N.B., Vitak, J., Gray, R., Lampe, C.: Cultivating social resources on social network sites: Facebook relationship maintenance behaviors and their role in social capital processes. J. Comput.-Mediat. Commun. 855–870 (2014)
5. Fanning, J., Mullen, S.P., McAuley, E.: Increasing physical activity with mobile devices: a meta-analysis. J. Med. Internet Res. e161 (2012)

6. Gamberini, L., et al.: Designing and testing credibility: the case of a serious game on nightlife risks. In: Proceedings of Persuasive Technology, pp. 213–226 (2018)
7. Gamberini, L., et al.: A gamified solution to brief interventions for nightlife well-being. In: Proceedings of Persuasive Technology, pp. 230–241 (2016)
8. Hamari, J.: Do badges increase user activity? A field experiment on the effects of gamification. J. Comput. Hum. Behav. **71**, 469–478 (2017)
9. Hamari, J., Koivisto, J., Pakkanen, T.: Do persuasive technologies persuade? - A review of empirical studies. In: Proceedings of Persuasive Technology, pp. 118–136 (2014)
10. Kasmel, A., Andersen, P.T.: Measurement of community empowerment in three community programs in Rapla (Estonia). J. Environ. Res. Publ. Health **8**, 799–817 (2011)
11. Martire, L.M., Franks, M.M.: The role of social networks in adult health: introduction to the special issue. J. Health Psychol. **33**, 501–504 (2014)
12. Oinas-Kukkonen, H.: Behavior 'change support systems: a research model and agenda. In: Ploug, T., Hasle, P., Oinas-Kukkonen, H. (eds.) PERSUASIVE 2010. LNCS, vol. 6137, pp. 4–14. Springer, Heidelberg (2010). https://doi.org/10.1007/978-3-642-13226-1_3
13. Putnam, R.D.: Bowling Alone: The Collapse and Revival of American Community. Simon and Schuster, New York (2001)
14. Räisänen, T., Oinas-Kukkonen, H., Pahnila, S.: Finding kairos in quitting smoking: smokers' perceptions of warning pictures. In: Oinas-Kukkonen, H., Hasle, P., Harjumaa, M., Segerståhl, K., Øhrstrøm, P. (eds.) PERSUASIVE 2008. LNCS, vol. 5033, pp. 254–257. Springer, Heidelberg (2008). https://doi.org/10.1007/978-3-540-68504-3_25
15. Rollo, M.E., Ash, S., Lyons-Wall, P., Russell, A.: Trial of a mobile phone method for recording dietary intake in adults with type 2 diabetes: evaluation and implications for future applications. J. Telemed. Telecare **17**, 318–323 (2011)
16. Ruijten, P.A.M., Ham, J., Midden, C.J.H.: Investigating the influence of social exclusion on persuasion by a virtual agent. In: Spagnolli, A., Chittaro, L., Gamberini, L. (eds.) PERSUASIVE 2014. LNCS, vol. 8462, pp. 191–200. Springer, Cham (2014). https://doi.org/10.1007/978-3-319-07127-5_17
17. Schoeppe, S., et al.: Efficacy of interventions that use apps to improve diet, physical activity and sedentary behaviour: a systematic review. J. Behav. Nutr. Phys. Act. **13**, 127 (2016)
18. Sherman, C.B., Sherman, C., Price, G., et al.: The Invisible Web: Uncovering Information Sources Search Engines Can't See. Information Today Inc., New York (2001)
19. Torning, K., Oinas-Kukkonen, H.: Persuasive system design: state of the art and future directions. In: Proceedings of Persuasive Technology, pp. 30:1–30:8 (2009)
20. Verduyn, P., Ybarra, O., Résibois, M., Jonides, J., Kross, E.: Do social network sites enhance or undermine subjective well-being? A critical review. J. Soc. Issues Policy Rev. **11**, 274–302 (2017)
21. Williams, D.: On and off the 'Net: scales for social capital in an online era. J. Comput.-Med. Commun. 593–628 (2006)

A Group Intervention to Improve
Physical Activity at the Workplace

Martijn Krans[1], Louis van de Wiele[1], Nicola Bullen[2], Mike Diamond[2],
Saskia van Dantzig[1(✉)], Boris de Ruyter[1], and Anouk van der Lans[1]

[1] Philips Research, High Tech Campus 34, 5656 AE Eindhoven, The Netherlands
saskia.van.dantzig@philips.com
[2] For All Our Wellbeing, London, UK
http://www.forallourwellbeing.co.uk

Abstract. We present an exploratory field study to investigate the
acceptability of a group intervention to promote physical activity. To
this end, a five-week group coaching program was developed, as well as
the technological infrastructure to deliver this program. People participated in teams, consisting of hospital staff working together in a ward or
department. Two teams of nurses and one team of facility support staff
participated in the study. The program contained two consecutive team
challenges; aimed at increasing daily step count and daily stairs taken.
Participants wore a FitBit One activity tracker to measure steps and
stairs. Personal information was delivered via a smart phone app, while
aggregated team information was shown on a large screen placed in a
common room at the ward. At the end of the study, group interviews
were held to elicit feedback on the acceptability of the concept and experience of the coaching program. Participants were enthusiastic about the
concept. They indicated that the group coaching caused bonding and
improved team cohesion. There was a clear need to communicate within
the team (now solved through WhatsApp groups). Furthermore, they
would have liked an element of competition between teams. Overall, the
results were positive, leading to the conclusion that team coaching at the
workplace is a promising strategy to promote physical activity.

Keywords: Group coaching · Physical activity ·
Workplace intervention · Digital intervention · Field study ·
Qualitative research

1 Introduction

People are living longer and as a consequence will have to work longer as well [15].
In 2017, 32% of Americans 65 to 69 were employed, while 19% of 70- to 74-year-
olds were still working [22]. This trend is likely to continue as healthcare evolves
and new medicines and technologies allow people to live longer and healthier
than ever before. In order to age healthily, it is important to maintain a healthy
lifestyle. Lifestyle factors at midlife, such as weight, smoking status, physical

© Springer Nature Switzerland AG 2019
H. Oinas-Kukkonen et al. (Eds.): PERSUASIVE 2019, LNCS 11433, pp. 322–333, 2019.
https://doi.org/10.1007/978-3-030-17287-9_26

activity, alcohol consumption, and diet, are related to healthy aging [3]. However, it is often not easy for people to commit to those healthy lifestyle patterns.
For example, health professionals often prematurely leave their jobs due to health
reasons [17,21]. A possible explanation for this could be that nurses have sur-
prisingly high rates of obesity and hypertension [24]. Flannery et al. [9] showed
that approximately 50% of nurses report that they engage in enough exercise to
meet the physical activity guidelines promoted by the World Health Organization [23]. However, physical activity data was self-reported via questionnaires;
therefore the authors expect measurement biases resulting in over-reporting over
daily physical activity. Blake et al. showed that almost half (45%) of NHS personnel does not meet the physical activity guidelines, and approximately 30%
reported to be sedentary at the workplace [4]. In the UK, health care employees are perceived as important role models for health behaviors for the general
public. Therefore these findings are of concern and warrant immediate interventions to improve health behaviors in the NHS workforce. The authors suggested
that this could be achieved by '*helping people to build activity into their daily
lives, particularly at their place of work by encouragement for, and promotion of
incidental physical activities such as brisk walking, increasing daily step counts
through pedometer challenges, cycling and walking to work.*' Another study of
Blake showed that a 12-week messaging intervention with employees of a UK
hospital increased the duration of moderate work-related activity and moderate
recreational activity, increased the frequency of vigorous recreational activity
and increased the duration and frequency of active travel. So they concluded
that minimal physical activity promotion can increase frequency and duration
of active travel and duration of moderate intensity physical activity at work
and for leisure. This effect was maintained up to one month after the messaging
ended [5].

1.1 Social Dynamics

Peer motivation, so getting and staying motivated because of your peers, helps
to start and maintain regular exercise. There is evidence that individuals who
exercise with others are better off in a number of ways. Dishman and Buckworth
reviewed more than 100 studies on physical activity interventions in various
settings (home, schools, work etc.) and concluded that interventions focused
at groups were much more effective than interventions at individuals [8]. The
mechanisms that lead to higher and better performance are robust for keeping
up motivation to participate in physical activity when used under the right conditions. One of the mechanisms involved is social support [11]; by participating
in sport activities together, people can mentally support and encourage each
other. Another mechanism that is powerful especially for high achievers is competition [6,10]. In light of these findings, a group intervention at work could be
a promising strategy to promote physical activity. After all, many employees are
already part of a work team. Even though they may also be part of other social
groups (e.g., a sports team or group of friends), they spend a significant amount
of time with their colleagues [1]. Thus, the social dynamics of (existing) work

teams could be used to leverage health interventions. Indeed, previous research has shown that group interventions at the workplace are effective in improving participant health. Furthermore, they can have beneficial effects on the social atmosphere at the work floor [6].

1.2 Study Objective

The objective of the field study was to gain insight into the acceptability of a group intervention to promote physical activity of hospital staff working together in a ward or department. Two teams of nurses and one team of facility support staff participated in the study. Their feedback on the acceptability and experience of the intervention was elicited through group interviews held at the end of the study. The study was executed in collaboration between Philips Research and For All Our Wellbeing (FAOW), within the context of the EIT Digital subsidy project ProVITA (Prolonging Vitality and Wellness at the workplace).

2 Method

2.1 Participants

Thirty employees of the Royal Free Hospital (London, UK) participated in the study (2 male and 28 female). There were two teams of nurses and one team of facility support staff. Each team consisted of ten participants. The age of the participants ranged between 20 and 65 (mean $= 37.2$, sd $= 13.5$).

2.2 Infrastructure and Data Flow

Figure 1 shows the infrastructure developed for the study. Physical activity data was collected with the **FitBit One**, an activity tracker that can be clipped onto the pants or chest pocket [2]. This device was selected because nurses are not allowed to wear any devices on their wrists for hygienic purposes. Participants wore the FitBit One as much as possible during study participation, both at work and outside working hours. Activity data was transferred from the tracker to the **FitBit app** installed on the participant's smart phone. Data was synced with the **FitBit Cloud**, from which it was retrieved via the FitBit API every 15 min and stored in a local backend. Next, the data was used as input for the **Coaching Engine** that determined the messages delivered to each individual and team. Using production rules, the coaching engine selected the appropriate coaching messages from the message database (e.g., 'if team step count exceeds 25% of target, then deliver reward message'). Personalized coaching was delivered to participants via the **Active Team** app. The app contained several tabs. The **Home** tab contained with 'data bubbles', showing the number of steps and floors taken by the user per day and summed over the week. The **Messages** tab showed a newsfeed of coaching messages. The **Settings** tab allowed the user to view their user profile, as well as the privacy policy of the app. Team coaching was delivered via the **Active Team Screen**, a large screen installed on the ward. The Active Team Screen was placed in a room where it was only visible for hospital staff. The team screen displayed a carousel of 5–7 slides, revolving each 10 s (Fig. 4 shows a screenshot of one of the slides). At each cycle, data was retrieved from the backend to populate the dynamic parameters on the slide with real-time information (e.g., current distance covered).

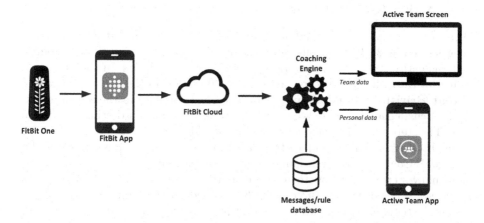

Fig. 1. System architecture and data flow

2.3 Study Design

The study took place in November and December 2017 in the Royal Free Hospital in London, UK. The Active Team program had a duration of five weeks and contained two activity challenges; one focused at increasing step count, and the other focused at increasing stair use (the program is described in more detail in Sect. 2.4). The Active Team program started on a Monday. In the week before the start of the program, participants joined an intake meeting, during which they were informed about the study purpose and method. The FitBit app and the Active Team app were installed on the participant's smart phone. The FitBit One was handed over and its use was explained. Also, participants completed a questionnaire regarding age, gender, height, weight, physical activity habits, department floor, number of working days, commute type, dietary habits, smoking habits and alcohol intake. In addition, participants signed the Informed Consent form. After the five-week Active Team program, participants were interviewed about their experience of the Active Team program. Interviews were held in small groups (approximately 4–5 participants) and guided by a researcher from Philips Research. Another researcher from Philips Research, as well as a member from FAOW were also present as observers. Interviews were semi-structured and addressed the acceptability of the concept. Using a bottom-up and top-down approach, common topics were distilled by the interviewers.

	Week 1	Week 2	Week 3	Week 4	Week 5	
Intake	Join next challenge Set personal target Vote for destination Daily Health Tip	Great British Step Challenge Team feedback on AT screen Personal feedback in AT app Daily Health Tip	Join next challenge Set personal target Vote for destination Daily Health Tip	Big Mountain Challenge Team feedback on AT screen Personal feedback in AT app Daily Health Tip	Feedback on Big Mountain Challenge	Interview

Fig. 2. Study design and setup of the Active Team program

2.4 Active Team Program

The Active Team program had a duration of 5 weeks and consisted of two challenges (see Fig. 2). Participants were instructed to wear the FitBit One throughout the entire study, both at work and outside working hours. In the first week (Monday through Thursday) participants could sign up for the first challenge; the **Great British Step Challenge**, which would take place in the second week. In this challenge, the team would jointly walk to a famous destination in the UK. The steps taken by each team member would contribute to the team's total number of steps. This would be translated in the distance covered towards the end goal. Contributions were anonymous, thus participants were not informed how many steps their fellow team members took. After signing up, participants could set a personal step target (Fig. 3a). Based on the personal step targets set by the team members, two virtual destinations were proposed by the system. The distance to destination A was determined as the sum of the personal targets, while the distance to destination B was 10% further than destination A. From Friday onwards, participants could vote for one of the destinations (Fig. 3b). In the second week the Great British Step Challenge was performed. Together the participants of each team walked to their virtual destination. Throughout the week participants received coaching messages to help them reach their goal. They received personal feedback on their performance in the Active Team app (Fig. 3c), and aggregated feedback on the Active Team screen (Fig. 4). The team member with the highest step count on a particular day was rewarded with a message on the following day. In addition, upon reaching 25% and 75% of the team goal, the team received a virtual reward (a badge). Upon reaching 50% and 100% of their goal, they received a real reward (a reusable water bottle, and a fruit basket for the team, respectively). In the third week, a rest week was incorporated. Participants could sign up, set their target and vote for the **Big Mountain Challenge**, which would take place in week 4. During the Big Mountain Challenge, participants collectively climbed a virtual mountain, by taking as many stairs as possible. Again, two destinations were proposed based on the personal targets of each team member. Destination A was the sum of the targets, and destination B was 10% higher than destination A. In week 4, the teams received the same coaching elements as in week 2; coaching messages, personal feedback in the app and aggregated feedback on the screen, a reward for the best climber (Fig. 3d), virtual rewards upon reaching 25% and 75% of their target, and real rewards upon reaching 50% and 100% of their target (free 15-min shoulder massage and a free team lunch, respectively). During the fifth week participants were informed on their results of the Big Mountain Challenge.

Throughout the entire program, participants also received daily educational messages (Health Tip of the Day). These health tips informed on the beneficial effects of taking enough steps and stairs, but also on other health behaviors, such as drinking enough water and eating fruit and vegetables.

Some of the essential aspects in the Active Team Program are:

- Individual and team goals. The team goal is set based on the individual goals of each team member. Individual goal setting is done via the personal communication channel (i.e. App) and is not shared with the team (in contrast to the team goal).
- Gamification elements. Rewards on team level (tangible and intangible ones) are unlocked upon reaching challenge milestones 25, 50, 75, 100%. Competition within team is not promoted, it's all about team effort.
- Peer pressure. The public team dashboard only indicates progress towards the goal to avoid naming/shaming of team members. Information about a team member's relative performance within the team is only provided to the best team performer after the challenge (only delivered via the personal message feed of this best performer).
- Social loafing. Group size is chosen not to be too large (max 10 members), to minimise the chance of social loafing.

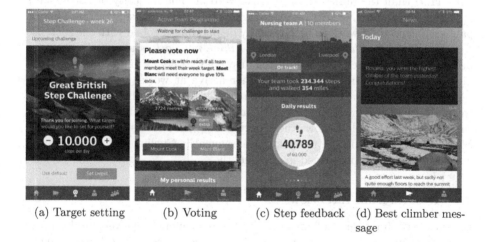

(a) Target setting   (b) Voting   (c) Step feedback   (d) Best climber message

Fig. 3. Screenshots of the Active Team app

3 Results

3.1 Participant Characteristics

Three teams participated in the study; one team of facility support staff, one team of nurses from an intensive care ward and one team of nurses from a preoperative care ward. On average, the facility support staff were older (M = 48.2,

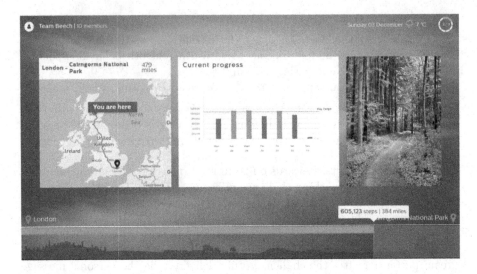

Fig. 4. Team feedback on Great British Step Challenge, displayed on the Active Team screen

SD = 11.9) than the nurses (M = 31.7, SD = 10.7). The majority of participants (16) had a normal BMI, 7 were overweight, and 5 were obese. Overall, participants reported their work to be physically demanding. Probed with the sentence *'In comparison to others of my own age I think my work is physically...'* twelve people answered 'much heavier', fifteen answered 'as heavy', and three answered 'lighter'. They also indicated to be rather active at work (see Table 1). They reported little sedentary time, and they reported to be standing and/or walking the majority of their working time. The majority answered often or always being tired after work. Table 2 shows the reported frequency of leisure time activities. Most participants reported to walk quite frequently. Cycling and playing sports were reported to be performed less frequently.

3.2 Results from Interviews

Overall, both hospital staff members and management were very enthusiastic about the concept. In informal talks with the researchers, hospital management expressed its enthusiasm about the concept, and asked the researchers to implement the concept more widely in the organisation.

Physical Activity Level. Most participants indicated that they became more active during the challenge weeks. Several participants indicated that the opportunity to get more active at work was limited, but that they became more active outside of work (e.g., by getting off the train a stop earlier and walking more). Two out of three teams succeeded in the Great British Step challenge, and all teams succeeded in the Big Mountain Challenge.

Table 1. Self-reported frequency of physical activities at work

Frequency	Never	Seldom	Sometimes	Often	Always
At work I sit	1	11	18	–	–
At work I stand	–	–	4	17	9
At work I walk	–	–	2	19	9
At work I lift heavy loads	1	2	13	11	3
After working I am tired	–	–	11	5	14

Table 2. Self-reported frequency of leisure time activities

Frequency	Never	Seldom	Sometimes	Often	Very often
During leisure time I play sport	9	9	10	2	–
During leisure time I walk	–	2	19	7	2
During leisure time I cycle	18	10	2	–	–
During leisure time I watch television	2	1	14	9	3

Team Building. Participants experienced a positive effect on team cohesion. Ward colleagues who were unfamiliar with each other before the study did get to know each other during participation. Some even mentioned that friendships were started during the study. One of the participants mentioned 'We started as a study group and ended as a team'. Although this was not the primary objective, the Active Team program did contain social strategies to promote team building, as a means to make people feel more committed to the team, and therefore more motivated to contribute to the team performance. Related to this, participants appreciated the 'real' rewards received at certain milestones during the challenges. They preferred rewards that could be shared with the team, such as the team lunch and fruit basket. This reflects the team spirit that was promoted by the program. The teams consisted of 10 people, which was seen as a good size. Participants also appreciated the fact that the teams were composed by the system, and how this allowed them to get to know new people.

Competition. Competition between the teams emerged, even though this was not an element of the program. The concept was primarily designed for team building, and the Active Team screen only showed the performance of the own team. Nevertheless, participants indicated to be motivated by competing with the other teams. The two teams of nurses checked each other's progress on the Active Team screen and also discussed the challenges with each other.

Communication. Participants indicated a need for communication within the team about the study. To address this need, each team created a dedicated Whatsapp group, in which they shared screen shots of the app and team screen. They would also notify each other whenever a new message appeared in the newsfeed of the app. The infrastructure did not cater for this need, as it did not include a communication channel (e.g., an in-app chat function).

Active Team App and Active Team Screen. Participants typically checked the app several times per day. The facility support staff didn't visit their common room frequently, and therefore checked the Active Team screen less often. To keep each other updated on the team status, team members would take pictures of the Active Team screen and share those with the team through Whatsapp. They also shared screenshots of the app at the end of every day. Participants mentioned that seeing the progress toward the destination (in the app and on the screen) motivated them.

Target Setting. At the start of the program, participants were unaware of their baseline activity level, which made it difficult to set a realistic target. As a result, some participants set targets that turned out to be too high. After learning from the first challenge, targets for the second challenge were set more conservatively. The majority of participants preferred the Big Mountain challenge. They did see more opportunities to take the stairs (instead of the elevator) during work than to walk more.

4 Discussion and Conclusion

Team Cohesion. A striking result of the study was that participants reported improved team cohesion and enhanced communication. This is in line with other studies that showed positive effects on the social dynamics on the workfloor. For example, a qualitative study by Joubert and De Beer showed that participation in organizational team sports was related to improved team commitment, enhanced communication, and increased trust at the work floor [12]. These beneficial effects could even have further implications; studies have shown that nurses who report better team cohesion also report higher job satisfaction [7,14]. Moreover, improved teamwork amongst nurses has even been associated with increased patient safety, improved quality of care, and greater patient satisfaction [13]. In addition, numerous studies have shown that organizations with a positive social atmosphere have healthier employees and lower rates of sick leave. Thus, this group intervention could act as a double edged sword. It could improve physical health directly, by motivating workers to become more active during the challenges, and indirectly, through strengthening the social environment at the workplace. However, when implementing such group interventions, it is important to enable every employee to participate. The flip side of stronger team bonding is that non team-members might feel excluded. Indeed, our study participants reported that their non-participating colleagues sometimes felt left out. Therefore, it is important to ensure that group interventions are suitable for employees with various physical abilities and fitness levels, including physically impaired employees. In a digital intervention, there are several ways to lower the barrier for participation for people with lower physical abilities or fitness. In our study, participants contributed anonymously to the team performance. Thus, their personal targets and achievements were not shared with the team. The Active Team screen only showed the aggregated group statistics. An other option is to measure people's performance relative to their capacity. For example, an intervention could start with measuring baseline levels of activity of each team member. Next, in a team challenge, each person's proportional increase from their baseline level is used, rather than their absolute activity level. This allows team members with diverse physical abilities to contribute equally much to the overall team performance. This could also prevent social loafing; the tendency for individuals to expend less effort when working collectively than when working individually [20].

Competition. Even though the Active Team program did not include a competitive element, a competition between the three teams emerged. Competition is a gamification strategy that is often used in physical activity programs. Shameli et al. [19] concluded that competition can lead to increases in physical activity level across a wide variety of user demographics. They also provide some recommendations for selecting competing participants:

- Competing participants should have similar pre-competition activity levels. Otherwise the effect of the competition on physical activity drops significantly.
- Competitions should have a balanced mix of both men and women.
- Competitions should ideally include some participants who have previously increased their activity in response to competitions to encourage the other participants.

Individuals differ in their preferred way of comparing themselves with others. Some people are motivated by comparing themselves to others who perform better than themselves (upward comparison), whereas others are more motivated by comparing themselves to people performing slightly worse than themselves (downward comparison). It is important to take these personal preferences into account; presenting users with the non-preferred type of social comparison may actually be counter-effective [16,18].

Active Team Screen. We expected that the Active Team screen would function as an additional touch point and visual reminder. Also, we expected that it might invite people to discuss the program (with team members and non-team members). In the nurses' common rooms, this was indeed the case. Team members as well as non-team members discussed the challenges and the progress. Participants appreciated the screen, especially seeing their progress toward the destination. Since the facility support staff visited their common room less frequently (they were working all over the hospital), they had less interaction with and in front of the Active Team screen.

Conclusion. Overall, the results of this field study were positive. Study participants as well as hospital management were very enthusiastic about the concept. Based on the feedback from the participants, we conclude that team coaching at the workplace is a promising strategy to promote physical activity. In the current field study, we only explored the acceptability of our concept. Next steps would be to improve the Active Team program based on the participant feedback and investigate the effectiveness of our concept in a randomized controlled trial.

Acknowledgments. This study was executed in the context of the EIT Digital project ProVITA (Prolonging Vitality and Wellness at the Workplace). We thank Ernst Hermens for managing this project. Furthermore, we thank Rik Bootsman, Frank Stokes, Hwang Kim, Abdul Nabi, Stijn Kooij, Jelte Bijkerk, Roberto Gamboni, Harijs Deksnis and Sandeep Kumar Pamujula for their contribution to the visual design and development of the Active Team app and Active Team screen. Finally, we thank the management and staff of the Royal Free Hospital London for enabling us to execute the study there.

References

1. American Time Use Survey (ATUS): Bureau of Labor Statistics. https://www.bls.gov/tus/charts.htm. Accessed 13 Nov 2018
2. Fitbit One. https://www.fitbit.com/eu/one. Accessed 22 Nov 2018
3. Atallah, N., et al.: How healthy lifestyle factors at midlife relate to healthy aging. Nutrients 10(7), 854 (2018)
4. Blake, H., Mo, P., Lee, S., Batt, M.: Health in the NHS: lifestyle behaviours of hospital employees. Perspect. Public Health 132(5), 213–215 (2012)
5. Blake, H., Suggs, L., Coman, E., Aquirre, L., Batt, M.: Active8! Technology-based intervention to promote physical activity in hospital employees. Am. J. Health Promot. 31(2), 109–118 (2017)
6. Brinkley, A., McDermott, H., Munir, F.: What benefits does team sport hold for the workplace? A systematic review. J. Sports Sci. 35(2), 136–148 (2017)
7. DiMeglio, K., et al.: Group cohesion and nurse satisfaction: examination of a team-building approach. J. Nurs. Adm. 35(3), 110–120 (2005)
8. Dishman, R., Buckworth, J.: Increasing physical activity: a quantitative synthesis. Med. Sci. Sports Exerc. 28(6), 706–719 (2006)
9. Flannery, K., Burket, T., Resnick, B.: Exercise habits of licensed nurses and nursing assistants: are they meeting national guidelines? Geriatr. Nurs. 35(2), 17–20 (2014)
10. Frederick-Recascino, C., Schuster-Smith, H.: Competition and intrinsic motivation in physical activity: a comparison of two groups. J. Sport Behav. 26, 240–254 (2003)
11. Houston, T., Cooper, L., Ford, D.: Internet support groups for depression: a 1-year prospective cohort study. Am. J. Psychiatry 159(12), 2062–2068 (2002)
12. Joubert, Y., de Beer, H.: Experiences of employees who participate in organisational team sport activities. J. Emerg. Trends Econ. Manag. Sci. 1(1), 51–59 (2010)
13. Kalisch, B., Curley, M., Stefanov, S.: An intervention to enhance nursing staff teamwork and engagement. JONA: J. Nurs. Adm. 37(2), 77–84 (2007)
14. Kalisch, B., Lee, H., Rochman, M.: Nursing staff teamwork and job satisfaction. J. Nurs. Manag. 18, 938–947 (2010)

15. Kontis, V., Bennett, J., Mathers, C., Li, G., Foreman, K., Ezzati, M.: Future life expectancy in 35 industrialised countries: projections with a Bayesian model ensemble. Lancet **389**(10076), 1323–1335 (2017)
16. Mollee, J., Klein, M.: The effectiveness of upward and downward social comparison of physical activity in an online intervention. In: 15th International Conference on Ubiquitous Computing and Communications and 2016 International Symposium on Cyberspace and Security (IUCC-CSS), pp. 109–115, December 2016
17. Rosen, J., Stiehl, E., Mittal, V., Leana, C.R.: Stayers, leavers, and switchers among certified nursing assistants in nursing homes: a longitudinal investigation of turnover intent, staff retention, and turnover. Gerontologist **51**(5), 597–609 (2011)
18. Schokker, M., et al.: The impact of social comparison information on motivation in patients with diabetes as a function of regulatory focus and self-efficacy. Health Psychol. **29**(4), 438–45 (2010)
19. Shameli, A., Althoff, T., Saberi, A., Leskovec, J.: How gamification affects physical activity: large-scale analysis of walking challenges in a mobile application. In: Proceedings of the International World-Wide Web Conference, pp. 455–463 (2017)
20. Simms, A., Nichols, T.: Social loafing: a review of the literature. J. Manag. Policy Pract. **15**(1), 58–67 (2014)
21. Skillman, S., Palazzo, L., Hart, L., Keepnews, D.: The characteristics of registered nurses whose licenses expire: why they leave nursing and implications for retention and re-entry. Nurs. Econ. **28**(3), 181–189 (2010)
22. Steverman, B.: More senior citizens working past retirement age (2017). https://www.insurancejournal.com/news/national/2017/07/11/457194.htm. Accessed 13 Nov 2018
23. World Health Organization: Global recommendations on physical activity for health (2010). https://www.who.int/dietphysicalactivity/publications/9789241599979/en/. Accessed 20 Nov 2018
24. Zapka, J., Lemon, S., Magner, R., Hale, J.: Lifestyle behaviours and weight among hospital-based nurses. J. Nurs. Manag. **17**(7), 853 (2009)

User Types and Tailoring

Combining Behavior Change Intentions and User Types to Select Suitable Gamification Elements for Persuasive Fitness Systems

Maximilian Altmeyer[1(⊠)], Pascal Lessel[1], Linda Muller[2], and Antonio Krüger[1]

[1] German Research Center for AI (DFKI), Saarland Informatics Campus,
Saarbrücken, Germany
{maximilian.altmeyer,pascal.lessel,antonio.krueger}@dfki.de
[2] Saarland University, Saarland Informatics Campus, Saarbrücken, Germany
linda_muller@hotmail.de

Abstract. The motivational impact of gamification elements differs substantially across users. To account for these differences, we investigate Hexad user types and behavior change intentions as factors to personalize gamifed, persuasive fitness systems. We conducted an online study (N = 179), measuring the perceived persuasiveness of twelve gamification elements using storyboards. Results show the applicability of the Hexad user type in the Physical Activity domain. Besides replicating correlations between gamification elements and user types, we also found correlations which were hypothesized in literature, but not yet shown. Our main contribution is to show that behavior change intentions influence the perception of gamification elements in general and affect the set of relevant elements for each user type. Since a static set of elements has been suggested for each user type so far, this is an important finding, leading to potentially more effective personalization approaches.

Keywords: Personalization · Gamification · Physical Activity

1 Introduction

Gamification, the use of game elements in non-game contexts [5], has been successfully used to engage users in various domains [9,11]. Among these, the Health domain is one of the most prominent [8], with gamification being frequently used to motivate people to lead a more active lifestyle [26]. Given that an increasing number of people lead sedentary lifestyles [24], investigating gamification for behavior change in this domain is important. While in general most gamified systems have been shown to be successful when adopting a "one-size-fits-all" approach [8,26], research has also found negative results [4,9,26]. This is unsurprising, given that the motivational impact of game elements differs substantially across users [3,29]. Therefore, understanding how to personalize gamified

© Springer Nature Switzerland AG 2019
H. Oinas-Kukkonen et al. (Eds.): PERSUASIVE 2019, LNCS 11433, pp. 337–349, 2019.
https://doi.org/10.1007/978-3-030-17287-9_27

systems has gained attention as a topic for research. To personalize gamified systems, static factors like personality [11], age [1,2] or gender [18] have been shown to influence the perception of game elements. Also, the Hexad model [15], a user type model specifically developed for gamified interventions, was shown to be a useful factor for tailoring gamified, persuasive systems [20,30]. However, psychological models like the Transtheoretical Model of Behavior Change ("TTM") [23] suggest that the behavioral intention to perform a behavior dynamically changes, with people passing through several qualitatively different, successive stages of change ("SoC"). When individuals progress through these stages, the type of motivation changes from extrinsic to intrinsic as behavioral regulation becomes more self-determined [17]. This potentially affects the perception of gamification elements. Therefore, the SoC might play an important role in personalizing gamified, persuasive interventions. Yet, to our knowledge, this has not been researched so far. In this paper, we contribute to this open question by using a storyboard-based approach, illustrating frequently used gamification elements for persuasive systems in the Physical Activity domain. After ensuring that these storyboards illustrate the intended gamification elements, we conducted a user study confronting participants with the aforementioned gamification elements ($N = 179$) and correlated their answers to their user type and TTM level.

With our findings we reproduce the set of relevant gamification elements for Hexad user types from previous research, showing its applicability in the Physical Activity context. We also found correlations between gamification elements and user types, which were hypothesized in literature, but not yet shown. As our main contribution, our results show that the SoC indeed influences the perception of gamification elements in general and changes the set of relevant gamification elements for each user type. This implies that the set of relevant gamification elements does not remain stable for each user type, but dynamically changes when behavior intentions change. This finding is important, as, so far, a static set of gamification elements has been suggested for each user type [30], not taking into account the dynamic process of behavior change [23].

2   Background and Related Work

After introducing the Hexad- and the Transtheoretical models, related work about individualizing gamified systems is presented in this section.

2.1   Hexad User Type Model

The Hexad user types model [15] was specifically developed for gamified systems [20]. It was shown to be an effective personalization tool for persuasive systems [20]. Also, a questionnaire was created and validated [28]. The Hexad consists of six user types that differ in the degree to which they are driven by their needs for autonomy, relatedness and competence (as defined by the Self-Determination Theory (SDT) [25]). **Philanthropists ("PH")** are socially-minded, like to bear responsibility and share knowledge with others. They are driven by *purpose*. Similarly, **Socializers ("SO")** are socially-minded, but they are more interested in interacting with others. *Relatedness* is most important for them. **Free Spirits ("FS")** are satisfied when acting without external control, with *autonomy* being most important for them. **Achievers ("AC")** are satisfied when overcoming difficult challenges or learning new skills. *Competence* is most important for them. **Players ("PL")** are out for their own benefits, and will do their best to earn rewards. *Extrinsic rewards* are most important for them. Lastly, **Disruptors ("DI")** are driven by disrupting systems and by testing its boundaries. Triggering *change* is most important for them.

2.2 Transtheoretical Model

The Transtheoretical Model by Prochaska et al. [23] describes the process of intentional behavior change. It posits that behavior change involves progress through five stages of change. In the **Precontemplation** stage, the subject has no intention to take action in the foreseeable future (usually 6 months), while subjects in the **Contemplation** stage intend to take action within the next 6 months. Subjects in the **Preparation** stage intend to take action in the immediate future (usually 30 days), and have taken some behavioral steps yet. In the **Action** stage, the subject has changed their behavior for less than 6 months, while in **Maintenance**, subjects have changed their behavior for more than 6 months. When individuals progress through these stages, their motivation becomes more intrinsic as behavioral regulation becomes more self-determined [17]. We expect that this has an effect on the perception of gamification elements.

2.3 Individualization of Gamified Systems

Individualizing gamified systems has been shown to be appreciated [13] and more effective than traditional "one-size-fits-all" approaches [4,12]. Consequently, research has been conducted on how gamified systems can be individualized. For instance, Jia et al. [11] investigated the relationship between personality traits and perceived preferences for several motivational affordances. They found multiple significant correlations (e.g. that Extraverts tend to be motivated by points, levels, and leaderboards) which help to personalize gamified systems. Similarly, Orji et al. [19] studied how personality traits can be used to tailor persuasive strategies within systems for health. They found that individuals' personalities indeed influence the perceived persuasiveness of persuasive strategies (which were explained using storyboards). Studies also revealed age [1,2] and gender as factors influencing the perception of motivational affordances [18,22]. For instance, Birk et al. [2] found that motivations to engage in games change with increasing age, from focusing on performance towards focusing on enjoyment, which is supported by findings from Altmeyer et al. [1]. Complementing these findings, Oyibo et al. [22] found relationships between age and gender for the game elements rewards, competition, social learning and comparison. One of the most promising approaches to personalize gamified systems is using the Hexad user types model [30], as it is the only model that was specifically developed for gamified systems (rather than for games) [20]. Also, the applicability of this model for gamified, persuasive systems has been shown [20]. Research has been carried out to examine whether different Hexad user types prefer different game elements or motivational affordances. Indeed, Tondello et al. [30] found several significant correlations between Hexad user types and the perception of game elements. In a follow-up work, Tondello et al. [29] propose a conceptual framework for classifying game elements based on an exploratory factor analysis of participants' preferences. In line with the previous study, they found several correlations to the Hexad user types. Furthermore, Orji et al. [20] showed that the Hexad user types play a significant role in the perception of persuasive strategies to change risky alcohol behavior. Thus, the Hexad user type model offers great potential for tailoring gamified, persuasive systems. However, the Hexad framework (and all aforementioned factors) does not take into account the dynamic process of behavioral intentions, which has been shown to affect the type of motivation a user develops towards an activity [17]. In this paper, we aim to reduce this gap by investigating whether the SoC has an effect on the perception of gamification elements in the Physical Activity context.

3 Gamification Elements, Storyboards and Validation

For the storyboards, we ensured to have at least one gamification element for each user type, based on [15,30]. This resulted in twelve different storyboards (showing the gamification elements as stated in Table 1). These were created using the guidelines by Truong et al. [31]. We decided to use storyboards since they provide a common visual language that is easy to understand and do not involve game- or technology-specific knowledge [21]. Due to space restrictions, only two storyboards are included in this paper (see Fig. 1). However, all created storyboards can be found on figshare[1].

Fig. 1. Virtual Character (a) and Custom Goal (b) storyboards

---

[1] https://doi.org/10.6084/m9.figshare.7380902.v1.

Table 1. Gamification elements included in the main study, a short textual description explaining what is depicted in the corresponding storyboard and the user types ("PT") we expect to be positively affected by them based on [15,30].

Gamification element	Short storyboard description	Expected PT
Virtual Character	*The appearance of a virtual character is linked to the amount of steps walked*	AC, PL
Custom Goal	*The user sets herself a custom step goal*	AC, FS
Personalized Goal	*The system personalizes the users' step goal*	AC
Challenge	*The user manages to reach a demanding goal*	AC
Badges	*The user reaches her goal three times, unlocking a new badge*	AC, PL
Points	*The system rewards the user with points for walking steps*	PL, AC
Rewards	*After reaching the step goal three times, the user receives a coupon code*	PL
Knowledge Sharing	*The user helps another user in a forum by answering a question*	PH
Unlockable Content	*After reaching the step goal three times, the app unlocks a new feature*	FS
Cheating	*The user decides to cheat by driving a car to reach her step goal*	DI
Social Collaboration	*A group of users have to collaborate, to reach their shared step goal*	SO
Social Competition	*A group of users are shown on a leaderboard, competing for the top position*	SO, PL

3.1 Storyboard Validation

To ensure that participants understand the storyboards, we conducted a qualitative pre-study in the lab.

Method. After answering demographic questions, the printed storyboards were shown to each participant in random order. A semi-structured interview followed in which all sessions were conducted by one researcher and audio recordings were made. First, participants were asked to describe the storyboards in their own words. When necessary, the interviewer asked questions to prompt participants to identify which activities are depicted by the storyboards. Questions included: *"What is the character's goal?"* and *"What means does the character use to achieve her goal?"*. Afterwards, participants were given a short textual summary of each gamification element. They were asked to assign each of the storyboards its respective element by placing the aforementioned pieces of paper (holding the textual summaries) next to the respective storyboard. Next, interviews were transcribed and analyzed by two independent raters ("R1", "R2"). They received the transcriptions for each storyboard, without revealing which gamification element was described by the participants. Their tasks were to evaluate which element was being described and to rate how well the element was understood on a 5-point scale (1-very poor to 5-very well).

Results. 8 German participants took part (4 female, average age 21.75). To ensure that the ratings can be interpreted objectively, we calculated the interrater agreement and found it to be Kappa $= 0.75$, which is considered as substantial [16]. Analyzing the ratings of the two independent raters, we found that the participants understood the storyboards very well ($M_{R1} = 4.90$, $Min_{R1} = 4$; $M_{R2} = 4.86$, $Min_{R2} = 4$). This was supported by the fact that both raters successfully assigned the correct game element based on participants' storyboard descriptions. Regarding users assigning the textual summaries to the respective storyboard, only one assignment was incorrect. However, this wrong assignment was not due to a misunderstanding of the game element, but due to the participant misreading the descriptions of one of the game elements. The participant assured us that the storyboard and respective game element were clear to him.

4   Main Study

We conducted an online survey, which was available in English and German. Participants were recruited via social media and Academic Prolific (paid 1.50 pounds). The study took 10–15 min to complete and was approved by our Ethical Review Board[2]. After asking for demographic data and gaming behavior, the TTM SoC was determined using a validated scale for the Physical Activity context [14]. For later analysis, participants were split into two groups: "Low-TTM" (participants who did not take action so far, having a SoC ≤ 3 [33]) and "High-TTM" (participants who did take action, having a SoC ≥ 4 [33]), according to the suggestions of Xiao et al. [33] on how to analyze the different TTM stages. Afterwards, participants' user type was determined using the Hexad User Types scale [30]. Finally, as the main part of the questionnaire, participants were shown the 12 storyboards in a randomized order. To measure the persuasiveness of each gamification element depicted in the storyboards, we adapted the perceived persuasiveness scale by Drozd et al. [6] in the same way as was done by Orji et al. [19]. The scale consists of four items to be answered on 7-point Likert scales. A Shapiro-Wilk test revealed that the persuasiveness items were not normally distributed, which is why we used non-parametric tests for our analysis. For correlation analysis, Kendall's τ was used, as it is well-suited for non-parametric data [10]. It should be noted that Kendall's τ is usually lower than Pearson's

---

[2] https://erb.cs.uni-saarland.de/, last accessed January 24, 2019.

r for the same effect sizes. Therefore, we transformed interpretation thresholds for Pearson's r to Kendall's τ, according to Kendall's formula [32] (small effect: $\tau = 0.2$; medium effect: $\tau = 0.3$; large effect: $\tau = 0.5$).

Table 2. Persuasiveness of gamification elements in the Low- and the High-TTM group and results of Mann-Whitney-U tests comparing them ("Diff. sig."). Significant differences from the neutral choice are colored (green = positive, red = negative deviations)

	Low-TTM	High-TTM	Diff. sig.
Virtual Character	M = 4.05, SD = 1.77, Mdn = 4.50	M = 3.94, SD = 1.81, Mdn = 4.25	-
Custom Goal	M = 4.34, SD = 1.49, Mdn = 4.63	M = 4.70, SD = 1.55, Mdn = 5.25	-
Personalized Goal	M = 4.88, SD = 1.44, Mdn = 5.00	M = 4.93, SD = 1.38, Mdn = 5.25	.
Challenge	M = 4.32, SD = 1.65, Mdn = 4.75	M = 4.88, SD = 1.27, Mdn = 5.00	p = 0.045, Z = -2.00, U = 3173.50
Badges	M = 3.95, SD = 1.57, Mdn = 4.00	M = 4.46, SD = 1.40, Mdn = 4.75	p = 0.028, Z = -2.19, U = 3108.50
Points	M = 4.39, SD = 1.46, Mdn = 5.00	M = 4.52, SD = 1.43, Mdn = 4.50	-
Rewards	M = 5.16, SD = 1.48, Mdn = 5.25	M = 5.50, SD = 1.39, Mdn = 5.75	-
Knowledge Sharing	M = 4.06, SD = 1.52, Mdn = 4.25	M = 4.26, SD = 1.51, Mdn = 4.50	-
Unlockable Content	M = 4.70, SD = 1.49, Mdn = 5.00	M = 4.84, SD = 1.53, Mdn = 5.00	-
Cheating	M = 2.12, SD = 1.16, Mdn = 2.00	M = 2.35, SD = 1.44, Mdn = 2.00	
Social Collaboration	M = 4.23, SD = 1.56, Mdn = 4.88	M = 4.81, SD = 1.61, Mdn = 5.25	p = 0.009, Z = -2.62, U = 2963.50
Social Competition	M = 4.09, SD = 1.74, Mdn = 4.50	M = 4.61, SD = 1.76, Mdn = 4.75	p = 0.048, Z = -1.98, U = 3180.50

4.1 Results

We excluded three participants who are unable to exercise or answered all gaming related questions with "Strongly disagree", leading to 179 valid responses. Of these participants, 44.1% were male, 55.3% were female and 0.6% identified themselves as "nonbinary". Most participants (38%) were aged 18–24 years, followed by 25–31 (34.1%), 32–38 (17.3%), 39–45 (6.7%) and younger than 18 (1.7%). The remaining participants were aged 45 and older (1.7%). Participants claimed to have a passion for video games (M = 3.70, SD = 1.11, Mdn = 4.00) and to frequently play video games (M = 3.58, SD = 1.24, Mdn = 4.00).

SoC and Gamification Elements. After splitting participants into two TTM groups (as suggested in [33]), 72 participants were in the Low-TTM and 107 participants in the High-TTM group. To investigate whether the perceived persuasiveness changes between these groups, we performed a two-sided Mann-Whitney-U test for each gamification element. Also, a one-sample Wilcoxon signed rank test was performed against the value 4 on the 7-point scale to investigate which gamification elements were perceived as significantly better or worse than the neutral choice. Table 2 shows an overview of these tests and the means and medians of the perceived persuasiveness for each gamification element. Overall, we found that some gamification elements were perceived significantly differently from the neutral choice in the High-TTM group but not in the Low-TTM group. Also, significant differences for four gamification elements were found. Badges and Challenges, both building on the need for mastery or competence [15], were shown to be significantly more persuasive for users at high stages of change than for users at low stages. This is explainable by goal-setting theory (as both elements require reaching a goal), stating that goals are most effective when users are committed to them [27], which is unlikely for users in the Low-TTM group. Another reason could be that participants in Low-TTM considered themselves not to be able to reach those goals [7]. Moreover, Social Competition and Social Collaboration, both building on the relatedness motive [15] were perceived as significantly more persuasive in the High-TTM group. A potential reason for this includes the fear to not be able to keep up with other users [7], detrimentally affecting users' motivation. These findings show that the SoC on its own is a relevant factor that should be considered in tailoring persuasive, gamified interventions in the physical activity context.

Table 3. Kendall's τ and significance between the Hexad user types and the gamification elements. Bold entries represent expected correlations (Table 1). *p < .05, **p < .01

	AC	DI	FS	PH	PL	SO
Virtual Character	-	-	-	-	**.237****	.114*
Custom Goal	**.205****	-	.132*	.119*	-	.106*
Personalized Goal	**.211****	-	-	.145**	-	-
Challenge	**.200****	-	.145**	-	.177**	-
Badges	**.122***	-	-	-	**.223****	-
Points	**.201****	-	.110*	.192**	**.169****	.105*
Rewards	.114*	-	-	.152**	**.250****	.109*
Knowledge Sharing	.123*	-	-	.234**	-	.175**
Unlockable Content	.140**	-	**.143****	-	.163**	-
Cheating	-	**.157****	-	-	-	-
Social Collaboration	.147**	-	.153**	.145**	.216**	**.314****
Social Competition	.105*	-	-	-	**.370****	**.204****

Hexad User Types and Gamification Elements. Table 3 presents the significant correlations of gamification elements to each user type. We found 16 positive correlations between user types and gamification elements out of 17 expected correlations (see Table 1). The positive correlation between the gamification element "Virtual Character" and the "Achiever" user type is the only correlation that was expected but not found. Given these results, we extend and replicate previous work [20, 30]: We show the applicability of previous findings in the Physical Activity context and contribute evidence for previously hypothesized, but not yet shown correlations, i.e. between the Philanthropist and the gamification element "Knowledge Sharing" and between the Disruptor and the gamification element "Cheating" [30]. In addition to expected correlations, some unexpected correlations were found. However, this is in line with previous research about the Hexad user types [20, 30]. Also, all but one unexpected correlations are weak ($\tau < 0.2$), which suggests that their actual effect is negligible.

Table 4. Kendall's τ and significance between the Hexad user types and gamification elements for the Low- and the High-TTM group. Colored cells indicate that a correlation is significantly stronger in one group than in the other group. *p < .05, **p < .01

	Low-TTM						High-TTM					
	AC	DI	FS	PH	PL	SO	AC	DI	FS	PH	PL	SO
Virtual Character	.218*	-	-	-	-	-	-	-	-	-	.304**	.183**
Custom Goal	.192*	-	-	-	.171*	-	.215**	-	.178*	.194**	-	-
Personalized Goal	-	-	-	-	-	-	.253**	-	.178*	-	-	-
Challenge	.182*	-	-	-	-	-	.214**	-	-	-	.249**	-
Badges	-	-	-	-	.215*	-	.161*	-	-	.141*	.276**	-
Points	-	-	-	.213*	-	.191*	.250**	-	.200**	.170*	.195**	-
Rewards	-	-	-	-	.182*	-	-	-	-	.144*	.303**	-
Knowledge Sharing	-	-	-	-	-	-	.191**	-	-	.327**	-	.248**
Unlockable Content	-	-	.222*	-	-	-	.154*	-	-	-	.230**	-
Cheating	-	.222*	-	-	-	-	-	-	-	-	-	-
Social Collaboration	-	-	.191*	-	-	-	.153*	-	-	.185**	.285**	.343**
Social Competition	-	-	-	-	.316*	-	-	-	-	-	.422**	.206**

SoC, Hexad User Types and Gamification Elements. To investigate potential effects of the SoC on the set of suitable gamification elements for each user type, we compared correlations of gamification elements to user types between the Low- and the High-TTM group. Table 4 shows these correlations for both groups. The analysis revealed that the set of significantly correlating gamification elements is different in both groups, suggesting that taking the SoC into account when tailoring persuasive systems for user types should improve personalization. To emphasize this, we also investigated whether the strength of correlations differs significantly between the Low- and the High-TTM groups. For this, we converted Kendall's τ to Pearson's r according to Kendall's formula described in [32]. Afterwards, we applied Fisher's z-transformation to these coefficients to check for effects. Supporting the main hypothesis of this paper, we found multiple significant differences between the groups for all user types but the Disruptor. Gamification elements for which the correlation coefficient significantly increased on a user type level are colored green in Table 4. For example, we found that the correlation between the "Virtual Character" gamification element and the "Achiever" user type is significantly stronger in the Low-TTM than in the High-TTM group. Similarly, we found that social competition is positively affecting for Socializers only when being in a High-TTM stage. Besides the Disruptor, we found similar findings for all other user types. Therefore, these results should be considered when making decisions about which gamification elements should be included in a system, in order to enhance its persuasiveness.

Discussion and Limitations. We investigated the effect of behavior change intentions on the perception of gamification elements in the Physical Activity domain. We contribute three main findings: First, we presented results about the individual impact of the SoC on the perception of each gamification element, leading to a set of well- and poorly perceived elements for each TTM group. We found that there are differences in this set, as many gamification elements are not perceived similarly across groups, showing that the SoC impacts their perception. This is supported by finding multiple significant differences between both groups, showing that considering the SoC for tailoring gamified, persuasive systems in the Physical Activity domain is important. Second, confirming previous findings [20,30], we found 16 out of 17 expected correlations between gamification elements and Hexad user types. Besides validating previous findings in the Physical Activity context, we contribute a set of new correlations, which were expected in previous works [15,30], but have not been shown. This might be due to using storyboards rather than textual descriptions as in [30] and because of using a concrete context rather than a general context, also as in [30], potentially leading to a more concrete idea of how the elements work. Additionally, we examined the "persuasiveness" of gamification elements, whereas past work by Tondello et al. [30] investigated "enjoyment". Third, by analyzing the effect of the SoC on the set of relevant gamification elements for each user type, we show that even though the user type itself may remain stable [30], the set of relevant gamification elements does not. This is important, as so far a static set of elements has been suggested for each user type [30], not taking into account the dynamic process of behavior change intentions [23]. However, our work has several limitations that should be considered. First, we used storyboards to assess the persuasiveness of each gamification element. Therefore, validating our findings using real implementations is an important next step. Second, even though we investigated atomic gamification elements, some aspects of the realization of these gamification elements are inherently a matter of interpretation, affecting the external validity of our results when implementing gamification elements differently. Third, it should be noted that combining gamification elements may create different experiences for the user, which should be analyzed in future work. Fourth, our participants reported to have experience in games, which should be considered. Last, we cannot say whether our findings generalize to different contexts besides Physical Activity. Therefore, further research should be conducted about the SoC as a factor for personalization in different contexts.

5 Conclusion and Future Work

We investigated the effect of behavior change intentions on the perception of gamification elements in the Physical Activity domain, both on their own as well as for each Hexad user type. We conducted an online study ($N = 179$) and replicated previous correlations between the Hexad model user types and gamification elements. This suggests the validity of previous results found in other domains [20] or in a general context [30]. Thus, we contribute a set of suitable gamification elements for each user type. Furthermore, we provide the first investigation of using behavior change intentions to personalize gamified, persuasive systems. As an overarching result, we show that the set of relevant gamification elements does not remain stable for each user type, but dynamically changes when behavior intentions change. This is important as, so far, a static set of gamification elements has been suggested for each user type [30]. In future work, gamification elements should be implemented to investigate in how far our findings are transferable to real implementations. Furthermore, our results suggest that investigating the effect of behavior change intentions in different contexts is worthwhile to consider in order to inform the design of persuasive systems.

References

1. Altmeyer, M., Lessel, P., Krüger, A.: Investigating gamification for seniors aged 75+. In: Proceedings of the 2018 Designing Interactive Systems Conference (DIS 2018), pp. 453–458. ACM (2018)
2. Birk, M.V., Friehs, M.A., Mandryk, R.L.: Age-based preferences and player experience: a crowdsourced cross-sectional study. In: Proceedings of the Annual Symposium on Computer-Human Interaction in Play - CHI PLAY 2017 (2017)
3. Böckle, M., Micheel, I., Bick, M.: A design framework for adaptive gamification applications. In: Proceedings of the 51st Hawaii International Conference on System Sciences (HICSS 2018), pp. 1227–1236 (2018)
4. Böckle, M., Novak, J., Bick, M.: Towards adaptive gamification: a synthesis of current developments. In: Proceedings of the 25th European Conference on Information Systems (ECIS 2017) (2017)
5. Deterding, S., Dixon, D.: From game design elements to gamefulness: defining gamification. In: Proceedings of the 15th International Academic MindTrek Conference, pp. 9–15. ACM (2011)
6. Drozd, F., Lehto, T., Oinas-Kukkonen, H.: Exploring perceived persuasiveness of a behavior change support system: a structural model. In: Bang, M., Ragnemalm, E.L. (eds.) PERSUASIVE 2012. LNCS, vol. 7284, pp. 157–168. Springer, Heidelberg (2012). https://doi.org/10.1007/978-3-642-31037-9_14
7. Fogg, B.J.: Persuasive Technology: Using Computers to Change What We Think and Do. Morgan Kaufmann Publishers, Burlington (2002)

8. Hamari, J., Koivisto, J., Pakkanen, T.: Do persuasive technologies persuade? - A review of empirical studies. In: Spagnolli, A., Chittaro, L., Gamberini, L. (eds.) PERSUASIVE 2014. LNCS, vol. 8462, pp. 118–136. Springer, Cham (2014). https://doi.org/10.1007/978-3-319-07127-5_11

9. Hamari, J., Sarsa, H.: Does gamification work? - A literature review of empirical studies on gamification. In: Hawaii International Conference on System Sciences, pp. 3025–3034 (2014)

10. Howell, D.: Statistical Methods For Psychology. Duxbury, Boston (2002)

11. Jia, Y., Xu, B., Karanam, Y., Voida, S.: Personality-targeted gamification: a survey study on personality traits and motivational affordances. In: Proceedings of the 2016 CHI Conference on Human Factors in Computing Systems - CHI 2016, pp. 2001–2013 (2016)

12. Kaptein, M., De Ruyter, B., Markopoulos, P., Aarts, E.: Adaptive persuasive systems. ACM Trans. Interact. Intell. Syst. 2(2), 1–25 (2012)

13. Lessel, P., Altmeyer, M., Müller, M., Wolff, C., Krüger, A.: Measuring the effect of "bottom-up" gamification in a microtask setting. In: Proceedings of the 21st International Academic Mindtrek Conference, pp. 63–72 (2017)

14. Marcus, B.H., et al.: Self-efficacy and the stages of exercise behavior Change. Res. Q. Exerc. Sport 63, 93–109 (2008)

15. Marczewski, A.: Even Ninja Monkeys Like to Play: Gamification. CreateSpace Independent Publishing Platform, Game Thinking and Motivational Design (2015)

16. Mchugh, M.L.: Interrater reliability: the kappa statistic. Biochemia Medica 22, 276–282 (2012)

17. Mullan, E., Markland, D.: Variations in self-determination across the stages of change for exercise in adults. Motiv. Emot. 21(4), 349–362 (1997)

18. Orji, R.: Exploring the persuasiveness of behavior change support strategies and possible gender differences. In: CEUR Workshop Proceedings, vol. 1153, pp. 41–57. BCSS (2014)

19. Orji, R., Nacke, L.E., Di Marco, C.: Towards personality-driven persuasive health games and gamified systems. In: Proceedings of the 2017 CHI Conference on Human Factors in Computing Systems - CHI 2017, pp. 1015–1027 (2017)

20. Orji, R., Tondello, G.F., Nacke, L.E.: Personalizing persuasive strategies in gameful systems to gamification user types. In: Proceedings of the SIGCHI Conference on Human Factors in Computing Systems - CHI 2018 (2018)

21. Orji, R., Vassileva, J., Mandryk, R.L.: Modeling the efficacy of persuasive strategies for different gamer types in serious games for health. User Model. User-Adapt. Interact. 24, 453–498 (2014)

22. Oyibo, K., Orji, R., Vassileva, J.: The influence of culture in the effect of age and gender on social influence in persuasive technology. In: Adjunct Publication of the 25th Conference on User Modeling, Adaptation and Personalization - UMAP 2017, pp. 47–52 (2017)

23. Prochaska, J.O., Velicer, W.F.: The transtheoretical change model of health behavior. Am. J. Health Promot. 12(1), 38–48 (1997)

24. Rajaratnam, S.M.W., Arendt, J.: Health in a 24-h society. Lancet 358, 999–1005 (2001)

25. Ryan, R.M., Deci, E.L.: Self-determination theory and the facilitation of intrinsic motivation, social development, and well-being. Am. Psychol. 55(1), 68–78 (2000)

26. Seaborn, K., Fels, D.: Gamification in theory and action: a survey. Int. J. Hum.Comput. Stud. 74, 14–31 (2015)

27. Tondello, G., Premsukh, H., Nacke, L.: A theory of gamification principles through goal-setting theory. In: Proceedings of the 51st Hawaii International Conference on System Sciences (HICSS), January 2018

28. Tondello, G.F., Mora, A., Marczewski, A., Nacke, L.E.: Empirical validation of the gamification user types hexad scale in English and Spanish. Int. J. Hum.-Comput. Stud. (2018)

29. Tondello, G.F., Mora, A., Nacke, L.E.: Elements of gameful design emerging from user preferences. In: Proceedings of the Annual Symposium on Computer-Human Interaction in Play - CHI PLAY 2017, pp. 129–142 (2017)

30. Tondello, G.F., Wehbe, R.R., Diamond, L., Busch, M., Marczewski, A., Nacke, L.E.: The gamification user types hexad scale. In: The ACM SIGCHI Annual Symposium on Computer-Human Interaction in Play (2016)

31. Truong, K.N., Hayes, G.R., Abowd, G.: Storyboarding: an empirical determination of best practices and effective guidelines. In: Proceedings of the 6th ACM Conference on Designing Interactive Systems, pp. 12–21. ACM (2006)

32. Walker, D.: Converting Kendall's Tau for correlational or meta-analytic analyses. J. Mod. Appl. Stat. Meth. 2(2), 525–530 (2003)

33. Xiao, J.J., O'Neill, B., Prochaska, J.M., Kerbel, C.M., Brennan, P., Bristow, B.J.: A consumer education programme based on the transtheoretical model of change. Int. J. Consum. Stud. 28(1), 55–65 (2004)

Engaging the Audience with Biased News: An Exploratory Study on Prejudice and Engagement

Alessandra G. Ciancone Chama, Merylin Monaro, Eugenio Piccoli,
Luciano Gamberini⬤, and Anna Spagnolli(⌧) ⬤

Department of General Psychology and HIT Research Centre,
University of Padova, Padua, Italy
anna.spagnolli@unipd.it

Abstract. The persuasiveness of a narrative is increased by the audience's engagement with it, which in turn depends on the extent to which its needs and goals are served by the narrative. This study considers whether indulging the audience's prejudice might be a way to serve their needs and increase engagement. Two different versions of a news videoclip, one neutral and one prejudiced, were displayed in a between-participants design (N = 44). The participants' familiarity with the topic and prejudice against it were measured, and their effect on the engagement with the two types of video was tested. The analysis shows an indifference for biased content, equally engaging than non-biased; they also show an effect of familiarity. These first results are relevant to the current debate about biased news and the potential manipulative role of personalized content recommendations.

Keywords: Engagement · Prejudice · News · Narrative persuasion

1 Introduction

Narratives describe the sequential connection between events. They are not only a natural format to organize and share information, explain new concepts, and provide justifications [3, 26]; but also one of a great persuasive power. Reporting events as sequential chains of cause and effect is one of the most renowned principle of persuasion [8]. DalCin et al. also suggest that the narrative format makes it more difficult to apply counterarguments [6]. Green and Brock found that the more participants reported to be transported into a story, the less false notes they found in it [14], regardless of whether the story was labeled as fact or fiction; it also activated story-consistent believes. According to Slater and Rouner, the engagement with a narrative makes the audience less aware of any hidden persuasive agenda [27].

Engagement is a multi-dimensional concept used to capture the experiential involvement with a media and its content [7]; it can be defined as a quality of the user experience characterized by the depth of the cognitive, temporal, behavioral, and affective investment in interacting with a digital system [21]. Among the factors that facilitate engagement in a narrative is the personal identification with it [6, 27]:

H. Oinas-Kukkonen et al. (Eds.): PERSUASIVE 2019, LNCS 11433, pp. 350–361, 2019.
https://doi.org/10.1007/978-3-030-17287-9_28

empathy with characters [4], prior knowledge or experience relevant to the theme of the story [13], a system of beliefs consistent with the media content selected. In the qualitative study carried out by O'Brien [19], at least seven interviewees out of 30 mentioned that a personal connection with the news makes them more engaging [19, 24]. A similar idea emerges from the study reported McCay and colleagues [18], who found that the participants' interest in the topic is a good predictor of their focused attention, more than the visual catchiness of the news presentation.

From the point of view of persuasion, this suggests that to make some piece of news more engaging (and then persuasive, according to [27]) one needs to facilitate the users' identification with it. This can be achieved by emphasizing topics that are close to the participant's personal sphere of interests (autobiographical familiarity); or by emphasizing aspects that are close to the users' beliefs and worldview (attitudinal closeness). Both strategies are at reach nowadays given the level of sophistication of the techniques to identify users' preferences and recommend content consequentially (e.g., [16, 17]). Within a larger project that aims at understanding users' response to biased content in the news, we report here an exploratory study in which we examine the effect of familiarity with the news topic and of holding a prejudice towards the news topic on the audience's engagement with news.

2 Study Method

The study consists of showing participants a video clip that reports a piece of news and then measuring their level of engagement with it. Neutral and prejudiced versions of the video are varied between participants. The participants' familiarity with the news topic and their prejudice against such topic are measured and related with the engagement level.

2.1 Video

In order to select the topic of the news, we carried out a preliminary small survey with participants similar to the ones involved in the main study, i.e., students enrolled in a university course at the University of Padova, mainly psychology. We were looking for a subject that was relevant to them, and that could be a target of prejudice for a part of them. We asked participants to (a) express their "level of concern" for a set of topics on a 5-point scale (1 = I am indifferent, 5 = I am very concerned); and (b) to provide up to three adjectives or words spontaneously associated with each topic. The first question gave us a rough idea of whether participants had a strong position about the topic, and the second was meant to collect terms that could be used in the video commentary. Since train transportation was one of the topics, we also asked participants if they were commuters or not. The questionnaire was administered in paper and pencil modality after signing an informed consent. 37 first-year psychology students (26 women) participated. Out of the five topics proposed (university tuitions, trains comfort and timeliness, animal testing in research, recycling efficiency at the campus, and male/female ratio in the students' population), we eventually selected trains comfort and timeliness, because for this topic most respondents avoided the middle value of the scale (8 respondents only out of 36) and 66.67% of the adjectives were negative (delays, crowded, expensive, dirty). We also noticed that being a commuter made concern more likely.

Following the lead provided by this short survey, we created a video about train service, in which new plans were announced fulfilling the needs of commuters in the region in which the data were collected. The video was created with Powtoon and comprised a sequence of images related to train transportation, an audio commentary and over-layered graphics (Fig. 1). Images of commuters and railway transportation were taken from the Internet. Audacity was used for sound editing. To obtain the two versions of the video, slight changes in the audio commentary were made to either exclude or include a few sentences betraying a strong prejudice against train transportation. For instance, the neutral sentence "I spend four hours a day on public transportation, so I value the quality of the services to commuters" became "I spend four hours a day on public transportation. Unluckily, I waste both time and money due to several disservices". Overall, each version of the video lasted about 2 min.

Fig. 1. Screenshots from the video used in the study (left) and from the IAT task (right).

2.2   Data Collection Tools

User Engagement scale. The most robust measure for engagement is the UES (User Engagement Scale). It has been used to test user engagement in a variety of digital domains including news [20, 22]. We used the version validated by O'Brien, Cairns and Hall [23] and covering four constructs. Despite the names of the constructs, which seem somehow restrictive in scope, the items are able to cover a large part of the user engagement experience: Focused Attention (FA) measures the extent to which the user feels immersed in the content (e.g. "I lost myself in this experience"), Perceived Usability (PU) measures the ease with which the content was experienced (e.g., "This experience was demanding."), Aesthetics (AE) measures the aesthetic pleasantness of the experience (e.g. "This application was aesthetically appealing") and Reward (RW) measures how satisfactory the experience was (e.g. "Using the application was worthwhile" or "This experience was fun"). Answers were collected on a Likert scale ranging from 1 to 5 (1 = strongly disagree). In order to employ this scale, certain wordings had to be modified to reflect the medium used in our study (for example "video" and "watching" replaced "application" and "using"). The scale was then translated to Italian following the Translation-Back translation method [2]: three different Italian native speakers with high knowledge of English translated the original scale to Italian separately; then they met to solve any discrepancy between their individual versions. A bilingual Italian and English speaker, who was not involved in the forward translation and had no knowledge in human-computer interaction or user engagement, translated the resulting version back to English. The discrepancy with the original UES scale were examined by the research team and adjusted to produce the final version, reported in Appendix 1. All translators were asked to choose the simplest and most straightforward translation, and to avoid the use of local or colloquial terminology.

Familiarity with Public Transportation and Other Self-reported Measures. Participants' familiarity with public transportation was checked with a set of items collected at the end of the session (Appendix 1). A few additional items checked that some inclusion criteria were met, i.e., that participant's mother tongue was Italian and that there was no left hand preference. Participants' age, and type of academic course in which they were enrolled were also collected.

Prejudice. An Implicit Association Test (IAT) was used to detect the presence of prejudice against public transportation. The IAT consists of presenting one stimulus at a time on a computer screen along with two labels (Fig. 1, right), which are positioned on the top-left and on the top-right areas of the screen [15]. The participant is asked to pick as quickly as possible the correct label to categorize each stimulus, for instance 'transportation' to categorize the image of a train, or 'pleasant' to categorize the word 'beautiful' (Table 1). The label is picked by clicking on it with the mouse, following Freeman and Ambady [9]. The central part of the IAT consists of two combined blocks of trials (block 3 and 5 in Table 1), where target and attributes are both used alternatively as stimuli, so that the same part of the screen can be occupied by labels referring to the target (transportation or food) and by labels referring to the attributes (positive or negative). When the participant needs to pick the attribute positioned in the same space of the screen as the target, the task performance is hampered if the attribute and target are competing and dissonant categories in the experience of the participant. For instance if "trains" and "smart" share the same button, and the participant has a negative prejudice against trains, the clicking behavior is slower [9]. As an alternative category to public transportation for the discrimination tasks we chose food; for the attributes, we had a set of positive ones (good, smart, beautiful, wonderful, pleasant) and of negative ones (bad, ugly, rude, horrible, annoying) fitting both types of target, i.e. transportation and food. The fourth and fifth blocks were displayed before or after the second and third, to counterbalance the order of tasks.

Table 1. The structure of the IAT tasks

	1st block		2nd block		3rd block		4th block		5th block	
Goal	Target discrimination		Attribute discrimination		First combined task		Reverse attribute discrimination		Reverse combined	
Labels	Left	Right	Left	Right	Left	Right	Left	Right	Left	Right
	Transportation	Food	Positive	Negative	Transportation/ Positive	Food/ Negative	Negative	Positive	Transportation/ Negative	Food/ Positive
Stimuli	Picture		Text		Picture or Text		Text		Picture or Text	
Trials	20		20		40		40		40	

2.3 Data Collection and Analysis

Procedure. The video and the questionnaire were displayed via OpenSesame v.3.2.5, while the IAT interface was provided by MouseTracker v.2.84 [9]. In both cases the participant could proceed autonomously from task to task by reading the instructions on the screen. At the time appointed for the data collection session, the participant was welcome, and was asked to read the information note about the study. After signing the consent to participate, the participant was randomly assigned to either the neutral video condition or the prejudiced video condition and the session started; the participant was instructed on the way to start the task and recommended to carefully read the instructions on the screen. The participant was left alone in the room and asked to call the researcher after the end of the IAT part in order to switch interface. The whole session lasted about 30 min. The response time (RT) in the compatible and incompatible blocks of the IAT was collected by MouseTracker in a log file, while the answers to the questionnaire were collected in a csv file via GoogleForm.

Data Preparation. To identify prejudice, the D index was calculated. The mean Response Time recorded during the incompatible block (the block associating transport and unpleasant attributes) was subtracted from the mean Response Time recorded during the compatible block (the block associating transport and pleasant attributes); this difference was then divided by the inclusive standard deviation of the two blocks [15]. Participants having negative D values ($D < -0.2$) are considered as holding a negative prejudice. The general UE score and the score of each UE subscale were also calculated, after reversing the score of items PU1, PU2, PU3, PU4, PU5, PU6, PU8, and RW3. An additional preparatory work consisted of recoding the willingness to watch longer (30 s = 1, 1 min = 2, 2 min = 3, 3 min = 4, 4 min = 5, Longer than 4 min = 6), and the frequency of using transportation (daily = 1, some times a week = 2, a few times a month = 3, never = 4).

Research Questions. The study is exploratory, and investigates the effect of familiarity, exposition to prejudiced content and holding a prejudice on the engagement with the news content. By engagement we mean: (a) the overall UE score; (b) the scores of all UE subscales (FA; PU; AE; RW); and (c) the willingness to watch the video longer. All statistics were run using R software version 3.3.3.

2.4   Ethics

During recruitment the study goal was described, generically, as assessing the audience reaction to multimedia content. Two consents were asked, one for participating in the study and one, after debriefing, to obtain permission to use the data collected; the participant kept a copy of each. A disclaimer was given at the end of the data collection session that all content in the video was fabricated for the sake of the study and the news was then not actually true. All data was pseudonymized and the file with the participants' identity was destructed four weeks after completing the data collection. No physical or psychological wellbeing was compromised by the procedure. No monetary or other compensation was offered. Common content was used for pictures and licensed software for programming (free or test).

2.5   Participants

Recruitment took place at the university campus as well as via dedicated social media platforms. Mandatory recruitment criteria were being an Italian native speaker (due to the categorization task with Italian words) and right-handed (to simplify mouse movement analysis); fulfillment of such criteria was checked during recruitment as well as via dedicated questionnaire items (Appendix 1). 56 participants completed the study; 12 participants were excluded from the analysis being left-handed or having incomplete data for some technical issue, thus leaving a total sample of 44 participants (29 women and 15 men, aged 25 years on average, SD = 2.29). They were mostly right-handed (93.18%), except for three participants who were ambidextrous. Most of them were enrolled in a psychology course (86.36%) and the remaining ones in other university courses. No one participated in the preliminary study.

3   Results

3.1   Overall Results

Regarding the video content, the scores expressing the engagement with it were overall positioned on the middle value of the scale (M = 3.18, SD = 0.50); higher values were observed in the items referring to one construct, PU (M = 4.11, SD = 0.56), which measured the ease with which the video was experienced (Fig. 2). The willingness to keep on watching the video longer after the end of the session was on average 2.6 min (SD = 1.37), which was not the shortest possible option and which was longer than the duration of the video itself.

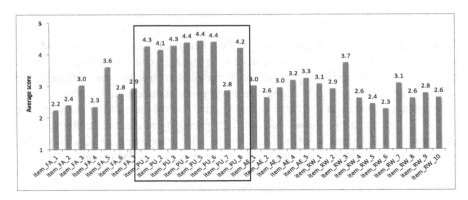

Fig. 2. The average scores achieved in all items of the user engagement scale

A negative prejudice against train transportation (D < −0.2) was found in more than a half of the sample, i.e. in 63.64% of the participants. Since 54% of them declared to use public transportation daily/a few times a week, and 77% declared to use trains at least a few times a month, we assumed that participants' prejudice might somehow be related to their personal experience. To examine whether this was the case, a Wilcoxon rank sum test with continuity correction was run to test the relation between the declared frequency of using public transportation and the presence of negative prejudice against it, returning a result close to statistic significance, W = 151, p = 0.06. Similarly, a significantly higher frequency of prejudice in heavy train users was found after running a Wilcoxon rank sum test, W = 92.5, p = .021 (Fig. 3); the 83.33% of the train commuters have shown a negative prejudice against train transportation (D < −0.2) versus only the 50% of participants who do not use the train. This suggests that, in our sample, the personal experience with trains tends to be accompanied by negative prejudice; however, negative prejudice are hold also by participants who do not use the train, reflecting a pervasive cultural stereotype.

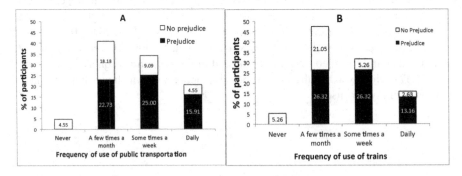

Fig. 3. The presence of prejudice among participants divided according to the frequency of use of public transportation in general (A, left) and of trains (B, right).

3.2 Factors Affecting User Engagement

We measured the relation between *familiarity* (the frequency of use of public transportation) with the overall UE score and the score of its sub-constructs with a Pearson correlation (overall UE score $r = .103$, $p = .507$; single constructs scores: FA $r = -.070$, $p = .653$; PU $r = .233$, $p = .127$; AE $r = -.091$, $p = .555$; RW $r = .181$, $p = .239$). We also measured the correlation between the frequency of using trains with the overall UE score and its sub-constructs (overall UE score $r = .065$, $p = .697$; single constructs scores: FA $r = -.110$, $p = .512$; PU $r = .246$, $p = .137$; AE $r = -.104$, $p = .535$; RW $r = .127$, $p = .449$). In this way we considered the effect of having a direct experience of public transportation on the engagement with the video and the willingness to watch it longer. According to the results reported above, no significant effect was found.

Regarding the effect of *holding a prejudice* against public transportation, we compared with a t-test the UE overall score, as well as the score of each UE subscale, in participants holding a negative prejudice vs. participants holding no prejudice. No significant difference was found (overall UE score $t = .347$, $p = .730$; single constructs scores: FA $t = .141$, $p = .888$; PU $t = 1.253$, $p = .219$; AE $t = .418$, $p = .678$; RW $t = -.476$, $p = .637$). The willingness of these two groups to watch the video longer was then compared with a Wilcoxon rank sum test, returning no significant difference, $W = 199$, $p = .536$.

Then we checked the effect of *prejudiced content* compared with neutral content on the same variables. Again, no difference was found (overall UE score $t = .186$, $p = .853$; single constructs scores: FA $t = .227$, $p = .821$; PU $t = 1.378$, $p = .176$; AE $t = -.038$, $p = .970$; RW $t = -.628$, $p = .537$). With a Wilcoxon rank sum test we also tested the difference between these two groups in the willingness to watch the video longer, and found no effect, $W = 265$, $p = .576$.

Finally, we focused on one subconstruct of UE that seemed more sensitive, PU. A multiple linear regression was calculated to predict the engagement subconstruct called PU based on two factors, the frequency of using public transportation (familiarity) and the presence of a prejudice against public transportation; the regression equation was not significant, $(F2,35) = 2.93$, $p = .067$ with an R^2 of .094. If the factors were considered separately, however, the *frequency of public transportation resulted to be a significant predictor of PU*, $t = 2.148$ $p = .038$, while prejudice was not significant, $t = -1.84$ $p = .074$. Also, if train commuters were split into groups, commuters versus non commuters, and a regression was run with train commuter and holding a prejudice as factors a not significant regression equation was found, $(F2,35) = 2.73$, $p = .079$ with an R^2 of .085. But the effect of *train commuters on PU was significant*, $t = 2.056$, $p = .047$, while prejudice was not significant $t = -1.76$, $p = .087$. The correlation with the willingness to watch the video longer tested with Spearman's rank correlation for the frequency of using public transportation (rho $= .088$, $p = .571$), and with Wilcoxon rank sum test for the difference between train commuters and non commuters ($W = 136.5$, $p = .196$) was not significant.

4 Conclusions

The analysis showed that both types of video, neutral or prejudiced, were received with great ease, and participants were willing to keep watching them. In other words, the presence of biased content in the video did not affect the engagement with it, which was no higher but also no lower than with the neutral video. Even participants who were void of any prejudice against public transportation did not seem disturbed by watching biased content. Of the two factors considered here, holding a prejudice or having personal familiarity with public transportation, only the latter affected engagement. This is consistent with the theory of narrative persuasion [27], according to which engagement increases if the narrative serves personal goals: prejudice might be of cultural origin and not derive from personal experience. In the future, we will try and see if these results are confirmed even if the difference between biased and prejudiced video is enhanced by including prejudice in the visual content and by using neutral and prejudiced topic. We will also see if engagement and credibility are affected differently.

The results of this first exploratory study allow to make some initial remarks about the persuasive power of narratives. First, users might feel engaged with news content just because it seems close to their own experience; the occurrence of this phenomenon is exacerbated by the pervasiveness of technological solutions that recommend on-line content based on past navigation history and preferences. This might lead in turn to the false impression that one's worldview and life experience is shared by many; or can accentuate that natural tendency to find confirmation for our own beliefs. The second remark regards users' seeming lack of awareness of the extent to which news can be biased and prejudiced; if participants, regardless of their position on a given topic, were not annoyed by content that is prejudiced, what would be the threshold they are willing to reach before eventually discarding a source as not credible? Persuasive interventions that have the goal of increasing users' awareness of narrative persuasiveness would be much beneficial, accompanied by regulatory provisions and safeguards against diffusion of forged news.

Acknowledgments. We thank Roberto Barattini for having recorded his voice as a narrator in the video.

Appendix 1. Questionnaire

Constructs	Items
1 UE-FA	I lost myself in the narrative (*Mi sono perso/a nel racconto*)
2 UE-FA	I was so involved in the narrative that I lost track of time (*Ero cosi coinvolto/a nel racconto che ho perso la concezione del tempo*)
3 UE-FA	I blocked out things around me when I was watching the video (*Mentre guardavo il video mi sono isolato/a da ciò che mi circondava*)

(*continued*)

Constructs	Items
4 UE-FA	When I was watching the video, I lost track of the world around me. (*Quando stavo guardando il video, ho perso la concezione del mondo intorno a me*)
5 UE-FA	The time I spent watching the video just slipped away. (*Il tempo speso a guardare il video è passato velocemente*)
6 UE-FA	I was absorbed in the narrative. (*Ero immerso/a nel racconto*)
7 UE-FA	During the narrative I let myself go. (*Durante il racconto mi sono lasciato/a andare*)
1 UE-PU	I felt frustrated while I watched this video. (*Mi sono sentito/a frustrato/a mentre guardavo questo video*)
2 UE-PU	I found the video confusing to watch. (*Ho trovato questo video disorientante da guardare*)
3 UE-PU	I felt annoyed while I was watching the video. (*Mi sono sentito/a infastidito/a mentre guardavo il video*)
4 UE-PU	I felt discouraged while I was watching this video. (*Mi sono sentito/a scoraggiato/a mentre guardavo questo video*)
5 UE-PU	Watching this video was mentally taxing (*Vedere questo video è stato mentalmente difficile*)
6 UE-PU	The narrative was demanding. (*Il racconto è stato impegnativo*)
7 UE-PU	I felt in control while I was watching the video. (*Mi sono sentito/a in controllo mentre guardavo questo video*)
8 UE-PU	I could not do some of the things I needed to do while I was watching the video. (*Non ho potuto fare alcune delle cose che dovevo fare mentre guardavo il video*)
1 UE-AE	This video was attractive (*Questo video era piacevole*)
2 UE-AE	This video was aesthetically appealing (*Questo video era esteticamente accattivante*)
3 UE-AE	I liked the graphics and images in the video. (*Mi sono piaciute la grafica e le immagini del video*)
4 UE-AE	The video appealed to be visual senses. (*Il video ha attratto i miei sensi visivi*)
5 UE-AE	The screen layout of the video was visually pleasing. (*Il layout dello schermo del video era visualmente piacevole*)
1 UE-RW	Watching the video was worthwhile (*È valsa la pena guardare il video*)
2 UE-RW	I consider this experience a success. (*Considero questa esperienza un successo*)
3 UE-RW	This experience did not work out the way I had planned. (*Questa esperienza non ha funzionato come avevo pianificato*)
4 UE-RW	This experience was rewarding. (*Questa esperienza è stata gratificante*)
5 UE-RW	I would recommend the video to my family and friends (*Raccomanderei il video alla mia famiglia e ai miei amici*)
6 UE-RW	I would continue to watch the video out of curiosity. (*Riguarderei questo video per curiosità*)

(continued)

Constructs	Items
7 UE-RW	The content of the video incited my curiosity. (*Il contenuto del video ha stimolato la mia curiosità*)
8 UE-RW	I was really drawn into the narrative. (*Sono stato/a veramente attratto/a dalla narrazione*)
9 UE-RW	I felt involved in the narrative. (*Mi sono sentito/a coinvolto/a dalla narrazione*)
10 UE-RW	This experience was fun. (*Questa esperienza è stata divertente*)
1 Willingness to watch longer	How longer would you keep watching the video without getting bored (*Quanto più a lungo avresti guardato il video senza annoiarti?*) RESPONSE OPTIONS: 30 s/1 min/2 min/3 min/4 min/Longer than 4 min
2 Background	How old are you (*Quanti anni hai?*)
3 Background	In what university course are you enrolled? (*A quale corso universitario sei iscritto?*)
4 Inclusion criterion	What is your mother tongue? (*Qual è la tua lingua madre?*) RESPONSE OPTIONS: Italian/Other
5 Familiarity	Are you a commuter (*Sei pendolare?*) RESPONSE OPTIONS: yes/no
6 Familiarity	How often do you use public transportation? (*Quanto spesso usi i trasporti pubblici?*) RESPONSE OPTIONS: daily/some times a week/a few times a month/never
7 Familiarity	Which public transportation means do you use more often? (*Quali mezzi di trasporto pubblico usi più spesso?*) RESPONSE OPTIONS: train, bus, tram, other (specify)
8 Inclusion criterion	What is you hand preference? (*Sei mancino o destrimane?*) RESPONSE OPTIONS: righthanded, lefthanded, ambidextrous
9 Familiarity	Have you ever been a commuter in the past? If you did, which transportation means did you use? (*Sei mai stato un pendolare regolare in passato? Se sì, con che mezzo?*) RESPONSE SCALE: Bus; train; car (you can select more than one)

References

1. Appel, M.: Fictional narratives cultivate just-world beliefs. J. Commun. **58**(1), 62–83 (2008)
2. Behling, O., Law, K.S.: Translating Questionnaires and Other Research Instruments: Problems and Solutions, vol. 133. Sage, Thousand Oaks (2000)
3. Bruner, J.S.: Actual Minds. Possible Worlds. Harvard University Press, Cambridge (2009)
4. Busselle, R., Bilandzic, H.: Measuring narrative engagement. Media Psychol. **12**(4), 321–347 (2009)
5. Cassidy, B.S., Sprout, G.T., Freeman, J.B., Krendl, A.C.: Looking the part (to me): effects of racial prototypicaly on race perception vary by prejudice. Soc. Cogn. Affect. Neurosci. **12**(4), 685–694 (2017)
6. Dal Cin, S., Zanna, M.P., Fong, G.T.: Narrative persuasion and overcoming resistance. In: Knowles, E.S., Linn, J.A. (eds.) Resistance and Persuasion, pp. 175–191. Erlbaum, London (2004)

7. Doherty, K., Doherty, G.: Engagement in HCI: conception, theory and measurement. ACM Comput. Surv. **51**(5), 99 (2018)
8. Fogg, B.J.: Persuasive Technology: Using Computers to Change What We Think and Do. Morgan Kaufmann, San Francisco (2003)
9. Freeman, J.B., Ambady, N.: Motions of the hand expose the partial and parallel activation of stereotypes. Psychol. Sci. **20**(10), 1183–1188 (2009)
10. Freeman, J.B., Ambady, N.: MouseTracker. Behav. Res. Methods **42**, 226–241 (2010)
11. Freeman, J.B., Pauker, K., Apfelbaum, E.P., Ambady, N.: Continuous dynamics in the real-time perception of race. JESP **46**, 179–185 (2010)
12. Freeman, J.B., Pauker, K., Sanchez, D.T.: A perceptual pathway to bias: interracial exposure reduces abrupt shifts in real-time race perception that predict mixed-race bias. Psychol. Sci. **27**(4), 502–517 (2016)
13. Green, M.C.: Transportation into narrative worlds: the role of prior knowledge and perceived realism. Discourse Process. **38**(2), 247–266 (2004)
14. Green, M.C., Brock, T.C.: The role of transportation in the persuasiveness of public narratives. JPSP **79**(5), 701 (2000)
15. Greenwald, A.G., Nosek, B.A., Banaji, M.R.: Understanding and using the implicit association test: I. An improved scoring algorithm. J. Pers. Soc. Psychol. **85**, 197–216 (2003)
16. Lavie, T., Sela, M., Oppenheim, I., Inbar, O., Meyer, J.: User attitudes towards news content personalization. IJHCS **68**(8), 483–495 (2010)
17. Masthoff, J.: Group recommender systems: combining individual models. In: Ricci, F., Rokach, L., Shapira, B., Kantor, P.B. (eds.) Recommender Systems Handbook, pp. 677–702. Springer, Boston, MA (2011). https://doi.org/10.1007/978-0-387-85820-3_21
18. McCay-Peet, L., Lalmas, M., Navalpakkam, V.: On saliency, affect and focused attention. In: Proceedings of the SIGCHI Conference on Human Factors in Computing Systems, pp. 541–550. ACM, New York (2012)
19. O'Brien, H.L.: Exploring user engagement in online news interactions. Proc. Am. Soc. Inf. Sci. Technol. **48**(1), 1–10 (2011)
20. O'Brien, H.L.: The role of story and media in user engagement with online news. In: Proceedings of the 41st Canadian Association for Information Science Conference, Victoria, British Columbia (2013)
21. O'Brien, H.: Theoretical perspectives on user engagement. In: O'Brien, H., Cairns, P. (eds.) Why Engagement Matters, pp. 1–26. Springer, Cham (2016). https://doi.org/10.1007/978-3-319-27446-1_1
22. O'Brien, H.L., Cairns, P.: An empirical evaluation of the user engagement scale (UES) in online news environments. IPM **51**, 413–427 (2015)
23. O'Brien, H.L., Cairns, P., Hall, M.: A practical approach to measuring user engagement with the refined user engagement scale (UES) and new UES short form. IJHCS **112**, 28–39 (2018)
24. O'Brien, H.L., McKay, J.: What makes online news interesting? Personal and situational interest and the effect on behavioral intentions. In: Proceedings of the ASIST Conference, Copenhagen, Denmark, 15–19 October 2016, 6 p. (2016)
25. O'Brien, H.L., Toms, K.K., Kelley, E.: The development and evaluation of a survey to measure user engagement. JASIST **61**(1), 50–69 (2010)
26. Ochs, E., Capps, L.: Living Narrative: Creating Lives in Everyday Storytelling. Harvard University Press, Cambridge (2009)
27. Slater, M.D., Rouner, D.: Entertainment-education and elaboration likelihood: understanding the processing of narrative persuasion. Commun. Theory **12**(2), 173–191 (2002)

Persuasive Technology, Social Representations and Ergonomics of Interfaces: A New Theoretical Articulation

Mathilde Barbier[1]([✉]), Ladislav Moták[2], Camille De Gasquet[2],
Fabien Girandola[1], Nathalie Bonnardel[2], and Grégory Lo Monaco[1]

[1] LPS, Aix-Marseille University, Aix-en-Provence, France
mathilde.barbier@univ-amu.fr
[2] PsyCLE, Aix-Marseille University, Aix-en-Provence, France

Abstract. This paper addresses the possibility to build on the success of digital development in order to design messages that will be seen by individuals as being the most relevant to the object being addressed. By studying the social representations status as well as ergonomic features of interfaces like the information elements' location and the color of background, we tried to determine whether persuasive technology can be a particularly effective medium to achieve favorable attitudes and behaviors towards organ donation. We recorded participants' ocular activity and administered them a self-reported measures questionnaire. Results show several significant effects, particularly on attitudes, intentions and behaviors. We demonstrate that to increase the persuasive impact of a message, it is better to mobilize central elements of the social representations of the object being treated and to place these elements in the middle of the screen. The blue background screen did not show the expected effects. However, regarding to the interaction between social representations' status and background's color, it seems that white is more appropriate than blue for technological persuasion. In the end, this research contributes to propose optimization tracks for public communication though technologies, for example in fields of health, commerce, education, environment, professional efficiency or social media marketing.

Keywords: Persuasive technology · Social representations ·
Ergonomics of interfaces · Behavior change · Organ donation

1 Introduction

Responses provided by users to computers follow the same characteristics in terms of emotions [40] and persuasion [38] as what can be observed in human-human interactions.

In this paper, we argue that, building on psychosocial concepts and combining them with design features for human-media interactions (HMIs), we could propose a better approach of the user's psychology.

The present study intends to rely on the fields of technological persuasion, social representations (SR) and ergonomics of interfaces in order to deliver the messages that

© Springer Nature Switzerland AG 2019
H. Oinas-Kukkonen et al. (Eds.): PERSUASIVE 2019, LNCS 11433, pp. 362–373, 2019.
https://doi.org/10.1007/978-3-030-17287-9_29

are most suitable for individuals in relation to the object being addressed. Our ultimate purpose is to investigate the effects of technological persuasion on changes in attitudes and behaviors, specifically regarding to organ donation.

In the following, we will discuss the interconnection between SRs and socio-cognitive process [6, 22]. Although works have shown that articulating the SR's status with commitment procedures and binding communication is particularly efficient to subsequently obtain attitudes' and behaviors' changes [15, 41], to our knowledge, no studies have yet explored the articulation between the theory of SRs and the field of technological persuasion.

Associating the salience's power of the central elements of the representations with ergonomic features would suggest us new ways for understanding technological persuasion implications.

2 Persuasion: A Dialogic Communicative Process

Persuasion can be summed up as transmitting a message from a source to a target with the aim to modify the attitudes and possibly the behaviors of this target [4].

Although we can think that they are independent parts, source and target might necessarily be engaged in an interactive process and transformed in and through communication and social thought [24]. Therefore, persuasion goes beyond the simple level of a content's diffusion. The dialogism of this communication involves multi-dimensional aspects and multiple purposes, reminding us of the mechanisms involved in HMIs.

Just as persuasive communication designs the strategies that are most suited to the objectives pursued, the systems contain tasks that each respond to specific goals. Consequently, it appears particularly appropriate to bring together what happens in the dialogical process of persuasive communication with that happens in human-machine interactions. The systems functioning is thus, very well-articulated with the fields of interpersonal communication and influence, and it can be related to research on decision-making in interaction [10].

Consequently, exposing users to elements that are supposed to be the most cognitively salient to them can be particularly relevant to enhance the persuasive impact [9].

In this paper, we refer to the theoretical field of SRs as a key to understand the ways in which individuals and groups communicate and behave (see [27]).

The content constituting SRs is structured in a dual system of 'central' and 'peripheral' elements [1, 26]. Central elements can be defined as a stable set of cognitions produced and shared by the individuals of the same group about the same object [1, 26, 33]. They have the particularity of being meaning markers. On their part, peripheral elements constitute the individualized part of the SR and thus, support the heterogeneity of the group [1, 26, 33]. They have the particularity of being context-sensitive [23, 35].

Because of their consensual and stable character, central cognitions could particularly appropriate to fulfill the epistemic function of the SRs [7]. They effectively make possible to provide the individual with a predictable and controllable vision of the world.

Maintaining that central cognitions contain more necessary and salient content than the peripheral [17], we can deduce that the individual will focus more closely her attention on the central elements compared to the peripheral when she is exposed to them. Therefore, individuals should be more motivated to process information containing central elements of the SR than peripheral leading them to further borrow a "central" processing of the information in line with the Elaboration Likelihood Model (ELM) [31, 34].

According to the ELM model, the strength in which a message is received by the target (i.e., as relevant, convincing) depends on the elaboration initiated by this target relating to the message's content.

Two ways of information processing are possible. About the first way (the "central route"), the individual is sufficiently motivated or able to treat the information, leading her to an attentive examination of the content. Thus, this way should lead to the production of positive cognitive thoughts and validation of these, allowing more attitudes' changes and expression of more attitudes' certainty [30, 32]. Interestingly, attitude strength makes more possible to predict the subsequent behavior [40].·

Regarding to the second way ("the peripheral route"), the individual engages in a superficial treatment. She uses heuristics allowing some cognitive economy and she focuses her attention on external conditions such as the source's credibility or the felt sympathy towards this source.

As we have seen above, it may be particularly interesting to operate on the cognitive salience of the message's content (by playing on the status of SR, for example). To facilitate the achievement of the objectives pursued in a context of persuasive technologies, it is also possible to work upon the ergonomic criteria.

3 Facilitating Decision-Making by Using Ergonomic Criteria

Digital interfaces reveal effective communication skills when it comes to influencing and persuading in a decision-making task involving HMIs [18, 37].

Although the final decision remains to the user, this one may need interfaces to guide her through information processing, in order to achieve the pursued behavior in a cognitively cost-effective manner. Working on the interfaces' architecture could overcome the limits of processing capacity. In this vein, we can wonder if designing aesthetic, satisfying and user-relevant digital interfaces could track the goal of reducing the individual's cognitive load during a decision-making process [36].

Several studies insist on the need to work on the "emotional design" [29] and on the user's feelings during human-computer interaction [21]. For example, works show that website design leads to a formation of positive consumer opinions [25].

The color of websites could be particularly useful in context of persuasive technologies. Thus, internet users express more preference with cooler colors such as blue [5]. From a cognitive point of view, mobilizing color can particularly draw attention based on this feature.

The location can be an additionally interesting way since it is possible to observe some constants in the way people approach a screen. Figure 1 shows as percentages, the proportion of Internet users who have traveled at least once in one of the designated areas when looking at a web page [28].

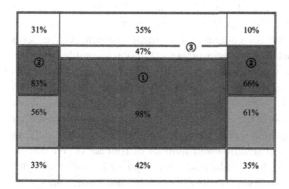

Fig. 1. Percentage of Internet users who have looked at the indicated area at least once (schema reproduced from [28], p. 33).

Figure 1 informs that it is better to place a message at the top and the middle of a page to maximize its visibility. Zones numbered 1, 2 and 3 (i.e., the "middle" of the screen) appear to be the most privileged location to broadcast a message with persuasive aims. Likewise, zones at 33%, 31% and 10% of visualization can be defined as the least viewed and named "the sides" of the screen.

Placing elements in locations that are spontaneously the first to be viewed will allow direct attention to the content of the information [20]. Given the mechanisms of selective attention, we are able to consider that a first element placed in the middle of a screen would function as an "information gateway". Indeed, this first element would invite attentional allocation in the central field, circumscribed and close to it. In doing so, design can help reduce cognitive workload by facilitating the processing of important data [11]. It should reduce compensation costs and improve performances.

4 Objectives and Hypotheses

This study aimed at analyzing the impact of a combination of ergonomics features about the interface (i.e., 'Location' and 'Color') with the SR of the participant about the object being addressed, particularly manipulating the 'Status'. In a specific way, we hoped to contribute enhancing the persuasive technologies outcomes.

For the variable Location, we expected that participants will focus more attention on elements placed in the middle of the screen than on the sides, in terms of number of fixations, fixation duration and number of rollbacks. Additionally, we expected that participants report more favorable attitudes towards organ donation, more attitudes' certainty, more willingness to become organ donors and finally, we expected that they will more perform this behavior when they were exposed to elements placed in the middle than on the sides.

For the variable Status, we expected that participants will focus more attention on the central elements of the SR than on the peripheral ones (i.e., number of fixations, fixation duration and number of rollbacks). We expected that participants exposed to central elements of the SR would take the "central route" in processing information. Also, we expected that participants will better memorize elements referring to the central status of the SR compared to elements referring to the peripheral one. In the end, we expected that participants report more favorable attitudes, more attitudes' certainty; declare more willingness to become organ donors and finally, we expected that they will more perform this behavior when they were exposed to central elements than to peripheral.

For the variable Color, we expected that participants focus more attention exposed with a blue background screen compared to a white one (especially, in terms of number of fixations, fixation duration and number of rollbacks). We also expected that participants express higher satisfaction when exposed to a blue background screen than a white one. For this reason, we finally expected that participants report more favorable attitudes towards organ donation, more attitudes' certainty, more willingness to become organ donors and finally, we expected that they will more perform this behavior when they were exposed to a blue layout than to a white one.

Also, we expected interaction effects of our three independent variables on attitudes, strength of attitudes, and behaviors.

5   Method

5.1   Preliminary Step

A previous study made possible to collect the content and the structure of the SRs. This previous study solicited the same population as in the main study. However, there were two separate samples.

Participants were asked to associate the four words or expressions that came to mind when we said to them "organ donation" [39]. Then, participants had to rank these words or expressions from 1 to 4 (i.e., from the most important word, according to them related to organ donation, to the least important). Crossing frequency and importance-rank of occurrences, a prototypical analysis provided centrality assumptions. To ensure verification of these assumptions, we performed a test of context independence [23].

Items included in their formulation the salient themes regarding to the prototypical analysis and were formulated on the following pattern: "In your opinion, is organ donation always, in any case, an act of generosity?". Participants had to situate their opinion among 4 propositions: "1 = definitely no, 2 = rather no, 3 = rather yes, 4 = definitely yes". A percentage of centrality of each element was obtained calculating the percentage of "rather yes" and "yes". Finally, the decisional threshold for defining centrality was calculated using a Kolmogorov-Smirnov table. Results provided: "help", "save lives" and "good deed" as being central elements of the SR of organ donation; and "generosity", "illness", and "evidence" as being peripheral elements.

5.2 Main study

5.2.1 Participants

Two hundred forty undergraduates people participate to the study (218 females, Mage = 19.27 yrs, SD = 1.68). All participants were students enrolled in the first year of psychology and receiving course credit for their participation. None of them was informed of the experiment purpose before performing it.

5.2.2 Procedure and Materials

For all participants, we gathered their attitude towards organ donation before exposure to the message, asking them how much they supported organ donation on a scale of 0 to 10.

Then, each participant was randomly assigned to one of the experimental conditions. There were 8 experimental conditions crossing the three independent variables with two modalities each: Location (in the center of the screen or on the sides), Status (elements referring to the central or peripheral status of the SR), Color (with a blue or a white background screen).

The participant installed herself in front of a computer and was exposed to the stimuli. The slide lasted seven seconds and introduced participants to one of the eight conditions.

Eye paths were recorded using the Tobii Studio®. For each participant, we were interested in (1) the total number of fixings; (2) the total visual time spent; and (3) the number of rollbacks performed on a same element during the exposure.

After being exposed to the message, participants were invited to answer an online questionnaire. This, first included a measure of satisfaction with the slide previously presented, rating on a scale of 0 to 10.

Then, the participants' cognitive thoughts and individual validation of these thoughts were collected [30, 32]. It consisted in asking them to write down all the thoughts that came to mind as watching the message; and by asking them to assign a valence for each of these thoughts (i.e., 'zero', 'plus' or 'minus' if their thoughts were 'neutral', 'favorable' or 'unfavorable' to them). The validation consisted in asking participants how much they were confident about their thoughts on a scale of 0 to 10.

We collected a measurement of explicit attitude, "At this time, on a scale of 0 to 10, how would you rate your support for organ donation?"; and just after measures of the attitude's strength (i.e., importance and certainty) [40].

We collected a behavioral intention measurement [2] about declaring as an organ donor on 0 to 10.

Last measures concerned free recall of the words as well as collection of the socio-demographic data.

Once the questionnaire was completed, we proposed to each participant to take a sticker on which was displayed the comment "I am an organ-donor" and to stick it on her phone.

6   Results and Discussion

Ad Hoc Behavioral Measure – Taking the Sticker. Out of 119 participants per condition, 105 took the proposed sticker within the *central status* condition while only 89 took it within the *peripheral status* condition, $\chi^2(1, N = 238) = 7.138$, $p < .01$. Furthermore, this effect occurred while the central status elements were contrasted against white [$\chi^2(1, N = 121) = 7.760$, $p < .005$] versus against blue colored background, $\chi^2(1, N = 117) = 0.982$, *ns.*; and, jointly, while these elements were located in the middle [$\chi^2(1, N = 60) = 6.405$, $p = .01$] but not aside, $\chi^2(1, N = 61) = 2.241$, *ns.* (both χ^2s are *ns.* within the *blue* condition).

This suggests that participants exposed to terms such as "help", "save lives" and "good deed" (central status; vs. "generosity", "illness", and "evidence" for peripheral status)–and mainly when these elements were contrasted against a white background and in the middle of the screen—were more willing, at the term of our experiment, to ostensibly adhere to organ donation. This implies that while SR issues are of importance when articulated with the commitment theory or with the binding communication paradigm [15, 41], this articulation is also relevant in terms of technological persuasion. Moreover, our study puts forward that the persuasive effect due to the social status of the representation does not happen independently of the interface layout. In addition, the location on the interface may sensibly underpin the reach of persuasive messages being displayed and this effect is increased with an appropriate color background, consisting in white in the context of this study (i.e., with the theme of organ donation).

Self-reported Measures. Based on the valence participants attributed to their cognitive thoughts as 'favorable' (+), 'unfavorable' (−) or 'neutral' (0), a one-way analyze of variance (ANOVA) could be performed. It revealed a significant effect, $F(1, 237) = 17.68$, $p < .001$, $\eta_p^2 = .07$, leading us to say that participants produced more favorable thoughts when exposed to central elements than to peripheral. Additionally, participants expressed a better confidence in their thoughts in the 'central elements' condition rather than in the 'peripheral elements' condition, $F(1, 238) = 9.85$, $p = .002$, $\eta_p^2 = .04$.

Also, a better confidence in the thoughts led to a stronger attitude towards organ donation (respectively for the certainty, $r(240) = .41$, $p < .001$, and for the importance, $r(240) = .37$, $p < .001$).

Finally, results showed a main effect of the structural status of SR on free recall, $F(1, 238) = 9.6$, $p = .002$, $\eta_p^2 = .039$. On average, participants recall more words when being central elements of the representation rather than peripheral.

These few results tell us that individuals who have been exposed to central Status paid attention to the presented elements and memorized them better. It appears consistent with the theory of treatment depth [12, 13]. Also, regarding effects on attitudes, these results provide relevance for the ELM model predictions.

Moreover, several previous models assume that human behavior result from previously formed intentions and, sometimes, attitudes [2, 3, 14]. In this vein, logistic regression indicated that the observed ad hoc behavior (i.e., in our case, declaring as an organ donor by taking a sticker) depend namely on attitudes ($p = .001$), on attitudes' certainty $(p = .01)$ and on intentions $(p = .001)$, *Nagelkerke's* $R^2 = .61$, $\chi^2(14, N = 240) = 70.25$, $p < .001$.

Furthermore, multiple analysis of variance (MANOVA) performed on all self-reported measures yielded interesting effects of Status, of Location and, marginally, of Status × Location × Color interaction (see Table 1).

Table 1. Results of MANOVA performed on Status, Location and Color, regarding effects on all self-reported measures.

Variables	Wilks' λ	df	F	p	η^2
Status	.938	6	2.52	.02	.06
Location	.942	6	2.34	.03	.06
Color	.923	6	3.15	.005	.08
Status × Location × Color	.955	6	1.78	.10	.05

Moreover, ANOVA revealed a significant Status × Location × Color interaction on attitudes' certitude, $F(1, 232) = 25.48$, $p = .02$, $\eta^2 = .02$ (see Fig. 2).

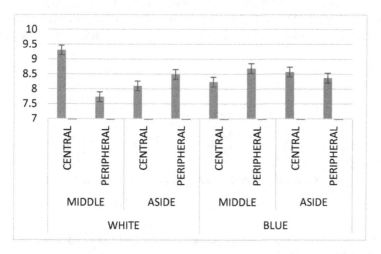

Fig. 2. Results of ANOVA performed on Status, Location and Color, regarding effects to the certainty of attitudes.

As Fig. 2 suggests, the most certain attitudes appeared while central elements were displayed in the middle of the screen and against white background. In all other conditions, peripheral elements were treated with more certainty or did not differ, in certainty of attitudes, from central elements. By the way, these central elements did not receive the same degree of certainty as in the first mentioned combination. Interestingly enough, the smallest differences appeared against the blue background, as if considering blue screenshot led participants to treat the color instead of different elements' characteristics.

Thus, if we previously showed, by examining the simple effects, that exposure to central elements led to an in-depth treatment, it seems to be that, when Status and Location are coupled with Color, we observe a focus of the users' attention on this latter. We can advance that the color "blue" may be sufficiently salient compared to locating elements in the middle of a screen or reading textual content involving central status' elements. The individual seems closely focused on the color, which in turn allows her to enjoy considerable cognitive economy and to drop the other factors summoned. As mentioned when discussing theoretical foundations of this paper, the ergonomics of interfaces can be particularly indicated to lighten the user's workload.

Finally, no significant interesting effects were found in satisfaction measures respecting to the layout and the color background, although we expected some ones.

Eye-Tracking Measures. MANOVA performed on eye-tracking measures including number of fixations, total fixation times and number of rollbacks yielded too, interesting results. Namely, there was a combined and of large magnitude Location effect [*Wilks'* λ = .750, $F(3, 223)$ = 24.84, p < .001, η^2 = .25]. Also, there was a marginally Status $\times$ Color interaction, *Wilks'* λ = .993, $F(3, 223)$ = 2.29, p = .08, η^2 = .03. In detail, ANOVA showed that number of fixations as well as total fixation times and number of rollbacks were more important when displayed in the middle (*Ms* = 56.57, 4.25 and 5.68 respectively) than when displayed aside, *Ms* = 50.70, 3.52, and 4.56, respectively, all $Fs(1, 225)$ > 10.32, all ps < .01, all η^2 > .04. Moreover, there was a significant Status $\times$ Color interaction, $F(1, 225)$ = 4.75, p = .03, η^2 = .02 (see Fig. 3).

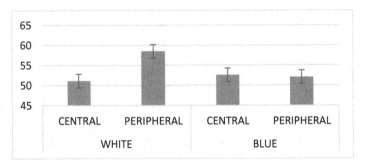

Fig. 3. Results of a two-way ANOVA performed Status and Color, regarding effects to the number of rollbacks.

As Fig. 3 indicates, whereas the number of fixations did not differ between central and peripheral elements against the blue background, there was a clear increase in fixations of peripheral (but not central) elements against the white background. This result is even more striking when considering the above-mentioned Status $\times$ Location $\times$ Color interaction on attitudes' certainty. Here, *in fine*, less is more, as a *lesser* number of fixations on central elements against white background yielded *stronger and more certain* attitudes than a greater number of fixations on peripheral elements against the same background, further suggesting a smooth interaction between persuasion through SRs on one hand, and the interface layout on the other.

7 Conclusion and Perspectives

The present study intended to deliver the most persuasive and attractive elements in the content and format displayed. This work sheds new light for future empirical contributions, including proposing to leverage the status of SRs in the field of interface design that have a user-centric approach. In particular, dealing with a theme such as difficult as organ donation in terms of thinking and performing behavior, results of our study appear very encouraging to think about future perspectives.

Disseminating information to a wide audience simultaneously [8, 19], systems relating to HMIs can be considered optimal for persuasive communication. So, we hope that this study will be able to join the existing workflow interested in serving many problems and social issues by using persuasive technologies media.

For the future, the challenge for us, regarding persuasive technologies, will be to have the means to reveal, analyze and discuss the human, social, cultural, ethical and political implications of attitudes and behaviors changed by technologies; referred by Fallman as "philosophy of technology" [16].

References

1. Abric, J.-C.: A structural approach to SRs. In: Deaux, K., Philogène, G. (eds.) Representations of the Social: Bridging Theoretical Traditions, pp. 42–47. Blackwell, Oxford (2001)
2. Ajzen, I.: The theory of planned behavior. Organ. Behav. Hum. Decis. Process. **50**(2), 179–211 (1991)
3. Ajzen, I., Fishbein, M.: Attitude-behavior relations: a theoretical analysis and review of empirical research. Psychol. Bull. **84**(5), 888–918 (1977)
4. Bettinghaus, E.P., Cody, M.J.: Persuasive Communication, 5th edn. Harcourt Brace, Fort Worth (1994)
5. Bonnardel, N., Piolat, A., Le Bigot, L.: The impact of colour on website appeal and users' cognitive processes. Displays **32**(2), 69–80 (2011)
6. Bonetto, E., Girandola, F., Lo Monaco, G.: Social representations and commitment: a literature review and an agenda for future research. Eur. Psychol. **23**, 233–249 (2018)
7. Bonetto, E., Lo Monaco, G.: The fundamental needs underlying social representations. New Ideas Psychol. **51**, 40–43 (2018)
8. Cassell, M.M., Jackson, C., Cheuvront, B.: Health communication on the internet: an effective channel for health behavior change. J. Health Commun. **3**(1), 71–79 (1998)
9. Chaiken, S., Eagly, A.H.: Communication modality as a determinant of persuasion: the role of communicator salience. J. Pers. Soc. Psychol. **45**(2), 241–256 (1983)
10. Cialdini, R.B.: Influence: How and Why People Agree to Things. William Morrow, New York (1984)
11. Cornish, L., Hill, A., Horswill, M.S., Beckera, S.I., Watson, M.O.: Eye-tracking reveals how observation chart design features affect the detection of patient deterioration: an experimental study. Appl. Ergon. **75**, 230–242 (2019)
12. Craik, F.M.I., Lockhart, R.S.: Levels of processing: a framework for memory research. J. Verbal Learn. Verbal Behav. **11**(6), 671–684 (1972)
13. Craik, F.M.I., Tulving, E.: Depth of processing and the retention of words in episodic memory. J. Exp. Psychol. Gen. **104**(3), 268–294 (1975)

14. Davis, F.D.: Perceived usefulness, perceived ease of use, and user acceptance of information technology. Manag. Inf. Syst. Q. **13**(3), 319–340 (1989)

15. Eyssartier, C., Joule, R.V., Guimelli, C.: Effets comportementaux et cognitifs de l'engagement dans un acte activant un élément central versus périphérique de la représentation du don d'organes. Psychol. Française **52**(4), 499–518 (2007)

16. Fallman, D.: Persuade into what? Why human-computer interaction needs a philosophy of technology. In: de Kort, Y., IJsselsteijn, W., Midden, C., Eggen, B., Fogg, B.J. (eds.) PERSUASIVE 2007. LNCS, vol. 4744, pp. 295–306. Springer, Heidelberg (2007). https://doi.org/10.1007/978-3-540-77006-0_35

17. Flament, J.C.: Consensus, salience and necessity in social representations. Pap. Soc. Rep. **3**, 97–105 (1994)

18. Fogg, B.J.: Persuasive Technology. Using Computers to Change What We Think and Do. Morgan Kaufmann, Amsterdam (2003)

19. Fogg, B.J.: Mass interpersonal persuasion: an early view of a new phenomenon. In: Oinas-Kukkonen, H., Hasle, P., Harjumaa, M., Segerståhl, K., Øhrstrøm, P. (eds.) PERSUASIVE 2008. LNCS, vol. 5033, pp. 23–34. Springer, Heidelberg (2008). https://doi.org/10.1007/978-3-540-68504-3_3

20. Léger, L., Chevalier, A.: Location and orientation of panel on the screen as a structural visual element to highlight text displayed. New Rev. Hypermedia Multimed. **23**(3), 207–227 (2017)

21. Lockner, D., Bonnardel, N.: Emotion and interface design. In: Ji, Y.G., Choi, S. (eds.) Advances in Affective and Pleasurable Design, pp. 82–98. AHFE, Danvers (2014)

22. Lo Monaco, G., Girandola, F., Guimelli, C.: Experiments inter-connecting the structure of social representations, cognitive dissonance, commitment and persuasion: past, present and future. Pap. Soc. Rep. **25**(2), 5.1–5.25 (2016)

23. Lo Monaco, G., Lheureux, F., Halimi-Falkowicz, S.: Le test d'indépendance au contexte (TIC): une nouvelle technique d'étude de la structure représentationnelle. Swiss J. Psychol. **67**(2), 119–123 (2008)

24. Marková, I.: Persuasion et propagande. Diogène **1**(217), 39–57 (2007)

25. Martínez-López, F.J., Luna, P., Martínez, F.J.: Online shopping, the standard learning hierarchy, and consumers' internet expertise: an American-Spanish comparison. Internet Res. **15**(3), 312–334 (2005)

26. Moliner, P., Abric, J.C.: Central core theory. In: Sammut, G., Andreouli, A., Gaskell, G., Valsiner, J. (eds.) The Cambridge Handbook of Social Representations, pp. 83–95. Cambridge University Press, Cambridge (2015)

27. Moscovici, S.: Psychoanalysis: Its Image and Its Public. Polity Press, Cambridge (2008)

28. Nogier, J.F., Bouillot, T., Leclerc, J.: Ergonomie des Interfaces: guide pratique pour la conception des applications web, logicielles, mobiles et tactiles. Dunod, Paris (2016)

29. Norman, D.A.: Emotional Design: Why We Love (or Hate) Everyday Things. Basic Books, New York (2004)

30. Petty, R.E., Briñol, P., Tormala, Z.L., Wegener, D.T.: The role of metacognition in social judgment. In: Kruglanski, A.W., Higgins, E.T. (eds.) Social Psychology: Handbook of Basic Principles, pp. 254–284. Guilford Press, New York (2007)

31. Petty, R.E., Cacioppo, J.T.: The elaboration likelihood model of persuasion. Adv. Exp. Soc. Psychol. **19**, 123–205 (1986)

32. Petty, R.E., Ostrom, T., Brock, T.: Cognitive Responses in Persuasion. Erlbaum, Hillsdale (1981)

33. Rateau, P., Moliner, P., Guimelli, C., Abric, J.C.: Social representation theory. In: Van Lange, P.A., Kruglanski, A.W., Higgins, E.T. (eds.) Handbook of Theories of Social Psychology, vol. 2, pp. 477–497. Sage, London (2011)

34. Rucker, D.D., Petty, R.E.: Increasing the effectiveness of communications to consumers: recommendations based on elaboration likelihood and attitude certainty perspectives. J. Public Policy Mark. **25**(1), 39–52 (2006)
35. Skandrani-Marzouki, I., Lo Monaco, G., Marzouki, Y.: The effects of unconscious context on social representations: evidence from the subliminal emotional priming paradigm. North Am. J. Psychol. **17**, 509–524 (2015)
36. Speier, C., Morris, G.M.: The Influence of query interface design on decision-making performance. MIS Q. **27**(3), 397–423 (2003)
37. Stock, O., Guerini, M., Zancanaro, M.: Interface design and persuasive intelligent user interfaces. In: Bagnara, S., Crampton Smith, G. (eds.) The Foundations of Interaction Design, pp. 193–207. Lawrence Erlbaum Publishing, Hillsdale (2006)
38. Takeuchi, Y., Katagiri, Y.: Social character design for animated agents. In: 8th IEEE International Workshop on Robot and Human Interactive Communication (RO-MAN 1999), Pisa, Italy, pp. 53–58 (1999)
39. Vergès, P.: L'évocation de l'argent: une méthode pour la définition du noyau central d'une représentation. Bull. de Psychol. **45**, 203–209 (1992)
40. Visser, P.S., Krosnick, J.A., Simmons, J.P.: Distinguishing the cognitive and behavioral consequences of attitude and certainty: a new approach to testing the common-factor hypothesis. J. Exp. Soc. Psychol. **39**(2), 118–141 (2003)
41. Zbinden, A., Souchet, L., Girandola, F., Bourg, G.: Communication engageante et représentations sociales: une application en faveur de la protection de l'environnement et du recyclage. Prat. Psychol. **17**(3), 285–299 (2011)

Author Index